CONFESSIONS OF A SPY

The Real Story of Aldrich Ames

Pete Earley

Hodder & Stoughton

First published in Great Britain in 1997
by Hodder and Stoughton
A division of Hodder Headline PLC

The right of Pete Earley to be identified as the Author of
the Work has been asserted by him in accordance with the
Copyright, Designs and Patents Act 1988

10 9 8 7 6 5 4 3 2 1

A CIP catalogue record for this title is available from
the British Library.

ISBN: 0 340 64707 8

Printed and bound in Great Britain by
Mackays of Chatham PLC, Chatham, Kent

Hodder and Stoughton
A division of Hodder Headline PLC
338 Euston Road
London NW1 3BH

FOR KEVIN MICHAEL EARLEY

CONTENTS

He had two lives: one open, seen and
known by all who cared to know . . . and
another running its course in secret.

—Anton Chekhov,
The Lady with the Dog

CONFESSIONS OF A SPY

To Whom It May Concern:

This letter will serve to introduce Mr. Pete Earley, a well-known and respected American author who is writing a book about my case. Mr. Earley's integrity and devotion to a fair and honest story convinced me that his will be the best and most successful book about it. Mr. Earley is the only author of a book with whom I am cooperating, through interviews and recommendations. I hope that any who value my opinion will do the same.

Any account of my career lacking the benefit of the knowledge of my friends, acquaintances and collaborators in Russia and the former Soviet Union would lack both completeness and balance. For that reason I earnestly hope that any in a position to assist Mr. Earley's research will be able to do so.

Mr. Earley is writing his own book — I have no editorial control or other influence over its content. Nor will I receive any compensation from him or his publisher, or in connection with his book.

Most sincerely,

Aldrich H. Ames

Allenwood, PA, 22 September 1994

PROLOGUE

THE DRAMA BEGINS

How do you break *into* a jail?

Aldrich Hazen Ames had just admitted he was a KGB spy in early 1994 and I wanted to interview him one-on-one for this book. But how? He was being held under tight security in the Alexandria Detention Center, a high-rise jail south of Washington, D.C., and the U.S. Department of Justice was already steaming about Ames and the media. He and I had met briefly shortly after he was arrested, when his clever court-appointed defense attorney, Plato Cacheris, had taken several television personalities and authors in to see his notorious client. In all, Ames had met briefly for off-the-record talks with three other authors and me. All of us wanted his exclusive cooperation. No one could pay him because the government would seize any such funds, and I wasn't about to offer him any editorial control over this book. Still, I knew Ames had plenty of reasons to talk. He was enraged over how the government was treating his wife, Rosario, and he claimed the CIA was unfairly smearing him as a drunk and a deadbeat. He was also savoring the notoriety.

On July 7, 1994, a gossip columnist at *The Washington Post* revealed that Ames had been meeting potential interviewers in his jail cell. Federal attorneys were outraged. Mark J. Hulkower, the assistant U.S. attorney in charge of prosecuting the Ameses, sent an irate letter to Cacheris. "Having learned of the parade of media personalities to the jail in recent days," he complained, "it seems that this would be an appropriate time . . . to iron out the details . . . of your client's future contacts with the media." Reminding Cacheris that it was *still* against the law for Ames to divulge classified information, Hulkower warned, "It is for the U.S. government, *not Mr. Ames*, to determine what is classified." From now on, Hulkower declared, Ames would not be permitted to meet with anyone from the media unless the CIA approved of the visit and had one of its censors attend the entire interview.

"I've got some good news and bad news for you," Cacheris quipped when he called me. "The good news is that Ames has decided to work exclusively with you on a book."

"And the bad news?" I asked.

"I don't know how you are going to get in to see him now without the CIA censoring everything he says."

I knew the government had good reason to be jittery about Ames. He had worked inside the CIA's Directorate of Operations, known by its initials as the DO, for thirty-one years. He knew many of the CIA's most sensitive secrets and he had played a role in many of its most daring Cold War spy games. His speciality was the KGB, the very organization that later had become his master. But I suspected the government had other reasons besides protecting national security for wishing to keep him quiet. From the moment of his arrest on February 21, 1994, the CIA and the FBI had engaged in a two-pronged public relations attack. Retired and anonymous CIA employees characterized Ames as an inconsequential, bumbling bureaucrat who spent most afternoons napping at his desk. The FBI, meanwhile, dazzled the media with a series of self-serving briefings. The bureau even granted New York author Peter Maas exclusive access to its special agents so he could rush the FBI's story into print. In the opening pages of his book *Killer Spy*, Maas boasted that the "real story" was not Ames and his spying, but "how Ames was pursued and captured by the FBI!"

Such government hogwash made me skeptical. If Ames was such an incompetent boob, why had the CIA given him access to its choicest secrets? And if the FBI had really done such a swell job, why had it taken *nine* years to catch him? There had to be more to this story than the public was being told.

It is usually easy to investigate a notorious figure, but Ames was different. Because he had spent most of his government career working undercover, the CIA could legitimately hide information about him from the public. There was only one way for me to learn who Ames really was and why he had become a traitor. I had to spend time *alone* with him. I had to learn what made him tick, how he viewed himself and the world.

But how? How could I get inside the jail, especially now that Hulkower had issued new rules restricting the media's access to Ames?

Or had he?

I'd spent most of my career in Washington, D.C., and one of the first lessons that I'd learned as a journalist was that federal bureaucrats liked to issue orders *without* consulting the people who actually have to carry them out. I figured Hulkower had notified the CIA and FBI about his new guidelines. But I wondered: *Had he bothered to tell anyone working at the jail?*

I drove to the Alexandria Detention Center and asked to speak to the sheriff. He was busy so his secretary suggested that I talk to Undersheriff Richard R. Ruscak, the jail's no-nonsense administrator. He welcomed me with the same coolness that one shows a door-to-door salesman. I explained that Ames had agreed to work exclusively with me on a book and that I wanted to begin interviewing him. Ruscak was not impressed. If he let me into the jail to talk to Ames, he said, he would have to let in everyone else in the media who requested interviews. "That's not something we are equipped to handle," he said firmly.

I noticed that Ruscak had not mentioned Hulkower's letter, so I decided to keep trying.

"But you really won't have to let everyone else in," I argued, "because Ames doesn't want to talk to anyone else—just to me."

Ruscak didn't reply, but I could tell from his expression that my argument had not changed his mind. And then I got lucky.

"I won't be a problem," I said. "I spent a year inside the maximum security prison in Leavenworth, Kansas, doing research for my last book, so I'm used to being around inmates and officers." I handed him a paperback copy of my book *The Hot House: Life Inside Leavenworth Prison.*

"Hey, I just finished reading this!" Ruscak replied. A friend had recommended it to him; even better, Ruscak had enjoyed it. For several minutes we talked about the main characters and how difficult running a jail was.

"When you walked in here, I was planning on telling you, 'No way are you seeing Ames!'" Ruscak said, "but I guess it will be okay—as long as Ames says he wants to see you, and his attorney doesn't object."

We shook hands and I started to leave, but then stopped. "I'd really like to interview Ames in the attorney/client room in the jail rather than in your normal visiting area," I explained. "If that's okay?" I knew that inmates had to talk to their visitors in the jail's visiting room over telephones while sitting on opposite sides of a thick window, and I had a hunch that Ames would refuse to speak over a telephone, for fear the government would tape-record his conversation.

"Sorry," Ruscak said, "that room is only for lawyers."

I asked Ruscak if I could start that night, and he promised to notify his captain. I was afraid to visit Ames during the day because the FBI and CIA were still debriefing him (he'd pleaded guilty earlier) and I didn't want to risk bumping into anyone who might tip off Hulkower. Around eight P.M., I strolled into the jail's empty lobby. Trying to look calm, I made my way to the jail's control center, a fortified glass booth that looked like the drive-in window at a bank. I was worried. What if Ruscak had telephoned Hulkower or gotten a copy of the prosecutor's letter about the new media guidelines governing Ames?

"Can I help you?" a deputy asked through an intercom.

"I'm here to interview Aldrich Ames. Undersheriff Ruscak approved it this afternoon."

The deputy flipped through a stack of papers. "Sorry," he said, "but I don't have a memo on this."

I could feel myself sweating.

"I'll have to call the shift lieutenant," he said.

Time slowed. I glanced at the clock in the lobby and watched the red minute hand slowly sweep around the dial. After several minutes, I heard a loud thump, the sound of a heavy steel bolt being turned inside a lock. A steel door to my left opened, and a petite woman dressed in a crisp white shirt and creased blue pants stepped forward. She was the lieutenant in charge of the jail at night.

"I'd like to interview Aldrich Ames," I said. "Mr. Ruscak approved it this afternoon."

"I know," she replied, "but there's a problem."

Damn! I thought. They found out about Hulkower's letter.

"No one wrote a memo about this," she continued, "but I was talking to Mr. Ruscak earlier today and he told me it had been approved, so I guess it is okay."

She spoke to the deputy in the control room and then turned to me. "Where would you like to interview him?"

"Uh, er, when I was here earlier with Mr. Cacheris to see Mr. Ames, we all met in the attorney/client interview room upstairs and it was really convenient."

She turned back to the deputy. "Have them take Mr. Ames to the attorney/client room. It's empty now so there shouldn't be any problem."

A few minutes later, I was standing inside the interview room waiting for Ames. Neither of us said anything when a guard brought him inside, but as soon as the officer left, we shook hands, and both of us grinned.

"You got in without a censor!" Ames exclaimed. "I didn't think you would! This is amazing, simply amazing!"

At that exact moment, the guard came back inside the room.

"Sorry, Mr. Earley," he said, "but the control center just called me."

I could feel my face turning red. I figured that someone had either found Hulkower's letter or been told that Ruscak did not want me talking to Ames inside the attorney/client room. I looked at Ames and noticed that his face betrayed nothing.

The guard handed me a legal form and pen. "You were supposed to sign this before coming upstairs." It was a standard release form. I scribbled my name and the guard left.

Ames burst out laughing. "I wonder," he said, "what would happen if two guys with Russian accents tried the same thing that you just did? Do you think the jail would let them in here to talk to me?"

For the next several weeks, we met nearly every night. No one ever questioned my comings and goings. We were left entirely alone in the attorney/client room. One night, Ames seemed distracted. I asked why, and he pressed a finger to his lips, indicating that we shouldn't speak. He bent down and examined the underbelly of the table that we were using. He was searching for hidden microphones. He examined both of our chairs next and then searched the walls. There were no obvious bugs. "I'm sorry, but I just can't believe the agency is letting you come in here night after night like this," he said. "It's crazy. This just doesn't make any sense. I could tell you everything!" He looked at me. "Last night I was wondering if you might be working for them, you know, trying to find out if I will tell you something different from what I am saying to them in the CIA/FBI debriefings."

"Well, I'm not," I replied indignantly. "No self-respecting journalist works for any government agency, particularly the CIA."

Ames laughed. "Is that what you really think?" he asked, hinting that I was being naive.

During our nightly sessions, Ames answered every question that I asked. No subjects were off limits, including questions about classified information. I tape-recorded more than fifty hours of our conversations. One night when I got to the jail, Ames announced: "They know we've been talking! The FBI told me that one of its agents saw your name on a list of visitors. I hope you got your tapes in a safe hiding place!"

I did.

"Don't tell me where," he said. "I don't want them to ask me."

"Why? You're not good at keeping secrets?"

My joke surprised him and he seemed to relax. "If I were in charge of this case, I'd arrest you tonight when you left the jail. I'd confiscate your tapes," he said.

I didn't know if he was teasing or not. "I don't think the FBI wants to arrest an author," I said. "Think of the first amendment implications."

"Trust me," he replied, "if the FBI knew what was on your tapes, they would want them destroyed."

I began feeling uneasy. Ames had asked only one concession from me in return for his exclusive cooperation. He had made me promise that I would leave for Russia immediately after we finished our interviews. "If you go to Moscow, the FBI and CIA will never be certain if I told you something that was classified or if you learned it on your own from the Russians," he had explained. "No one will be able to trace anything back to me."

That night the jail's elevator seemed to take forever to descend from the interview room to the lobby. Would the FBI be waiting with handcuffs? The doors opened. I peeked out—no one was there but the guard in the control booth. I hurried to my car, glancing over my shoulder as I walked. No one followed me nor was the FBI waiting at my home.

The next morning, my telephone rang.

"This is Mark Hulkower. I'm the assistant U.S. attorney prosecuting Aldrich Ames. I've been told that you have been interviewing him in the jail—going in to see him at night—all alone."

"Yes," I replied.

"That should never have happened. You should not have been allowed in there with him," Hulkower grumbled.

I didn't reply, and for a few seconds the line was quiet.

"I can promise you, Mr. Earley," he continued, "you will never be allowed to see him again without someone being in the room with you. No one is supposed to be interviewing him alone."

A few days later, Ames was taken to a maximum security federal prison in Pennsylvania, where he was kept isolated from other inmates. As far as I know, he has never been allowed to speak to anyone in the media while he has been in prison, without a CIA censor being present in the room.

I kept my promise to Ames a short time later by boarding a British Airways jet for London, the first stop on my trip to Moscow. I went to England to interview Oleg Gordievsky, a former high-ranking KGB officer who had been working as an agent for the British Secret Intelligence Service, known as MI-6, for eleven years, before he was mysteriously recalled to Moscow and accused of being a traitor. Ames had been accused of telling the KGB about Gordievsky. If MI-6 had not helped Gordievsky escape from Moscow during a daring daytime operation in 1985, he would have been executed.

I met Gordievsky in an English pub, where we sipped dark ale and talked about his days as a spy. "The KGB still uses drugs to make people talk," he warned. "They drugged me at lunch by spiking my drinks. So please be especially careful when you are in Moscow, particularly if they invite you to lunch."

The next morning, I left for Russia. I had never been there. I do not speak Russian. I had no idea of what to expect. Ames had given me a letter of introduction to give to the KGB.* Ames urged the KGB in his letter to let me read its files about him. He had told me that the KGB would be suspicious of my visit and assume that I was a CIA spy. "You will have to convince them that you aren't," he warned.

On the flight to Moscow, I was suddenly struck by the sheer craziness of what I was doing. Here I was, an author, flying into Moscow after meeting for more than fifty hours *alone* with a KGB mole who was still being debriefed by the CIA and FBI. What was I getting myself into?

A German foreign correspondent, a friend of mine, had given me the home telephone number in Moscow for Boris Aleksandrovich Solomatin, a retired KGB general. For nearly twenty years during the height of the Cold War, Solomatin had overseen most of the KGB's anti-American spy operations. He had been the KGB's chief *rezident* in Washington, D.C., in 1967 when U.S. naval officer John A. Walker, Jr. had volunteered to become a

---

*After the breakup of the Soviet Union, the KGB underwent a number of reorganizations. In 1994, spying outside Russia was conducted by the Russian External Intelligence Service, or *Sluzhba vneshney razvedki* (SVR). Inside Russia, the KGB's functions were taken over by the Ministry of Security and Internal Affairs or *Ministerstvo bezopasnosti I vnutrennykh del* (MBVD). For the sake of simplicity, I will refer to Russian intelligence as the KGB in most places in this book.

KGB agent.* Solomatin had personally overseen the Walker spy case for an incredible *eighteen* years. Once again, luck was on my side. I knew Walker personally. He had been the subject of my first nonfiction book, *Family of Spies: Inside the John Walker Spy Ring*, and I hoped to use my relationship with him to interest Solomatin in meeting with me.

"Please tell me, how is my friend John Walker?" Solomatin asked as soon as I introduced myself over the telephone. His voice sounded friendly. I started to explain why I had come to Moscow, but when he heard the name Rick Ames, Solomatin cut me off. "Let's not discuss such matters over the telephone." The next day we met in the lobby of a popular Moscow hotel. Short, square-shouldered, his voice deep from years of chain smoking, Solomatin was now seventy years old, yet he remained a handsome man with a finger-cracking handshake, piercing eyes, and a quick mind. I told him that I wanted to interview the KGB officers who had "handled" Ames. He chuckled.

"My government has never said that this Mr. Ames was spying for us. It is our intelligence service's policy to never make such comments. What is to be gained by such admissions? Nothing! So I am telling you that you will not have any success in Moscow getting anyone to discuss this case."

"General Solomatin," I continued, dropping my voice to a whisper, "last month I spent fifty hours talking to Aldrich Ames in his jail cell without anyone else being present. Just him and me, and he told me that he wants your government to talk to me about his case. He has given me a letter." I handed him an envelope. He opened it slowly and read the message carefully. It was the note that Ames had given me, asking the KGB to cooperate with me.

"Your country's FBI and your CIA permitted you to talk to this man in jail?" he asked.

I told him how I had gotten in to see Ames, but I could tell by his reaction that he didn't believe me.

"Someone will call you," he said, tucking the letter into the pocket of his heavy wool coat. "Please enjoy your stay in Moscow."

It was midnight when the telephone rang in my rented apartment.

"A car will come for you at ten o'clock tomorrow," a voice said. "Please be standing outside your building."

The English was excellent, without a trace of a Russian accent. I didn't

---

*The CIA and KGB both use the word "agent" to describe someone who is spying for them. Employees are called officers, as opposed to the FBI which calls its employees special agents.

sleep that night. The next morning at exactly ten, a white Volga limousine arrived outside the apartment building. The driver, who stood well over six feet and weighed close to three hundred pounds, opened the rear door. I bent down and peered inside.

"Hello, Mr. Earley, won't you please join me?"

It was the same voice I had heard on the telephone. I stepped into the car.

"You may call me Yuri," my host in the back seat said, extending his right hand. "It is a name Americans can pronounce without too much difficulty." We shook hands and he said: "It would be better if we do not talk while we are in the car."

The Volga moved across the snow-covered streets in silence for about twenty minutes before we arrived outside a nondescript apartment building. "General Solomatin has invited us for some refreshments in his apartment," the man I was told to call Yuri explained.

The general's wife, a pleasant woman wrapped in a heavy pea-green coat, was kissing Solomatin on the cheek and leaving as we stepped from the elevator. Solomatin welcomed us inside and led the way into a living room, where two bottles of Coca-Cola and homemade apple strudel waited. Yuri sat across from me and listened without interruption, as I explained again how I had gotten into the jail to interview Ames. When I finished, Yuri spoke to Solomatin in Russian for several minutes.

"Forgive me for being rude and speaking in Russian," he said, "but your story seems so, well, so, so simply impossible to us."

Yuri began questioning me, looking for some error, a slip-up that would expose me as a liar. A few minutes later, he spoke again to Solomatin in Russian. Their discussion grew loud and animated, and it appeared to me that they were arguing.

Addressing me, Solomatin said in English: "In our country, what you did, getting in to see this man—why it just could not be done. My friend here seems to believe that it could not have happened in your country either."

Both looked directly at me. "Well, it did," I replied, sounding a bit peeved. "And if either of you really understood how the bureaucracy in Washington, D.C., works—you would know it is true."

"May I ask you a few questions about Mr. Ames?" Yuri said politely. Without waiting for me to reply, he began interrogating me. It became clear that Yuri either had met with Ames in the past or had been intimately involved in the KGB's handling of him. He simply knew too many details about Ames to have gleaned them from news accounts. I apparently passed his test, because he eventually stopped grilling me about Ames. "What do you want from our government?" he asked.

"I want to meet Ames's handlers, the men in the KGB who actually controlled him. I want to interview them for my book. I want information about the agents Ames exposed—the men who were executed by your government."

This time it was Solomatin who spoke in Russian to Yuri for several minutes, as I waited, completely clueless about what was being said.

"I will come for you in two days. We will have lunch and talk about your requests," Yuri said abruptly.

His driver took me back to my apartment.

Two days later, at precisely ten o'clock, the same Volga arrived, with Yuri sitting in the backseat. Only this time, the car zipped in and out of Moscow's heavy traffic, darting up and down several narrow streets. We rode together in silence for nearly an hour before we arrived at a dreary concrete slab apartment building. I had assumed that we were going to eat in a restaurant, but Yuri said it was not a good idea for the two of us to be seen together in public. The entrance to the building was dark—only one of the three light bulbs in the lobby was lit, there were no windows near the entrance, and even though it was midmorning, it was an overcast day. Someone had urinated on the linoleum floor in the tiny elevator.

Yuri and I stepped inside and he pushed the seventh-floor button. The elevator groaned as it climbed upward. Yuri led me to an apartment without a number on the door. A thin woman, blonde and attractive, opened the door. She was young and wore a black skirt and dark blue blouse. There was no ring on her right hand where Russian women traditionally wear their wedding bands. Yuri kissed her on both cheeks. She blushed. She shook my hand and led us into a room where a table had been prepared for lunch. She pulled out my chair, and as I sat down, I noticed that Yuri and I were not sitting directly across from one another. He was about five inches to my left. It was then that I saw an antique walnut buffet directly behind him. In the center of it, at my eye level, was a mirror. I was staring at my own reflection and immediately suspected that there was a video camera hidden behind it. Our lunch was going to be recorded.

The woman poured us vodka. I declined, but Yuri insisted that we toast "world peace." She handed me a cut crystal glass. I raised it to my lips, but Oleg Gordievsky's warning in London kept me from drinking the contents. The woman brought appetizers and after Yuri and I sampled them, he removed a note card from his jacket.

"Please tell me why Mr. Ames thinks he was caught?" he began, reading from the card.

"He blames you," I replied. "I mean, the KGB."

"Why?"

"Because as soon as he began telling you the names of the KGB officers who were working for the CIA, you arrested them and had them shot. He told me it was as if you had put a big neon sign directly over the CIA building in Langley with the word *mole* written on it."

"But, my friend," Yuri said, "let's not forget that your government says Mr. Ames began spying in 1985. Most of the executions in my country took place that same year or the next. If we are guilty of putting up a big neon sign, as you say Ames claims, then why did it take your CIA and FBI nine more years to arrest him?"

"I don't think the CIA wanted to admit that it had a traitor working for it, and I don't think the FBI is as clever as you do."

"Pete, c'mon, how can this be possible?" Yuri said, in a friendly voice. "Think about what you are asking me to believe. Intelligence services all over the world know that they can be penetrated. They watch for the very first sign, the very first hint of such treason. Surely the CIA is not so inept as to not see this big neon sign. No, my friend, perhaps there is another reason why in 1994 they suddenly arrested Mr. Ames."

"Like what?"

Yuri paused. "Did Mr. Ames mention anything to you about someone in my country, perhaps here in Moscow, possibly turning him in—telling the CIA about him? Does he believe that he was sold by us to the Americans?"

This line of questioning was making me nervous. "No," I answered. "Ames never said anything to me about that. Besides, I thought Ames gave you the names of everyone in your government who was working for the CIA. Surely he was aware of the danger of someone in Moscow exposing him."

"Yes, of course," said Yuri, "but, my friend, maybe this person was not an agent. Maybe it was someone in our government who sold out Mr. Ames. If this is true, then perhaps Mr. Ames would not have learned about this person until after his arrest. I assume he is being debriefed. Did the people debriefing him give him any clues?"

I didn't like the direction our conversation was going. "I simply don't know," I replied. "If there is such a person in Moscow, Ames certainly did not mention his name to me. Do you think that Ames was betrayed by someone in your government?"

Yuri's reply was noncommittal. "In politics and spying, there is much treachery."

He moved to the next question on his card. Some thirty minutes and dozens of questions later, he finished. At that same moment, our hostess entered with the main course. "Come, let us eat and then I will tell you what you want to know," Yuri said. When we finished, he removed another index card from his pocket.

"Are you ready?" he asked.

"Yes," I replied eagerly.

"My government will not comment officially on whether or not Mr. Ames was working for the KGB. However, I have been authorized to tell you unofficially that we believe there is sufficient proof to show that Mr. Ames is not responsible for the identification of these traitors who were arrested in 1985 and later executed. In each case, these men were captured because of mistakes which they made, or that the CIA or other U.S. agencies made, and this is what brought them to the attention of our well-trained KGB officers. I am now willing to discuss with you how each of these spies was exposed. Let us begin with the traitor Oleg Gordievsky."

Yuri was following a carefully crafted script, and for the next twenty minutes he provided me with detailed explanations designed to exonerate Ames completely. I could not hide my frustration. Ames had admitted to me that he had sold the KGB the names of more than twenty agents, including a woman, who were working for the CIA and FBI. Yet Yuri was insisting that Ames had not helped either the KGB or the Soviet Union's military intelligence service, known as the GRU, or *Glavnoye razvedyvatelnoye upravleniye*, identify any of these agents. I suddenly realized that I had been naive to think that the KGB would be willing to discuss the Ames case with me. At the end of his monologue, Yuri asked if I had any additional questions. I turned my eyes away from him and stared directly into the mirror across from me.

"Only one," I said. "If Aldrich Ames didn't provide the KGB and GRU with a single bit of worthwhile information, then why was he paid more than two million dollars—the most ever paid to an American traitor?"

Yuri did not flinch. What proof did I have that the former Soviet Union had ever paid Ames? he asked. There was absolutely nothing in writing that could be traced to the KGB or the GRU. Of course, the FBI had claimed that it had found notes in Ames's apartment after his arrest that suggested he was a KGB agent, but how could anyone be certain that they were genuine?

I saw no point in arguing, but I couldn't resist one final jab. I shut my notebook.

"What you say may be true, but I don't think so. I am certain that Mr. Ames was spying for your government, if for no other reason than because he has personally told me that he was."

Yuri shrugged. "Do you have any other questions?" he asked.

"No."

Our hostess returned, and Yuri gushed over the meal. "Tell me Pete, wasn't this meal wonderful?" he asked.

I nodded.

"And Russian women," he continued. "Tell me, are there any women as beautiful as Russian women?" The young woman smiled.

Neither of us spoke as we waited for the elevator. I was irritated. When the elevator's doors opened, I noticed that the urine on the floor was still damp. It smelled. I suddenly felt as if the entire building reeked. I almost gagged. As the elevator slowly descended, Yuri spoke to me in a voice that was barely a whisper.

"Come now, my friend, did you really think my government was going to admit Ames was one of ours? Don't you remember how your president and Congress reacted when Ames was arrested? How angry they were? What good would it do us to make such an admission? How would this help us? Please don't think we are so stupid."

He had been looking straight ahead, but now he turned to face me. "Pete, I like you. You seem like an honest man. Perhaps I can be of some help to you—how do you say it in Washington, D.C.—off the record?"

"Unofficially," I said, "without anyone ever knowing your name."

The elevator doors opened. The temperature outside had dropped a few degrees, and I was glad that the driver had kept the engine running so it was warm inside. Yuri gave him instructions in Russian. The Volga rolled forward, its tires making a crunching sound as the driver maneuvered through the apartment's vast parking lot. I could see no order to how the cars had been left. There were no straight lines of bumpers facing bumpers. Instead the vehicles were parked haphazardly, as if their owners had simply driven them as far as they wished or could, and then stopped. Some were ice-encrusted, their sides splattered with grime. Others, not driven recently, were buried under mounds of dirty snow. Together, they formed an unintentional maze through which we now weaved.

We rode in silence. My thoughts were on Aldrich Ames and one of our last meetings in jail. I had been worrying aloud about the other authors who were hurrying to write books about him. I knew that they would move up their deadlines in a race to be the first to publish. I did not want to compete in this market-driven rush. Although Ames was cooperating exclusively with me, I was not going to blindly accept everything that he told me. It would take time to verify his claims, to interview his friends, his critics. Ames had laughed at my stewing.

"Don't worry," he told me, "no one will ever get the complete story unless they talk to me and the KGB."

He had then taunted me. "You were good enough to find a way into the jail. Now the question is, can you get the KGB to cooperate with you?"

"Do I really need the Russian side?" I remembered asking.

He had looked disappointed. "Of course you need it! There are things that have never come out about this case. There are still secrets that only a few know."

I had immediately asked him to elaborate, but he had refused.

It had been a suspenseful moment between the two of us that night in jail, and Ames had squeezed from it every bit of drama that he could. " . . . *Things that have never come out about this case . . . still secrets that only a few know.*" I could hear his voice in my head. At the time, I had thought that he was simply being melodramatic. He loved theatrics. But as I sat next to Yuri in the back seat of the Volga as it slipped onto a major Moscow artery, I looked out of the car window and saw the majestic outline of the Kremlin in the distance. At that moment, I began to suspect that Aldrich Ames had not been exaggerating, not at all.

PART ONE

THE
SEEDS

The villainy you teach me I will execute,

and it shall go hard but I will better the

instruction.

—William Shakespeare,
The Merchant of Venice

CHAPTER 1

Why did he commit treason?

"Treason?"

He repeats the word out loud as if he is shocked by it. The word itself sounds evil, doesn't it? he says. He prefers spying. It is easier on the ear, exotic even, much more civilized. He chuckles. Wasn't that part of the game, one of the tricks learned at the CIA's legendary training school known as the Farm, a few hours south of Washington, D.C.? His job as a CIA case officer was to make the unthinkable sound pedestrian, to persuade a target that there was nothing sinister about sharing his nation's most closely guarded secrets with a foreign superpower. Of course the pitch always sounded better if the recruiter himself honestly believed it were true and appeared sincere when he spoke about how their actions would "promote world peace" and "usher in democracy." Rick Ames had been a believer—once. There was a time, early on, when he had been faithful to the cause. But later? Ah, no, no. Too much had happened. By then he had come to see the intelligence wars differently. "They are mostly a silly game," he explains. Adults wearing children's masks, trying to sneak peeks at each other's cards, like schoolboys cheating at penny ante poker. What purpose does it all serve? Who really gains? He pauses, composing his thoughts.

Who is the greater fool? he asks, his voice intense. The man who believes his own lies and spends his nights rationalizing the obvious contradictions in his life? Or a man who sees the lies for exactly what they are and, recognizing them, uses them for his own purposes? He chuckles, and just as quickly begins to cough, the result of too many cigarettes. He has smoked since he was a teenager, and he is not going to stop now that he is in his mid-fifties and confined in jail. There are too few pleasures behind bars.

Treason. Why did Rick Ames betray his country?

He toys with the question, addressing it in the third person, as if he himself is curious to discover an answer. Was it some event that sparked Rick Ames to become a traitor or had the seeds for it always been in his blood, slumbering inside some defective DNA, waiting to burst free? The conversation amuses him. Could his betrayal have been preordained? Which of our actions are truly our own? he asks. Which are determined before our birth? Were his parents somehow to blame? Or some childhood trauma long repressed?

Treason.

He shuts his eyes. "I assume you want to know about my past." That is where everyone always begins, isn't it? An author must find an explanation for his subject's criminal behavior, some hidden defect that explains the monster his subject has become. The public expects it, no, the public *demands* it, doesn't it? he says. A social autopsy must be performed. Someone must declare: "Ah, this is why Rick Ames did what he did!" His imperfections must be magnified, put on public display, vigorously condemned. Otherwise, readers might wonder: *Could I have done what he did?*

Treason.

The cough returns. He allows his mind to drift back through the years to when he was a boy. Where to begin? Where to begin? He wishes he had a cigarette, but he smoked his last one an hour ago. He coughs again, and then he starts.

━━━

Dolly had one good eye. Rick was four when he ran up on the plowhorse's blind side. He had watched his father harness Dolly the day before and he wanted to get her ready by himself. Startled, Dolly kicked, and her right hoof caught Rick in the chest, knocking him several feet through the air. He hit the ground unconscious. His father found him. His mother thought he was dead. After a few minutes, Rick came around, and the doctor later decided that there had been no permanent damage, although he was certain that if the kick had been an inch higher, it would have killed the boy. This is Rick Ames's earliest memory of his own life.

During World War II the Ames family rented a farm on the outskirts of River Falls, Wisconsin, then a town of four thousand residents, located about twenty-six miles southeast of the Twin Cities Minneapolis and St. Paul, Minnesota. Rick's parents, Carleton and Rachel, tended chickens and grew vegetables for themselves and to sell. The money supplemented the $37.50 per week that Carleton earned teaching European history and sociology at the River Falls Teacher's College. As soon as the war ended, Carleton quit farming and moved into a bungalow at 423 East Cascade Avenue. It was only a few blocks from the college and the grand house on Squirrel Knob Street where Carleton's parents, Jesse Hazen Ames and his wife, Louise, lived. Jesse was not surprised when his son gave up farming. It was another one of Carleton's foolish escapades.

Everyone knew Jesse was a hard man to please. By the end of the war, Jesse was completing his twenty-eighth year as president of the teacher's college. Town historians would later credit him with single-handedly transforming a lackluster ordinary school into a thriving, nationally accredited, four-year institution. It was River Falls' biggest business. Even before he had accepted the college presidency in 1917, Jesse had distinguished himself by coauthoring a series of successful American history textbooks with his brother, Merle. Jesse was perhaps the town's most important citizen and he played that role well. He gave orders only once and demanded perfection. That was how he ran the college and, everyone assumed, his home.

Jesse's wife, Louise, was at least a foot shorter than her rail-thin husband and was as gregarious as he was dour. The daughter of a Canadian congregationalist preacher, Louise was an accomplished musician who had sung with a professional opera company while still in high school. The couple had two sons and two daughters. Of them, Carleton always seemed the most promising. He was River Falls High School valedictorian in 1922, and few were surprised when he announced that he intended to be a teacher, like his father. Three years later, Carleton graduated from college with a teaching degree and then something completely unexpected happened. He announced that he was going west in search of adventure. A few days later, he left town without any real idea of where he was going. Occasionally he wrote home, but Jesse was so angry he refused to read the letters. Louise kept them. Carleton worked briefly for an undertaker, taught at four different high schools, landed an acting job at the Pasadena Playhouse in California, and joined the

Army Air Corps, only to wash out of pilot training because of poor hand-eye coordination. At one point, he worked as an organizer for a teacher's union and befriended Golda Meir, who was also working as a union organizer.

After twelve years, Carleton returned home, broke and jobless, and Jesse arranged a teaching job for him at the college. On his first day as a professor there, he met Rachel Aldrich, an amazingly self-poised and beautiful twenty-year-old coed. Her father, John Aldrich, was a Harvard graduate who had moved to Wisconsin to operate a dairy farm. Her mother, Mabel Luckman, was a voracious reader and liberated freethinker clearly ahead of her times. From the start, Mabel disliked Carleton Ames. It wasn't because he was thirteen years older than her daughter. Mabel pegged him as a loser. Despite Mabel's warnings, however, Carleton and Rachel were married in 1938. Rick Ames was born on May 26, 1941, about the same time that his mother graduated with a teaching degree. Everyone called him "Ricky," although his real name was Aldrich. Carleton liked first names and last names that began with the same letter. A second child, Nancy, was born one year after Rick, and another daughter, Alison, was born in 1945.

Carleton and Rachel's best friends in River Falls were Mel and Margaret Wall, whose son, Charles "Chuck" A. Wall, was the same age as Rick. The two couples played bridge, attended campus lectures and theatrical plays, went on picnics. When Carleton decided to form a band to perform at the college's annual Faculty Frolics talent show, Mel and Margaret Wall joined right in. The men recruited six other professors, and since none of them could afford the five dollars to rent a tuxedo, they wore their academic caps and gowns when they performed. They called themselves the Tuneful Tooters. Rachel and Margaret cajoled another professor's wife into forming a singing trio. They were the Teacher's Pets, and they went along with the band to various weekend gigs, at other schools mostly. Carleton played the trombone and three other instruments. He also wrote plays. His best, *Birds Have Nests*, was performed twice by students at River Falls. It described the housing shortage during the war. Carleton directed the productions. Rick thought his dad was swell.

Remembering those days later, Ames would describe a childhood so innocent that it sounded as if it had come directly from an *Ozzie and Harriet* or *Leave It to Beaver* 1950s television script. Nearly every Saturday, Rick and Chuck Wall spent their afternoons at the local movie theater, watching a Superman serial and Bugs Bunny cartoon followed by a Western. The price was twenty-seven cents, about half of Rick's weekly allowance. He spent the remainder on candy bars. At age nine, Rick and Chuck started camping overnight by themselves along Pete's Creek, which meandered through the college campus. Everyone knew everyone else in River Falls. If the boys had a problem, they could run to the closest house.

Ames could not recall ever seeing or hearing his parents argue or fight or gossip or even swear during his childhood. On a typical weekday night, Carleton and Rachel would sit in the living room after dinner, with the radio playing classical music or jazz, and read. Rick and his sisters usually joined them, each with his or her own book. By age ten, Rick was reading three or four books each week, and Alison routinely shocked her baby-sitters by reading bedtime stories to *them!* She was three.

There were a few malicious moments, but not many. Cousin Louise from Minneapolis always visited for two weeks in July, and she would later recall how Rick had surprised her one summer morning when she was using a rope bridge to cross over a creek. Rick had run ahead, and started rocking the bridge when she was about halfway across.

"Please, Rick," she screamed. "Stop. I'm scared! Stop!"

But he rocked harder—so hard that Louise burst into tears and fell to her knees. The next day, Rick took her to a neighbor's house, where there was a moving sale going on. The young girl bought a tiny teapot and she and Rick played together all day with it. When she left that summer for home, she told Rick that she was naming her new teddy bear after him. Most days Rick was really fun to be with, but every once in a while he would do something really mean, Louise said later. He always seemed so sorry afterward, though, that you just had to forgive him.

In 1949, Carleton began spending his summers at the university in Madison, working on his Ph.D. It was a move that would eventually lead to dramatic changes in his and his family's life. Carleton's doctoral thesis, which he defended in 1951, described Burma's struggle for independence from the British, and his academic adviser, Paul Knaplund, was so impressed by Carleton's understanding of Burmese politics that he quietly forwarded a copy to a friend who worked at the CIA. The agency had an immediate interest in Burma because it had been operating a covert operation there that had turned into a disaster. "Project Paper" had started in 1949, shortly after Mao Zedong had forced Chiang Kai-shek's nationalist followers out of China, which had ended a bloody civil war. The bulk of Chiang Kai-shek's troops had fled to Taiwan, but five thousand soldiers had crossed China's southern border into Burma, where they took refuge in the country's remote northern mountains. General Li Mi controlled these troops, and the CIA had immediately started sending him money, supplies, and weapons, because it wanted him to return to China and unseat Mao. Between 1949 and 1951, Li Mi's soldiers crossed the border twice but they were no match for the communists. In December 1951, China accused the United States of trying to overthrow its government by secretly funding the general's troops. Secretary of State Dean Acheson hotly denied the charge, but a few days later, the *New York Times* published evidence that showed General Mi was, indeed, on the CIA's payroll. Acheson was forced to retract his denial, badly embarrassing the Truman White House, and the CIA had been ordered to stop funding its secret war. The Burmese government had panicked. The prime minister of Burma, U Nu, worried that China might use the debacle as an excuse to invade his country, so he announced that Burma would no longer permit any U.S. foreign aid programs to operate inside its borders. The CIA had been using aid programs to smuggle shipments to Mi's troops. As soon as the CIA stopped supporting Mi, he abandoned his plans to invade China. Instead, he used his troops to seize control of the region's lucrative heroin trafficking operations. Overnight, with the help of weapons the CIA had provided, the general became one of Southeast Asia's most lethal drug lords.

In early 1952, a stranger appeared on the River Falls college campus asking for Carleton. He had come to offer him a job. U.S. aid programs were still banned in Burma, but the government allowed academics to do research there. If Carleton would apply for a sabbatical from his teaching job, the CIA would arrange for him to receive a study grant from the privately funded Catherwood Foundation to conduct research in Burma, the stranger explained. As far as anyone would know, Carleton would be writing a college textbook, a natural follow-up to his doctoral thesis, but he would actually work as a CIA officer. The agency would give him the names of Burmese politicians and military leaders it wanted interviewed. He also would be expected to deliver cash to publishers in Rangoon whose newspapers were secretly being bankrolled by the CIA.

Carleton was thrilled. The agency was offering him a chance to serve his country, earn a better salary and travel overseas. Rachel agreed that it was a great opportunity. Although they were not supposed to tell anyone, Carleton and Rachel told their parents. Rachel's mother was horrified. "There has to be something wrong with a job if a person isn't supposed to tell anyone the truth about what he actually does," she snapped. Jesse Ames proved equally reticent. Why couldn't Carleton be satisfied working at the college in River Falls, just as he had done?

On March 17, 1952, Carleton officially sought leave of absence. "I have been requested to spend some time in the service of the U.S. government,"

he bragged. "This is in the intelligence service, probably in the Far East."
A few weeks later, the Ames family moved to Washington, D.C., where
Carleton was trained to be a case officer. They left for Burma in early Sep-
tember 1953. Rick was twelve years old, Nancy was eleven, Alison was eight.
None of them had a clue about what was really going on.

Because Carleton was supposedly doing private research, he did not
move into the U.S. embassy compound but instead rented a spectacular
house in one of Rangoon's most affluent neighborhoods. Surrounded by a
high privacy wall, the house had been used during the war as headquarters
for a Japanese cavalry regiment. The two-story villa came with an array of exotic servants: Ba Win, a dignified and aloof Burmese bearer; Sammy—no
one knew his real name—a black Madras cook who plunged his hand into
boiling water while cooking to determine how hot the water was; Ba Nee, the
Ames family's chauffeur who had been a machine-gunner with the Burma
Independence Army, fighting first with the Japanese and later against them;
and a procession of maids, clothes washers, and housekeepers. In all, there
were thirty-one servants and family members living in the compound.

The Ameses arrived during the Festival of Lights, a local holiday, and at
dusk a troupe of dancers came to perform a *pews*—a Burmese drama in
which performers make up their lines extemporaneously without anyone
knowing how the show will end until it is over. Rick stayed up all night, mesmerized by this strange new world.

As part of his cover, Carleton joined the very fashionable, Europeans-
only Kokine Swim Club in Rangoon; the very British and proper Rangoon
Yacht Club; and another exclusive for-men-only club. He and Rachel began
hosting elaborate dinners for the country's most influential politicians, its
war heroes, various U.S. embassy officials, and members of Burma's avant-
garde, including a popular Burmese film actor, Maung Maung Tau. Each
Sunday, Carleton would send his children off to the yacht club and meet privately with his CIA contact. Sometimes the officer gave him money to deliver; more often he quizzed him about cocktail chitchat and interviews that
Carleton had done. It was during one of these Sunday sessions that Carleton
mentioned a Russian named Victor M. Lessiovsk,* whom he had met at a
cocktail party. Carleton's CIA boss was flabbergasted. Most Soviets were

---

*Lessiovsk would continue to be a prime CIA target. After leaving Burma, he eventually was as-
signed by the KGB to the United Nations, where he became a popular dinner guest among New
York City's social elite. Jacqueline Kennedy would later ask for his assistance in arranging a private audience for her with Pope Paul VI during his 1965 visit to the city. The KGB found the fact
that a Kennedy had to seek the help of one of its officers to meet the Pope especially hilarious.

afraid to fraternize with Westerners, for fear that someone in Moscow would become suspicious of their loyalty and immediately call them home. The fact that Lessiovsk was a known KGB agent made Carleton's encounter with him even more tantalizing. Was Lessiovsk trying to recruit Ames? Carleton was ordered to get as close as he could to Lessiovsk, and during the next few weeks, he tried several times, but always failed. His boss made a notation in his file: Carleton Ames was not good at recruiting. It was a tag that would later come to haunt his son too.

At the CIA's request, Carleton did manage to befriend Edward Michael Law Yone, the founder and editor of Burma's biggest English-language newspaper, called *Nation*. He was an adviser to Prime Minister U Nu and a useful source for gossip. Rachel Ames helped by becoming good friends with Law Yone's wife, Eleanor. They got along so well that the two women went on a long summer vacation together in 1954. The Law Yones' children, Bryon, Marjolaine, and Wendy, were about the same ages as Rick, Nancy, and Alison, and during the tedious train ride north from Rangoon to Kalaw, a former British resort in the mountains, the youngsters instinctively paired up. "I was surprised at how adventuresome Rick was," Bryon Law Yone said later. "He wanted to experience everything there was about Burma, to eat every dish, see every pagoda."

Carleton took Rick with him that fall on a trip to meet Kyaw Saw, commander of the North Burma Army and the chief rival of Ne Win, commander of the South Burma Army. During the trek north, Carleton explained how the two commanders had once been friends. Both were members of Burma's famed Thirty Comrades, thirty young men who had been smuggled out of the country before World War II and taken to Japan for combat training. When the war started, they returned home to fight the British and, later, the Americans. Eventually most of them changed sides and fought the Japanese. Now they were fighting each other. This flip-flopping struck Rick as strange. When they arrived in Kyaw Saw's camp, the commander invited both father and son to dinner. That night, Kyaw Saw entertained them with war stories.

In 1955, Carleton's two-year tour in Burma ended. Rachel called the children together. They were not returning to River Falls, she announced. They were going to live in the Washington, D. C., area. She didn't explain why. All three children were scared.

"You have nothing to fear about moving into a new community," Carleton lectured them. "You are Ameses. You are special. You are smart and you will do well."

Years later, Ames would recall his father's pep talk that day in Burma with crystal clarity, as if the ghost of Carleton Ames himself had appeared in the Alexandria jail to repeat it. His father had not spoken arrogantly; rather his lecture had sounded as if being a member of the Ames family was more of an obligation, some might say a burden, than a reward. Rick had not questioned for an instant his father's judgment. He genuinely believed that he and his sisters *were* different. Grandpa Jesse Ames had been a leader. An entire town had looked up to him. Rick had watched his father dine with Burmese generals and movie stars. It seemed obvious to him that Carleton was someone who mattered. Did that mean he was also destined to become someone important? Of course! He was going to leave his mark on the world.

THE WORDS OF RICK AMES

My father smoked Chesterfields and sometimes a pipe. I remember he smelled of pipe tobacco. He always read to us a lot, and my most vivid recollection is him sitting in his living room chair in River Falls and me sitting on his lap or on the footstool, listening to him reading me Wizard of Oz *stories. I could smell the smoke in his smoking jacket and there was a smoking stand with a zinc-lined humidor compartment next to the chair, and I remember how wonderfully safe it was having him hold me and read to me about Dorothy and Toto.*

My parents always seemed super-busy and happy. I don't remember any tense times. On weekends, we'd pile in their bed in the mornings and Dad would read the comics. But manners! Oh, manners! There was absolutely no talking back, no door-slamming, and we learned that Dad didn't buy every fad toy. I remember my bitter disappointment when "all the kids" had blue Civil War-style forage caps and Dad refused to buy me one. He said a fad was no reason at all, that being like all of the other kids was not something to aim for.

I was told that I was a good child, but, of course, I had faults. I was caught stealing a candy bar at O'Brien's Cafe, the adult hangout, on Main Street, and Dad marched me down to return the candy bar and to apologize to Mr. O'Brien personally. I never shoplifted again. Another time, I shot out the elementary school principal's car side windows, all four of them. It was on my birthday and I used my brand-new Red Ryder BB gun, which I never saw again.

Everything seemed to revolve around, not just us kids, but the house, the home, family. We had relatives everywhere. Holidays were big family events. In the summer, big Ames family picnics were held at Uncle Ken's farm outside River Falls. Autumn and winter holidays were big dinners, at our house mostly. In the summer, we'd also drive up to my great-grandparents' cottage on Sand Lake. My great grandfather had built boats there in his machine shop. He'd invented a log peeler, too, and I can recall that he played the violin with tremendous vigor and enthusiasm, even though he was quite old.

Grandpa and Grandma Ames lived close by, and I spent a lot of time with them on weekend mornings and after school in the afternoon. Grandpa Ames was immensely dignified and always formal, even to me, but Grandma was warm and, I remember, always organizing something. She would set up a card table and tell me it was a sheriff's office or a bank or a lemonade stand. Once she told me it was an insurance business and I ended up writing a policy for Grandpa's cigarette holder. He smoked Old Golds in a holder like FDR's. While he was much too dignified to get down on his knees and play, he would tell me stories about American history.

Funny, I don't remember much about my father's relationship with his father. We did not speak much about feelings and there was never any gossip. I know all of this sounds pretty routine but when I look back on it, it seems to me that we were different from other families. Mom and Dad always impressed us with the need for manners, ideas, integrity. They were friends with the only Jewish couple in town, and I remember Dad explaining to me about Jews, anti-Semitism, and the evil of prejudice. When I saw a black man for the first time in St. Paul, Dad told me about slavery and discrimination. There was also a flavor of being not better than others, but being held to different, and implicitly higher, standards. I see it almost as a class distinction now, though Mom and Dad were devoid of what could be called snobbishness or reserve, much less pretending to be from better origins. The idea was that individual integrity and worth was of paramount importance. Also independence, and a refusal, the way I got it anyhow, to whine, beg, draw attention to oneself, brag, or push forward. Stoicism was the virtue, and one's own efforts and sense of value sufficient reward. Praise, though we got it and knew our parents' pride in us, was worth nothing by itself, and shouldn't be pursued for its own sake.

I spent a lot of time with Dad. He always included me. He knew all about tools and fixing things and had a workshop and always had some project going. Dad and I built a large model train setup in the basement. Still, his love was his books. I remember a review that he wrote for Wisconsin Historical Review, *in which he tore to pieces a book about Paul Bunyan. During the thirties, American folk heroes were promoted heavily and kids were immersed in tales of* big John Henry, Pecos Bill, Paul Bunyan and the like. Dad saw it for what it was: commercialism and somewhat politicized New Deal, American populism. In his book review, he showed that Bunyan was the creation of a lumber company publicist. Dad drew on interviews with his grandfather and other retired loggers to argue that no such folk stories about Paul Bunyan had ever been told or known in logging camps. I was struck deeply by his insistence on the truth and on the significance of that truth.

It is hard for me to describe the sense of comfort and security which we had there in River Falls, nestled as we were in the midst of the college, relatives, and in our own home. It seemed so safe, so closed off from the rest of the world. As I grew older, I used to think that those days there really were from a different time, as if my parents were actually from a generation twenty years behind their own.

Of course, the big adventure was Burma, and it marked all of us. It really contributed to this feeling of being different. We didn't go to the embassy school, didn't live in an American house, and Mom and Dad socialized very little with the official Americans.

Weekends were terribly exciting. On Saturdays we'd go swimming or sailing, sometimes both. Sundays were far more structured. First, the swimming club, where I played center forward on the men's water polo team, after playing in the kid's water polo game. I was tall and fast enough for both! Then to the sailing club, where I crewed for the adult A-license races and then sailed in B races by myself.

I quickly learned the streets and immersed myself in the culture. I munched sugar cane, drinking its juice, and occasionally smoked a cheroot, more for effect than enjoyment. I rode my bicycle all over and took the buses—old lorries with rickety wooden bus bodies—downtown to the library and the military post. I usually went by myself, and a favorite spot was the Shwe Dagon pagoda, only a fifteen-minute walk from our house. It was an incredible place, especially at night. The real fascination was the covered staircases rising from the street entrances. They were lined with booths, shops, and vendors, selling everything to the crowds moving up and down under hundreds of bare electric light bulbs. A half-dozen times or more, I would sneak out of bed and the house around ten or eleven and wander up and down those stairs, drinking in the exciting sounds, smells, and sights, all the while eating constantly.

Here is a shameful secret, which I've never before admitted. I ate like a horse at home but was always hungry, never satisfied. My allowance went a long way in buying snacks on the street and at the swimming and sailing clubs.

But two or three times, I remember being ravenously hungry and no doubt greedy for a big Chinese meal. I knew where Dad kept his money and so I liberated, feeling guilty as hell, the equivalent of a couple of dollars in kyats. I took the bus downtown and walked to a side street near the Sule pagoda and went into a big, popular Chinese restaurant. There I would stuff myself in solitary greed, returning home to eat dinner a few hours later, feeling fat, satisfied, and guilty. Some people, especially women, hate eating alone, but I never have minded it.

Every so often, Dad would take us out to Nam Sin's Chinese restaurant. Our cook at home made Indian, Anglo-Indian and Burmese dishes, but not Chinese, so this was a real treat. Even today, I remember those meals as perhaps the best Chinese food I've ever eaten. We always ate at a big circular table in one of the private dining rooms, and Dad would talk to us about world events. Dad had always talked a lot about the life and death struggle taking place between the free and communist worlds. But one night he stunned me with a particular application of it. He depicted the suppression of freedom and the brutal conditions of life under communist regimes as being so inhuman and dehumanizing that he said [he told Nancy and me because there was just the three of us there that night] that he would rather see us dead than living under communism. Dead! Can you imagine? Amazed, in helpless disagreement with his premises, I had no response, but I wondered about it for years. The brutality of Dad's words was utterly surprising, and despite my belief in his ideals, I think I recognized and was reacting to the implicit denial of humanity to those hundreds of millions of people. And, finally, I didn't believe it and, in a way, didn't believe Dad, either, that he could, however hypothetically, wish Nancy and me dead.

Over these years, I've thought from time to time of that conversation and my silent, stunned reaction. And my rejection of Dad's assertion stayed with me in many ways. What emerged in me was a belief that whatever the evils of a government and the sufferings inflicted upon a people, no human beings can simply be written off. Regardless of the amount of human cruelty and brutality under communism, we all share a common humanity, whether we were the oppressed or the oppressors. In the end, we are all human creatures.

That conversation sticks in my mind, even now, because for perhaps one of the first times in my life, I found myself passionately disagreeing with my father. Of course, I did not speak out. I was young. I simply finished my meal.

THE WORDS OF OTHERS

He was an awkward boy. I remember he used to run after me and try to kiss me! He wore a sarong for a few days, but he didn't know how to sit properly. Most Burmese men pull up the bottom of the sarong to keep from exposing themselves when they sit with their legs spread but Rickie pulled up the top layer and completely exposed himself one day to my sister and me. He got so embarrassed he never put on a sarong again!

—Wendy Law Yone

He has no redeeming values. I don't see any hope for him to ever improve. I don't blame him as much as I blame our headquarters for sending him out here.

—Evaluation of Carleton Ames,
CIA station chief in Burma

When I first read his father's file, I was shocked at the parallels. Here was this father from River Falls, Wisconsin, I mean, we aren't talking Chicago here, and he is teaching at what really was a community college at the time, and he comes to Washington, D.C., with three kids and a wife and all that responsibility and he gives up a steady job and changes careers in his mid-forties to run off and become a spy in Burma. I mean, the guy obviously was chasing some dream, but he didn't achieve it, and I think Rick followed right in his footsteps.

—Sandy Grimes, CIA

Rick Ames devoured a series of books by the British author Leslie Charteris about the swashbuckling fictional hero Simon Templar, "the Saint." The Saint was the James Bond of his day, a dashing, debonair British adventurer who traveled the world rescuing damsels in distress, smoking cigarettes, drinking highballs, and solving mysteries. In Burma, Rick Ames signed himself "Simon Templar."

—David Wise, *Nightmover* (one of four books published
about Ames the year after his arrest)

Espionage is a drastic thing to do. You turn your back on your country, your own mother and your father, and everything of value you have been taught in school and growing up. It was easy for us to see why someone in a repressive sys-

tem would do this—but Rick Ames? Look at his past. What possible reason could he have?

—Jeanne R. Vertefeuille, CIA

Mom and Dad told us that we were gifted—we had our health, brains, good looks, and strong family affections. They told us we had unlimited opportunities awaiting us. Rick and I have talked about this at length. There was no arrogance when they told us these things. It was explained to us almost as if having these gifts were an obligation. You were expected to do more.

—Nancy Ames Everly, Rick's sister

Rick Ames would have known exactly what he was doing in betraying the information: he was sentencing the victim to death. He knew any important source he passed on to the Russians would be shot. . . . He has the blood of a dozen officers on his hands. He would have had my blood, too, had I not managed to escape.

—Oleg Gordievsky,
KGB officer working for the British, who claimed he was betrayed by Ames

CHAPTER 2

Carleton Ames told his son the truth in the spring of 1957: "I work at the CIA." The agency operated a summer jobs program for its employees' children, and Carleton wanted sixteen-year-old Rick to apply. Rick had believed his father was a State Department bureaucrat. He was shocked. Carleton told Rick that he couldn't tell anyone else. Ames would later remember his father's explanation. "You and I both know that lying is wrong, son," Carleton had told him. "But if it serves a greater good, it is okay to lie. It is okay to mislead people if you are doing it in the service of your country, but it is never okay to lie or mislead people for your own personal benefit."

Rick worked as a clerk at the CIA that summer in an old government office in Washington, D.C., where he spent most of his time making fake money that was used in training exercises at the Farm. Rick tacked a map of the world on his bedroom wall and stuck pins in every country where there was a conflict. Someday he would be a CIA officer just like his father.

Unbeknownst to Rick, his father's career was floundering. The Rangoon station chief gave him such a negative performance review that the agency required Carleton to undergo a six-month probationary period after he returned home. He passed muster, but was never again sent overseas. Carleton would garner some praise for his knowledge of the Communist Party in Indonesia and his skill at writing "black propaganda"—news reports that appeared legitimate but were actually stories planted by the CIA in foreign newspapers, usually to stir up anticommunist feelings. But for the most part, Carleton was pushed into a desk job and quietly forgotten. He had started drinking heavily in Rangoon and, back home, his family soon began witnessing the degeneration that comes with chronic alcoholism. Armed with a six-pack of beer, he would escape to his study to drink alone at night and read. When rumors about Carleton's drinking leaked back to River Falls, few were surprised. Of Jesse and Louise Ames's four children, three were alcoholics.

In contrast, Rachel Ames bloomed after she was hired to teach English at a new suburban high school in McLean, Virginia. "Rachel was a beacon," one of her former students would later recall. "We worshiped her. She was the absolute best teacher most of us ever had." Rachel and a fellow history teacher decided to teach American history and English together as one class, and their team-teaching approach earned them national recognition. Rick was banned from taking his mother's classes, however, and since she taught all of the school's college prep English courses, that meant he got stuck in the regular English program. Ames would later credit this slight with helping him make friends with two dissimilar groups, those who were college-bound and those who weren't. Rick's best buddies in the "smart set" were Wes Sanders and John Souders, both "CIA brats" just like him. The three were nicknamed the Triumvirate, because they went everywhere together, and each had played a role in the drama club's performance of *Julius Caesar*. Rick was also close friends with Margaret "Peggy" Anderson, on whom he had a crush during high school. "We considered ourselves very mature," Anderson, now a history professor at the University of California at Berkeley, said later, "and we actually were for our age. We all smoked and had endless arguments about politics. We weren't beatniks, but we thought of ourselves as being coffeehouse intellectuals."

Rick's pals in the noncollege group were Bob Duncan and Chuck Windley. "Bob was brilliant, but neither of us cared about our grades," Windley said later. "We simply did what we wanted to do in school and we had absolutely no respect for authority. None whatsoever." Duncan and Windley loved playing pranks and drinking beer at the Brickskeller, a D.C. bar that claimed it had more brands of beer than any other saloon in the nation's capital. "Rick and Bob Duncan were always playing fantasy games," said Susan Seeley, Duncan's sweetheart in high school. "When Bob and Rick and I would go out someplace together, we would pretend that we were wealthy socialites or that we were on some secret mission. We would never go as ourselves. What was so witty about Rick was that he would take on these characters and actually become them."

Rick always wore a trench coat to school. Everyone knew he wanted to be a spy. Rick and Windley even developed a secret way of communicating. Certain words had double meanings. If you blew smoke through your nose while you were smoking and telling a story, it meant that you were lying. Rick used to tell Peggy Anderson some real whoppers while Windley tried to keep from laughing. Windley had never known anyone who could seem as sincere as Rick was when he was lying.

Even though Windley was still in high school, he was an accomplished magician, having performed on a vaudeville stage in New York City at age fourteen. "Rick had no interest in actually doing magic," Windley said, "but he loved the deception aspect of it. He became my secret shill." One weekend, Windley led a seance at a party in the basement of Bob Duncan's house. About ten teenagers held hands and formed a circle around a table. Windley put a glass milk bottle, with a string and fishing weight hanging inside it, in the center of the table, and flipped off the lights. He said the spirits would answer the group's questions by moving the fishing weight so it would clink against the glass. One clink meant yes, two meant no. Seconds after Windley started chanting, everyone heard a clink. Windley announced that he was in contact with a notorious killer, which produced a lot of laugher when the teenagers began asking what it had been like for him to be executed in an electric chair. Near the end of the seance, Windley fell into a trance, and a voice that didn't sound anything like his own revealed that the murderer had used a candle to mark his initials on one of the rafters in the unfinished basement. The teenagers turned on the lights and began their search. "Here it is!" a girl squealed. The killer's initials had been marked in candle-black on a rafter, just as the voice had said. Everyone accused Bob Duncan of being part of the scam, since the party was in his house, but Duncan seemed genuinely shocked. Windley never told his classmates how he had pulled off the stunt, even when he was asked about it twenty years later at a high school class reunion. But Ames knew. "It was Rick who was moving the card table with his foot—shaking the weight so it clinked against the glass," Windley said. "Everyone was trying to catch me, so they weren't watching him." Before the seance, Windley had distracted Duncan long enough for Rick to sneak downstairs and write the initials on the rafter. "I used Rick a lot in my magic and he never ever told a single soul about his part. *Never!* Do you know how rare that is? Most people want to take credit, but Rick got his kicks from fooling people."

No one was surprised when John Souders and Wes Sanders were inducted into the National Honor Society because of their excellent grades.

But Rick didn't get asked to join, even though he was a National Merit Test semifinalist. His grades were mediocre because he didn't do his homework. "I'd procrastinate and I was lazy," Ames later admitted. But the real reason for his poor marks was his attitude. "I have a character flaw that never got corrected. If someone says, 'Hey, you got to do this,' and I don't want to, I don't argue about it, I simply don't do it. What's odd is that I react this way without ever really considering the consequences. I never look ahead. I just do what I want."

One weekend, when a group of kids went raspberry-picking in West Virginia, Rick doubled over in pain. His appendix had ruptured. He was rushed to a local hospital, but the doctor there couldn't find Rick's appendix. Rather than make a larger incision, the doctor just probed around with his fingers until he found it. Afterward, Rick couldn't eat without vomiting. He was hospitalized again and nearly died. Another operation revealed that the first doctor had "misarranged" Rick's internal organs, blocking the passageway to his stomach. Sanders visited Rick at the hospital and was shocked when he saw how emaciated he was. Sanders was afraid Rick was going to die, but Rick joked about it. "I remember listening to him in the hospital and thinking that he had real problems with intimacy," Sanders said later. "John Souders and I could talk about our feelings, but that was really difficult for Rick. I began to think that he used his wit and jokes as a shield to keep other people from really getting to know him."

Their senior year, Sanders was chosen Most Talented. Souders was named Most Likely to Succeed. Rick was declared Wittiest. A few weeks before graduation in 1959, Windley announced that he was taking his magic show on tour that summer, and he asked Rick to go with him. They had been putting on a popular two-hour performance in a local church on Saturday mornings that featured magic by Windley, and a melodrama with Rick playing the much-booed Snidely Whiplash. Rick wasn't certain his parents would approve, so Windley came to dinner at his house and pitched the idea. Carleton thought it was great, but Rachel was appalled. The next morning, Carleton made Rick an offer. "You don't have to go to college," he said. If Rick wished, he could spend the summer touring with Windley and then move to New York to pursue an acting career. Carleton was willing to give him the money that had been saved for Rick's college tuition. "Everyone deserves a chance to chase a dream," he told Rick. "I'll handle things with mother." Rick didn't know what to do, so he didn't do anything. When school ended, Windley left town without him.

In August 1959, Rick enrolled at the University of Chicago. He wrote to Peggy Anderson nearly every week at the Virginia college she was attending. Nearly forty years later, she would still have his letters. In them, Rick writes excitedly about how much fun he is having as a member of the Blackfriars, a student drama group, and how he is spending all his time at the theater. Rick barely passed his first year. He flunked out his second. "I knew I was going to flunk out but I just gritted my teeth and refused to do anything about it. I was having too much fun working at the theater." Carleton and Rachel were upset. "They put a real guilt trip on me because I didn't have a scholarship and it had placed a real financial burden on the family," Ames recalled. Worse, it was the first time that anyone in the family had failed academically. "Both of my parents were trained teachers. They couldn't believe that I had flunked."

Rick stayed in Chicago, performing bit parts in a few plays at night, working at a temporary employment service during the day. He began using the name Al, started drinking heavily, didn't shave, moved into a cheap rooming house in one of Chicago's worst neighborhoods, and became best buddies with a marijuana-dealing pothead. Horrified, his parents begged him to return home. Rick told them in a nasty note to leave him alone. Not long after that, he was held overnight in jail on a car theft charge but was released when the police learned the car belonged to one of his friends. A discouraged Rick woke up late one morning in December 1961 with a hangover and his rent due. He hadn't eaten in three days and his shoes had cardboard tucked inside because of holes. He rode the bus home. Carleton was waiting, just as his own father, Jesse, had been when he had returned to River Falls after twelve years of wandering. Carleton told Rick not to worry. He would help him get a job at the CIA.

CHAPTER 3

Rick moved into a cheap apartment in Washington, D.C., with Bob Duncan, his buddy from high school, who was studying chemistry in college and getting high on marijuana. Rick stuck with beer. The worst thing the agency learned about Rick when it did a routine background investigation was that he and a buddy had gotten drunk once and gone for a joy ride on a stolen bicycle. Rick was hired as a clerk-typist in what was then called the Records Integration Division of the DO. He helped file cables that were being stored because they were no longer needed. Most were from the CIA's overseas stations, and Rick spent every free moment that he had reading them. The other clerks only worked in the file room temporarily while they were waiting for openings in the agency's Junior Officer Training (JOT) program, but Rick wasn't eligible because he didn't have a college diploma. He enrolled at George Washington University but got sidetracked the following summer when a friend in Chicago offered him a job as the technical director at a summer theater. Rick told the agency's personnel department that he needed a leave of absence to enroll in a foreign language course that was only being offered at the University of Chicago. The CIA approved his request. No one checked to see if he was lying.

Rick had fun, but the theater had lost its appeal. He wanted to become a CIA officer. When he returned to work that fall, a young blonde woman was sitting at what used to be his desk. Rick was shocked when he saw her face. She could have been a twin of his sister, Nancy. They even had the same first name. Nancy Jane Segebarth had just graduated from an Ohio college and was from Orchard Park, a suburb of Buffalo, New York, where her father was a bank executive. She was waiting for an opening in the JOT program. Rick used the desk next to hers, and they began going to lunch together and became friends. "We didn't begin dating for at least a year and a half, just before she left for the JOT program."

In 1964, Rick's youngest sister, Alison, became so despondent that Carleton and Rachel were afraid that she might kill herself. Psychiatrists said the twenty-year old was suffering from schizophrenia, but Rachel blamed herself. She decided that she had demanded too much from all three of her children. That was part of the reason why Rick had flunked out of college and why Alison was now depressed. Everyone in the family visited Alison as often as the hospital allowed, except for Rick. He went once and that was it. "I just can't handle this," he told his mother.

That same year, the American School in Karachi, Pakistan, contacted Rachel and offered her a job teaching English for two years. Carleton offered to stay behind to take care of Alison. He didn't want to apply for early retirement at the agency and he had lost all interest in living overseas. Rachel took the job, and Rick moved in with his father to keep him company. Carleton's drinking was worse than ever. At work he was often caught sleeping at his desk. "It had all seemed so idyllic in River Falls during the 1950s," Ames recalled. What had happened? One afternoon when Rick was searching through some old boxes in the attic, he found a love letter that Carleton had written Rachel before they were married. Carleton described how wonderful their life together was going to be; they would travel and have experiences in foreign countries that others in River Falls only could dream about. Rick tucked the note back in the shoebox where he had found it. He never mentioned it to his father.

Rick's driver's license was suspended after he was arrested three times for alcohol-related violations. He was drinking a lot at night. Without a car, he couldn't commute from the Virginia suburbs to the agency and college, so he moved back in with Duncan in the city and rode a bicycle everywhere. In September 1967, he graduated with a solid B average from George Washington University, and immediately applied for the JOT program. Carleton retired from the CIA, after working fifteen years there, during the same month in 1967 that Rick was accepted by the JOT program. There were more than seventy members of his JOT class, making it one of the largest ever, and nearly all of them were white men. The Vietnam War was gobbling up intelligence officers as fast as the CIA could send them overseas.

At the Farm, students were divided into two groups after they completed a couple of weeks of basic instruction. Employees who wanted to work as analysts in the Directorate of Intelligence (DI) were sent back to Langley for specialized training. Those who had signed up to become case officers in the DO were given paramilitary training and taught how to work as spies. As in other government bureaucracies, the CIA had developed a step-by-step procedure for teaching employees how to do their jobs. Rick was taught that he was supposed to follow these steps when recruiting a spy: Step one, the "assessment stage," consisted of (1) deciding what sort of information the agency needed to obtain; (2) identifying people who knew this information; (3) determining who among them you could get close to; and (4) picking one of these people as your "target." Stage two was "evaluation": What was the best way to take advantage and exploit the target—money, intimidation, blackmail?

"The entire focus was on identifying a person's weaknesses," Ames said later. "Once you learned where a target was vulnerable, you could develop a plan to take advantage of him or her." The third step was called development. "You had to find some clever way to get close to the target, so that he would not suspect you. You needed to befriend him or her," said Ames. If a CIA officer was interested in recruiting a Bulgarian who played tennis, the case officer would find someone who belonged to the same tennis club as the Bulgarian, and arrange an introduction. The club member who made the introduction was called an "access agent," because he was giving the officer access to the target. The "approach" and the "pitch" came next. It could take months of preparation before an officer would make a pitch. A good case officer had to be patient. The hardest pitch for a target to turn down was a request from a friend, Rick was told. "The better friends that you became with a person, the better the chances of using him."

The CIA told its case officers that a good way to make a potential target feel at ease was by asking him or her for nonclassified material first. "We didn't give a damn about the papers," Ames explained. "We wanted to get the target used to bringing us documents. In a lot of cases, we would pay outrageously generous amounts for totally worthless documents." The cash was how the CIA got its hook into an agent, because it made him or her obligated to the case officer. It also provided the agency with evidence of that person's spying.

After a successful pitch was made, the case officer had to "handle" the agent. "You had to keep the target producing and safe." The next step, considered by many the ultimate test of a good recruiter, was when the case officer turned over the agent to someone else to handle. "Most recruitments are made on the basis of a personal friendship," Ames said. "If you were able to turn over an agent to someone else, that meant a change in the relationship had occurred. The handler had developed the agent so well that he was now working for the agency instead of an individual." There was one final step. "Termination" happened when the CIA decided an agent was no longer needed. Someone had to tell the agent that he was being cut from the payroll.

Rick enjoyed the lectures by veteran CIA officers at the Farm the best. These were the real Simon Templars of his boyhood dreams. One of his favorite speakers was the case officer who had handled Colonel Oleg Penkovsky, one of the CIA's most important Soviet agents. In 1962, a U-2 spy plane flying over Cuba had taken photographs that showed that launch sites for Soviet-made missiles were being constructed on the island. However, U.S. intelligence officials were not certain what sort of missiles were being sent to Cuba, or what stage the construction process was in. Penkovsky had provided that information, which proved vital to President John F. Kennedy's decision to blockade the island. Penkovsky had been caught and executed by the KGB shortly after he helped the US.*

"At the Farm there was a great emphasis on camaraderie, and there was a subtle effort made to dissolve any moral misgivings that you might have about right and wrong," Ames claimed later. "You were told that you were now part of an elite service, that you were selected because you were one of the best and brightest, and that your job was paramount to the very survival of the United States. Because of these things, you were entitled to lie, cheat, deceive. You did not have to obey laws in any foreign countries. Only the laws of the U.S. had any jurisdiction over you. Of course, we were told there were some lines the agency would never cross, such as trying to assassinate someone. That was something the Soviets might do, but not us. What we

---

*Rumors surfaced after his death that Penkovsky had been executed by being lowered alive into a blast furnace. The KGB had supposedly filmed his execution to show to recruits as a warning. Over the years, this story has been reported as fact in numerous books and magazines. After Ames was caught, one author claimed in a book about the case that the KGB had lowered an agent betrayed by Ames into a blast furnace. These blast furnace stories are complete nonsense. Penkovsky was shot by the KGB, and none of the agents whom Ames betrayed were ever lowered into furnaces, according to the CIA, FBI, and KGB.

didn't know at the time was that there had already been a number of CIA assassination attempts."*

Some of his classmates, especially those with strong religious convictions, began dropping out of the DO program, Ames said later. "They just couldn't tolerate the duplicitous nature of the job, as well as the widespread, and I mean widespread, drinking that went on." Rick drank a lot at the Farm, often with his CIA instructors. In his eyes, it was part of the DO's macho image. The highlight of the DO's training program was the Live Problem Exercise, a role-playing game. Students were told that a disastrous series of political events had resulted in the United States being carved into different nations. The Republic of Virginia was the last remaining stronghold of democracy. The northeastern states were under the control of the communists. The South was a modern-day Confederacy. There was a People's Republic of West Virginia and an equally redneck independent Republic of Texas. California was under the control of anarchists. Rick and his classmates were divided into teams and given assignments. One squad was told to learn whether or not the Confederacy had nuclear weapons, another was ordered to recruit an agent. The entire exercise took place in the neighboring town of Williamsburg.

Near the end of his training in 1968, Rick asked to be assigned full-time to the Far East (FE) division, a hot spot at the time because of the Vietnam War. He spoke passable Chinese, which he had studied in college, but his interview with FE division officials went badly, and he had to fall back on his second choice, the Soviet Bloc, later renamed the Soviet Eastern Europe (SE) division. He worked at the SE branch in Langley for four months and was then offered his first undercover assignment. He was being sent to Ankara, Turkey, to see if he could put what he had learned at the Farm into practice. His job would be recruiting. His targets were the Soviets. Rick was ecstatic. He was finally going to be a CIA spy.

There was only one hitch. He and Nancy Segebarth had been dating exclusively for some time, and Rick knew if he didn't ask her to marry him before he left for Turkey, he would probably lose her. She was now an analyst in the DI. "Was I madly in love with Nan? No. Was I committed? Yes. Was there a great deal of affection? Yes. And there was certainly physical attraction. Yes, that was there," Ames said later. "But passion? No, not in the be-

---

*According to testimony by the agency before Congress, the CIA has been involved in assassination attempts in Cuba, Zaire, and the Dominican Republic. All three failed.

ginning and never afterwards, and I think the same was true on her part. It was more of a mature fondness for each other. I remember that we didn't have sex until after we were married, even though she was twenty five and I was a year older. Neither of us pushed for it, which should have been a warning sign to me. But we enjoyed each other's company and we never had any huge arguments. We were both intellectually well suited for one another, and we both felt it was time for us to get married, and that seemed to be enough."

A problem surfaced. The CIA had an opening in Turkey for Rick, but there wasn't one for Nan. If they married, she would have to resign. Once they got to Ankara, the CIA could rehire Nan as a "contract employee," but she would lose her seniority and other benefits. "We spent hours discussing it, and finally, Nan agreed that she would give up her job." Their wedding was on May 24, 1969. "Looking back, I think I felt a certain obligation to get married. It was what I had always believed you did, and I think all of the problems that were happening to my parents at home and with my sister, Alison, contributed to some basic need which I had for some sort of family stability, some sort of reassurance in the family system. I guess deep down I wanted my parents to see that I had turned out okay, to be proud of me. I had finally finished college and had gone to work at the CIA and this would be the next logical step—settling down by getting married."

In family discussions, Rick called his bride Nan, to distinguish her from his sister, Nancy. Nan's family liked to vacation on North Carolina's Outer Banks, so she suggested that they honeymoon near the resort town of Duck. One morning while they were walking along the beach, Rick spotted a teenager thrashing in the waves. He swam out and brought the boy back to the beach. Later that afternoon, he saw another swimmer, who had been caught in a riptide and was being pulled out into the ocean. He saved that boy's life, too. After he was arrested for being a KGB mole, Rick would think a lot about those two boys. It made him feel good to know that their lives had been saved because of him.

THE WORDS OF RICK AMES

It's funny about actors, you know. I've always thought of Ronald Reagan this way and I noticed this in me, too, and in other people whom I have known as actors. If you play a role, say you play a role as a pilot in a play and you get wrapped up in it, in a funny way you think you really have become a pilot. You think you know something special, something expert and real about being a pilot! Of course you can't fly a plane, but you convince yourself that you are a pilot. I always thought Ronald Reagan was playing the role of a president even when he was the president. He became the role that was in his head. Once he figured out what that role was, he knew exactly what he was supposed to do. That made playing the role—being the president—easy for him.

QUESTION: Do you feel more comfortable playing a role, say, as an actor, than in being yourself?

Role versus self, huh? Many answers come to mind.

- *Don't we all play roles in life? Maybe the question actually should be who assigns us these roles and why do we accept them?*
- *What's the difference between playing a role and being yourself? Doesn't the fact that you choose a role for yourself reveal some truth about who you are? Reagan as president.*
- *Or are you asking me if I am playing a role right now? Am I spinning an illusion for you and your readers? Hiding my true self? Am I trying to manipulate you into creating an image of me in your book that I am concocting as we speak?*
- *Do I even know for sure what my own feelings are? Have I become my perceived role? Or is the role that I perceive, the true me?*

None of this is easy for me to answer because I know that I often feel artificial as a person, as if I am somehow forced into playing some role or have drifted into playing roles that are different from who I actually am. Sometimes it's because I don't like or want to do what I'm doing; sometimes it's because I feel that somehow, in ways not clearly understood or articulable in speech and action, I'm not doing or being what I am, feel to be, or want to be. But I don't know, honestly, whether I am more this way than other people.

So.

Please note I did not say "So what?" or even say "So there!" I simply said "So." I mean, what's the point here?

[Long pause]

You must understand that self-exposure does not come easy for me. I have always seen myself as someone who is friendly and candid in almost all circumstances, and yet I recognize that I am often unable to open myself up fully or allow any true familiarity to show in many situations. I am not the sort of man who can talk easily about his feelings or gush with strangers during the cocktail hour. Because of this, some people will tell you that I am consciously or unconsciously arrogant when, in fact, I am simply reserved.

Again, I say, so.

[Long pause]

Now the relationship between acting and theater, and role-playing in espionage, now that is interesting. The crucial difference is this: in the theater there is a willing suspension of disbelief. An audience voluntarily suspends its disbelief when watching a performance, and in this way it joins the actor in creating an entertaining illusion. This is not the case in espionage. Let me preface this by saying that most agents volunteer and come into the situation knowing fully what they are accepting, the risks, et cetera. But in some instances, a case officer will choose a role to play. He becomes an actor. The purpose of his performance, however, is not the mutual construction of an entertaining illusion, it is exploitation through deception. And this is where another talent, or trait, is required that goes beyond acting. It is the ability to assess a person's vulnerability, figure out your target's desires and then to purposefully construct a reality or a scenario that entices that target. This demands role-playing at an extreme because the purpose is to deceive and manipulate. It is also a betrayal of trust.

What you must understand is that the essence of espionage, even the most innocuous sort, is betrayal of trust. One might almost say that this is the defining element, because without it, there is no espionage. A soldier doing reconnaissance behind enemy lines may be shot as a spy, but he is not betraying a trust. But an American military attaché who assiduously acquires the friendship and trust of his Iraqi counterpart on the diplomatic circuit and uses it not for the traditional exchange of military gossip but to support a CIA recruitment attempt is betraying a trust. And when an academic acquires the private and compromising views of his Chinese host and passes them on, he is betraying a trust. Now the extent to which this variety of behavior is reprehensible, corrupting, and justifiable is open to discussion, certainly. But the defining element is always a betrayal of trust. That is what is at the core of the intelligence officer's world—betraying another person's trust in you.

How does this relate to me personally? I lacked the talent and skills of a naturally gregarious person. What I did have, however, was the ability to focus on a target, establish a relationship, manipulate myself and himself into the situation or frame of mind I aimed for, and then to construct and make the ap-

proach. This I was good at and I had the ability to do it as myself or as another person altogether—businessman, academic, rich, poor, married, unmarried, liberal, conservative. A lot of otherwise successful recruiters have trouble with this. Now it may be that some extra layer of role-playing, a false or altered identity, helped me to be more successful, just as it might hinder case officers who feel simply being themselves and inviting a target to a family cookout is the best way.

Now, how does this role-playing affect me personally? This becomes confusing. I blame Stanislavsky and the Method for forever muddling these together, in the sense that many are tempted to believe that successful acting means the ability to merge, substitute, or even assume the personality of the actor with that presumed to be the character's. This is simply not so. Acting is an art in which techniques determine almost everything and, once again, there is no such thing as a one-man show—the audience must choose to participate. So what am I saying here?

I guess what I am saying is that I had no problem slipping into roles in my professional life, no problems playing roles. I could do it in my personal life, as well, also with great ease. I guess the difference is that in my personal life it was a defensive mechanism, I think. Deception was involved, but more for my own protection than for manipulation.

Of course, deception always involves manipulation, doesn't it? Hmm. I guess the role playing was essentially to hide who I really am. But again, how different is that? This is how we all are, is it not?

THE WORDS OF OTHERS

The bottom line is that our job as recruiters is to exploit people. That is what we do and the only way you can justify that is if you believe in what your side is doing. If you don't believe that what you are doing is not only the right thing for your country, but is also right with your sense of justice and your sense of what needs to be done to protect democracy, well then, there is nothing to keep you from crossing the line. I think Rick simply lost those feelings—if he ever had them. I'm not sure he did.

—R. Patrick Watson, FBI

Aldrich Ames? I hope he rots in hell forever!
          —Son of a Russian executed after Ames exposed him as a CIA spy

Did Rick do something immoral? He hurt his son, but that was about it.
Look, all of those spies who were executed knew what they were doing. Just like
him, they were taking a chance. I don't feel sorry for any of them, and as for
Rick, hey, he's my friend and I don't know anyone who could have pulled off
something like this as well as he did!

—Chuck Windley, high school friend

At a Christmas party on December 20, 1973, Ames became so drunk that
he had to be helped to his home by employees from the CIA's Office of Security.
The following Christmas, Ames also became intoxicated and was discovered by
an agency security officer in a compromising position with a female CIA em-
ployee.

—Select Committee on Intelligence report,
United States Senate

I thought I'd be shot. I never knew any story of people arrested by the KGB
who ever got out again. I never knew anyone who went into Lefortovo prison
and got out alive.

—Vladimir Potashov, a spy identified by Ames for the KGB

Rick was certainly not materialistic when he first joined the agency and was
married to Nan. He was really, well, just unkempt. His hair in particular was
hanging down to his shoulders and I swear he just cut it with scissors by him-
self. It was certainly not groomed or stylish and it didn't even look clean or any-
thing. He had these old glasses that were clearly out of style. He had bad teeth
and he smoked all the time. He loved to talk about ideas. He was not the kind
of guy who you would sit around with and talk about the weather or what the
cafeteria had for lunch that day.

—Jeanne R. Vertefeuille, CIA

John Souders called and told me that Rick was going to go to work full time
at the CIA. I asked him where? And John said, "Rick wants to join the DO." I
remember saying, "Oh, God!" You see, both of my parents worked at the CIA,
and I know what it can do to the people who work there. People in the CIA di-
vide themselves into two lines—analysts and those who go into operations, like
where Rick was going. There is nothing immoral or amoral about the analyti-
cal side, the so-called DI, but everyone knows that the Directorate of Opera-
tions exists in a complete and total moral vacuum. People who go covert have
to suspend all of the moral categories by which other people live their lives. You

can't tell your neighbors what you do. You have to lie to people every day, but the worst thing is that you really enter an ethical wasteland. It's the real-life Machiavellian world of The Prince, *where decisions about human beings and international politics are made exclusively on the basis of Realpolitik. Rick was one of my closest friends and I was afraid for him. I was afraid of what might happen to him when he disappeared into that murky world.*

—Wes Sanders, high school friend

CHAPTER 4

The KGB was reluctant to share its technology, even with its satellite republics, but the CIA was generous in the late 1960s when it came to doling out telephone wiretapping devices. "The Turkish intelligence service was cash-strapped, so we gave it a half million dollars' worth of wiretap equipment and taught its people how to use it," said Ames. "They repaid us by tapping the lines at the Soviet embassy and then giving us the tapes. This happened not only in Turkey but all over the world, particularly in Central and South America."

Before leaving Langley, Rick pored over the intelligence reports that were being sent from Ankara, and he noticed that several mentioned a young officer in the GRU. A French businessman had become friends with the GRU officer and had told the CIA about him. "I devised a rather complicated plan for recruiting this GRU target," Ames recalled. Rick wanted to frighten the GRU officer by making him believe he was about to be arrested as a spy by Turkish intelligence officers and booted out of the country. Rick figured the young officer would panic. The Soviet would not want to return to Moscow, where living conditions were harsh. GRU officers who were expelled from a country often had trouble leaving the Soviet Union again once they had been identified as an intelligence officer. "The idea was to make him vulnerable and desperate. Then we would step in and offer to save his ass by intervening with the

Turks," said Ames. "The entire threat would be a scam, but he wouldn't know it." Ames said his bosses approved of his scheme, but when he arrived in Ankara, he was told that a more senior case officer had been chosen to run the operation. "This guy needed his ticket punched—something on his resume that would get him his next promotion—and I was told that my turn would come later," Ames said.

Rick didn't get upset until he discovered that the case officer didn't speak Russian and knew only a few words of Turkish. Those were the only two languages that the GRU officer spoke. "There was absolutely no way we were going to be able to successfully pitch and recruit this guy, since our man wasn't going to be able to even talk to him coherently," said Ames, who had taken a crash course in Turkish before being sent to Ankara. "Everyone knew it wasn't going to work, but no one cared. The point was that the station would be able to report that it had made a recruitment attempt, and everyone would be congratulated." Just as Ames predicted, the Russian didn't understand the pitch, and the ruse failed. "The CIA case officer got his promotion, so it didn't matter to him that we hadn't recruited anyone."

In Ankara, Rick used his actual name, but he told everyone that he was a civilian employee working for the United States Air Force. To help with the masquerade, he worked in Ankara at the headquarters building of TUSOLOG, an acronym for the Turkish United States Operations and Logistics Command center. He was supposedly involved in some sort of long-range logistical study, but he spent all his time hunting for targets to recruit.

Before arriving in Ankara, Rick had envisioned himself playing a cat-and-mouse game with the KGB as it tried to catch him rendezvousing with a Soviet agent in some exotic, poorly lit Ankara bar. Instead, he found himself sitting at a desk, filling out intelligence reports and answering cables.

"After Richard Nixon won the 1968 elections, word went out that the new president wanted the agency to stop being a Mr. Nice Guy when it came to the Soviets. The incoming administration was tired of the Russians screwing around with us, and every station was ordered to get creative and come up with some serious covert action plans. I thought, *At last we are going to go out and actually recruit a Soviet.* But our station chief had a different definition of what getting tough meant." The Soviet Union had invaded Czechoslovakia and ousted Czech leader Alexander Dubček in August 1968, so the station chief in Ankara printed thousands of stickers that protested the invasion. Ames spent his workdays strolling through the city, slapping "Remember Dubček, Remember '68" stickers on walls and the windows of office buildings. "We wanted to make it look as if the Turkish people were really outraged by the Czech invasion." Rick spent several weeks distributing stickers and still had a large box of them left over. One afternoon, he and another case officer climbed onto the roof of a tall downtown building and dumped the boxes over the side that overlooked Ankara's busiest intersection, treating the lunchtime crowds to a momentary deluge of pro-Dubček stickers. "We wrote this up as a big station accomplishment!"

Nancy Segebarth Ames found life in Ankara just as frustrating as her husband did. In a perfect example of bureaucratic absurdity, the same CIA personnel office that had required her to resign as a DI analyst did not object when she was hired in Ankara to work as an administrative assistant in the same office as Rick. She soon had a reputation for being smart, aggressive, and outspoken. At home and in the office, she seemed to dominate her husband.

One year into his assignment, Rick finally got to test his recruitment skills. An American college professor teaching in Ankara volunteered to introduce Rick to a Turkish student who was a member of DEVGENG, a radical student organization dedicated to overthrowing the Turkish government. The student, who Rick was supposed to recruit, was a close friend of Deniz Gezmis, one of DEVGENG's leaders. The CIA was interested in penetrating DEVGENG because Turkey was being rocked by unrest. Prime Minister Suleyman Demirel had been forced to resign and the country was under martial law. Newspapers were being censored, books were being banned, illegal arrests were being made, and there were rumors that government execution squads were kidnapping dissidents at night from college campuses. Rick personally favored most of the democratic reforms that were being advocated by the government's critics, but he knew the United States was not about to challenge the established government. The National Security Agency used Turkey as a site for numerous listening posts built to intercept Soviet communications. Turkey was where the United States stockpiled some of its nuclear arsenal, and the Turkish government was a vital supporter of NATO. Having an informant inside DEVGENG would give the CIA a hefty bargaining chip to use when trading favors with those in power.

The American college professor who knew Rick's target was confident that she would help them, mainly because the professor was having a sexual affair with her. Rick decided to pose as a State Department official interested in pursuing democratic reforms in Turkey. He chose a restaurant away from the university for the meeting and arrived early enough to make certain it was safe. He would later recall what happened. He had chosen a table in a back corner and had passed the time by watching the smoke from his cigarette vanish into the stale air. The cafe smelled of grilled lamb and human sweat. An unintelligible babble rose from the men and women speaking rapidly at several tables near the restaurant's entrance. Rick was anxious. Would she come? He silently cursed himself for choosing such a seedy place. The student was in her early twenties and a former beauty contest winner. The professor had shown him a photograph. She was going to stand out in this haunt of watermelon-bellied men and dowdy women.

As he had feared, everyone stared when the student stepped inside, but she didn't seem worried when he waved her back to his table. Rick had never felt relaxed around attractive women, and still didn't, even now that he was married. He still wore thick black glasses, had a permanent cowlick and found it difficult to make polite chitchat. "I believe we both want the same things here," he told her. It was the opening to a speech that he had been rehearsing for several days. He assured her that the United States wanted to push for reforms, but explained that it had to work behind the scenes because of its relationship with the existing government. His main priority was preventing bloodshed, he said. He didn't want her or her friends arrested, tortured, or murdered, but he couldn't help them unless he knew more about DEVGENG and its plans. He was lying, of course. He did not plan on helping her or DEVGENG. But he would later recall that he had sounded earnest and convincing that day in the restaurant, and she had swallowed the bait.

"The key to recruiting someone is always to offer that person exactly what they want from you, while making it appear as if there is no downside for them," Ames later explained. After he made his speech, he had slid an envelope that contained seventy-five dollars across the table. "We know you are not doing this for money but what I am asking will take your time and I want to compensate you for that," he told her. "I want you to have this to help with your expenses each month." Rick knew seventy-five dollars a month was a large amount for her. It meant the difference between struggling to survive and being able to live comfortably. She tucked the envelope in her pocket. At that moment, he knew he had her.

A few days later, Rick met her in his car at a corner near the university. As they drove around Ankara, she told him the names of the other students in DEVGENG, as well as the date of the group's next meeting. He passed along this information to his chief of station, who contacted Turkish intelligence. Much to the CIA's surprise, the Turks weren't interested. They already had several sources in DEVGENG. Rick met with his agent twice more but she didn't tell him anything useful, so he was ordered to terminate the relationship.

They met in the same cafe where he had pitched her. She was late and seemed upset. He didn't ask why. Instead he slipped her an envelope that contained two hundred dollars. "My country is grateful for your help but I do not think there is much else we can do working together," he would later recall telling her. "We want you to know that what you did was very helpful." If she ever wanted to contact him again, all she had to do was go to any U.S. embassy and ask to speak to an intelligence officer. "Just give your name," he said. She seemed shocked. He wasn't sure, but he suspected that it was because she had only now understood that she was dealing with the CIA, and that her name was in some file somewhere ready to be called up if she ever were needed.

The woman asked if Rick had spoken to their mutual friend, the college professor, and Rick said that he hadn't. "Did you know that he stopped seeing me?" she asked. Before he could reply, she continued, "He found himself a new girl, a younger student." They drank the rest of their coffee without comment, and then she left. Rick had not known how she was going to react. He had been warned that some agents panic when they are told that their monthly stipend is going to end. Some are relieved. Others offer to do more. He had been worried that she was going to be angry, since he had not done anything to help her or DEVGENG. "The whole process had been much easier than I thought, actually," he said later. "That was my first recruitment."

Rick attempted another one a few weeks later. "It was the classic setup. Nan and I invited this fellow and his wife to dinner. He worked in the Turkish foreign ministry and I had spent quite a bit of time developing a friendship with him. We had gone fishing, been on picnics with our wives, gone sailing, all that sort of thing, and when I felt comfortable enough, I decided to pitch him." Rick began complaining about his job and how he was having trouble getting reliable information that he needed for a special report. He was really being pressured to get the report written, he said. His next promotion depended on it. His dinner guest asked Rick what sort of information he was trying to find. "It has to do with intelligence estimates about the Soviet military," he replied matter-of-factly. "That sort of thing." Rick implied that the report was being written for NATO, and he subtly reminded his friend that both the United States and Turkey were NATO members. "I wanted him to think we were all on the same team," said Ames. Finally, Rick asked his pal if he could get the information for him from the Turkish intelligence service. "I remember that he agonized and agonized over it. It took him several days, but he finally gave me some material and I gave him some cash." At the CIA station, Rick got credit for another recruitment.

"You quickly learn that everyone you meet is a potential target. That is the way you always think, so while you can develop a personal relationship with people and these can be genuine and can grow, these relationships are always an offshoot of your original and primary mindset, which is to evaluate every person and use the ones that you can use. What's odd is that I discovered I was fairly good at manipulating people, but I was never good at using those skills for self-promotion within the agency. I never cultivated my bosses, never suggested that they come over for dinner. I never felt comfortable doing that sort of thing and I always had problems with authority. I have never felt at ease with people who are senior to me."

Rick was ready to return home when his two-year tour ended, but the Ankara station was shorthanded. Despite his protests, he was told that he had to extend his tour for another six months. He sulked, and became even more depressed when his parents visited and he learned that Carleton had inoperable cancer and a short time to live. Rick's father and mother had reunited after Rachel's teaching tour in Pakistan had ended. Alison had been treated and released for her mental troubles and was doing better. The family seemed to be pulling itself back together.

In July 1971, Dewey Clarridge arrived in Ankara as the new deputy chief of station, eager to shake things up. "Dewey ordered me to get out and recruit some Soviets. We really didn't have many Soviet agents. He said, 'Throw a few parties, mingle more with the Turks,' but I didn't feel comfortable with that and simply dragged my feet. Dewey got really pissed off when I ignored his instructions." Before Clarridge arrived, Rick had received excellent performance ratings from his bosses and had been promoted twice. Clarridge rated Rick as low as possible. Worse, he wrote in the evaluation form that he really didn't believe Rick would ever be an effective case officer. Rick had trouble working "face-to-face . . . with unknown personalities who must be manipulated," Clarridge noted. He also wrote that Rick's personality was too reserved for him ever to become a successful recruiter.

Clarridge's evaluation was devastating, especially since Rick's job was recruiting Soviets. "Nan and I talked about whether or not I should switch over to the DI analytical side or try to move into the foreign service at the State Department. Nan didn't want to get her old job back at the agency. She had had enough of the CIA, and I should have left the agency, too. Instead, I just sort of soldiered on and headed back to headquarters, not knowing exactly what was going to happen next. That was typical of me. But when I got back, I was told that I had been chosen to spend a year in the foreign language school studying Russian, and that meant I was being groomed for another promotion. I thought, *Wow, I guess that lousy rating by Clarridge didn't hurt me at all.*"

THE WORDS OF RICK AMES

When Nan and I returned to the states in 1972, we moved into a house in the Virginia suburb of Reston, which was one of the first planned communities, and much to my surprise, Nan really got involved. It started when she went to a couple of Reston Community Association meetings, and then out of the blue she volunteered to help Joe Fisher, a Democrat, campaign for a local congressional seat against Joel Broyhill, a longtime Republican conservative. She did one hell of a job! She went out and really ginned things up, you know, knocked on doors and found a big latent talent as an organizer, and it made a big difference in helping Joe win the upset. After Joe won, he hired her to do some sort of analytic study, and the next thing I know she is running for a seat on the Reston Community Association board. It was a side of her I had never seen. She got real involved in getting the county to build lower-cost housing in the community for minorities and the poor, and I supported her in that.

My father died that summer. He was sixty-seven. It bothered me a lot. He told me when he came to Ankara that he was proud of me. You know, proud that I was serving my country. Mom was still in Hickory, North Carolina, and she was getting involved in local politics, too.

Nan and I were still getting along okay. Maybe in Turkey, you know, we started to realize that we just didn't find each other as interesting sexually as before, but there were never any fights or arguments. We decided not to have children. I didn't feel like I wanted children and when the subject came up, we would both decide "Well, maybe later," but later never came. I don't know why I didn't want them, because later with Rosario, I did. I guess I thought that

Nan didn't want children, and maybe she thought I didn't want children; of course, later on I learned that she had wanted children. The truth is we were fooling each other and fooling ourselves. I mean, we deceived the hell out of ourselves during our marriage in terms of what we wanted and our ability to communicate that to each other. We weren't really communicating and listening to each other, but each of us just sort of pretended that everything was okay and acted as if we ignored the problems, then they would not exist. Of course, by the time we realized we were both pretending, it was too late.

In Turkey, we had gone to a party and I had overindulged and had gotten a bit too relaxed. I wasn't falling-down drunk or anything, but I got kind of loud and slurry, and Nan really was embarrassed and got on me for it. If I even had two drinks at a party after that, I would hear about it, because she didn't drink at all. And, of course, after she got on the Reston Community Association board, there were parties and she would always be apprehensive about whether I'd drink too much or not.

Drinking has always been a struggle for me. I have vacillated between considering myself beyond self-help and total denial. Before I left home for college, I don't think I'd consumed more than a dozen beers and glasses of wine. I'm quite sure I never even tasted anything stronger. My first autumn at Chicago, I got drunk on Scotch with friends in the dormitory, but quickly switched to gin for our weekend parties. By the next spring, I had drifted into the theater group's circle, dropped the dorm parties, and drank beer when I could afford it at the taverns favored by the theater people. For many years after that, I seldom drank liquor, only beer and wine, which gave me plenty of opportunities to feel high and, often, drunk.

I guess I should mention that an enduring pattern to my drinking has been its social aspect. I have always felt inhibited, uncommunicative, unable to make small talk and to enjoy intimacy with others, even friends and colleagues. Social drinking, together with the effects of alcohol itself, made me feel more able to relate to and deal with others. As time went on, I noticed two things. I always seemed to drink more and longer than most, and often got drunker. Others seemed more in control and able to pick up and leave. I couldn't. I always was a bitter-ender. While still in college, I had blackout episodes, when the last hour or so of a binge would be completely lost to me the next morning. I guess nothing disastrous ever happened. I was told that I was always a friendly and sentimental drunk.

CHAPTER 5

"I'm pregnant," the woman could be heard crying in Spanish on the tape recording.

"I'll take care of you, don't worry," came the answer, in clumsy Spanish with a heavy Russian accent.

Such talk normally did not interest officers of Colombia's intelligence service, known by the acronym DASS, but when they recorded this brief exchange over the telephone, they decided to investigate. The woman was calling from Madrid and speaking to someone at the Soviet embassy in Bogotá. He said he couldn't speak freely over the embassy line, and suggested she call him at a nearby public telephone.

DASS agents were watching later when Alexander Dmitrievich Ogorodnik cautiously approached the ringing receiver. The conversation confirmed what they suspected. Ogorodnik was having a sexual affair with Pilar Sanchez,* a Colombian visiting relatives in Spain. Shortly after Sanchez returned home, two DASS agents demanded that she introduce them to Ogorodnik. If either she or the Russian refused to cooperate, DASS would make their affair public. Sanchez would be humiliated, and Ogorodnik would be recalled to Moscow. Sanchez agreed to cooperate, but Ogorodnik balked. He would only deal with the CIA, he said. Two weeks later, Ogorodnik

*Not her real name.

and a CIA case officer met in a Turkish steambath in downtown Bogotá. The Soviet agreed to spy for the agency. In return, the CIA promised to pay Sanchez's childbirth expenses, move her and her newborn daughter to Spain, and give her enough money to open a child care center.*

The CIA desperately needed Soviet "assets." For six years, the agency's SE division had been ravaged by the paranoid rambling of James Jesus Angleton, the CIA's legendary mole hunter, whose obsession with catching a KGB agent inside the agency had ruined the careers of several innocent employees and crippled recruitment efforts. William Colby, the agency's newly appointed director, was in the midst of firing Angleton in 1974, and had just given the SE division a kick in the pants when Ogorodnik surfaced. "The Soviet division still wasn't producing agents to operate against the Soviets," Colby told Tom Mangold in *Cold Warrior.* "I had to give them speeches to stress the importance of their mission. 'Let's go, let's go!' I told them. 'Let's recruit all over the world!' It must have had some effect because one of the guys went off and promptly recruited a Russian in a steambath!"

Now that Ogorodnik was aboard, Havilland Smith, the chief of the Latin American (LA) branch in the SE division, needed someone to "handle" him. A CIA officer in Bogotá would retrieve whatever information Ogorodnik left at dead drops (prearranged sites where an agent and his handler could leave packages for each other), but a desk officer in Langley would ultimately be responsible for sorting through Ogorodnik's deliveries and finding ways to use him best. Smith chose Rick, who had just completed learning Russian at the agency's language school and needed an assignment. No one knew whether or not Ogorodnik would turn out to be much of a spy, and Smith was curious to see how Rick would perform as a handler. Ogorodnik was given the cryptonym KNIGHT, and because he was from the Soviet Union, the prefix AE was automatically added to that codename. AE was used to identify Soviet assets. The new spy was listed in directories as a low-level diplomat, but everyone thought he was KGB.

"In the 1970s we were sure that every Soviet who was allowed to travel outside the USSR either was KGB or GRU or controlled by them," Ames said, "but Ogorodnik kept insisting he was a genuine diplomat. Our station chief in Bogotá finally called him a liar to his face, so Ogorodnik says, 'Okay, you're right. I am KGB!' and he gives us this long description of KGB operations in Bogotá. When we checked, we discovered his stories were a bunch

*She and her daughter still operate it today.

of baloney, because he really was a diplomat. Rather than being thrilled, everyone was disappointed, because the mind set was that only information about the KGB, GRU, and the Soviet military was worth collecting." That view quickly changed when analysts in the DI read what KNIGHT sent them. The Soviet embassy in Bogotá was hardly a hot diplomatic post, but the ambassador was privy to a continuous flow of cables from Moscow that explained the Kremlin's attitudes toward Latin America and matters being debated in the United Nations. "The stuff was dynamite, and then our agent's access got even better," Ames said. Seven months after Ogorodnik became an agent, he announced that he was being recalled to work in the Global Affairs Department of the Ministry of Foreign Affairs in Moscow. It was one of the Soviet Union's most important and well-guarded bureaucracies. Every Soviet ambassador was required to submit an annual report to the ministry analyzing the local political situation in his country, along with an appraisal of what the embassy was doing to further the goals of communism. Through Ogorodnik, the CIA would be able to see the world *exactly* as the Soviet leadership was viewing it.

The CIA issued Ogorodnik special writing pads to use. Each pad had its own individual encryption code. Only a person with an identical pad could decipher the message. The CIA also issued him a T-100 spy camera disguised as a tube of lip balm, but capable of taking one hundred photographs. Ogorodnik was given a new crypt, too. There was always a chance that the KGB had somehow discovered that a CIA mole known as KNIGHT was working in the Soviet embassy in Bogotá. If KNIGHT suddenly was mentioned in cable traffic to and from Moscow, the KGB would deduce that KNIGHT was someone who had recently moved to Moscow from Colombia. Ogorodnik's new name was TRIGON, and to further protect him, a new prefix was added. Unlike AE, his new prefix, CK, did not refer to a specific country but simply meant the case involved an SE division agent. Overnight, Rick found himself in charge of a hot case.

He was frequently called on to give briefings to the top DO brass. One morning, Havilland Smith was waiting when Rick reported to work. TRIGON wanted a suicide pill to swallow if he were caught in Moscow, Smith announced. Rick was surprised. He didn't know that the agency made "L" (lethal) pills, but Smith told him that they had been issued in rare cases during World War Two to officers being sent behind enemy lines. Smith suggested that Rick convince TRIGON that he didn't really need one. He tried, but TRIGON was adamant, so the CIA's technical branch hid an L pill inside a cigarette lighter and sent it to TRIGON. A few months later, TRIGON sent word he needed another suicide capsule because he had lost the lighter. The agency sent him one hidden inside an expensive ink pen.

In Moscow, TRIGON began photographing hundreds of Soviet diplomatic cables, including candid reports written by the current Soviet ambassador to the United States Anatoly Dobrynin, who was stationed in Washington, D.C., and by the Soviet ambassador to the United Nations, Oleg Troyanovsky, in New York City. TRIGON's material was so important that the CIA implemented a separate system to distribute it. The diplomatic reports that TRIGON photographed were translated and printed verbatim on paper with a blue edge. They were dubbed the Blue Stripe Reports and were delivered by couriers to the White House, the State Department, and the National Security Council. Henry Kissinger reportedly studied them closely.

Rick's handling of TRIGON impressed Havilland Smith, so much so that he decided to take Rick with him to New York for a meeting with a Soviet diplomat. Smith had recruited this agent and was personally handling him. If the Russian, who worked at the UN Secretariat, liked Rick, Smith planned to turn the case over to him. New York City was a Mecca for recruiters. The CIA had sixty employees in its office there. They worked closely with the FBI field office, which had two hundred special agents on call just to shadow Soviets. Some of the G-men didn't even have desks in the FBI's Manhattan office because they spent all of their work days on the streets. The CIA and FBI estimated that of the seven hundred Soviets who were employed at the UN, the Soviet Mission, or the UN Secretariat, at least half were either KGB or GRU officers.

Smith and Rick arrived early at a CIA safe house in the Bronx, near a subway line that many Soviets used to commute between the UN headquarters in Manhattan and the Soviet residential compound in Riverdale. Sergey Fedorenko, whose CIA crypt was PYRRHIC, was late.*

"Is something wrong?" a concerned Smith asked. "Were you followed?"

Fedorenko grinned. The cocky Soviet had always bragged that he didn't need the CIA to tell him how to keep from being caught by the KGB.

"Is anyone ever on time in New York?" he quipped. Roguishly handsome, Fedorenko was thirty years old, two years younger than Rick. He was a Camel

---

*By this time, the CIA had changed the AE prefix that it used to identify the Soviet Union to GT. It frequently changed these prefixes. For simplicity's sake, I have chosen not to include the prefixes in the remainder of this book.

cigarette-smoking, straight-talking, quick-witted rebel with a cause. He had a reputation for being absolutely fearless, some might even say reckless. No one was going to force him to take Rick as his new handler unless he wanted him. Over several bottles of beer, the Russian sized up Rick. He liked what he saw. Rick's hair fell over his ears, and he was wearing black boots. Based on those two observations, Fedorenko decided Rick was not a typical Washington bureaucrat. He also liked Rick's curiosity.

"I am an idealistic idiot," Fedorenko proclaimed. "When I was a small boy, my grandfather used to read me a quotation that went like this: 'Don't be afraid of your enemies, because all they can do is kill you. Don't be afraid of your friends, because all they can do is betray you. But always be afraid of silent indifference, because that is where all crimes will be committed.' I refuse to be silent or indifferent toward what the KGB is doing to my country."

That night Fedorenko expressed feelings that Rick would hear repeated by other Soviets during the coming years. Fedorenko said he loved his country, but despised the corrupt Communist Party system, and especially hated the KGB. His grandfather had spent ten years in a forced labor camp in Siberia because he had used a piece of newspaper as toilet paper that had Joseph Stalin's photograph printed on it. A KGB informant had been next in line at the communal toilet and had received extra privileges for retrieving the soiled newsprint as evidence and reporting the insult. "That's the service I want to destroy." At the end of their meeting, Fedorenko told Rick: "I will work with you. I am now placing my life in your hands." After pausing for a moment, he added, "Please don't screw up."

Rick began making bimonthly trips to New York to meet the agent, and during the next two and a half years, the two men became close friends. Often, after they finished their long sessions together, they would relax over glasses of wine, and Fedorenko would tell Rick about what life had been like growing up in the USSR. He had a talent for storytelling. Fedorenko had been born during the Great Patriotic War (World War II), when much of Russia was starving. He had been illegitimate and unwanted. His mother wanted an abortion, but the town doctor refused to end the pregnancy because she was already several months along. His mother abandoned her unnamed newborn in an overcrowded, underfunded public orphanage, where he nearly starved to death twice—but Fedorenko proved to be a survivor. As a teenager, he showed an unusual skill at playing chess and was blessed with a keen mind for mathematics. A teacher arranged for him to enter Moscow's prestigious Aviation Institute, which was responsible for the successful Soviet space program. Fedorenko became an expert on guided missiles, which were being seen as the weapons of the future, and his work soon came to the attention of one of the Soviet Union's most important diplomats, Nikolai Fedorenko.

The senior Fedorenko had served as the Soviet ambassador to the UN, spoke flawless Chinese, and had served as an interpreter when Mao Zedong first visited Stalin. He was also the father of Yelena Fedorenko, one of the most sought-after women in Moscow. In 1964, *Vogue* published a photograph of Yelena. "Vivid, with a deeply romantic Russian look, Yelena Fedorenko is a refreshing blend of brains, grave poise, and young exuberance. A world traveler at nineteen, she has lived, with her diplomat parents, in China, Japan, the United States—and naturally Russia." Sergey and Yelena fell in love, and after they married, the new husband adopted his famous father-in-law's last name since the elder Fedorenko did not have any sons and did not want his name to die out. Yelena's father arranged for Fedorenko to become the youngest member of the Soviet's SALT I treaty negotiation team, and had pulled the necessary strings to get him hired at the UN by Arkady N. Shevchenko, who in 1972 became Under Secretary General of the UN, the second most important person there. Fedorenko could have had an easy life, but his hatred of the KGB and his rebel's attitude was always leading him into trouble.

Fedorenko told Rick that the KGB had visited him and Yelena in Moscow shortly after it learned that he had been chosen to work at the UN. "They expected me to help them spy, but I told them I would be too busy to play their dirty games and kicked them out of my apartment." Fedorenko's father-in-law was called, and the younger Fedorenko was summoned for some parting advice. "Tell the KGB in New York that you will be happy to help, and then do whatever they ask you to do so poorly and so stupidly that they will leave you alone," the diplomat suggested. It was good advice, but Fedorenko was too stubborn to follow it. The KGB's *rezident* in New York City was Boris Aleksandrovich Solomatin, and he reacted quickly when Fedorenko snubbed his officers. He called Yelena into his office and berated her for doing a lousy job as a switchboard operator at the Soviet mission, where she had been put to work. By the time he had finished, she was in tears, and her husband got the message. "He was showing me how the KGB could make life for my family difficult."

A short time later, a KGB officer asked Fedorenko to drive to New England and look at a radar station that was under construction. Most Soviets working in the United States had to get special permission from the State Department to travel more than twenty-five miles from their diplomatic posts, but Fedorenko worked at the UN Secretariat, and its employees could travel freely in the United States without permission. Fedorenko thought the trip would be a waste of time. "The radar site will be surrounded by a fence. I will not be able to see anything," he replied. This time, however, he suggested an alternative. He volunteered to snoop around at the Hudson Institute, a New York think-tank with close ties to the Pentagon, the National Security Council, and the State Department. The KGB officer was thrilled.

Fedorenko telephoned Donald Brennan, the institute's director of studies, whom he had met earlier at the SALT I negotiations, and the two agreed to meet for lunch. Brennan was a prime KGB target. His expertise was nuclear weapon systems, and his wife was the daughter of a top executive at the Boeing Corporation, the major builder of the B-1 bomber and a leader in developing Stealth technology. The KGB wanted Fedorenko to befriend Brennan and win his trust. Once that was done, Federenko would introduce Brennan to a KGB recruiter. But when the two met for lunch, it was the Soviet who volunteered to become a spy for the American. "Don, can you introduce me to some of your friends in Washington?" Fedorenko asked. A month later, Brennan arranged for Fedorenko to speak at a scientific seminar in the nation's capital. Havilland Smith was seated in the front row and stayed late to speak with Fedorenko.

One of the first revelations that Fedorenko had told Smith was that three KGB officers were trying to penetrate the Hudson Institute. The FBI was already aware of attempts by two of the men, but no one had suspected the third because he was a respected Soviet scientist. He had befriended several institute members, including Brennan, who was stunned when he learned that the scientist was a spy.

During interviews with me, Fedorenko, who now lives in the United States, would insist that he had never provided the CIA or the FBI with any information about the Soviet military. His entire reason for spying during the mid-seventies had been to damage the KGB by exposing the names of their officers and clandestine operations. Ames and the FBI agents who debriefed Fedorenko would claim that the Russian had done more than talk about the KGB. "Sergey told us all about the SS-4, the intermediate range missile that the Soviets had tried to install in Cuba, and about other missiles too," Ames said. His most valuable contribution at the time, however, was his explanation of how the Soviet defense industry actually worked. "We didn't have a clue about how the Soviets decided which weapon system they were going to build or how they chose who got what contract. We didn't even know who actually made those sorts of military decisions." Fedorenko's expertise was so pivotal that the Pentagon completely revised its estimates of the Soviets' overall military strength in the late 1970s because of what he said, Ames claimed.

"I don't want your money," Fedorenko said, when he first volunteered to Smith. "I don't want to be obligated to you. I am doing this on my own and I will do it my way." Just the same, the CIA began putting aside cash for him.*

In the fall of 1973, Fedorenko told Rick that a KGB officer named Valdek Enger was pressuring him to steal documents from the Hudson Institute. After his initial meeting with Brennan, Fedorenko had convinced the KGB that security was too tight there for him to steal anything. Enger wanted him to try again. Rick suggested that Fedorenko avoid Enger, but the feisty spy didn't like that advice. It might make Enger suspicious. He wanted to begin feeding Enger bits and pieces of information. That way it would make the KGB less suspicious of him. Rick checked with his bosses, and they agreed. During the coming months, the agency arranged for several scientific reports to be funneled through Brennan to Fedorenko, who then presented them to Enger. "These were not classified, but they were very sexy," Fedorenko said later. As expected, Enger was elated, so much so that he began spending more time with his new source. Despite his hatred of the KGB, Fedorenko soon found himself liking Enger. "He was harmless, almost an idiot, but lovable." He also learned that Enger was an excellent source for KGB gossip. Because of his position, Enger was privy to which Soviets were having sexual affairs, which were drunks, which were suspected of being disloyal: information that Fedorenko passed on to Rick.

One night, Fedorenko arrived at the CIA safe house still chuckling over

*Ames later helped Fedorenko open a checking account after he defected to the United States. Because Fedorenko did not have a permanent U.S. address at the time, he listed Ames's home address as his own. It was the discovery of this account that made public Fedorenko's spying during the 1970s. The *Washington Post* inadvertently exposed Fedorenko when one of its reporters noticed that the FBI had found a joint checkbook with Fedorenko's name on it when it collected evidence at Ames's house. The reporter wrote a story raising questions about Fedorenko's links to Ames, and within days Fedorenko's relationship with the FBI and CIA was made public. Fedorenko was furious, because he was afraid that the Russian government might punish his relatives in Moscow, but none of them was arrested or questioned.

an exchange that he and Enger had had earlier. KGB *rezident* Boris Solomatin's tour was over, and his successor, Yuri Ivanovich Drozdov, was eager to prove himself. He had demanded that his officers recruit more Americans. "Enger is under tremendous pressure, so he asked me if I would invite an American diplomat over to my apartment for a cookout," Fedorenko told Rick. "Enger says to me: 'We can grill some shiskabobs and then pitch him.' I said, 'Valdek, what can we offer him to spy?' and he says, 'Well, we don't have any money, but maybe we could give him a nice Russian fur hat.' I said, 'Valdek, you aren't going to get a man of his caliber to betray his country for a fur cap,' and he says, 'Well, who could we get to betray his country for a fur cap?' I told him, 'Only one of our people!'"

Fedorenko and Rick laughed all night.

Rick's commute to New York soon became routine. He would leave Washington before dawn on a commuter train and take a taxi to the FBI's New York field office, where he would chat with R. Patrick Watson, a special agent who was also assigned to handle Fedorenko. Oftentimes, Watson and Rick would eat lunch and discuss the questions they would ask their agent later that night. Rick would buy some steaks and wine for the evening and then take the subway to the safe house to prepare dinner for himself and Fedorenko. One afternoon in 1975, while riding on the subway to the safe house, Rick fell asleep. He woke up just as the subway car was about to pull away from his exit. Rick bolted out the doors just as they were closing and started down the ramp. Then he realized he had left his briefcase on the train. Inside it were snapshots that Fedorenko had taken at a recent party. He had written the names of the Russians in the photographs on the back of each picture. "There were over three hundred Soviets living in the Soviet residential compound and it was near the end of the line. I knew most of them rode the subway. It was clearly a hot zone." If Rick's briefcase were found by the KGB, Fedorenko was sure to be identified and arrested. Rick was only a couple of stops from the end of the subway line, so he raced to the other side of the tracks and waited for the subway car that he had been riding to return. When it arrived, he raced inside, but his briefcase was gone. "I ran to the safe house and called Watson."

Neither Rick nor Watson said anything about the missing briefcase when Fedorenko arrived at the safe house that night. Neither warned him that he could be in grave danger. As far as they knew, KGB agents could have been examining Rick's case at that very moment. When Fedorenko left, as carefree as ever, Rick was terrified that he would never see him again. The next morning, Watson called Rick. "We got it!" A woman had found the case and had looked through it for some sort of identification papers. When she saw the photographs and read the Russian names on them, she had become frightened. The next morning, she called the FBI. Rick's bosses put a reprimand in his personnel file. "That night was one of the worst in my life," he said later. "I can still remember how upset I was, because I thought I was going to be responsible for getting Sergey killed."

Despite that screwup, the agency promoted Rick to its New York City office and gave him an even bigger case than Fedorenko. He was assigned to help handle Fedorenko's boss, Ambassador Arkady Nikolaevich Shevchenko, the number two man at the UN. Originally, Shevchenko had wanted to defect when he first contacted the agency in 1975, but the CIA had sent one of its best recruiters to meet the diplomat, and he had convinced him to postpone his defection and work as an agent.

"We had Shevchenko, who had access to a wealth of diplomatic cables and information. We had TRIGON in Moscow photographing many of the same diplomatic cables that Shevchenko was telling us about, and we had Sergey Fedorenko giving us information at the UN too," Ames said later. "None of them knew about the other. We also had a fourth source, an agent whose crypt was FEDORA. He was supplying us with stuff from the Soviet residency in New York. It was just a gangbuster time!"

Rick and Nan moved into a glitzy one-bedroom apartment in a building called The Revere at 400 East 54th Street in Manhattan. From their living room they could see the East River. Despite their new surroundings, they were flat broke. They'd lost Nan's salary when she'd quit her job to move with Rick, and the prices in midtown Manhattan were much higher than they were used to paying. "We were so busted that when we went to visit Nan's folks in Pennsylvania, we had to take the bus." One of Rick's relatives would later recall visiting him and Nan in New York. "Rick was wearing really old clothes and the two of them were barely scraping by, but neither seemed to care. Money just wasn't that important to them."

Nan found a job working for the lobbying group Common Cause, and Rick got a pay raise. Still, he was peeved. He didn't think that he was being promoted as quickly as he should have been, and he thought he knew why. "I was not punching the right bureaucratic tickets. I was handling really important cases, but the promotion panels only paid attention to one thing— recruitments. I wasn't recruiting anyone, so I was not on the fast track." Ames began trolling the city in search of vulnerable Soviets. The CIA's main office was in the Pan Am Building, but he worked undercover from a dummy corporate office in a skyscraper on Lexington Avenue and 42nd Street. When he met Soviets, he was supposed to tell them that he was a businessman from the Midwest who came to New York frequently. "It was a really poor cover. I mean, what's a businessman from Ohio going to have in common with Soviets?" Despite his best efforts, he couldn't find anyone to recruit. "It didn't bother me, because I really didn't have time anyway to develop any contacts. I was too busy with Fedorenko and Shevchenko."

Technically, Rick was not Shevchenko's handler. That job belonged to the deputy chief of the New York station, but he was busy and let Rick do it. In mid-1977, James Dudley Haase took over the deputy's job and he decided to take control of the case. Haase was a forty-six-year-old heavyset ex-Marine. Shevchenko was a refined, piano-playing, and poetry-reading diplomat. They didn't hit it off. "Shevchenko had an awful lot of personal problems with his marriage and his drinking, and whenever he would get drunk with us and become weepy, Jim's reaction would be 'C'mon, quit sniveling, straighten up and be a man!' and that would just make Arkady even more miserable, so I would sort of hold his hand and quietly build him back up so we could send him out the door again."

Rick developed a personal fondness for the diplomat. "The first thing every CIA officer is told is 'Never fall in love with your agents.' And that is always exactly what happens anyway. I'm not talking about a sexual relationship. I'm talking about letting down your professional guard so that you begin believing everything that the agent tells you and begin worrying more about his best interest instead of your country's." Shevchenko was given the cryptonym DYNAMITE, and it proved a fitting tag. "He'd walk into the safe house and say, 'I've had it. I've done enough! I'm ready to defect,' and Jim and I would begin talking to him and getting him excited about what he was doing and get him to promise to hang on until the next session at the UN ended or whatever. He was too good a source to lose."

Shevchenko kept the CIA apprised of the ongoing feud in the Kremlin between Leonid Brezhnev and Aleksey Kosygin about how friendly the USSR should be toward the United States. He told them what the Kremlin was ordering Soviet ambassador Anatoly Dobrynin to do at the UN, what the Soviets' position on arms control talks were, even the Soviets' fallback positions in the SALT I talks. He provided details about how the Soviets' commitment to the fighting in Angola was weakening, top secret data about Soviet economics, even reports about the rapidly declining reserves in the oil fields in the Volga-Ural region. "Shevchenko's access was unbelievable. All we had to do was ask and he could get us an answer."

Not long after he began working with Shevchenko, Rick learned that Sergey Fedorenko was being recalled to Moscow. "Suddenly, I had Sergey wanting to defect, too, and one of my biggest accomplishments was convincing him to go ahead and return home," Ames recalled. "Of course when it came time for my next promotion, I once again got turned down because I hadn't recruited anyone. It was a joke. I was responsible for keeping Fedorenko on board, but that didn't count." Fedorenko was being assigned to work in the same foreign ministry office as Alexander Ogorodnik, TRIGON, when he returned to Russia. "We actually took Sergey into New Jersey and put him through an abbreviated version of the internal training program that we put our own officers through at the Farm," Ames said later. "That's how much we valued and trusted him. We'd never done that before." Rick gave Fedorenko a man's black leather purse as a gift at their last meeting. They hugged each other.

"Be careful," Rick said.

Fedorenko laughed. What did he possibly have to fear?

CHAPTER 6

MOSCOW

On July 15, 1977, Martha Peterson, a young CIA officer serving undercover at the U.S. embassy in Moscow, casually strolled across a bridge that spans the Moscow River. When she reached the grass on the opposite side, she paused, glanced around, and then stooped over. She was about to put what appeared to be a rock on the ground when a black Volga shot forward and screeched to a stop in front of her. Its back door flew open and a Russian woman bolted out. Without saying a word, she grabbed Peterson, spun her around, and ripped open her blouse, revealing a radio receiver taped to her chest. Peterson had been using it to monitor KGB surveillance, and had mistakenly thought that she had "gone black," agency lingo for getting out of the embassy without being followed, a nearly impossible task in Moscow at the time. Two men shoved Peterson into the car and drove to Lubyanka, the KGB's imposing headquarters near the center of Moscow.

The rock that Peterson was putting on the ground was a CIA concealment device with rubles hidden inside it. She had been leaving the money for Alexander Ogorodnik, better known as TRIGON.

"I am a United States diplomat!" Peterson protested, when she reached Lubyanka. "I have diplomatic immunity." But the KGB questioned her for two hours before begrudgingly freeing her. She was declared persona non grata that same day and ordered to leave the USSR. TRIGON, meanwhile, had vanished.

Sergey Fedorenko read about Peterson's expulsion in the Soviet newspaper *Izvestia*. The KGB gave the newspaper photographs of the fake rock, secret writing materials, and a miniature camera that it said the CIA had provided its spy.

A friend from the foreign ministry telephoned Fedorenko later that same day. Had Fedorenko heard who had been arrested? the caller asked. Before Fedorenko could reply, his friend announced: "It was Ogorodnik!" Fedorenko felt betrayed. "Why did they need two of us working in the same department?" he complained later. The next day, he received more jarring news. He was being removed from his job and assigned to a different place to work. Fedorenko tried to stay calm. He kept reassuring himself that just because the KGB had arrested Ogorodnik, that didn't mean it knew that he was a CIA agent, too. Still, a thousand "hads" nagged at him. Had Ogorodnik done something stupid to expose himself? Had the CIA made a mistake? Or had someone inside the CIA betrayed its spies to the KGB? It was that last possibility that terrified Fedorenko the most. He had always prided himself on being smart enough to elude detection. But if there was a mole in the CIA, he was doomed. Fedorenko went to see his powerful father-in-law at his dacha outside Moscow. On his son-in-law's behalf, Nikolai Fedorenko had asked a few questions of his old friend Boris Solomatin, and had been given a warning. "The general says there is a whore lying in your files," Nikolai Fedorenko said. The younger Fedorenko understood the expression. Someone in the KGB had raised questions about his contacts with Americans. He was suspected of being a spy. That was all Solomatin had said. During Fedorenko's return drive to Moscow, he reviewed all of his recent contacts with Rick and Watson. Had he made a mistake? He couldn't think of anything that he had done wrong, and once again, he wondered if he had been fingered by someone inside the CIA. Who?

Yelena was still at work when Fedorenko entered their quiet apartment. He poured himself a drink and sat down to think. Suddenly he sensed that something was wrong. Nothing seemed out of order in the apartment, yet he suspected it had been searched. He hurried over to his collection of jazz records. More than three thousand of them sat upright in a row that stretched along one entire wall. He kept them arranged according to his eclectic tastes. Several, he noticed, were out of order. Someone had removed them, probably grabbed a handful at a time, and not put them back correctly. He was sure the KGB had been there. He slipped an LP out of its cover, removing the two sheets of white paper that protected it from being scratched. Good, he thought. The KGB had missed his trick. Before he came to Moscow, he had been given sheets of secret writing paper by the CIA. The paper was treated with a clear chemical substance. Whatever he wrote would vanish and could only be recovered when the paper was "developed" with another chemical. He had hidden these special papers in his albums, making the separate sheets look as if they were the sleeves for his records. He removed all the albums that contained the secret sheets and dashed into the bedroom where he had hidden his spy camera. He packed the spy gear into an empty tennis ball can and, later that night, after Yelena was asleep, he tucked the container inside his jacket and took his dog outside for a walk. By the time he reached a nearby park, he felt confident that he was not being followed. Using his pocketknife, he punched holes in the ends of the tennis can and then buried it. He estimated that it would take about a month for enough water to seep inside to ruin the contents. That gave him time to retrieve the spy gear if he decided he was being paranoid. He would later recall that as he hurried back to his apartment that night, there was only one loose end that remained. "I hoped like hell that the CIA was smart enough not to try to contact me."

Six weeks after Peterson was expelled from Moscow, the CIA confirmed through various diplomatic sources that TRIGON was dead. Several stories have surfaced over the years about how he died. The most popular first appeared in the 1983 book *KGB Today: The Hidden Hand*, by John Barron, a writer with friendly ties to the CIA. According to this account, Ogorodnik was arrested and taken to Lubyanka, where he immediately admitted that he was a spy and began lecturing inquisitors about the evils of communism. Having delivered his own eulogy of sorts, Ogorodnik asked the guards if he could use his own fountain pen to sign his confession. When they foolishly handed it to him, he snapped it open and swallowed the suicide capsule that was hidden inside. He died instantly. Another version popular among American writers has Ogorodnik committing suicide after he is tortured for several hours. In this version, Ogorodnik is again portrayed as a gallant anticommunist, faithful until death. There is no mention in either of these versions of his love affair with Pilar Sanchez or the money that the agency was giving him in fake rocks.

I went to Moscow twice to conduct interviews for this book, and during my month-long trips, I spoke to nearly two dozen retired and active KGB officials. One of these men claimed that he had been on the team sent to arrest Ogorodnik. "Luckily for me, I was assigned to drive the car that day," he said, laughing. "We had just put the traitor Ogorodnik in the rear seat—two of our officers were seated next to him—when he managed to remove a pill from his pocket. He swallowed it before our men noticed. I became aware of what was happening when Ogorodnik began thrashing around wildly, and I heard my comrades cursing at each other while trying to subdue him and make him vomit. I drove as fast as the car could go to a hospital, where doctors tried to drain his stomach, but it was too late. We later discovered that he had gotten a pill, perhaps from a fountain pen. I was able to avoid punishment because I was merely the driver, but my comrades were demoted."

Admiral Stansfield Turner, who was then the director of the CIA, ordered Leonard McCoy, the deputy chief of counterintelligence, to investigate why Ogorodnik had been caught. Almost immediately, McCoy's probe got sidetracked. A few weeks before Ogorodnik disappeared, he had delivered a roll of microfilm to the CIA in Moscow. The film contained photographs of diplomatic cables, including one written by the Soviet Union's ambassador to the United States, Anatoly Dobrynin, describing a private conversation between himself and Secretary of State Henry Kissinger. According to the cable, Kissinger was furious because Jimmy Carter had been elected president and was replacing him with Cyrus Vance. Kissinger was quoted in the cable viciously attacking both men, whom he reportedly described as "amateurs." He was then quoted giving Dobrynin advice about how he could outsmart Vance and his negotiators during the SALT II treaty talks. SALT I was scheduled to expire in October 1977. If the cable were genuine, and if what Dobrynin had written was an accurate reflection of their talks, then Henry Kissinger had committed, in the opinion of some CIA officials who read the cable, an act of treason by aiding the Soviets in the SALT negotiations.

Not everyone, however, felt the cable was genuine. The cable could have been disinformation planted by the KGB to embarrass Kissinger. No one knew for certain when Ogorodnik had been arrested, and it was possible that the KGB had found the microfilm, manufactured a fake cable, and added it to the film intentionally to embarrass Kissinger and confuse the CIA.

For several days, a closeknit group of senior CIA officials debated whether or not the cable was real and, if it were, whether the former secretary of state had betrayed his country. Both superpowers knew that Kissinger and Dobrynin had a special relationship, dating back to when Kissinger had been President Nixon's national security advisor. Historians would later credit the two men's "back channel" communications with helping pave the way for détente. It made sense to those who thought the cable was genuine that Kissinger would be angry about being removed from his perch on the world stage, and that he would lash out at Carter and Vance. They also pointed out that the controversial cable was found in the middle of a roll of microfilm. The documents on either side of it were clearly genuine. Why would the KGB jeopardize these other documents just to embarrass Kissinger? Finally, the men who thought the cable was legitimate argued that the Kremlin had no reason to blast Kissinger, since the Soviets had wanted Gerald Ford to continue as president and Kissinger to stay on as his secretary of state.

Those suspicious of the cable rejected all these arguments. The KGB was notorious for being anti-Semitic, and Kissinger was Jewish. The hard line KGB wanted détente to fail. What better way to undermine the SALT negotiations and détente than to leak a document that raised questions about Kissinger's loyalty? As for the other cables, exposing them was necessary in order to make the Dobrynin cable seem legitimate.

After several heated debates, the CIA bureaucracy decided to simply pass the buck. A carefully written memo about the Dobrynin cable was sent to the Carter White House. What happened next is unclear. To this day, the CIA has never acknowledged that the Dobrynin cable ever existed. Nor did the Carter White House ever comment on it. Periodically, stories about the cable have leaked out. The first detailed mention of it was made in the 1989 nonfiction book *Widows*. Retired navy admiral Elmo R. Zumwalt, Jr., referred to the cable briefly in a column in *The Washington Times*. But no one has ever been able to explain what happened to the cable. Ames claimed in interviews with me that he knows. "Kissinger still had friends in powerful places and they took care of him," Ames said. "All traces of the cable conveniently disappeared." Ames told me that he had looked for the Dobrynin cable in 1984 after he had reached a position in the SE division where he had access to Ogorodnik's case file. "I had heard so many rumors that I decided to investigate. I found the actual negatives from the microfilm that Ogorodnik had sent us, but there was one strip missing. It contained the photographs of the Dobrynin cable. I asked what had happened to that strip, and I was told that the strip had simply disappeared." According to notes in the files, several inquiries had been made to learn who had removed the strip, but no one had ever been able to identify who had taken it.

A retired senior CIA officer from the SE division, who was familiar with the Ogorodnik file, confirmed for me in an interview the gist of what Ames said. This officer acknowledged that the strip of negatives that contained the Dobrynin cable had indeed been removed and was presumed to have been destroyed. No one knew by whom.

I tried to find Dobrynin's original cable in Moscow at the foreign ministry, but despite repeated attempts, I failed. At one point, I asked an aide to Yevgeny Primakov, who in 1995 was the head of the External Intelligence Service (SVR), which succeeded the KGB, if I could have a copy of the cable. After several weeks, the aide told me that such a cable did exist, but that it would not be made public. He suggested that I not "emphasize its importance" in this book. "Ambassador Dobrynin had a reputation for sometimes exaggerating his own importance, much the same, I believe, as Mr. Kissinger did," the aide said. "Because of this, you should not assume that our leaders paid as much attention as you might expect to such a cable."

Someday the Dobrynin cable may surface in Moscow, if it still exists, but even if that happens, I am certain no one will know whether or not it is genuine, or if what Dobrynin supposedly wrote was an accurate reflection of what he and Kissinger said.

After the CIA washed its hands of the Dobrynin memo, McCoy again set out to discover why TRIGON had been caught. He decided that the spy himself was to blame. Sources in Moscow told the agency that hidden cameras inside the foreign ministry had caught Ogorodnik photographing diplomatic cables with his spy camera. The investigation of TRIGON's arrest was closed.

Five years later, the CIA would discover the real story behind Ogorodnik's arrest. In 1973, the same year that Ogorodnik became a spy, the CIA hired a man named Karl Koecher to work as a translator and assigned him to work in the SE division. A loud, hot-tempered Czechoslovak, fluent in Russian, French, Czech, and English, Koecher seemed to be a rabid anticommunist with excellent credentials. He was a naturalized American citizen who, along with his wife, Hana, had immigrated to New York City in 1965 to avoid religious persecution in his homeland. Koecher's mother was Jewish. Both Karl and Hana had passed routine lie detector tests and CIA background investigations. No one had any clue that the couple were actually "illegals"—Czech spies trained to infiltrate foreign governments. Surprisingly, the Koechers did not try to blend into the bureaucracy, as one might suspect. At least twice a week, the forty-year-old Karl and Hana, who was ten years his junior, swapped spouses with other couples or attended sex parties in the

Washington suburbs, according to investigative reporter Ronald Kessler, who based his 1988 book, *Spy vs. Spy*, in part on exclusive interviews with the couple. The Koechers frequented New York City sex clubs, and Hana would later brag of having had sex with numerous CIA employees, a U.S. senator, reporters from several major newspapers, and Pentagon officials.

Just how the Koechers discovered TRIGON's actual name remains in dispute. Some claim Hana learned it during one of her sexual trysts with an agency employee. More likely it was Karl who identified Ogorodnik, after being assigned to work at SCREEN, a crypt for a translation and analysis unit in the SE division. His job there was to translate stolen written reports and telephone conversations that had been secretly tape-recorded by the agency. Most of these materials were in Russian or Czech. Some were from TRIGON.

Koecher left the CIA before Ogorodnik's suicide, but he returned occasionally as a part-time employee to work on special projects. The FBI would later claim that it had become suspicious of Koecher after he was spotted giving documents to a known Czech spy. But Ames told me that explanation was a cover story used by the CIA and FBI to protect one of its sources. "We caught Koecher because a Czech source of ours working in their intelligence service told us about him." The Koechers were arrested in December 1984, and Karl confessed, but his statement was inadmissible in court because the two FBI agents and the CIA officer who had interrogated him made promises that they never intended to keep. The Justice Department couldn't risk taking the case to trial, so it agreed to swap the couple for the release of Soviet dissident Anatoly Shcharansky.

In interviews with me, Ames would insist that there was yet one more mystery about Ogorodnik that has never been made public. "We always assumed that Ogorodnik had lost the first suicide pill that we gave him [the one hidden in the cigarette lighter]," Ames confided, "but after he killed himself, we began hearing stories that he had actually used the pill to murder a woman in Moscow. It was a girlfriend whom he wanted to get rid of. Of course, the agency decided this was just Soviet disinformation, because none of us wanted to admit that we might have been responsible for giving him the means to kill an innocent woman."

When asked about this story, the KGB showed me a death certificate for a woman who had been found in her Moscow apartment in mid-1976. According to this document, the woman had died after ingesting a poison thought to be cyanide. There was no record of the woman having any living next of kin, so there was no way for me to learn much about her or prove that she had been Ogorodnik's girlfriend or that she, indeed, had even been murdered.

What is known is that TRIGON's suicide rattled the CIA officers who worked in Moscow. They were afraid that the incident might prompt the KGB to try a "provocation," a term used to describe a trap when one intelligence service sends an officer to pose as a potential spy and then arrests the person who comes to recruit him. Sure enough, a short time after the CIA learned about Ogorodnik's suicide, a CIA officer working in the U.S. embassy found a note tucked under the wiper of his car. The writer claimed he had access to military information that was so valuable it could "tip the balance of power." He said he worked at the Research Institute of Radiobuilding, the scientific branch responsible for developing and improving the USSR's radar systems, and he wanted to meet a CIA officer.

At around this same time, a CIA officer was ambushed by the KGB on his way to a meeting with a Soviet agent known by the cryptonym BLIP. The officer was booted out of the USSR, and the agency subsequently learned that BLIP had been arrested. CIA director Turner ordered the entire SE division to "stand down." All meetings with "assets" in the Soviet Union and Eastern Europe were postponed. Obviously, something was wrong, and he didn't want any more Soviet assets disappearing on his watch.

Gus Hathaway, the CIA's chief of station in Moscow, thought Turner was overreacting. An aggressive manager, Hathaway asked for permission to contact the mysterious note-writer, who seemed eager to volunteer his services. But Turner and his advisors suspected the note was part of a trap, and Hathaway was told to remain in "stand down" status. A few weeks later, another note appeared. This time, the writer enclosed some technical details about one of the Soviet's radar systems, but even that disclosure was not enough to convince Director Turner that the volunteer was genuine. Hathaway began to fume. Someone needed to contact the note-writer, he argued. Turner said no. A month later, a thin, grim-looking man ran up to a CIA officer when he stopped his car at a light near the U.S. embassy and tried to hand him a third note. Horrified, the officer sped away. Now the director was confident that this was a KGB provocation. Everyone knew that the KGB watched the American embassy twenty-four-hours per day and tailed most CIA officers who worked there. What sort of fool would risk such a direct approach? Only someone who had nothing to lose because he was not a genuine spy. Two weeks later, the same man made another unsuccessful attempt to talk with a CIA officer. In a strongly worded cable, Hathaway offered the director's office a compromise. He asked for permission to call the note-writer at a number scribbled at the bottom of one of his notes. Director Turner reluctantly agreed.

"There's a package waiting for you," Hathaway told the man who answered the telephone. It was hidden at a telephone booth near the radar institute. The CIA was watching when the thin man hurried to the public booth and grabbed the package. It contained a list of questions about Soviet radar, detailed instructions about how and where to leave the answers to those questions, and a five-hundred-ruble note, worth about five hundred dollars at the time. A week later, the thin man left his reply at another telephone booth. Inside that package, the agency found detailed answers to all of its technical questions. All doubts about whether or not the note-writer was a double agent quickly vanished. The information he provided was so secret that the agency knew instantly the KGB would never have risked releasing it. A CIA officer was sent to greet the agency's newest volunteer.

"My name is Adolf Tolkachev," the Soviet told the officer. Overnight, Tolkachev became one of the agency's most important spies. He provided the United States with detailed information about the electronic guidance systems used in the Soviet MIG fighters, as well as details about the countermeasures the MIGs used to elude U.S. aircraft. Even more important were the technical drawings he gave the CIA of the Soviet's Stealth technology. The CIA had lost an extremely valuable asset in TRIGON, yet despite its own best efforts to ignore him, the agency had gained a new spy as important, some might say even more valuable, in Tolkachev.

CHAPTER 7

Arkady Shevchenko was frightened. He asked Rick and Jim Haase to meet him at the CIA safe house they used for emergency meetings. It was an apartment in the same building where Shevchenko and his wife lived. On March 31, 1978, a Friday, the ambassador hurried down the three flights that separated the two units and burst inside. He had received a cable calling him back to Moscow, he said, and he didn't want to go. For twenty-seven months, he had been a spy. He was ready to defect.

Shevchenko would later write in his 1985 book, *Breaking With Moscow*, that he hadn't been certain why he was being called home, but Ames and others in the agency told me that the diplomat had been afraid that his wife, Lina, had gotten them into trouble. She was friendly with Lidiya Dmitriyevna Gromyko, the wife of the Soviet foreign minister Andrey Andreyevich Gromyko, and the two of them had been engaging for months in "speculation." Lina Shevchenko would buy fur coats and antiques in New York City and ship them to Lidiya Gromyko for resale at inflated prices in Moscow. This was illegal, and Shevchenko had warned his wife to stop, but she had called him a coward and insisted that all the *nachal'niki* (bosses) used their overseas tours to get rich. "We had been worried for weeks about Arkady's continuing inability to get a hold on his own life and his deteriorating relationship with his wife," said Ames, "and we had decided a few weeks earlier to take him on a short vacation out to a cabin in the woods. We were going to have the director of the CIA give him a medal and pump up his ego."* Rick and Haase tried to get Shevchenko to change his mind about defecting, but he was adamant, so the agency decided to hide him at the cabin it had already rented. Rick asked Shevchenko if he had told his wife that he was going to seek asylum. "No," he replied. He had been afraid that she would turn him in to the KGB. She was asleep upstairs. Rick suggested that Shevchenko write his wife a letter. They sent him up to his apartment to leave it in an obvious spot where she would find it in the morning. Making him return to his apartment was a good way to check how serious he was, Rick and Haase decided. A few minutes after he left them, Shevchenko reappeared, carrying an overnight bag. "Let's go," he said. Rick and Haase hurried him downstairs to a waiting car, which sped out of Manhattan.

Everyone was too nervous to sleep when they got to the cabin. They knew the defection of the number two official at the UN would spark worldwide headlines. At first light, Shevchenko called his apartment to ask Lina to join him. The FBI was waiting to help her defect. A man answered the phone.

"Lina?" Shevchenko asked.

"*Yeeyo nyet doma.* [She's not at home.]"

Shevchenko dropped the phone. He was sure it was the KGB.

His defection was the lead story on television that night and front page news the next morning. "We had everyone trying to find where we were hiding him," Ames recalled. "The Russians, the media, everyone was after us." The agency decided to move Shevchenko after a truck from a television station was spotted in the area. They took him from one hotel to another. Rick continued to be his escort. The Soviets demanded that Shevchenko meet with them in person to insure that he had not been kidnaped. A meeting was arranged in Manhattan. Shevchenko was taken there in a convoy of FBI cars. Soviet ambassador Dobrynin and Soviet UN ambassador Troyanovsky were the only Russians allowed to meet with him. Troyanovsky told Shevchenko that his wife had been flown back to Moscow and was horrified by what he had done. The KGB was questioning Shevchenko's grown daughter and son, Troyanovsky added. He suggested that Shevchenko rethink his decision. Shevchenko demanded that his wife and children be released, otherwise he

---

*Intelligence services often issue awards to spies to boost their morale. Sergey Fedorenko was given thank-you notes that he was told had been written by Henry Kissinger, and the KGB awarded John Walker, Jr., the honorary rank of admiral in the Soviet Navy for his spying.

would not resign his post at the UN, which the Soviets were demanding that he do. The meeting turned into a heated exchange of insults, and Shevchenko stormed from the room. A second meeting held a few days later was equally tense. Worried that the KGB might try to kidnap Shevchenko, the FBI instituted even more security. "When we left the second meeting and were crossing the Brooklyn Bridge, the FBI agents in the back of our convoy simply stopped and parked in the middle of the Brooklyn Bridge," Ames recalled. "They blocked all of the traffic trying to cross the bridge for about ten to fifteen minutes while we got away."

As the negotiations between the Soviets and Shevchenko continued to drag, tempers flared. "The pressure was incredible and none of us was happy," Ames said. He and Shevchenko found themselves alone one afternoon in the living room of a guest house on the grounds of an estate owned by a wealthy businessman outside New York City. "Arkady lost it. He had been threatening to redefect all day, and finally, I lost it, too. I said, 'Listen, Arkady, if you want to go back, we can get in that car outside, and I will personally drive you up to 67th Street and hold the door open for you in front of the Soviet mission! If you can't control yourself and see yourself functioning in the United States, then say the word and we'll leave right now.' Arkady started screaming at me. 'Who do you think you are—talking to me like that?' Which is exactly the reaction I wanted. I wanted to remind him that he was someone who was extremely important and capable of taking control. For about a half hour, we shouted at each other, and then we calmed down. We were both exhausted. Afterwards we had some stew, and he asked me what I would have done if he had said, 'Take me to the mission!' I laughed and said I would have driven him as far as 64th Street before turning around."

Eventually the furor died down, and the agency arranged for Shevchenko to return to his apartment. The KGB had stripped it bare. There was no trace of anything personal from his previous life. A few days later, Shevchenko was informed that Lina was dead. The KGB said she had become so depressed that she had committed suicide. He didn't believe it and still doesn't. The agency decided to buy Shevchenko a house in a Washington, D.C., suburb. Rick rode from New York City with Shevchenko to a Sheraton Hotel in Washington, D.C., which was to be his temporary quarters until he chose a house. "We shook hands, and on an impulse I took out a pad and I wrote my home phone number on it. I had never given anyone else my real phone number and I was breaking a rule, but I told him that if he ever needed anything he could call me. I really meant it and he thanked me and got out of the car, and that was the last time I ever saw him. I was immediately relieved to be rid of him, because I hadn't been home for a month, but I really was moved by my experiences with him."

Nan had saved newspaper clippings about Shevchenko for Rick, but they only talked briefly about it after he got home. Nan had a new job and was busy. "She was consumed with her own work, and her interest in what I was doing was at the vanishing point. We didn't talk much. If I was at home, we would watch television or go to a show. We were drifting apart, but neither of us seemed to care. It was like, 'Why bother'. At least that is how I perceived us." They had been married nine years.*

Rick began drinking at night before he went home. He also began calling Peggy Anderson, his old high school pal. She was married, but not happily. Rick would babble about how he wished he had married her instead of Nan. "He was very lonely," Anderson said later. Rick started dating other women. Initially it was for sex, but his one-night stands soon led to more serious betrayals. He had two love affairs, both with women at work. If Nan knew, she never let on. There were no angry accusations, no screaming fits.

Rick and Nan were close friends in New York with David and Angela Blake. Occasionally David would see Rick with other women, but because Rick was a CIA officer, David assumed the women were part of some cover story. "Nan and Rick liked going to the opera and they had a wonderful collection of classical and opera records," said Angela Blake. "But most weekends, they would invite us over for dinner and Rick would cook Chinese. We would just sit around and discuss things. We did notice that you rarely saw any affection between them, but neither of them were very demonstrative. There certainly was no indication that either of them was miserable."

Said Rick, "Because we didn't argue and fight, it appeared as if we were content, but there was no passion, and certainly not much sex. I felt Nan and I were simply playing the role of a husband and a wife. I just figured this was how things were after a few years. Besides, I was really busy at work."

The SE division was in the midst of another crisis, this time about the pending publication of *Legend: The Secret World of Lee Harvey Oswald*, by Edward Jay Epstein. CIA officials had obtained an advance copy of the book and were enraged, because it revealed that the CIA had two high-ranking

*Nancy Segebarth Ames declined to be interviewed for this book.

Soviets spying for it. Epstein had learned about them while investigating the assassination of President Kennedy. According to the book, shortly after the assassination, the agency had questioned a key Soviet source known as FE-DORA about Oswald. Epstein said that the CIA had access to another important Soviet, known as TOPHAT, if it wished to do additional checking on Oswald's possible ties with the KGB. The agency had never faced a problem like this before. Epstein was about to reveal the cryptonyms of two Soviet agents who were still active agents. "People were livid," said Ames. "The book was not only going to put FEDORA and TOPHAT in real danger, it was going to terrify our other Soviet sources. They were going to wonder if their cryptonyms were going to be published next. What made the matter worse was that we all suspected that we knew the name of Epstein's source: James Jesus Angleton. We felt certain that he had betrayed us."

Few within the agency were as legendary, controversial, or ruthless as Angleton. The bony, bespectacled counterintelligence chief had been convinced that a KGB mole had burrowed himself into the agency, and during the 1960s and early 1970s, Angleton had led an obsessive witch hunt for this phantom traitor. One of the reasons top CIA officials believed Angleton was the source behind the leak was that he had always suspected FEDORA and TOPHAT of actually being under the KGB's control. Of course, by 1974, when he was finally fired after serving twenty years as the nation's top spy-catcher, Angleton had become convinced that nearly every Soviet recruited after 1960 was a double agent. Senior CIA officials knew in 1978, when they obtained an advance copy of Epstein's book, that Angleton was a deeply embittered man. Still, even his harshest critics had not thought that he would reveal information about two active agents. "I can't stress enough how utterly shocked everyone was," Ames said later. When Angleton was confronted by the agency, he denied that he was Epstein's source and instead blamed William Sullivan, a high-ranking FBI official, for the leaks about FE-DORA and TOPHAT. Inside the agency, however, Angleton remained the chief suspect.

"I remember wondering during all of the uproar," Ames said, "how a man who had been so close to the heart of the CIA could have done what he did. I can't emphasize enough what an extraordinary betrayal it was at the time."

The agency knew that trying to block publication of the book would only call attention to it, so the CIA decided to warn the two agents and offer both a chance to defect. FEDORA, whose real name was Aleksey Isidorovich Kulak, was in the most danger because he lived in Moscow and was mentioned in several of the book's passages. The other spy, TOPHAT, was Dmitri Fedorovich Polyakov, a GRU general stationed in New Delhi, India. The agency decided that Gus Hathaway, who was still the Moscow chief of station, needed to contact FEDORA. Although Hathaway refused to be interviewed for this book, Ames and others still in the agency confirmed that Hathaway went to elaborate steps to leave the U.S. embassy without being followed. He then telephoned FEDORA from a pay telephone, stunning the spy. Choosing his words carefully, Hathaway warned him that something was going to appear in the United States that could endanger his life. He offered to ex-filtrate FEDORA and his family from the USSR, and promised that FEDORA's "friends" would make certain that he was well provided for in his new home. Despite the danger, FEDORA decided to stay put. "We will never contact you again," Hathaway was later quoted as telling him. The agency sent another officer to warn Polyakov and make him the same offer. He, too, declined the agency's help. A short time later, Epstein's book was published. Neither FEDORA nor TOPHAT was arrested, but Polyakov's tour was cut short and he was ordered to return to Moscow. Later, Polyakov would be told by a friend that he had come under suspicion for being a spy because of the book. Neither man was of any use to the United States again as an agent. "Angleton was never punished," said Ames.

Shevchenko's defection left Rick spyless, so the agency assigned him another promising Soviet to handle. He was a prominent Russian scientist who had been recruited by an FBI agent in San Francisco, but was now working in New York. His crypt was BYPLAY.* Rick liked BYPLAY, and the two men soon became friends. Rick's work in New York impressed his bosses. In late 1978, the chief of the CIA's African division, Clair George, asked Rick if he was interested in becoming the deputy chief of station in Lagos, Nigeria. The chief there would be Milton A. Bearden, a personable, cowboy-boot-wearing Oklahoman whom Rick really liked. "Lagos was one of the largest and most active African posts, and it was one of the spots where the agency sent officers who were clearly being groomed for better jobs," Ames said later. He rushed home to tell Nan, but she was not enthused. She had just gotten a promotion at her job, and she reminded him that she had already

---

*BYPLAY has never been identified publicly nor was he ever arrested by the KGB, even though Ames would later admit that he had told his KGB handlers about him. The CIA does not know why BYPLAY was not arrested. I attempted to interview him in Moscow but was told that he did not want to meet with me. I have chosen not to reveal his name or provide readers with any information that might endanger his life today.

tossed away one career because of their marriage. She was not going to leave New York. "I really agonized over what to do," Ames said later. "I thought about going without her. She just sort of said, 'Well, you have to do what you have to do, and I have to do what I have to do,' but that always seemed to mean that I ended up doing what she wanted." Rick turned down the Lagos offer. A few months later, Rick was offered a job at the Moscow station, but he turned it down for the same reasons as before. "I went to see Clair at headquarters after that, but it seemed clear to me that my refusal had muddied the waters. My decisions showed I was not willing to sacrifice everything for the company."

Rodney W. Carlson, the New York branch chief, warned Rick that no one in the SE division got to stay in Manhattan forever. At about this same time, BYPLAY was called back to Moscow, once again leaving Rick without any agents to handle. He began trolling. After Ames was arrested, the CIA would insist that he had never recruited a single Soviet as an agent during his entire career, but Ames would insist that he had recruited several Soviets. None, however, turned out to be very productive. Such was the case during 1979, and Rick grew restless. One night, while he was attending a party given by a wealthy American businessman, Rick met Thomas Kolesnichenko, a senior correspondent for *Pravda*. Rick introduced himself as Frank Madison, one of the aliases that he used, and told the heavyset, gregarious Russian that he was a Sovietologist employed by a nonprofit think tank in New Hampshire. Rick invited Kolesnichenko to lunch a few days later, and the two men soon started meeting regularly for meals in some of the city's most expensive restaurants. Because of his position as a senior *Pravda* correspondent, Kolesnichenko knew many of the rising young leaders in the Communist Party, including Mikhail S. Gorbachev. "I remember having lunch with Thomas after Yuri Andropov left his post as head of the KGB and accepted a spot on the central committee. Thomas told me, 'The deal is done. My country's next leader is going to be Andropov.' And by God, he was right!" Ames said.

Rick began filing detailed reports after his sessions with Kolesnichenko, but none of his bosses paid any attention to them. They dismissed Kolesnichenko as a "party hack" and "propagandist" and questioned why Rick was wasting so much time with him. Rick got angry. He argued that Kolesnichenko was "an insider" who understood how his country worked better than nearly all of the CIA's so-called experts. "Thomas knew his country was going to radically change once [Leonid] Brezhnev and the members of the Kremlin's old oligarchy died," Ames later said. "But the agency was only interested in finding out who was in the KGB and what the KGB was plotting. I began to realize how shortsighted this was." Under Kolesnichenko's tutelage, Rick began to see the USSR through different eyes. "I began to learn that what held the vast Soviet system together, and ensured it would all creak roughly in unison, was not merely the Communist Party. It was a highly evolved network of personal and institutional relationships, mostly developed after 1953, and the result of a myriad of political, economic, personal, and other sorts of pulling and hauling. It was this *nomenklatura* which defined the Soviet system and that was something which Sovietologists and historians had understood almost since World War II, but which we in the agency still did not comprehend."

Although the agency had made it clear that it did not consider Kolesnichenko's views worthwhile, Rick continued to file memos crediting the reporter with important insights. "No one listened. Having a guy explain Soviet foreign policy in Soviet terms, like Thomas was doing, was perceived within the agency as nothing but a big yawner."

Rick began losing interest in his job. "All the CIA wanted to do was catch spies, it really didn't want useful intelligence." In October 1980, he was reprimanded for leaving a safe unlocked that contained top secret documents. "When my first two-year tour in New York ended, I thought, 'Hey, this is fun, I'll stick around for another tour. Then when the next one ended, I thought, 'This is still fun, besides where can I go?' But by 1980, it was not much fun anymore. I felt stuck because of Nan, and I began to resent it, although I never told her that I did."

One morning, Rick was walking down Second Avenue from his apartment to his Manhattan office, when he turned a corner and looked west along 42nd Street. "The street sort of drops away beneath you, and as I made the turn and was standing up there, I looked out and there were about forty thousand people moving up and down the sidewalk, and all of a sudden, I thought, *I've got to get out of here!*"

In January 1981, Rick was told to report to Langley for a meeting with Gus Hathaway, who had returned to headquarters after finishing his tour in Moscow. He told Rick that a young case officer in Mexico City had been caught stealing money. The officer had claimed that he had recruited a Soviet diplomat, but was actually pocketing the money that the CIA was giving him for his agent. The officer had been fired, leaving a slot in Mexico City vacant. Did Rick want it?

"It seemed like the perfect solution," Ames said later. Mexico City was only a few hours away by airplane. Nan could stay in New York. He could live in Mexico. They could get together once or twice a month for weekend visits. Lots of professional couples had commuter marriages, he told himself. "I talked it over with Nan, and we agreed it was a good idea, so I took the job. I don't think either of us had any idea about what was going to happen when we began living apart. We were just blithely going along, pretending that nothing was wrong."

THE WORDS OF RICK AMES

By the time I left New York, I was really beginning to change how I perceived the agency and intelligence. Beginning with TRIGON and later with Arkady Shevchenko, we were getting really good—and I mean first-class—political information about the Soviets. We were getting really top-notch military information from Tolkachev and Polyakov, too. I mean we were getting it all. Don't forget we also had our spy satellites sending us back intelligence. And do you know what all of this data—from human agents and the satellites—kept telling us over again and again and again and again? It told us that we were disproportionally stronger than the Soviet Union and the Warsaw Pact. It told us that Soviet forces couldn't compete with us. The bottom line was that with only the most minor exceptions, we were consistently superior militarily to the Soviets. It didn't matter whether we were talking about our bombers, our nuclear warheads, our megatonnage, our missiles—in every damn area—whether it was the quietness of our submarines, the quality of our aircraft avionics, the training of our pilots—everything you could think of—we were light-years ahead of them. The only military advantage the Soviets had was bodies. They had more men.

You must understand that this reporting was consistent in the intelligence community starting right after World War II and going up to the collapse of the Soviet Union. We did our job. We consistently drew a picture of a Soviet Union and Warsaw Pact that never would decide to fight a war against us. And yet, decade after decade, the political leadership in both parties ignored that intelligence. They were committed to running around screaming, "The Russians are coming! The Russians are coming!" Every administration pushed the Soviet threat. Every administration misread it. Every administration overestimated it. It wasn't just Reagan, it was Carter before him and Ford before him and Nixon and JFK before him. Why? Why did they do this? Because it was good politics! No president wants to be seen as being weak on communism and that translates into being strong on defense. Americans had to be Number One no matter if the other superpower was incapable of striking back. I read TRIGON's reports, and those diplomatic cables showed a feeling of helplessness among Soviet policymakers. They believed that they were under terrific pressure. Their cables were filled with statements about how the Soviets felt that they were losing in every way. They knew they were falling behind—were being passed by the United States economically and militarily. And yet Henry Kissinger and Gerald Ford and later the Democrats all blustered about a resurgence in Soviet aggressiveness and military power. The Russians are notorious for blustering and then backing down. We knew this.

TRIGON died. He gave us fantastic political intelligence and it cost him his life. What good did it do? Not one damn bit of good, because none of it mattered. That was the CIA's dirty little secret. Every White House ignored what the evidence overwhelming showed was true. They preferred to push the myth. They preferred to say the sky was falling. TRIGON died. Why? For what? When I left New York City, I knew that much of what I was doing was for nothing. Soviets were risking their lives to tell us information that our leaders didn't want to hear and refused to use. I knew it, and I began to realize that much of what we were doing really was just part of a silly game.

THE WORDS OF OTHERS

Henpecked, lazy, a nerd with an attitude, Ames, 52, sounded like a small-timer on the FBI tapes that led to his arrest last week on charges of espionage.
—*Newsweek* cover story, March 7, 1994

What really amazed me about Rick is that I thought he had a feeling of loyalty to the people whom he dealt with and that is the betrayal that I can't understand—the personal betrayal. I can understand why he didn't have any loyalty to the agency. I can understand how he could have lost his way so that there came a point when it didn't matter to him if he was the recruiter or the recruitee. But what I can't understand is how he lost his loyalty, not only to his coworkers, such as me, but his friends, people like Sergey Fedorenko! How can you ever justify betraying the people closest to you?
—R. Patrick Watson, FBI

The National Intelligence Estimates were not inaccurate or misleading, former CIA director Stansfield Turner said, but were simply "irrelevant" to the president in making policy. . . . "How could we have thought we possibly needed more [missiles]?" former CIA director Stansfield Turner asked. He said the agency should have told President Carter there was no need to build more weapons, except for purely political reasons. "What it should have said to him, in my view, was simply two words: 'Too much.' We and the Soviets both have too much firepower to need any more," said Turner.

—The Washington Post, December 3, 1994

After his arrest, Ames made it sound as if the Soviets were never a military threat. Obviously, he forgot about what they did in Afghanistan, Nicaragua, and Angola.

—Senior CIA official, SE division

Nan was very cold. My husband and I went to look at a rug she and Rick were selling before they moved to New York City, and she was basically rude. She was not a nice person at all, and that surprised me, because he really was.

—Sandy Grimes, CIA

Valdik Enger came to Moscow on a holiday in 1978 and I met with him. He was depressed. He told me that a U.S. serviceman had offered to spy for the KGB, but he suspected it was an FBI trap. Still, he was ordered to keep meeting with this man. I asked Enger why he was being told to take such a risk, and he replied, "Politics!" The KGB's rezident agent in New York City was being pressured to recruit American spies so Enger was told to keep up with the meetings.* I saw Enger after he was released from an American prison and had returned to Moscow. The KGB had abandoned him. He was bitter. "Sergey," he said. "I meant nothing to them. My life meant nothing." I was angry. The FBI already knew Enger was KGB because I had identified him for them. Rick and I had fed Enger information. Why did they have to arrest him? What did it accomplish? All it did was make the KGB more suspicious of me in Moscow because I had met with Enger. The KGB wondered if I had betrayed him. His arrest was stupid.

—Sergey Fedorenko, CIA

---

*In May 1978, Enger and Rudolph Chernyayev were arrested in a wooded area of New Jersey searching for a package. The FBI had caught them in its trap. Neither Russian was protected by diplomatic immunity. They were found guilty and sentenced to fifty years in prison, but were released as part of a diplomatic exchange one year later.

I'm sorry, but I really can't help you. To tell you the truth, I don't remember much about him at all.

—Arkady N. Shevchenko, after Rick Ames's arrest.

He was not a male chauvinist. He wasn't strong enough to be one. When his first wife, Nan, got into politics, suddenly Rick got into politics. We used to warn him about getting into trouble, because he was a government employee and wasn't supposed to campaign. Looking back on it, I now see that it was Nan's personality that he latched onto. He was seeking her approval, trying to please her, no, it was more than just that. It was like he was trying to become just like her, because he was too weak to have a personality of his own.

—Sandy Grimes, CIA

PART TWO

LOVE AND BETRAYAL

Love looks not with the eyes, but with
the mind,
And therefore is wing'd Cupid
painted blind.

—*A Midsummer Night's Dream*
William Shakespeare

CHAPTER 8

The CIA station in Mexico City was a mess when Rick arrived in October 1981. The chief was preoccupied with planning his upcoming marriage to a Mexican woman half his age. His deputy was a heavy drinker who disappeared, sometimes for days at a time, on suspected binges. On his second day at work, Rick was taken by the deputy to lunch with a coworker at a nearby restaurant and bar. They began with a round of rum and Cokes and then ordered another. Four hours later, a famished Rick asked if they were ever going to eat something. Raising his glass, his coworker replied: "This is lunch."

Rick began avoiding the deputy. As the senior SE Division officer in the station, Rick had plenty to do. Mexico City was a prime meeting spot for the KGB and its U.S. spies. It was close, simple for U.S. citizens to enter, and, once there, a spy could easily disappear into the city's population of fifteen million. The wake-up call for the CIA and FBI had come in 1975, when Andrew Daulton Lee, a California dope dealer, had waltzed into the Soviet embassy in Mexico City and sold the KGB the operating manual for the Rhyolite system, the most technologically advanced spy satellite at the time. His best friend, Christopher Boyce, had stolen it from his employer, TRW Inc., the satellite's manufacturer. Both had been arrested in 1976 and sentenced to prison. After that fiasco, the FBI and CIA tried to beef up security in Mexico City, but it was the Defense Intelligence Agency (DIA) that came up with the best way to under-cut the natural advantages that the Mexican capital offered its Soviet guests. It began flooding the Soviet embassy with so many volunteer spies that the KGB must have wondered if the entire U.S. military was for sale. The trick, of course, was that these walk-in spies were double agents, com-pletely loyal to the United States. Rick had heard about the military's dou-ble agent program, but even he was stunned when he discovered how many agents were being dangled in front of the KGB during the 1980s. "World-wide, we had more than one hundred double agent cases going on at all times, and the majority of them were in Mexico City," he said later.

About once a week, military intelligence would send some low-ranking Air Force, Army, or Navy noncommissioned officer to Mexico City with or-ders to volunteer as a spy. These walk-ins often brought classified docu-ments with them as proof that they were legitimate traitors. The documents were real, but they had not been stolen. A special Pentagon panel, whose only job was to sift through stacks of classified information for the double agent program, had decided nothing would be lost by leaking the docu-ments to the KGB and GRU. It usually took the KGB and GRU several months before they could be certain a walk-in was a double agent, and by then, the United States had already sent another double agent to volunteer. One of the purposes of this revolving door was to ensure that the Pentagon always had a pipeline ready for feeding disinformation to the enemy if a war broke out. But the main benefit was that it helped U.S. intelligence identify which Soviets in the embassy were KGB and GRU officers, and what proce-dures the Soviets used when someone volunteered. The constant turnover in volunteers also wasted the Soviets' resources and kept them confused.

"The funny thing was that the Soviets knew our program was effective, but they couldn't duplicate it," Ames said. KGB and GRU defectors told the CIA that it was difficult to get the Soviet military to turn loose classified documents. "Even if a document were of no real value, no one in the Soviet military was willing to sign off on releasing it, knowing that it was going to be passed to the West," Ames said. "They were afraid that a few months later, they would be called before some Stalinlike tribunal and be shot for treason."

Rick was eager to prove himself in Mexico, and he soon came up with two ideas. The agency had tried repeatedly, without success, to plant micro-phones inside the Soviet's motor pool. At one point, it had planted bugs in several luxury cars that were being shipped to a new car dealer in a Texas border town. The agency persuaded him to offer the cars to the Russians at bargain prices. The Soviets bought the cars, but the KGB dismantled each vehicle in Mexico City and removed all the microphones.

It was Rick's idea to use the double agent program to plant a bug in an embassy car. Because the KGB couldn't tell if a volunteer was a legitimate spy or a fake one when he first walked into the Soviet compound, it always had to assume that he was an actual traitor and that meant he had to be smuggled out of the embassy without being seen by the FBI and CIA. The KGB generally dressed a new volunteer in a heavy coat, pushed a hat over his head and slipped him into the back seat of an embassy car, which then whisked out of the Soviet compound into the winding streets of Mexico City. Once the driver was certain that he wasn't being followed, the new spy would be dropped off at a taxi stand. Rick figured a double agent could hide a microphone in an embassy car while he was being driven around the city. The risks were obvious. If the KGB found a bug, it would know the walk-in was a double agent. But if Rick's plan worked, the agency would be able to listen to private conversations by anyone who later used the car. The DIA agreed to give one of its walk-ins a microphone, and he successfully hid it under the front seat of a Soviet car. It worked perfectly, but only until the car returned to the Soviet compound. Rick learned later that the KGB carefully swept each vehicle for bugs each time it was driven outside the embassy grounds.

Rick's second scheme was a bit more complicated. He had noticed from reading CIA case files that most U.S. citizens who were spying for the Soviets had come to Mexico City to meet with their handlers on a Thursday afternoon or Friday morning, and had returned to the States the next Monday. This extended weekend schedule gave them enough time to contact the KGB and GRU and negotiate a deal. Rick suggested that the agency use its computers to identify passengers who were flying to Mexico for weekend jaunts. The agency could then compare this list to military personnel records. "If someone—say from the army—showed up on both lists, then we would do a bit more checking and find out what he was doing in Mexico City." The CIA implemented the operation, but only for a few months. It was scuttled after the agency's in-house lawyers began questioning whether the CIA had the authority to review travel records of innocent U.S. citizens who were not suspected of breaking any laws.

In January 1982, Rick received a flattering cable praising his performance. It was written and signed by the CIA's new Latin American division chief, Dewey Clarridge, the same officer who had given him a damning evaluation years earlier in Ankara! A few weeks later, Rick was promoted to the government rank of GS-14, a grade level for senior employees. "It had taken me forever to get my other grade promotions in New York City, and here I was suddenly being promoted the first time I became eligible. I thought, *Hey, I am still competitive in my career after all.*"

Rick was also having fun. For the first time he was working under the guise of the State Department, which meant he had entree to the city's vast diplomatic circuit and its formal receptions, cocktail parties, and elegant dinners. His status gave him access to a much higher level of potential recruits than when he had posed as a businessman from out of town visiting New York, or when he was in Ankara working as a civilian Air Force employee. Rick had more spending money, too. He was earning $44,029 a year now, but that wasn't why he had more cash in his pockets. Rick had his entire paycheck automatically deposited in the New York checking account that he shared with Nan. He didn't need it, because the agency paid his rent in Mexico City and gave him another $360 a month in overseas premium pay. Plus he had an expense account for entertaining. Rick moved into a comfortable one-bedroom penthouse in a building that housed a bookbinding company, in a semi-industrial area of the city. He had decided to rent it as soon as he saw it. When the air wasn't filled with smog, he had a great view of the city. Besides, it seemed almost predestined that he would live there. All but three letters of the Spanish word for penthouse had worn off the elevator button. The remaining three were: C-I-A.

Despite their promise to one another, Rick and Nan were so busy with their jobs that neither of them took time to meet. Rick began dating Helen Riggs, an American businesswoman working in Mexico City.* He tried to keep his affair secret from his coworkers by never taking her to any embassy functions. His closest pals at work were a group of men with whom he ate lunch once or twice a week. Both Irwin Rubenstein and Richard Thurman worked for the State Department. David T. Samson, who was Rick's closest friend in Mexico City, was identified as a State Department employee, but was a CIA officer like Rick. Tall, slender, with jet-black hair and a radio announcer's smooth voice, Samson was in his early thirties and had a reputation for recruiting women as agents, usually by romancing and bedding them. He had arrived in Mexico City four months before Rick, and was un-

---

*Not her real name.

der the direction of the Far East (FE) division, which had sent him there to recruit Asians working in embassies. But he had been given a new assignment shortly after he had arrived. "A fast-tracker had wanted my job, so I had been reassigned," Samson explained later. A fast-tracker was someone who was being promoted as quickly as possible. In this case, it was an employee whose father-in-law happened to be one of the CIA's division chiefs. "It was pure nepotism, and I found it really disgusting," Samson recalled. "At one point, this guy left a briefcase full of intelligence reports in a Mexican taxi. That's how incompetent he was. It was a security violation for him to even take them out of the embassy, and he ended up losing them, but because of who his father-in-law was, everyone just looked the other way. He wasn't even reprimanded, and Rick and I both were furious about that."

Samson had been put in charge of recruiting informants inside Mexico's fledgling Communist Party, a task that often involved Rick, the embassy's top Soviet expert. During the 1950s and 1960s, the FBI and CIA had successfully recruited a large number of informants inside the Communist Party in Mexico, but during the 1970s, priorities had changed, and most of these sources had been cut from the payroll. Now that Ronald Reagan was president and his longtime friend, William Casey, was running the CIA, infiltrating the Communist Party in Latin America had become a top priority once again.

Finding new informants turned out to be tougher than anyone had imagined. Rick and Samson were both having trouble recruiting spies. Anti-American feelings were running strong in Mexico, which made Samson's task difficult. And Rick was having trouble even meeting Soviets stationed in Mexico. The Carter administration had irritated the USSR by supporting the rebels in Afghanistan, and President Reagan and Director Casey were backing the contras' efforts to overthrow the communist government in Nicaragua. "It was damn hard to find a Soviet who was willing to come outside his embassy and even talk to you in 1981," Ames complained. "They were hiding in their compound, and you can't recruit them if they never come out in public."

One morning, Samson suggested that Rick join him at a luncheon being hosted that afternoon by the Asociación Mexicano de Consejeros, Secretarios y Agregados Diplomáticos, better known by its acronym, AMCOSAD— the diplomatic association in Mexico City. Most nations belonged, including the United States and the USSR. Once a month, each embassy would send a cadre of diplomats to the association's luncheon meeting. The group also hosted periodic social outings, such as trips to various Mexican cultural sites and resorts. The purpose of AMCOSAD was to encourage "good will," but most intelligence services used it as a way to watch each other and meet potential recruits. The USSR always sent a large contingent to AMCOSAD, and the CIA was certain that Igor Shurygin, who was listed as the cultural attaché at the Soviet Embassy, was actually the "head of the KR-Line" in Mexico City. (That was the KGB's term for the officer in charge of counterintelligence.) Rick and Samson guessed that Shurygin's main function at AMCOSAD lunches was to watch other Soviet embassy employees.

Years later, after Ames was arrested, a noted author, and even some FBI agents, would insist that it was Shurygin who had first recruited Ames in Mexico City. They would report that Ames and Shurygin had become good friends and drinking buddies in Mexico City and had spent hours together. While sensational, neither the facts, CIA intelligence reports, nor Ames's own statements support such wild speculation. "My relationship with Shurygin was quite perfunctory," Ames told me in interviews. "I recall one five- to ten-minute conversation with him at an AMCOSAD party. Otherwise, we never exchanged more than polite greetings at AMCOSAD lunches. The idea that the two of us went off drinking together is a complete fabrication, and rather farfetched if one thinks about it."

A high-ranking CIA official directly involved in investigating the Ames case would insist during interviews with me that Ames was never seen drinking with Shurygin, nor had Ames ever reported having any long sessions with the Russian, as was reported in some books and news articles. David Samson also told me that he doubted the so-called Shurygin recruitment theory. "Rick and I were scared to death to be alone with a guy like Shurygin," Samson said, "and I am sure he would have been scared to be alone with us, too." The reason: neither side wanted to be pitched by the other. "If you get pitched, your own people become suspicious. They wonder what the other guys are seeing in you that makes them think you are vulnerable," said Samson, "and the Soviets, in particular, often sent anyone whom we pitched back to Moscow whenever they heard about it." Other CIA case officers in interviews with me said that the agency did not always become suspicious of an employee who was pitched, but "eyebrows were raised" whenever it happened. On the other side, retired KGB general Boris Solomatin told me that being pitched by the CIA could ruin a KGB officer's career.

At AMCOSAD lunches, the sharks such as Rick, Samson, and Shurygin gave each other wide berth and instead looked for smaller fish to swallow. Such a target appeared in early 1982, when Maria del Rosario Casas Dupuy attended her first AMCOSAD luncheon.

Rosario was the new cultural attaché at the Colombian embassy, and she caused quite a stir in the male-dominated diplomatic corps. "She was like a breath of fresh air entering a room stale with cigar smoke," recalled one State Department employee. Richard Thurman remembered her this way: "Rosario was clearly a cut above most women who came to these events. She was single, attractive, and she arrived with impressive academic and intellectual accomplishments. Everyone wanted to engage in conversations with her."

Although Rosario was twenty-nine years old and an intellectual, she had spent her entire life cloistered in academia, and many of the hardened diplomats who met her thought she was incredibly naive. "It was clear that she was new to the diplomatic world from the way that she spoke," Rick's State Department friend, Irwin Rubenstein, said later. "Our first reaction was that she must have had some important relative who got her a political appointment, because few people go out as cultural attachés without first serving as junior officers. So there was an immediate assumption that she was well connected politically, and in Latin America, that usually also meant that her family had money."

Samson first noticed Rosario when he overheard her speaking English. It was flawless and he assumed that she was a new State Department employee as he pushed his way through a crowd of men who had encircled her at her first AMCOSAD appearance.

"We must be colleagues at the U.S. embassy," he said, sticking out his hand. "I'm Dave Samson."

Rosario laughed. "I'm Colombian."

They began chatting and Samson learned that she was living at her aunt's house in Mexico City because she had not yet found an apartment. She also didn't own a car. He offered to show her around town, and they made a lunch date. "I found her immediately interesting, both personally and professionally," he later recalled. "The best time to befriend and recruit a woman is when they just get into town, because they are looking to make friends and they will not have established a routine or be hooked up with a boyfriend yet. This is when most women are the most vulnerable."

Samson began wooing Rosario. When she didn't receive her first paycheck because of a bureaucratic foul-up, he loaned her money. When she needed a ride, he drove her wherever she wanted to go. Rosario had no idea that he was looking at her as a potential recruit. "I thought he just wanted to be my friend," she said later. "Dave seemed to want to listen to a lot of what I had to say. He used to joke. He'd say, 'I'm not trying to get romantically involved with you, because I don't feel comfortable with women who are far more intelligent than I am.' When I decided to get my own apartment, he said, 'Do you have hangers?' and when I said, 'No,' the next day he showed up with hangers and light bulbs. He was very generous."

Whenever they were together, Samson was constantly filing away information about Rosario. He learned that she had a history of tragic romances. While she was teaching at a college in Bogotá, Rosario had fallen in love with an older, married professor. That affair had ended after he had refused to leave his wife for her. Samson discovered that one reason Rosario had moved to Mexico City was because she was having an affair with a married airline pilot who had been transferred to Mexico. Not long after they met, Samson and Rosario became lovers, even though he warned her that he had a steady Mexican girlfriend. She told him that she didn't mind, because she was still seeing her pilot boyfriend. She was waiting for him to leave his wife and marry her.

Not long after they became lovers, Samson told her the truth about his job. She was shocked. "When you hear the words CIA and you are Colombian," she recalled later, "you shiver because the image is so totally negative. But then I knew this person, and he's a normal human being, so I said, 'Oh, that's nice' and simply let it slide."

A few nights after he made his confession, Samson asked Rosario if she would do him a favor. "One of my jobs is to watch the Soviets and the Cubans and to try to figure out what the communists are doing, and you know all of these people, and it would be helpful if you could share with me some of your insights and tell me the sort of things that they tell you, so that I can figure them out," he said.

Rosario was confused. "What exactly do you want to know?" she asked. "What do you want me to tell you? Just gossip?"

"Sure, anything you might hear," he replied, with a shrug. Samson would later recall her response: "She said, 'Okay, if it will help you out.' And that is just what I expected her to say. You see, I knew she would have a difficult time telling me no, because she was a friend, and most times when you approach a friend subtly like that, it is an easy sell because a friend will be embarrassed to turn down what seems to be such an innocent request."

Rosario soon became a helpful source, according to the intelligence reports that Samson wrote about her at the time. In his reports, which are still on file at the agency, Samson said Rosario routinely told him about her meetings with Latin American diplomats as Colombia's cultural attaché. Most of the information she provided was gossip, rumors about who was sleeping with whom, but Samson also reported that Rosario had told him which of her friends still living in Colombia belonged to leftist groups that the CIA considered anti-American. Samson soon asked Rosario for another favor, this one a bit more risky. He needed an apartment where he could meet one of his sources in the afternoons without being seen. "I knew Rosario needed money, so I pitched it to her as something that we could do which would help both of us." Samson offered to pay her $200 per month and assured her that he would always tell her in advance when he was coming, would only meet his source on days when Rosario was at work, and would always leave the place so tidy that she would never know anyone had been there.

"I thought it was weird," Rosario said later, "but he was my friend, so I said, 'Okay,' and gave him a key."

Samson used her apartment for meetings with a retired Mexican federal police officer who had worked off and on as an informant for the FBI since the early 1950s. The officer had been part of the network the United States had used to keep track of what was happening inside the Communist Party, and Samson was paying the officer to help him rejuvenate that old system of informants. "This old fart had a big estate outside the city and when I first met him, he took me to a cave on his property that had a set of iron bars across the entrance. He told me that the FBI had built it for him back in 1951 or 1952, when the communists had a big international Communist Party meeting in Mexico City. He had gotten his men to kidnap Gus Hall (the head of the American Communist Party) and put him in that cave. They held him there for four days, until the meeting ended, because the FBI didn't want Hall speaking at that meeting."

Rosario's apartment was a perfect meeting spot for Samson. Because the Mexican was well known, Samson didn't want to meet him in a hotel, nor did he want to use one of the agency's safe houses in Mexico City. "Neighbors are always curious when they hear that the home next to them has been rented, yet they know that no one is living there," he said. "You can bet that they will be watching when someone does show up."

In the fall of 1982, Samson and Rosario both ran for seats on AM-

COSAD's four-member board of directors. Traditionally, AMCOSAD's president was from Mexico, the host country. Two of the seats were reserved for a Soviet and a U.S. diplomat. The last slot was taken by someone from Latin America. Samson was elected treasurer, Igor Shurygin was chosen vice president, and Rosario was elected secretary. How much Samson had to do with Rosario's decision to campaign for the secretary's slot is impossible to discern now. In interviews, Rosario vehemently denied that Samson had anything to do with her decision to run. He also insisted that Rosario had sought the office entirely on her own. "I didn't exploit her in this incident. . . . She was my friend." At the same time, Samson later admitted that Rosario's election to the board created a quandary for him. Igor Shurygin was always wary whenever someone from the U.S. embassy was near him. But what was he like when he thought he was with other foreigners? The Soviet spoke excellent Spanish. Would he let down his guard when he was with Rosario, an attractive, single, Spanish-speaking Colombian who was obviously not an experienced diplomat? Would he tell her gossip that would be useful to the CIA, or even attempt to recruit her to spy on the U.S.?

"There is no doubt that the situation with Rosario was really ripe for exploitation by either side, because she was just so incredibly naive," Samson said. "She didn't understand what she had really gotten into. She thought she was just doing me these simple little favors and she didn't have a clue where she was being led. And this really gets to the heart of the problem that all of us in the intelligence business face: How far are you willing to go to exploit someone who you really care about? The question for me was how far did I want to push her."

As it turned out, Rosario's access to Shurygin did not end up mattering much. The reason was Rick Ames.

CHAPTER 9

David Samson introduced Rick to Rosario at an AMCOSAD tour of
the National Anthropological Museum in Mexico City, but both of
them were busy and didn't pay much attention to one another. In
November 1982, a mutual friend from the Canadian embassy invited them to a dinner party in her apartment. They ended up sitting on the living room floor discussing Umberto Eco, Carlos
Fuentes, Gabriel Garcia Marquez, and other authors they both
liked. Rick thought Rosario was brilliant and beautiful. She thought
he was sweet and better-read than any American she had ever met.
Someone turned on some music and Rick asked her to dance.
Rosario didn't know he was married. He hadn't mentioned it and
didn't wear a ring. She thought he was a diplomat. He didn't own a
car, but she had bought a used one, so she offered him a ride home.
He invited her up to see his penthouse. They spent that night together. "Sex between us was fantastic," Ames said later.

He promised to telephone her the next day, but didn't. By this
time, Helen Riggs, his businesswoman girlfriend, had returned to
the States, but he was dating a coworker at the U.S. embassy. Three
weeks went by, and when Rosario didn't hear from Rick, she got angry. She was between boyfriends. When her affair with the married
pilot had ended, she had thought that she and Samson might become a couple, but he was still seeing his Mexican girlfriend. "Rick
pulled a disappearing act," she complained later. "The guy just totally vanished."

Rosario didn't have a date to AMCOSAD's Christmas gala, a formal affair, but she felt obligated to attend because she was a board member. She arrived feeling lousy. A doctor had just removed a mole from her arm and the incision still hurt. Samson waved her over to his table. He was there with his girlfriend and Rick was sitting next to his date. The only unoccupied chair was next to Rick. He jumped up, pulled out the seat, and spent so much time talking to her that his date became visibly annoyed and demanded that he dance with her. Rosario said goodnight. "I was old enough to realize that he wasn't obligated to call me, but it was strange how he had vanished and then after the Christmas dance, he did the same thing again. He acted interested, but then vanished and never called." Rosario spent Christmas Day at her aunt's house in Mexico City. Rick spent it working. On an impulse, he decided to fly home to spend New Year's Eve with Nan, and surprised her at their New York apartment. She was about to meet friends, and she didn't invite him to join her. He sat alone in the apartment, drinking, and flew back to Mexico City on New Year's Day. *It is gone. My marriage is over*, he told himself during the flight. Yet he still wasn't certain he wanted a divorce. "I was feeling sorry for myself—in a passive semi-state of denial."

Rosario's mother, Cecilia, who was visiting from Bogotá, answered the telephone when it rang in Rosario's apartment the next morning. "It's an American," she announced. Rosario assumed it was Samson.

"Dave, I thought you were going out of town for New Year's," Rosario said.

"This is Rick, Rick Ames." He was irked that she had assumed it was Samson. He asked her to dinner.

"No, I'm sorry, but I just can't. I've got to wash my hair," she replied.

Rick nearly laughed. He hadn't heard that excuse since high school. He asked again and then begged. Finally, she agreed. He arrived that night armed with flowers and chocolates, and spent fifteen minutes flattering Cecilia while waiting for Rosario to appear. Over an expensive dinner, they discussed T. S. Eliot and Emily Dickinson. Since her mother was staying at her apartment, Rosario didn't invite him up. He wanted to suggest that they go to his apartment, but he figured she would say no because he had not called her after their last lovemaking session. They kissed outside her apartment like teenagers, and later that night she wrote in her diary that she really liked him, but doubted if he would ever call her again. He seemed afraid of relationships. A few days later, Rick telephoned and invited her to dinner again. Rosario said she didn't want to go out. She asked him to come to her place. She was a gourmet cook. After they ate, they went to bed.

"Rosario and I went out last night," he told Samson the next day at work. "I thought you ought to know."

Rick knew Samson was using Rosario's apartment as a safe house. "It was Rick's way of telling me that he was serious about Rosario. On the one hand, Rick is my buddy and I was happy for him. On the other hand, I thought, 'Hey wait. Rosario is mine.' But I didn't love her and really wasn't interested in pursuing her, so I thought this was a great way out for me and it was good for Rick, too."

Rick began dating Rosario steadily. She was the one bright spot in a tour that was quickly turning bad. Director Casey had put Dewey Clarridge in charge of the agency's ill-fated efforts to help the contras fight the leftist Sandinista government in Nicaragua, and that meant Clarridge was constantly dropping in on the Mexico City station, which he often used as his Latin American base of operations. Clarridge hadn't liked how the station was being run, so he had put a new station chief in charge. Albert D. Wedemeyer was a veteran LA division officer and West Point graduate with a famous father, General Albert C. Wedemeyer, who had been commander of the U.S. forces in China during World War II. Clarridge had chosen John W. Sears, a veteran LA hand, to work as Wedemeyer's deputy. Both men made pleasing Clarridge their top priority. "Rick's bosses didn't want to waste station resources recruiting Russians. Everything was being focused on the contras or Cubans," recalled Diana Lynn Worthen, who worked for Ames in Mexico City as an intelligence assistant. "The Soviets were not a high priority. In fact, they didn't even make it on the priority list." Rick's conduct didn't win him any sympathy. While his new boss, John Sears, watched, Rick got drunk at a diplomatic party and began yelling at an equally drunk and obnoxious Cuban diplomat. A short time later, Rick was in a car accident and was so intoxicated that he didn't recognize the embassy security officer who'd been sent to smooth over things with the Mexican police. Sears sent a cable to Langley recommending that Rick receive counseling for alcohol abuse as soon as he returned to the States.

Rick seemed cursed at work, even when he was trying to do his best. Before Wedemeyer took charge, Rick was given permission to hide listening devices in the apartment of a Soviet diplomat. A CIA technician flew to Mexico City to pick the lock on the diplomat's apartment and plant the bugs, but he couldn't get the lock to open, so he made a mold of it and returned to Langley to make a duplicate key. By the time the technician was ready, Wedemeyer was in charge, and he didn't think the operation was worth the risk. Rick threw a fit and finally got his approval to go ahead. The technician returned and, this time, easily opened the door. Rick had chosen a night when he knew the diplomat and his wife would be attending a reception. Just to make sure that no one surprised the technician, Rick called in the station's "close support team" for help. This team was a group of five to ten Mexicans who were paid by the CIA to help during clandestine operations. Mostly, they were used to shadow targets. The listening devices were installed and worked fine. Rick was thrilled and then, twenty-four hours later, all of the bugs went dead. Everyone assumed there had been a mechanical failure. Wedemeyer was upset—the entire operation had been a waste of time—but Rick smelled a rat. He noticed that the Mexican who had been in charge of the close support team during the operation had never been given a polygraph examination or undergone a routine background investigation, even though he had worked for the agency for more than ten years. Rick suggested that he be given a lie detector test. It showed that he had been lying when he said that he had never worked for any other intelligence services except the CIA. A follow-up investigation confirmed that he had been under Soviet control for years and had been tipping off the KGB every time the close support team had been called upon for help.

"It was a really big scandal," said Samson, "and the station just covered up the entire mess, because the Office of Security at the embassy and LA division were so embarrassed about it." Rick was outraged. The station was blaming him for the bungled bugging operation and covering up the real culprit. After that, Rick had started drinking heavily.

"All of us were concerned about Rick," said his State Department friend Richard Thurman. "He was depressed and beginning to express some real skepticism about what our country was doing in Latin America. He was a bright and sensitive guy and I was afraid that we were going to lose him, literally, because of his drinking. And then Rick started going out regularly with Rosario and he really became crisp and clear again and seemed to focus. She really made him cut back on his drinking." Rick's other lunch partner from the State Department, Irwin Rubenstein, also noticed the change. "Rick told me that he was seeing Rosario and it was beginning to get serious. I was pleasantly surprised, because he clearly needed somebody, and I thought she would be good for him—you know, among other things, help him cut back on the drinking."

In March 1983, Rosario discovered that Rick and Samson were planning a weekend away in Acapulco. Samson was taking his girlfriend, Katarin, but

Rick hadn't said anything to Rosario about joining them. She knew that Rick and Samson had planned the trip months in advance, before she and Rick had become a couple. Still, she wanted to go along, so she asked Rick why he hadn't invited her. A red-faced Rick apologized and immediately asked her to join them. But she could tell something was bothering him as soon as they checked into their beachfront hotel in Acapulco on Friday night. The next morning, Rick said he had an upset stomach and disappeared for a few hours. Later, when the four of them were sitting by the pool, he again said that he needed to go inside and take a nap—alone. Rosario couldn't figure out what was wrong. A few minutes later, a porter told Samson that he had a telephone call. He handed him a telephone.

"Oh God," Samson said jokingly to the women. "I hope there hasn't been a revolution somewhere." It was Rick calling.

"I'm in the hotel lobby," Rick gasped. "You've got to help me! You've got to keep Rosario busy shopping all day!"

Helen Riggs, Rick's former girlfriend, was staying in the same hotel. He had originally invited her to join him in Acapulco, and he had not wanted to hurt her feelings by telling her about Rosario. The rest of that day, Rick raced back and forth between his two dates. He spent Saturday night with Rosario and Sunday morning apologizing to Helen about how he had gotten drunk and fallen asleep on the beach. Just when it looked as if he was going to pull off his escapade, Riggs appeared by the swimming pool when Rick and the others were having a drink. Rosario later recalled what happened next. "This woman comes walking over and Rick jumps up and he introduces Dave and his girlfriend, Katarin, and then he turns to me and says, 'And this is Katarin's friend.' I was totally humiliated, especially afterwards when it became clear who this woman really was."

Rosario was furious, but on the flight back to Mexico City, Rick apologized, and by the time they had landed, she had forgiven him. They began spending all their free time together and Rosario was sure that Rick was in love with her. Then one night while she was cooking dinner for him at the penthouse, Rick got a call from Helen Riggs. She was coming to Mexico City on business and wanted to make a lunch date. Rosario kept waiting for Rick to tell her that he was romantically involved with someone else, but he chatted away as if he were all by himself in the apartment, and even said that he was looking forward to seeing her when she got to town. "I was angry as hell," Rosario recalled, "but Rick says to me: 'What's the point in hurting her feelings?' I said, 'Her feelings? What about my feelings?' And he said, 'Why do you worry? I'm with you, aren't I? You're my choice. The hell with her.' That was supposed to be enough."

A few days later, Rosario told him how she felt. "Rosario dropped a bomb on me because she just came out and said that she had fallen in love with me and that she needed me and that I needed her and, by God, she was going to win my heart," said Ames. "I almost stood up and ran out the door. She wanted commitment, and I agonized and agonized over what I should do. No one in my family had ever gotten a divorce before. You just didn't do that. I also knew that I would have to face Nan and I would have to have a confrontation with her. I didn't want that. Besides, I kept asking myself, *Do I really love this woman?* I mean, what is love anyway? I had thought that I had loved Nan once, hadn't I?" Rick told Rosario that he needed time to think about what she had said.

Not long after that, Rick and Rosario went to Acapulco again with Samson and his girlfriend. While the women went shopping on a beautiful Saturday morning, the two CIA officers sat in beach chairs drinking Bloody Marys. Rick told Samson about TRIGON and Shevchenko, and how they had delivered top-notch political information to the agency. "No one gave a damn," Rick complained. He talked about how smart Thomas Kolesnichenko, his *Pravda* friend, had been. "No one in the agency wanted to hear what Thomas had to say." Pretty soon, Samson was complaining about the CIA, too. He said that Director Casey was furious because he didn't think the station was providing him with enough information about the Mexican economy. "I was sent here to recruit Chinese, not to write reports about the value of the peso!" he grumbled. The morning soon turned into one long, drunken gripe session. "I always thought that I was just as cynical as Rick was, because of some of my bad experiences," Samson recalled later, "but it suddenly dawned on me during our talk that Rick's cynicism about the agency had turned into pure hatred. He really had come to detest the agency, not just the people he worked for, but the institution itself and what it stood for."

During their beachside talk, Rick mentioned that Henry Steger, a translator at the U.S. embassy, had been pitched by the Soviets. Igor Shurygin had offered Steger, who worked for Rick, $50,000 in cash to become a KGB spy. By this time, Rick and Samson had drunk enough that both of them were feeling high, but Samson would later claim that he had no trouble remembering what they discussed next. "I said to Rick, 'How would you do it if you wanted to sell secrets to the Russians?' Rick had obviously thought about it, because he said, 'Well, here's how I'd do it,' and then he explained how he would only deal with them through a 'cut-out'—a false identity—and through dead drops, so that they would never know who he was. He didn't ask me how I'd do it, and we just sort of let the subject drop. But I kept thinking, 'You know, Rick has really given this matter a lot of thought.' It really struck me, but then I figured that part of his job was understanding the Soviets and how people contacted them."

When the foursome returned from that trip in late June, Rick told Rosario that he was finally ready to tell her how he felt.

"I love you and I am ready to make a commitment," he announced. "I will tell Nan that I want a divorce, but there is something you need to know about me first." Without warning, he blurted out that he worked for the CIA.

Rosario was speechless. "I kept thinking, 'This can't be true. I fell in love with a diplomat, not a spy!'"

If they were going to get married, Rick explained, Rosario would have to become a U.S. citizen, or he would have to quit his job, because CIA case officers couldn't be married to foreigners. Rosario wasn't listening.

"Does this mean you work with Dave?" she asked. "Do you mean to say that you've known about my apartment all along—that he was paying me?"

"Yes, and I'm very proud of you," he replied.

"Why?"

"Because you told Dave that you would never tell anyone what he was doing and you didn't even tell me—so we knew that you could keep secrets."

Rosario felt betrayed. "What are you doing with these creeps? Why are you wasting your time, your talents? You're supposed to be a diplomat."

"Look, it's something that's not forever," he said. "I can probably retire soon."

Rosario kept thinking about how he and Dave had been testing her, smugly knowing that she was a paid informant. She thought it was nauseating.

Rick's tour in Mexico City was scheduled to end that September, but he was actually leaving the embassy before then because he wanted to take a short vacation. He had rented a rustic bungalow in Playa del Carmen on the Gulf of Mexico, which in 1983 was still largely undeveloped. "This was going to be my dream vacation. I was going to take a whole bunch of books to read—all of Dickens's works—and a whole lot of booze to drink, and I was going to sit there on the beach and just drink and read and be by myself."

Already upset about Rick leaving, Rosario became even more distraught when Rick announced his plans.

"What about me?" she asked. "What about us?"

Reluctantly, he invited her along. Rosario called it their "honeymoon." Together on the beach they planned their future. He would return to Washington, where he was being reassigned, and find them an apartment to live in. As soon as his divorce was final, Rosario would quit her job and join him. They would get married. He would resign, find another job, and they would live happily ever after.

Rick didn't trust Mexico's postal system, so he asked Diana Worthen, his intelligence assistant, if she would make certain that Rosario got his letters. He'd mail them to her through the embassy diplomatic mail pouch. Worthen liked Rick. She had met Rosario at an embassy party but did not know her well. Rick and Rosario spent a tearful night together, and then he left Mexico City. A few days later, Worthen called Rosario. A letter from Rick had arrived. The two women met for lunch, and Rosario gave Worthen a letter to mail to Rick. Before long, the two women were meeting so often to exchange letters that they became friends.

It was an odd coupling, even though the two women were about the same age. Worthen was shy, conservative. She had been reared in the Midwest and had gone to work in the agency's secretarial pool fresh from college. She didn't date much. Rosario was happy to have a friend. She had not realized how much of her social life had revolved around Rick and Samson, who also had been transferred. She wasn't interested in dating anyone else, so she and Worthen began going to various diplomatic functions together and spending their weekends shopping. Rosario seemed to know every curio shop and boutique in the city, and she loved going from one shop to another, comparing prices, even though neither of them had much money.

Worthen had never known anyone quite like Rosario. Her new Colombian friend could speak five languages fluently and was able to talk about almost any subject as if she were an expert in it. She was a Colombian blue blood. Her father, Pablo Casas Santofimio, was from a family that had once owned thousands of acres of land in the Colombian state of Tolima, but he had turned his back on the family's wealth as a young man and chosen a career as a teacher. He was the first Colombian ever to receive a degree in mathematics from Bogotá's National University, and that is where he had met Rosario's mother, Cecilia Dupuy de Casas. She had been a dashing beauty in college, a mixture of French and South American bloodlines. Her ancestors had arrived in Colombia in the late 1800s from Corsica and had made a fortune selling the latest imported goods from Paris to Bogotá's wealthy upper class. Cecilia had been studying philosophy and literature when she met Pablo. He had found her to be a rather eccentric woman. She loved nothing better than to dance all night to the hot sounds of Cuban salsa and listen to avant-garde artists and writers argue about the meaning of life. Tears came to her as easily as laughter. She was self-centered, sometimes neurotic, but she had a lust for life that he envied. In 1949, Princeton University awarded Pablo a full scholarship, so he and Cecilia moved to the States. They returned home three weeks before Rosario was born in December 1951.

Rosario had adored her father and endured her mother. When she was small, her father's colleagues at Bogotá's National University used to joke that she was the safest child in the city: If she ever got lost, the police would know instantly where to take her, because she looked so much like him. Rosario was always eager to go with him to his office, and when he came home from the university, she was waiting at the door.

"What's the most important thing in the world?" he would ask her. Beginning at age four, she would repeat the correct answer: "To be orderly."

It was something that her mother never was. Rosario continued to favor her father as a young girl. Like him, she learned to love mathematics and literature, and she grew up believing that there was no profession as profound as teaching, no better place to spend one's life than inside the ivy-covered towers of a university. It wasn't the knowledge as much as it was the simple act of learning that she was taught to value. Rosario had been shy as a teen, completely introverted except when she was in the classroom. She was the student always determined to earn the highest marks, the one whose hand shot up instantly whenever the teacher asked a question.

Her mother, Cecilia, cajoled and dominated her. Why didn't she have boyfriends? Why was she always so stuffy? Rosario's younger siblings, Claudia and Pablo, eventually rebelled against their mother's hovering, but Rosario never did.

In 1969, Rosario graduated from the American School in Bogotá, where the majority of students were the sons and daughters of U.S. embassy employees. At the high school graduation, Rosario gave her valedictory speech in Spanish, even though English was the official language at the school. It was her way of declaring her pride in Colombia and Latin culture. "I will never marry an American," she told her best friend. "Americans think they are better than anyone else." Rosario enrolled at the University of the Andes in Bogotá but dropped out during her first year after she contracted a life-threatening case of malaria. By this time, her father had left teaching for politics, and she went to live with him on an island under Colombia's control off the coast of Nicaragua. He had been appointed its governor. Her father and mother were living apart, but were not divorced. Under her father's care, Rosario recuperated but remained depressed. She felt as if she had failed. Her father sent her to Europe. She spent six months there and then enrolled at Princeton University, but was soon unhappy and returned home. She moved in with her mother, and both of them enrolled as students at the University of the Andes. Her friends and relatives began to remark that Rosario seemed to be turning into almost a twin of Cecilia. They received their diplomas together in January 1976. The university hired both of them as professors. Rosario taught Greek and worked on her Ph.D.

By the spring of 1982, she had spent twelve years in college, either as a student or teacher, and she wanted a change. Her father was now the president of a university in Tolima, and he invited her to a lunch honoring Colombian president Julio Cesar Turbay Ayala. Afterward, Turbay offered Rosario a ride back to Bogotá aboard the presidential jet, and she told him that she was thinking about moving to Mexico. She did not mention that she had fallen in love with a married pilot who was being transferred there. President Turbay invited her to lunch at the presidential palace a few weeks later and offered her the job of cultural attaché. That was how she had come to Mexico City.

Diana Worthen knew Rosario was a member of Colombia's social elite. Yet she clearly didn't have much money, and that struck Worthen as odd. "In Latin America if you are a wealthy woman, you don't work," Worthen said later. "It was just not something a Latin woman ever did, and I knew Rosario was putting in long hours at her job, so that told me that her family was not wealthy."

Rosario later explained the inconsistency. "My mother likes to call us 'impoverished aristocrats.' I grew up around people with wealth, but we never had it." Her father could have taken millions of dollars in bribes when he was a politician, she said, but he refused. She went to top schools, but only because she was awarded full tuition scholarships. When she toured Europe, she had stayed with relatives and had ridden everywhere on the bus to save her money.

"What you have to understand about Rosario is, when I first met her in Mexico City, she was very nice, very sensitive and very unassuming," Worthen said later. "She never flaunted her education or her family connections. She wasn't a snob at all. In fact, she went out of her way not to be snobby to people."

Rosario and Worthen shared a hotel room during an AMCOSAD outing to Cozumel, Mexico. Rick called her at the hotel. Rosario was ecstatic. She had been afraid that he was going to vanish again as soon as he got back to the States. Rick invited her to spend Thanksgiving with him in Washington, D.C., where he was living with his sister, Nancy, and her husband. Rosario accepted. Rick's younger sister, Alison, and his mother spent Thanksgiving day at Nancy's too. Everyone loved Rosario. Rosario assumed that Rick had told his wife that he was in love with another woman, but he hadn't. In fact, Rick hadn't told Nan a thing about Rosario. When he had first returned to the States from Mexico City, Rick had spent a week with Nan in New York at their apartment, but he had not been able to muster enough courage to tell her that he wanted a divorce. He had saved that for a letter that he mailed to Nan after he moved into the basement at Nancy's house. He blamed himself in the letter for their marital problems. He said there was an "emptiness and hollowness" in their marriage. A week later, Rick went to meet Nan face to face. "She was stunned and shocked that I wanted a divorce," he said later. "She didn't understand why, and that really surprised me, because I figured she was as unhappy as I was. I insisted, and she agreed, sort of. I got the feeling that she wasn't going to push it."

Rosario asked Rick over the Thanksgiving holidays if he had filed for divorce. He mumbled something about how he was still working on it, and she returned to Mexico thinking that he would soon be rid of Nan and ready to remarry. Cecilia decided to spend the Christmas holidays with Rosario in Mexico City, and by chance, David Samson was on the same flight leaving Bogotá as she. They chatted and he wished her Merry Christmas when they landed. An upset Rosario called him the next morning at the U.S. embassy. Her parents' maid in Bogotá had found Rosario's father dead in his bed that morning of natural causes. Rosario and Cecilia were hysterical.

"Call Rick," Samson suggested. She did.

Rosario and Cecilia flew home that same day to arrange the funeral. A week later, Rosario returned to Mexico City. Her father had always been the rock in her family. Rick was waiting at the airport.

"Pack your bags," he said. "I want you to come live with me."

Rosario collapsed into his arms.

"Promise you will take care of me," she said. "I need someone to take care of me."

He held her close and spoke to her as if she were a child.

"I will. Don't worry, I'll always take care of you."

THE WORDS OF RICK AMES

Nan, my first wife, seldom drank more than a glass of wine at dinner, and we never drank at home at all. I would go to parties and sometimes get a definite high. The drinking got more serious in New York and on foreign trips. It wasn't boredom or loneliness that made me drink, rather the attraction was having a timeout period just for myself, when I could relax and lose myself for an afternoon or evening. I always took care to arrange these binges at times when I didn't need to work and would not be called. Typically, I would just sit in a hotel room with a book and read and drink myself to sleep, consuming most of a fifth of vodka or cognac in one sitting. I don't think anyone at the agency knew about this binge drinking when I was traveling.

Things got worse in New York. I began drinking in various bars without her knowledge. I seldom got fully drunk and only did this once or twice each month, except when I knew she was going to be away. I didn't crave alcohol, but it seemed to be answering some need I had for a timeout away from everything— work and Nan, too. We were beginning to go in different directions.

By the time I went to Mexico, I had developed quite a repertoire of drinking behavior, and Mexico City gave me much fuller opportunities for getting drunk, because I had no wife or home to rush back to at night. I had lots of free time and I spent lots of it binge drinking. My colleagues in Mexico were much harder drinkers than in New York. Parties were more frequent, and booze was cheap. I began taking long lunches with my colleagues, and I was getting drunk alone at night in my apartment at least once or twice every week. Of course, by this time, people were beginning to notice, and I was getting a reputation for overdoing it in social settings, but no one really said much. You have to realize that hard drinking had been an accepted part of the CIA culture for many years. James Angleton was famous for getting loaded every day at long lunches. There was still an element of macho pride in being an officer who could go drink-for-drink with other men.

Rosario was used to and enjoyed social drinking, and at first I don't think she was alarmed by my habits. In practice, I used her willingness to drink with me as a license to drink freely, without guilt, always stopping short of total drunkenness. I also used to egg her on, but only managed to get her to the point of a social high three times. By 1984, she stopped drinking, except for a glass of wine at dinner or at a party. She said it was because of her weight, but I think it was her attempt to get me to stop. I tried and even promised several times to not drink at home. But I always cheated, sneaking in a bottle of liquor and then concealing it or lying about it. Because Rosario disliked me drinking at home, I took up the practice of drinking alone at lunchtime, when I would consume four or five double vodkas at least once a week, sometimes twice. I really had no choice, since Rosario kept close tabs on me at night. This created problems, because I not only had to hide my drinking from my colleagues at work but also keep it from Rosario.

THE WORDS OF OTHERS

He's a greater traitor than Benedict Arnold.

—R. James Woolsey, CIA

Here is my hypothesis. Rickie is drawn to the CIA. His father worked there, and he sees the agency as having a certain glamour. But then he gets into it, and he discovers that it is a government bureaucracy just like all the other government bureaucracies. Now some are good, but most are filled with time-servers—people who get promoted because they have been there a long time or they have rubbed the right apple. I can see Rickie, who was always very creative but never good in a bureaucratic setting, not doing well and waking up one day and saying to himself, Is this how I should spend my life? The sad thing about Rickie is that I don't think he would have had the gumption to do what any decent person would have done at that point, which is to simply get out. You see, Rickie always avoided confrontation, and I think basically that behind his mask, he is a very fearful person. This is not wimpiness. Obviously he took a lot of risks being a spy. So I don't mean that. Rather it is a basic gutlessness—an inability to take his life in his own hands and take responsibility for his own actions.

—Margaret "Peggy" Anderson, high school friend

Of course we drank, but I never saw him falling down drunk like the CIA and FBI have claimed. He was always in control of his faculties. I never knew he was married, though. He kept that hidden, and when my wife and I had dinners with him, he always arrived with a new woman on his arm, and he always made it clear from the way that he touched her that they were more than just friends.

—Thomas Kolesnichenko, *Pravda*

I think Rick really wanted to make an impact on history. I think this was important to him. Now, the normal person might dismiss this as megalomania, but I think he genuinely thought that he had a chance to affect history by doing what he did. How many people have a chance to nudge history in one direction or the other? Not many. But he did. He really did!

—David T. Samson, CIA

When sentenced to what Russians euphemistically refer to as vyshaya mera [*the highest measure of punishment*]*, the condemned person is taken into a room, made to kneel, then shot in the back of the head. It is part of the Stalinist tradition.*

—Death of the Perfect Spy [Dmitri Polyakov], *Time* magazine

The branch chief job was a make-or-break job for him. He had really done well in New York, while Mexico had been a mediocre tour, you had to count it as a loss, so the jury was still out on Rick Ames.

—Jeanne R. Vertefeuille, CIA

CHAPTER 10

In September 1983, Rick seemed like an excellent choice for his new job as counterintelligence branch chief in Soviet operations. He spoke and read Russian, had a flair for writing clear, crisp, and thorough reports, was considered to be a KGB specialist, and, most important of all, was remembered by those in charge as someone who had done exceptionally well in New York handling big Soviet cases. No one paid any attention to his lackluster job performance in Mexico City or his periodic alcoholic outbursts.

"Everyone knew that no SE officer was going to do well in Mexico City," a retired SE division officer said later, "because the entire station was focused on the contras and Nicaragua. I think members of the review panel just sort of skipped over the negative evaluations Rick got in Mexico City and looked back on his New York years."

It was Rodney W. Carlson, Rick's last boss in Manhattan, who first recommended him for the branch chief slot at CIA headquarters. Carlson was reorganizing the counterintelligence functions in the SE division. Rick would oversee the operations in the USSR, and Jack P. Gatewood would handle those in Eastern Europe. The two men had worked for Carlson in New York and had gone through the agency's career training program together.

Carlson had not selected Rick by himself. The SE division's Personnel Management Committee, which was composed of the SE division chief, his deputy, the chief of SE operations, the chief of external operations, and the chief of internal operations, had voted on the choice. Federal investigations would later discover that no one on the committee was aware of Rick's drinking problem or that he felt alienated from the agency and its mission. The criticisms that John W. Sears, the deputy chief in Mexico City, had cabled to headquarters, after Rick had gotten into a drunken shouting match with a Cuban diplomat, had been routed to the CIA's medical operations office, which provided employees with alcohol abuse counseling. But no one on the personnel committee was shown a copy of the cable. Nor did the committee members know that Rick was living with a foreign national and one-time CIA source.

Rick had finally arrived. As branch chief, he had access to nearly all the agency's sensitive Soviet cases, including the actual names of most of the Soviets' "human assets." He had access to details about the agency's clandestine operations in the USSR, and he would be told whenever the agency recruited a new agent there. In short, little about the CIA's Soviet operations was being held back from him.

On his first day at his new job, he read the agency's files about the two agents whom he had handled in New York, Sergey Fedorenko—PYRRHIC— and the Soviet scientist BYPLAY. According to the files, Fedorenko had not been in contact with the agency since 1977, when he had been called back to Moscow. But there was a note in his file that said a diplomat had spotted him at an arms control meeting in Moscow in 1981, so the agency knew he was still alive. He was reportedly working at the Institute of USA and Canada Studies, headed by Georgy A. Arbatov, at the USSR Academy of Sciences. The agency had not been in touch with BYPLAY since he had returned to Moscow. However, he had been seen at a scientific conference. Rick wasn't surprised that both had lost contact with the agency. It wasn't unusual for a Soviet to help the United States only to vanish after returning to Moscow. Though clearly dangerous, spying outside the USSR was not nearly as threatening as dropping off a package of classified materials at a dead drop in the KGB-infested center of Moscow.

Rick began reading the dossiers of other Soviets spying for the agency. He discovered that a new generation was now under his protection. In the late 1950s and early 1960s, Colonel Oleg Penkovsky, the GRU officer who had helped President Kennedy identify missiles in Cuba, had been the agency's premier agent. After he was executed, the spies FEDORA and TOPHAT had stepped forward. They had been forced into retirement after publication of the book *Legend: The Secret World of Lee Harvey Oswald*. No sooner had those men fallen from the screen than TRIGON, Arkady Shevchenko, Fedorenko, and other lesser-known spies had appeared. Adolf Tolkachev, whom the agency called SPHERE, was currently its hottest asset. He was the electronics expert the agency had turned away repeatedly in Moscow in 1977. Since then it had paid him more than two million dollars for information. That was a paltry sum compared to the *billions* of dollars in research costs that Tolkachev had saved U.S. taxpayers. "Around the agency, people liked to say that Tolkachev paid the rent," Ames said later. "Everything else we did was nice, but Tolkachev made the entire CIA budget worthwhile! He basically handed us the entire Soviet avionics system. If a war in Europe had started, we would have had unquestioned air superiority."

The SE division's second most important source in 1983 was not a human asset but a technical one known as TAW. It was so secret that the file Rick was given to read only contained bits and pieces of information. In 1979, the CIA had discovered that the Soviets were building a super-secret communications center twenty-five miles southwest of Moscow near a town named Troitsk. Underground tunnels connected the center to the KGB's first chief directorate headquarters and its main headquarters in Lubyanka. These tunnels contained the cables for telephones, fax machines, and teletype messages, and were thought by the Soviets to be secure. The CIA, however, had managed to bribe a member of the construction crew, and he had given the CIA a blueprint of the tunnels. In 1980, a CIA technician was hustled out of the U.S. embassy in Moscow hidden in a van. After the driver was certain that he was not being followed, he drove out of Moscow to a remote area, where the technician jumped from the van, and hid in the woods. He located the communication tunnel, crept inside, and installed a sophisticated monitoring and recording device. From that point on, the CIA was able to obtain recordings of the KGB's most important messages. It was one of the most astounding and successful operations ever launched by the CIA. "The Soviets didn't have a clue what was going on," Ames told me during our private conversations, disclosing the existence of TAW for the first time ever in a book.

Ames learned about another fantastic clandestine operation by reading agency files. It was called ABSORB, and it sounded as if it had come from the pages of a James Bond novel. By 1983, the CIA had identified the precise location of every permanent ground-based nuclear missile in the USSR. But it wasn't sure how deadly these missiles were, especially after the Soviets began developing MIRVs (multiple independently targeted reentry vehicles). Some MIRVs could hold as many as ten warheads. CIA scientists began looking for ways to tell how many warheads were in each missile, and they soon came up with a scientific formula. They knew that each warhead emitted a tiny amount of radiation. By measuring the amount of radiation being emitted by each MIRV, one could tell whether it contained ten, six, or four warheads, and how powerful each warhead was. That left the agency with only one problem: How to get an accurate radiation reading? Sending a spy into a missile-launching silo with a Geiger counter was unrealistic.

At this point someone noticed that most Soviet nuclear warheads were manufactured in the western USSR and shipped over the Ural Mountains to the Far East, where they were installed in sites for firing at the United States. The only practical way for the Soviets to move the warheads was on the Trans-Siberian railroad, which begins in Moscow and travels some 5,750 miles east until it reaches the seaport of Vladivostok. Branch lines connect Moscow with the rest of Europe. At some point along the route, a train traveling from Vladivostok to Moscow had a good chance of passing an eastbound train carrying a nuclear warhead. Although the trains might only be together for a few seconds, a souped-up Geiger counter, if the agency could find a way to put one on a train car, might be able to get a reading from the warhead.

That was the theory behind ABSORB, and by 1983, when Rick first read about it, the agency had already spent close to fifty million dollars on the project. It still had not perfected its Radiation Detection Device (RDD), but it had done some interesting test runs using the railroad. In one test, the agency had hidden a number of sophisticated cameras inside a false wall built in the side of a cargo container like those pulled by semitrailers, which can be loaded onto trains or ships. Through a friendly Japanese company, the agency had arranged to have this container shipped across the USSR from Vladivostok to eastern Europe. The cameras had been rigged to snap photographs whenever the train crossed an adjoining track. Many of these tracks connected the railway to military manufacturing plants, so each time a train went by a weapons plant, the cameras snapped a photograph for the CIA. Thanks to those missions, the agency knew that ABSORB was possible. The trick was to perfect the RDD so that it would switch on whenever it began to detect minuscule amounts of radiation, and then flip itself off. The CIA was on the verge of sending an RDD across the USSR when Rick took charge. It had sent a rigged cargo container to Japan, where it was being included in a shipment of containers filled with ceramic vases that were being transported from the coast to Hamburg, Germany. As with TAW, details about ABSORB were revealed by Ames during our talks.

As Rick read through the stacks of Soviet files, he began to realize that he was in an extraordinary position. The CIA had more spies working inside the USSR in 1983 than at any previous time in its history. Besides Tolkachev, Ames was aware of at least twenty other agents and some one hundred covert operations, although few were as exotic as TAW and ABSORB. Most were minor operations, such as planting listening devices in a Moscow apartment owned by Soviet officials. The enormity of the CIA's access to Soviet secrets was breathtaking. "My God," he later explained, "We had penetrated every aspect of the Soviet system. We had spies in the KGB, GRU, Kremlin, scientific institutes—everywhere." Like a piece of Swiss cheese, the USSR was riddled with holes dug by moles. If he needed more proof, Rick got it when he read about a CIA-controlled agent working in Moscow known as MEDIAN, the cryptonym for Vladimir Potashov. He worked at the same institute in the same department as Sergey Fedorenko, PYRRHIC, although neither spy knew about the other. "We had spies working on top of our other spies!"

Besides the files of agents working inside the USSR, Rick also had access to information about Soviets who were working for the CIA *outside* the Soviet empire. Two caught his eye. Both were stationed inside the KGB offices at the Soviet embassy in Washington, and both were providing the FBI and CIA with incredibly good intelligence about what was happening there. Valery F. Martynov, whose cryptonym was GENTILE, was a KGB lieutenant colonel assigned to Line X, the KGB division charged with stealing scientific and technical intelligence. He had been recruited by Rick's boss, Rodney Carlson, and he was still personally handling the agent. According to notes in his file, Martynov had agreed to spy for political reasons after he had become disillusioned about widespread corruption inside the KGB.

High ideals were not what had made KGB Major Sergey Motorin, known as GAUZE, switch sides, however. He had been blackmailed by the FBI shortly after he had arrived in the States in 1980. FBI agents had tailed Motorin to an electronics store in suburban Chevy Chase, Maryland, where he had tried to buy an expensive combination television and stereo record player on credit. Because he was a foreigner and had diplomatic immunity, which meant the store owner couldn't file any civil claims against him in court, his application for credit was rejected by the store. After Motorin left the store, the FBI rushed inside and convinced the store owner to help them entrap Motorin. The owner called Motorin and suggested another way for him to buy the electronics that he wanted. The owner said he was willing to let Motorin pay part of the $950 price with cases of Russian vodka, which the KGB officer could buy through the embassy duty-free for $4.50 per bottle. At the time, Russian vodka was selling for $12 per bottle in U.S. liquor stores. Motorin agreed and when he returned to the store with several cases of Russian vodka, the FBI was waiting with its video cameras. It confronted Motorin as he was leaving and reminded him that it was against the law in the Soviet Union to sell or trade duty-free goods abroad. Motorin quickly agreed to spy.

In his new job, Rick was not expected to handle day-to-day spy operations. Rather, it was the branch chief's job to sit back and study ways those operations could be improved. He was also responsible for devising new ways to protect the CIA's agents. Rick noticed a pattern in the files that he studied. In nearly every case, the CIA had caught Americans who were spying for the KGB and GRU because of information provided to it by KGB and GRU traitors who had been recruited by the United States. The same was true in reverse. In nearly every case, the KGB and GRU had learned about the CIA's "human assets" because someone in U.S. intelligence had tipped them off. A prime example involved William Kampiles, a former low-ranking CIA officer who had strolled into the KGB *rezidence* in Athens, Greece, in 1978 and offered to sell the Soviets a technical manual for the KH-11 (Keyhole) satellite, a new secret communications satellite being used by the military. What Kampiles had no way of knowing was that the duty officer who met him when he stepped into the Soviet compound was a spy for the CIA. The agency had recruited Sergey Ivanovich Bokhan, whose crypt was BLIZZARD, several years earlier. He passed a message to the CIA about Kampiles, who was arrested when he returned to the States. "The biggest threat to each side's spies are agents coming over from the other side and snitching on them," Rick said later. It was as simple as that.

Rick began coming to work early and staying late. He was getting excited about his job again. One afternoon, he asked Rodney Carlson for permission to root through the agency's SAWDUST records. Even today, few files are as embarrassing to the CIA as SAWDUST, the codename given to James Jesus Angleton's agency-wrecking mole hunt in the 1960s and 1970s. "Anyone who knew any agency history had heard about SAWDUST, and the management that was running the agency in 1983—folks such as Rod Carlson—had been absolutely traumatized by the damage that Angleton had done. I wanted to read the actual documents myself, and Carlson told me to go ahead."

For several days, Rick pored over the yellowing papers. It was a grim and ruthless tale. In the early 1960s, Angleton had become so convinced that a defector named Yuri Nosenko was a double agent still working for the KGB that the counterintelligence chief had arranged for the CIA to hold Nosenko prisoner for *four years and eight months!* At first Nosenko had been locked in an attic room stripped of everything except a bed. He had been fed only weak tea, watery soup, and porridge. Later he was blindfolded and taken to a concrete cell at the Farm that had been built just to hold him. There he underwent what agency officials would later euphemistically describe to Congress as a "hostile interrogation." Kept in total isolation from the out-side world, Nosenko was not allowed to have a watch, reading material, or anything that he could use to keep himself entertained. At first he was given toothpaste in a tube, but it was confiscated after he was caught trying to read the writing on the tube while hiding under his blanket. The lights in his cell were turned off and on at weird intervals to disorient him, making it im-possible for him to keep track of when it was day or night. The agency gave him massive shots of Thorazine, a powerful drug used in prisons to make in-mates complacent, and other psychotropic drugs. Nosenko would later charge that he had been given LSD, but the agency would deny it. Three times during his incarceration Nosenko was given lie detector tests, but the first two tests were rigged so that the machine showed that he was lying re-gardless of what he said. At one point he was kept strapped in a chair for seven hours, with the lie detector equipment still attached to him, while his examiners took a long break. He was told that he was going crazy, that he had been abandoned by everyone who knew him.

When the agency was later forced by Congress to defend its vicious treat-ment of Nosenko, Angleton and his superiors said that they had been con-vinced that he was a double agent and were simply trying to get him to admit to it. It turned out that Nosenko was a genuine defector. His state-ments were much more credible than those being told by Anatoly Golitsin, the Russian who Angleton was convinced was the only Soviet defector not being manipulated by the KGB. "I was struck by the sheer insanity that had gone on," said Ames. "I remember reading the files and thinking to myself, *How could people who consider themselves to be moral do such things?* And the answer that came back, of course, was that they were not moral at all. That is why they could do what they did."

Nosenko was not Angleton's only victim. In July 1967, he deliberately betrayed one of the CIA's own agents, Yuri Loginov, by telling the South African intelligence service that Loginov was a KGB spy. Arrested by the South Africans, Loginov was held in prison for two years, during which time Angleton steadfastly denied that Loginov had ever worked for the CIA, even though he had served the agency loyally for eight years. Angleton was angry because Loginov had told his handler that Nosenko was a legitimate defector and that Golitsin was a liar. In 1969, Angleton arranged for Loginov to be sent back to Moscow as part of a swap for dissidents, even though the spy didn't want to go, and the agency suspected that he would be executed if he were sent home.*

"Most of what I was reading in the SAWDUST files had already come out during congressional investigations of the agency," said Ames, "but seeing the actual cables and seeing Angleton's handwritten notes—I mean, God damn, this was history that I was holding!"

Because Rick had oversight of various operations in Moscow, he was told about a clever idea that had been implemented two years earlier at the CIA station there. It was called the "clean slot" operation and was the brainchild of Burton Lee Gerber, who had been the agency's chief of station in Moscow at the time. Gerber had noticed that it was nearly impossible for his officers to leave the U.S. embassy without being followed by the KGB, but several low-ranking State Department employees seemed to come and go as they pleased. One reason the KGB always knew who to follow was because the CIA employees worked out of the CIA's offices in the embassy and were generally senior agency employees who had already served abroad elsewhere, often in jobs where they had recruited Soviets. The KGB already had collected thick files about them before they arrived in Moscow. Gerber decided that a CIA officer fresh from the Farm, who had never been overseas, would not be so easy for the KGB to identify, particularly if this employee was assigned a full-time State Department job and told to avoid the CIA's offices. To further keep this employee's real job a secret, only his fellow CIA colleagues and the ambassador would know about him, and he would only be used during emergencies, when the station chief needed to get someone out of the embassy without a KGB tail.

Gerber's suggestion was greeted with skepticism by his bosses. They were reluctant to send a novice officer to Moscow and they hated to have one of their employees working full-time for the State Department. But Gerber

*The CIA later learned that Loginov had somehow survived.

eventually won over his critics and a clean slot officer was sent to Moscow in late 1981. Rick was told that the clean slot operation had proven to be a real success, enough so that the agency had decided to send a second novice employee to Moscow in early 1983 as a replacement for the first. This new officer was Edward Lee Howard, a thirty-one-year-old former Peace Corps volunteer, whose maturity had impressed his teachers at the Farm. Because no one was certain what sort of emergency Howard might be called upon to handle, he had been briefed about the Moscow station's most important operations, including TAW, and had been told about the human assets working there, including Adolf Tolkachev. In April 1983, about five months before Rick arrived at headquarters as the new branch chief, a routine polygraph test had revealed that Howard had lied when he was asked about his past drug use while in the Peace Corps. Without warning, the agency had fired him in May and had chosen another fresh recruit to take his place. Rick was told that Howard's replacement was being hurried through the process so he could get to Moscow as quickly as possible.

Rick didn't bother to read Howard's file. Since he was no longer employed by the agency, it didn't seem important. Only much later would Ames come to realize just how important Edward Lee Howard was to become in his life.

THE WORDS OF RICK AMES

When I became branch chief, I collected all the studies the agency had written on Soviet cases over the previous ten to fifteen years. As I studied these cases, it suddenly occurred to me that no serious thought had ever been made by the agency to examine the overall philosophy of what was happening. And because that had never been done, there was no serious understanding of the KGB. Now here I am, maybe six to eight months into my job, and I'm thinking, My God, I'm the biggest expert on the KGB that this entire division has! Why should that be? How can that be? *I had read all of the KGB investigation manuals. I had read all of our reporting, and, knowing what I had learned, when I read our counterintelligence reports and our analysis, I said to myself,* These things lack a real connection with what the KGB really is. None of these people has a grasp of the reality of the KGB, the Soviet Union and how it works.

At first I thought, Is it possible that I am just smarter than everyone else? *While that was very satisfying, deep down I knew it couldn't be true. I really respected and admired many of my colleagues. And then I figured out what was happening. You see, no one really took seriously what all of the Soviet agents who we had handled over the years had told us. Now I'm not kidding about this. This is the truth. Let me give an example. Regardless of what we were told by our KGB sources, we always assumed that the KGB had all of the resources in the world, that if the KGB needed ten thousand officers to do surveillance and go around and find a needle in a haystack—why, it could come up with ten thousand officers. When everything else failed, we always decided that the reason a case got compromised was because someone from the KGB had seen our source at a dead drop or meeting with his handler. We never wanted to blame ourselves for our failures, so we always painted this mythical picture of the KGB as some huge tiger that was nearly invincible.*

Do you know how many officers the Seventh Directorate of the KGB in Moscow really has working for it full-time doing surveillance? It has 250 full-time agents assigned to follow people. That is not many. Believe me, you would be shocked to know how many the FBI has just to follow Soviets in New York City alone. Did you know that the KGB doesn't have enough tape recorders for its officers to use? And it certainly doesn't have enough transcribers fluent in English to sit around and listen to every American telephone call that comes into Moscow. The KGB is like any government bureaucracy— it has limited resources and it has to use them the best way that it can. But we never wanted to believe this because it was important for us to believe in the myth of the invincible tiger. Why? Because we wanted to be an invincible tiger too, and we couldn't justify ourselves to Congress and the American public unless we told them that the KGB was an invincible tiger that had to be stopped.

Now don't misunderstand me here. I am not saying that the KGB was a paper tiger. It was a real tiger with real claws and real teeth. I do not now nor did I ever have any illusions in 1983 about that. Let me tell you a story. Once upon a time in San Francisco a KGB officer [Boris Yuzhin, whose cryptonym is TWINE] at the rezidency began photographing documents for us with a neat little camera we gave him. One day, he loses the camera. Everyone panics in Langley, but nothing happens, and eventually this guy goes back to Moscow. In 1985, Vitaly Yurchenko defects, and he tells us about this case. A cleaning woman found the camera and gave it to the KGB. So now the KGB knows there is a spy in its midst. The KGB narrows it down to two suspects: the real guy and *a fellow who works in the foreign ministry.* The KGB calls both back to Moscow. It begins watching both but it can't tell which one is the agent. So what does it do? The first thing it does is search both men's apartments, but neither has anything incriminating. Now the KGB knows that we communicate with our agents in Moscow by sending them brief messages over shortwave broadcasts, and both of these suspects have shortwave radios.*

Now at about the same time the KGB is searching for our agent, one of our engineers at the agency discovers that you can electronically trace our shortwave radio broadcasts. This engineer gets everyone in the agency in an uproar by creating this image of the old World War II radio cars going up and down the streets of Moscow listening to broadcast frequencies and determining which radios are tuned to our frequency. He wants to completely redesign the shortwave radios that we give to our agents and put a special shield in each one to keep the Soviets from tracking signals to it. I argued against this idea, because it was more dangerous to give our agents shortwave radios that obviously had been altered by the agency than to believe the KGB was capable of zooming in on a specific radio during one of our transmissions. Why did I feel this way? Because Moscow is a huge city composed of huge apartment complexes and ten million people. Even if the KGB had the technology—is it really capable of zeroing in on a single radio in a single apartment? This is what I mean when I say seeing a huge tiger when one didn't exist.

I asked Yurchenko if the KGB had caught the spy, and he told me that it had taken each man's shortwave radio and put a microphone in it, so that officers could sit in the apartment next door and monitor what each of the suspects listened to. Now that is the real tiger! The KGB didn't have the technology to do what the invincible tiger would do, but it did do something.

The funny thing is that the KGB never heard anything of value, because we did not send this fellow any messages. I asked Yurchenko who he thought the agent was, and he told me it was the foreign ministry guy—the wrong one. Of course, the KGB did end up arresting our agent, but not because of anything it did electronically. I told the KGB his name. That's how the real tiger found out.

---

*The Russians later told me this was Igor Samsonov.

CHAPTER 11

Love was enough. At least at first.

Just before Christmas 1983, Rick and Rosario moved into a modest apartment in Falls Church, Virginia, a suburb. Rick owned a 1974 Volvo, but not much else. Except for his clothes and a few books that he had brought back from Mexico City, everything else was still in the New York apartment with Nan. Rick and Rosario picked out furniture at a discount store and began buying cooking utensils and dishes. It was really astonishing how much it took to furnish a place, Rick thought. He used his and Nan's American Express card to cover most of the costs. A few weeks later, he had to spend another $800 when the Volvo broke down. Rosario was still grieving about her father's death and worried about how her mother was coping in Bogotá. She telephoned Cecilia nearly every day. Rick didn't complain, even though their monthly telephone bills soon exceeded $400. He got a second credit card and immediately ran it up to the maximum $5,000 limit. It didn't matter. For the first time in years, he was happy. Rosario seemed happy too. She baked bread, bought a typewriter so she could work on her Ph.D. dissertation, and fussed over him as soon as he walked through the door. She didn't have any friends, but she didn't complain. They had each other.

At night, they planned their future. She wanted children and, much to his own surprise, he told her that he wanted them, too, even though he was now forty-two. He had promised her during their vacation in Playa del Carmen that he would quit the CIA as soon as they could afford it, and he had meant it. He hadn't decided yet what he would choose for a second career. Maybe he would work as a journalist. He loved to write. Or perhaps he could get a consulting job somewhere. Maybe he would become a businessman. "The world is ours," he told her. She liked how that sounded, but she was quick to remind him that Bogotá would always be her home. "Sometimes I think I'm Colombia's last patriot," she joked. "Everyone else wants to be just like the Americans!" Colombia was where she would raise her children, where she planned to grow old.

He liked the idea of being an expatriate, a citizen of the world. Before Rick had gone to Mexico, he had belittled Latin America and its culture. Nearly everyone he knew had done the same, especially in the government. It didn't matter if you worked for the CIA or State Department, assignments in Latin America were considered second rate. Nothing seemed quite so ludicrous, Ames said later, as watching Henry Kissinger, Cyrus Vance, or some other State Department official during a rare visit south of the border, uncomfortably professing the gravity and importance of Latin America to their daily concerns. Ha! The self-perceived elites in the DO were the Soviet folks, and everyone knew it. They were the front-line warriors who did battle with the real enemy. The Middle Eastern group dominated by Arabists came next in Rick's mental ranking, because the Arab–Jew conflict always kept the area on the front burner. Next came the Asia hands, losing ground since the Vietnam War, but still powerful. Of course anyone who asked to be sent to Western Europe was viewed as an ease-seeking dilettante. Still, because of Europe's bi- and multilateral ties with the United States, an ambitious officer could do well there. The African nations were seen inside the CIA as the province of cowboys who didn't really have to work for a living. Who really cared if Zaire, or whatever it was being called now, fell to the communists? That left Latin America as the safe and comfortable refuge for the mediocrities. Rick hadn't cared that Latin America wasn't seen within the DO as a good job when he had gone to Mexico City, because the assignment had seemed to be the perfect compromise with Nan. But now he felt as if he had been transformed in Mexico. In retrospect, he saw his entire experience there as exhilarating, bewitching. He had been reborn in Mexico City. A completely new creature had crawled from a cracked cocoon into a bright new world there. The food, drink, travel, conversation—everything in Mexico City had awakened his senses and contributed to his feeling of new life.

In Mexico City he had felt as if he could re-create himself, not only professionally, but personally, and that is what he had done.

Rosario was the catalyst. Falling in love with her and being in love—
something he had thought was impossible after his sterile marriage to Nan
and his empty sexual affairs—now made him feel as if everything and anything were possible. In one swift burst of clarity, he had seen a way out of his
humdrum existence, a vision of what he thought could be, not what was. He
had wanted desperately to strip himself clean of the past, which hung like a
dead skin clinging to his frame, pulling him down. He wanted desperately to
rid himself of his dead-end marriage to Nan, his growing sense of a lack of
purpose in his life, his bad habits of drinking and aimlessly drifting, and his
general lack of human vitality. Rosario! Ah, she is what had saved him. In
Mexico, he had not only fallen in love with her, but with everything that she
represented and was. He had never been to Colombia, but why did that matter? Rosario said it was a fantastic place to live. He saw it through her eyes
and that was good enough. How could he not be happy there? It was part of
her.

With this new sense of pride in Colombia and fascination with Latin
American culture, he had started to recognize for the first time just how
strong a sense of political and cultural alienation he now felt from the
United States. He absolutely hated Ronald Reagan and his Hollywood vision
of America, as proclaimed in sixty-second sound bites beamed through television sets to families enslaved by their adherence to a mass culture that proclaimed how great life was for those who wore the correct deodorant, drove
the snappiest car, and drank beer brewed the old fashioned American way.
"Reagan's presidency, politics, and rhetoric are absolutely abhorrent to me,"
he complained to Rosario. "I can't stand to hear his sentimental and hypo-
critical words, and I feel nothing but complete revulsion for most aspects of
popular culture in the United States." Ah, but in Latin America, surely
things there were different. Rosario loved books, fine art, gourmet food,
good conversation. Now there was a culture they could share! He felt sure
that Latin America was where he now belonged.

Rick had been sent to Mexico City to clean up a mess left by an officer
caught lying and stealing. When he returned to headquarters, he not only
felt that he had accomplished that professional task, but had also started to
clean up his personal life and become an entirely new person. That was how
his new year began in 1984, full of expectations, hope, and confidence.

And then the Volvo broke down again. A mechanic said it wasn't worth repairing, but Rick had the work done anyway. Rosario wanted a new car, so he bought her a Honda Accord financed by a loan from a credit union. As the weeks turned into months, Rick began to worry. Rosario seemed sad. She was lonely. In Mexico City, she had been overwhelmed with her duties at the embassy, fawned over at diplomatic receptions, questioned about her views on world affairs at dinner parties. Now she had little to do but wait for him. She couldn't work, because she was in the States on a tourist visa. Every six months she had to leave the country and then apply for reentry. The first time she returned to Bogotá to see her mother, Rick wondered if she might stay there permanently. The six-month provision began to grate on them both. She resented dividing her life into six-month chunks. She began to complain. Who was she now? They weren't married. She didn't have a job. She wasn't going to school. The few times that they went out, Rosario cringed each time they met someone, and Rick stumbled over the introductions. Sometimes he called her his friend from Mexico City. Other times she was his girlfriend, as if they were teenagers. Finally, he began introducing her simply as "Rosario," with no other title, and to her that seemed sadly fitting. She was losing her identity, she complained. In Mexico City she had never been the "other woman," but now she was—and that was all she was.

As required by agency regulations, Rick had submitted an "outside activity" report to the Office of Security shortly before they began living together. In it, he had formally notified the CIA that he was engaged in a serious relationship with a foreigner and one-time CIA asset. On April 17, 1984, he filed another report, informing the agency that he intended to marry Rosario. This triggered a background check of her. The agency telephoned five people who Rosario had listed as references on a CIA form. All vouched that she was a good person. Investigators would later learn that at this point the agency's security system broke down. The chief of the counterintelligence (CI) division recommended that Rick be moved to a less sensitive job if he went through with his marriage. This recommendation was given to the CIA's director of personnel, but he did not believe that it was his responsibility to decide who should and shouldn't be working in critical areas because of their spouses. That decision needed to be made by the chief of the SE division. And that is where the system failed. The personnel director never sent the counterintelligence chief's recommendation to the SE division chief. Consequently, none of Rick's bosses was told about the suggestion, and Rick's marriage was okayed without comment.

The fact that the CIA had to approve of her was insulting to Rosario.

What right did the agency have to ask questions about her? Rick laughed and reminded her that the background check was merely the first step. CIA employees weren't permitted to marry foreigners. She still had to become a U.S. citizen. Rosario hadn't said much about that requirement when he had first mentioned it in Mexico, but now that it was time for her to actually renounce her Colombian citizenship, she cringed. The State Department didn't have any such rule about spouses, she complained. Diplomats could be married to foreigners. Why did she have to turn her back on her beloved Colombia? It wasn't fair.

"You know I'm not a diplomat," he told her.

"The man I fell in love with was," she replied icily.

Rick got all of the appropriate naturalization papers and gave them to Rosario. He also reminded her that she had to pass a written exam before she could become a citizen. The night before the test, he asked if she wanted to review some of the sample questions.

"Of course not!" she replied, insulted. "This is a test they give to ignorant immigrants who have just stepped off a boat and they pass it, so obviously it is a very silly exam."

Rick was afraid to ask how she had done after she got back from taking the test. She mentioned it herself. She had gotten a perfect score. Rick asked if she wanted him to go with her to the swearing-in ceremony. "Some people really make it a big celebration," he said encouragingly. As soon as those words left his lips, he knew he had made a mistake.

"I don't care what I say when I raise my hand or what papers I sign," she snapped, "I'm not an American and I will never be one and no ceremony will change that." She did not want him at the "funeral," she added. Rick felt guilty. Several times a day, it seemed, she would remind him that she had fallen in love with a diplomat, not a CIA bureaucrat.

In 1984, David Samson was reassigned to agency headquarters, and he often stopped to see Rick and Rosario. "The walls of that apartment were slowly closing in on her," he recalled later. Rosario's best friend from Mexico City, Diana Worthen, also returned to Langley to work for Rick, and she noticed how unhappy Rosario was. "I felt so sorry for her," Worthen said later. "Rosario was bored. There was nothing for her to do and she had no friends." Worthen came by one Saturday to take her shopping. Rosario turned down her offer. She and Rick could barely afford to buy groceries, she complained. Rick noticed that Rosario had started to talk about how much better life was in Colombia, how much more fun they had had in Mexico City. What had happened, she asked, to the "old" Rick—the one who always wanted to try a new restaurant or jet off to Acapulco for a weekend? A big evening now was a trip to his sister Nancy's house for popcorn and a game of Trivial Pursuit. After her father's death, Rosario had wanted someone to take care of her. Rick had been doing that fine at first. "He babied me, which I liked," she said later. Now Rosario felt abandoned. Rick's priority, she grumbled, was his work.

Rosario had always assumed that Nan knew about her. But Nan called the apartment shortly after Rosario and Rick had moved in together, and it became clear from what Rosario heard Rick saying that his wife had no idea that they were living together.

"Rick, she's going to find out, and then she will be bitter," Rosario warned. "Why not tell her? Are you ashamed of us?"

"No," he replied. In Virginia, a couple without children had to live apart for six months in order to qualify for a no-fault divorce, he said. What was the point of telling Nan that he had fallen in love with someone else, particularly since Nan lived in another city? "I just don't see why I should hurt her feelings," he said. Rosario seethed. It was the same thing he had said about Helen Riggs, his old girlfriend in Mexico City.

One afternoon, Rosario answered the door, and a process server stuck an envelope in her hands. Nan had found out about them and had filed for divorce, charging him with mental cruelty. Rosario was livid, and when he got home, she confronted him.

"It really doesn't matter who files, does it?" he replied, "as long as one of us files."

It mattered to Rosario. "Look, the way his family explained things to me was that I was not to blame for the failure of his marriage," Rosario said later. "The whole situation with Nan had been an unbearable one for years and years and years, but he never had the guts to go face that lady. It was a big cop-out not to tell her the truth, and I realized exactly what he was doing. It was easier on him if she thought he was leaving her for some other woman, because then *I* was the one to blame. *I* was the home wrecker. *I* had destroyed their perfect marriage. It was so much like Rick to do that. To let *me* take the blame."

By late 1984, other pressures besides Rosario's grumbling had started to shatter Rick's vision of his rebirth. He was sinking further into debt. He got a signature loan from the CIA credit union for $7,500 but it provided only temporary relief. He soon had close to $34,000 in unpaid credit card bills.

Nan, whose name was still on the charge cards, made it clear that she wasn't going to help pay for her husband's love nest. Rick's annual salary was about $45,000. He figured that he needed nearly twice that per year to keep up with just the basics that he and Rosario seemed to need. Depression set in.

A frightened Rosario called Rick's sister, Nancy, late one night. "Rick hasn't come home!" she explained. "I don't know where he is. I think he may be out drinking." Nancy tried to reassure her. Rick would be home later. Staying out having a few drinks was his way of letting off steam. Rick eventually staggered in. Rosario cried.

In September 1984, Rodney Carlson asked Rick if he wanted to spend four weeks in New York with two other officers, helping the station there, because the UN General Session was about to start. Rick immediately agreed. He wanted to take Rosario with him. She was excited. They stayed in the San Carlos Hotel in Manhattan, and Rosario spent her days visiting museums and her evenings eating with Rick in different restaurants. The CIA picked up the tab. It felt like old times, but three weeks into the assignment, Rick was called before John MacGaffin, the chief of the station. One of Rick's fellow agents had complained: How come Ames gets to bring his girlfriend with him to New York?

"Do you have a woman staying with you?" MacGaffin asked.

Rick said he had gotten permission to bring Rosario, but he couldn't remember who at headquarters had told him it would be okay. He and Rosario were getting married as soon as his divorce became final, he added. MacGaffin didn't like it. He had no choice, he said, but to report Rick to Burton Lee Gerber, who was now the chief of the SE division.

"No need to bother him," Rick told MacGaffin, "We'll move out of the hotel today." He would use the standard per diem that the government paid its employees for out-of-town travel to rent a room on his own. MacGaffin still didn't think it was right. The agency already was renting a room for Rick. Why should he charge the government for another one? He said he was going to report Rick anyway. Rick didn't tell Rosario why they were checking out of the hotel. He knew she would be humiliated. When Rick returned to CIA headquarters a week later, Gerber took him aside.

"Why was everyone upset with you up there?" he asked.

Rick told him about Rosario.

"Is she your wife?"

"Going to be," said Rick.

Gerber asked if she was a foreigner. Rick said she was going to renounce her Colombian citizenship as soon as they married.

"Rick, taking her with you was not good judgment at all," Gerber lectured, giving him a verbal reprimand. "I expect more out of you than this."

Although he didn't show it, Rick was incensed. He really admired Gerber, and his criticism had stung. "What was the big deal?" he later complained. "Most guys up there were screwing their secretaries or women they would pick up in bars, but everyone got excited because I took Rosario with me."

If Rick had any doubts about how much Rosario preferred living in a large city and how much she despised their suburban apartment, they vanished after the New York trip. Rosario chattered nonstop about how great it had been to be in a city which had decent restaurants, plays, culture. All anyone in Washington, D.C., ever talked about was politics and the Redskins football team. One afternoon in the fall of 1984, Rick heard that a job in the CIA station in Rome was coming open in 1986. He asked Rosario if she wanted him to apply for it. "Yes!" she replied with excitement. She had always wanted to live in Rome. The more they talked about it, the more both of them became enthusiastic about the move. A tour in Italy—the idea reminded both them of their days in Mexico City! Rosario would enjoy living in such a historic city, and he would finish out his CIA tour in an exotic foreign post.

In late September 1984, Rick rode the train to Manhattan for a meeting with Nan and her divorce attorney. Rosario had given him a pep talk before he left. She was afraid he wouldn't be tough enough. She reminded him that Nan earned a higher salary than he did and there were no children to support. Rick promised that he'd be firm, but as soon as he walked into the attorney's office, he shrank. He couldn't get over how angry Nan was. She felt betrayed. Rick agreed to pay the $33,350 in credit card charges and other debts, to sign over all of their joint property, and to pay Nan $300 per month for forty-two months beginning in June 1985. In return, Nan agreed to give up any claims she had on his CIA retirement pay.

Rick knew Rosario was going to be furious when she learned what he had done. On the train ride home, he thought about what he would tell her. Did the settlement really matter? The most important thing was that the marriage was over. He and Rosario were free of Nan. Rome awaited them. Life would be good. Then he thought about the debts. How was he going to pay them? He didn't like the idea of asking for professional help from one of the agency's credit counselors. After all, he was in management. What would his supervisors think if they found out that he could not manage his own finances? For a moment, he thought about applying for a second job. He had seen a help wanted sign that very morning at a 7-11 convenience store near the apartment. He pictured himself standing behind the counter ringing up a sale on the cash register, and he wondered how it would feel if one of his colleagues came in. He just couldn't picture himself wearing a uniform and dispensing lottery tickets and Slurpees. As the train moved closer to Washington, he had another thought. "I decided I could rob a bank." That was where the money was, as the old joke went. For about half an hour, Rick plotted exactly how he would stick up the branch bank where he had his checking account. In this Walter Mitty fantasy, he saw himself putting on a disguise, driving his car to a safe spot where it wouldn't be seen, dashing inside. He didn't own a handgun, but he assumed he could buy one cheap somewhere. He could even use a toy one. He really wasn't going to hurt anyone. The only question in his mind was, did he really have the guts to go through with it? He convinced himself that he did. After all, he was desperate. How much money would he get? "I thought about it for a while and I decided it wouldn't be enough." He would have to rob several banks, and that idea scared him. He needed $34,000 to pay his debts and another $12,600 to pay off Nan, in total about $47,000. That figure stuck in his mind. $47,000! Where could he get $47,000? Suddenly he thought of another figure. "Fifty thousand—that's what Igor Shurygin had offered Henry Steger in Mexico City when he pitched him. That would be more than enough to pay off my debts."

By the time the Amtrak train pulled into Union Station in downtown Washington, Rick had abandoned the bank robbery idea and was imagining himself as a KGB agent. In his mind, he had played out the steps that he would need to take. He had seen himself flying to Vienna and walking into the Soviet embassy there to volunteer. He would have an edge over most traitors, he had thought, because he would know whether or not the CIA had any of its spies working in that embassy. "At this point, this all was just a fantasy, a mind game. It was like the bank robbery, not something I really intended to do."

That soon changed.

THE WORDS OF RICK AMES

I returned to Washington from Mexico City excited by the prospects of renewal, deeply in love with Rosario, and thinking of a future full of new possi-

bilities. I was looking forward to caring for and being cared for in ways I had never thought of before. I was vividly aware of how I, myself, had thrown away my first marriage. I blamed myself for my inability to love, share, and depend upon another person. But I was sure that all of this was going to change once Rosario and I were together.

Okay, okay, I know I'm getting a little wrought up here, but I really looked at myself as an exile of sorts, looking ahead as an immigrant to a new life. At the same time, there were practical problems: confronting Nan, getting a divorce, getting Rosario here and adjusted to our new life. Still, I felt confident.

The reality was both promising and rebuffing. Being intensely in love, I found, did not solve or ease all my difficulties. The divorce dragged. I felt anxious and finally desperate over my financial prospects. My study of Spanish languished, and I began to feel as if I had overestimated my ability to "Latinize" myself. Would I really be able to live in Colombia? Could I become this new person and recreate myself? My insular, isolated personality was resistant to my and Rosario's desires to be real, open, and honest. I was finding it hard to learn how really to love. And then there was the drinking. None of this was, to me, at least, delusional, but it gnawed at my confidence in renewal and, I think contributed to my feeling of desperation. I know this sounds a bit analytical, perhaps objectified and depersonalized in a way, but it is difficult for me to describe it in any other terms.

Let me tell you something really fascinating. It tells a lot about me, but I'm not sure what. After I was arrested, and the FBI was debriefing me, this guy asked me how much I was in debt because of the divorce settlement. I immediately said, "Oh, fifty to seventy thousand." Then he brought out the papers. Yeah, I had to pay off the debts, but they were only about $35,000. The rest was $300 per month over a three-and-a-half-year period. Now that is still a lot of money, but the point is that when he showed me those figures, I was shocked. In hindsight, my financial situation was not really as desperate as I had remembered. I could have gotten some guidance, but instead I convinced myself that I was in this huge hole and didn't have any choice but to do what I did. Now? Now I see things differently. The truth is that things weren't really that desperate, even though I convinced myself that they were. That says something about me. You see, I really didn't have to do what I did. I didn't!

So why did I do it?

It's a damn good question. At the time, I told myself that I was doing it for the money. And that is what I still tell people. I say, 'Let's be clear about this. There is no question. I did it for the money.' But now I am wondering if that is *really an accurate answer. Was it just for the money? Or was getting the money just a way for me to excuse or justify what I had wanted to do all along?*

[Long pause]

Okay, let's think this through. I am certain that I was genuinely feeling desperate. My God, I was going to rob a bank. So I was genuinely desperate. I rejected the bank robbery idea because it wouldn't give me enough money. So obviously I was feeling desperate and I was feeling desperate because I needed money. So we know that both of these feelings are accurate recollections of what I was experiencing at the time. But this continues to beg the real question, doesn't it?

Why did I immediately think that I had to do something illegal? I never even thought about sitting down with a credit counselor. Why did I descend immediately into thinking of selling out my country? Why?

Now that's the real question, isn't it? Why did this betrayal come so easily to me?

I just don't know. Let me think.

CHAPTER 12

Opportunity knocked just before Thanksgiving in 1984. It was Rodney Carlson at the door. Was Rick interested in helping the FBI recruit a Soviet press attaché?

Of course, Rick replied. "Who's the target?"

"Sergey I. Divilkovsky," Carlson replied. "He knows your old buddy, Thomas Kolesnichenko [the *Pravda* correspondent who had been friendly with Ames in New York]."

Divilkovsky had recently been transferred from the UN to the Soviet embassy in Washington, and when the FBI surveillance team that watches the embassy noticed him, it sent a "tracer" to the CIA, asking for information about this new face. Carlson knew plenty. When he had been the station chief in New York, he had befriended Divilkovsky. In a lengthy cable, Carlson gave the FBI a background sketch that included such insights as the fact that one of Divilkovsky's close relatives had been arrested recently for shoplifting. The FBI reacted to Carlson's cable by suggesting that he renew his friendship with Divilkovsky, but Carlson balked. He had been posing as an out-of-town businessman in New York, and he was afraid that Divilkovsky would get suspicious if he suddenly reappeared in Washington. Carlson was also already handling GENTILE, Valery Martynov, and he didn't think it was wise for him to handle two agents in Washington. What if the KGB found out about one of his informants? It might follow him to a second source. Carlson talked it over with John Murphy, the CIA station chief in Washington, and he agreed that someone new needed to be brought in. Rick's name came up. Carlson called Divilkovsky and suggested that he have lunch with Rick Wells, the alias Rick was using. He told the Soviet that Mr. Wells worked at a think tank and was really interested in learning more about the USSR.

Divilkovsky met Rick six times during November and December, but the lunches were always awkward. "I was a little too pushy at our meetings," Ames said later. "I'm pretty sure I scared him." Just before Christmas, Divilkovsky announced that he didn't have time to continue their lunch meetings, but another embassy employee, Sergey D. Chuvakhin, might be willing to meet with "Mr. Wells." Rick and his bosses were surprised. Why was Divilkovsky pushing Rick off onto one of his coworkers? That just wasn't done. In a sense, Divilkovsky would be vouching for Rick, saying that he was worth meeting. Carlson, Murphy, and Rick talked about whether it might be a KGB trap, but Chuvakhin was not thought to be KGB. He was reportedly a diplomat who specialized in arms control. Rick called Chuvakhin. Although friendly, Chuvakhin said he was much too busy to meet for lunch. He suggested that Rick call him in another month when he might have more time. Rick called in January 1985, but got nowhere. In February, he called twice, and both times was put off. What neither Rick nor the agency knew was that Chuvakhin had no intention of ever meeting Rick. "Divilkovsky had become suspicious of this Rick Wells," a retired KGB officer, who was stationed at the Soviet embassy in Washington in 1985, told me during an interview in Moscow. "So Mr. Divilkovsky did a very wise thing. His way of getting off the hook was by offering Mr. Wells another fish: Mr. Chuvakhin. What the Americans didn't know was that Chuvakhin, while a brilliant man, was known to have the disposition of an angry snake, and he abhorred most Americans."

Sometime in February, Ames would later claim that he couldn't remember the exact date, he and several of his CIA colleagues went to London on an agency trip, and one night while they were drinking in the hotel bar, one of the women officers announced that she was a practicing witch. "I've learned how to use my powers to tell when someone is a traitor," she declared. Rick began teasing her, but she was serious. "I looked at her and almost laughed in her face," Ames recalled later. "Here she is telling me this while I'm sitting there thinking about how I might betray my country. I said to her, 'Well, maybe you will have a chance to prove your powers someday.'"

Ames has always told the same story when asked how he became a spy. "One of our sources in the USSR had told us that the Soviets were going to have two or three double agents approach us and volunteer to spy. Well, wonder of wonders, these double agents popped up. I remember one of them approached one of our military attachés while he was traveling in the Ukraine. This was very important, because it gave me an idea. I had been thinking about how I could contact the Soviets, but I didn't want to really harm anyone. I thought, *Gosh, I could tell the KGB about these three cases and demand fifty thousand dollars. The KGB would have to pay me, because if it didn't, it would be admitting that these were double agents. So I'd get my money without really harming anyone because these weren't real traitors.* It was the perfect scam."

Rick called Chuvakhin and bullied him into agreeing to meet for lunch on April 16, at the Mayflower Hotel, which was only a few blocks away from the Soviet embassy. An hour before their lunch date, Rick typed a note demanding $50,000. "I wrote down: 'I am Aldrich H. Ames and my job is branch chief of Soviet counterintelligence at the CIA. I served in New York where I used the alias Andy Robinson. I need $50,000 and in exchange for the money, here is information about three agents we are developing in the Soviet Union right now.' I then attached one page from the CIA's SE division internal telephone roster to the note. I underlined my name."

Ames wrote his note to a specific person at the embassy: KGB general Stanislav Androsov, the KGB *rezident*. However, Rick did not refer to Androsov by name. Instead, he addressed him by his KGB pseudonym, *KRONIN*. The KGB, like the CIA, never used its employees' actual names in internal correspondence, for fear the messages might be intercepted by the enemy. In all CIA correspondence, Ames was referred to as Winfield Leggate. "I used his KGB name because I wanted to make it clear that I knew a lot about him." The agency had learned Androsov's KGB codename from Valery Martynov, GENTILE, one of the spies it had working in the Soviet embassy. Ames put his note inside an envelope, which he then addressed to "Gen. Androsov. KGB *Rezident*." He put this envelope into another envelope which he left blank. Ames planned to hand the blank envelope to Chuvakhin during lunch. He assumed the diplomat would open the letter, see Androsov's name, and then deliver it to him without opening it and reading the contents.

Rick arrived at the Mayflower half an hour early. "I had two or three double vodkas just to relax." Chuvakhin was supposed to join him at one o'clock. At two o'clock, Rick was still waiting. By two-thirty, he realized he had been stood up. He had been drinking vodkas nonstop to calm his nerves. "I kept trying to figure out what to do. I thought, *Okay, giving him the letter is a crazy idea. I'll just forget the whole thing.* But I had already made my decision, and I had convinced myself that it was the only way to solve my financial problems. Then I thought, *God, I can keep calling this guy forever, and he may never come out for lunch.* So I decided to improvise. I decided to walk right in the Soviets' front door. I knew the FBI would be watching the embassy, but I figured I could explain it to them later, because they knew I was supposed to be recruiting this guy, so I had another stiff drink and stepped outside."

When he reached the Soviet embassy, Rick hurried through the iron gate and rushed into the building's lobby. He was stopped by a guard sitting behind a reinforced glass wall. "I asked him if Mr. Chuvakhin was in. I said, 'We were supposed to have lunch.' The guard says, 'I'll get him on the phone,' and he does, and then he says that Chuvakhin will be down to see me in a minute."

Rick moved away from the glass partition and stood in a corner. It was now or never. Screwing up his courage, he walked over to the guard and pulled out the envelope. "I tore it open and took out the envelope that had Androsov's name printed on it. I slid it through the opening in the bulletproof glass to the guard. He grabbed it, looked at it, did a double take, and then he put it down and I just looked away. Chuvakhin came down, and I went over and told him that I had been waiting for him at lunch and asked why he hadn't showed."

Chuvakhin said he had forgotten. He didn't apologize. Rick told him that he wanted to reschedule their lunch. "I'll call you in a few weeks," he said.

"I'll be busy," Chuvakhin replied.

Rick grinned. "We'll see."

He left and went to a bar, where he downed some more vodkas. The next day, Ames apologized to the CIA's station chief, John Murphy, for not warning the FBI in advance about his trip to the embassy. "Murphy was really pissed, so I said, 'Look, the guy stood me up at lunch, so I improvised. There was no time to call the FBI.'"

Rick figured it would take the KGB several days to investigate him. It would also need time to collect his money. He waited two weeks, and then called. "Chuvakhin tells me, 'I'm still really busy, why don't you call me next week.' But I could tell by the way he said that, that he was not just brushing me off this time. I felt sure he had been told to tell me this." One week later, Rick telephoned the embassy again, and Chuvakhin agreed to meet him at the Mayflower Hotel for lunch on May 17. "Before we hang up, Chuvakhin says to me: 'Could you stop in at the embassy and pick me up before we go?' I said, 'No problem' but my mind is going, *What the hell is going on? Why do they want me to come there again, and what is the FBI going to think?*"

Ames decided to protect himself by calling Murphy and telling him about Chuvakhin's request. "I figured the FBI had probably monitored the call from the embassy and I acted as puzzled as everyone else about what was happening. I knew that none of these guys in the FBI or CIA would be suspicious of me, because I was a senior officer and had been doing this for so long. We all sat around trying to figure out what Chuvakhin was up to."

Rick was about to celebrate his forty-fourth birthday. He had worked at the agency twenty-three years. He had no regrets. "I knew exactly what I was doing, and I was determined to make it work."

This time, Chuvakhin was waiting in the lobby when Rick walked in. He motioned for Rick to follow him down a hallway which led to a large conference room. Rick stepped inside and Chuvakhin, remaining outside, closed the door, leaving Rick alone in the room. "Another Soviet came in . . . we shook hands, and he took a letter out of his pocket and handed it to me. He was afraid the room might be bugged, so he indicated with his hands that he wanted me to open and read it. It said 'We accept your offer and are very pleased to do so' or something like that. Then it said, 'Mr. Chuvakhin is NOT a KGB officer, but we have evaluated him and consider him reliable and mature, and he will be able to give you the money and be available to lunch with you if you care to exchange more messages.' I stood up and scribbled on the back of his note: 'Okay. Thank you very much.' We shook hands, and then I went out of the room, and Chuvakhin says, 'Let's go to lunch.'"

"Chuvakhin and I walked over to Joe and Mo's restaurant and we talked about arms control, and then, as he was getting ready to go, Chuvakhin says, 'Oh, here are some press releases that I think you will find interesting,' and he hands me this shopping bag with releases in it. I said thanks and left." Rick hurried to his car but he didn't look inside the bag until he was safely on the road driving away from the city. He pulled off onto a scenic overlook along the George Washington Parkway next to the Potomac River. What he was looking for was wrapped in brown paper at the bottom of the bag. He tore open a corner. "There were one-hundred-dollar bills wrapped tightly inside. Every one of them was a hundred-dollar bill! It was fifty thousand dollars. I was totally exhilarated. I had pulled it off."

That night, he hid the money in his closet, and on May 18, he deposited $9,000 into his checking account. He didn't want to deposit all of the cash, because he knew that banks were required to report deposits of $10,000 or more in cash to federal treasury agents. There was no way he would have been able to explain to investigators where he had gotten so much cash. Telling Rosario about his newfound wealth, however, had been easy, Ames claimed later. The $50,000 was a loan with no interest that he had gotten from an old college chum named "Robert" who owed him a big favor. "I told Rosario that Robert worked for a labor union and lived in Chicago, and the reason I was saying this was because I wanted her to assume that he was connected to organized crime or doing something that wasn't quite legal, so she wouldn't ask me too many questions." Rosario didn't, Rick recalled. "She figured this guy was a friend, and this was between him and me."

Two days after Ames made his first bank deposit, the FBI arrested John Walker, Jr., in a Maryland suburb of Washington. Walker had left a bundle of classified documents stolen from the U.S. Navy for the KGB in a grocery bag filled with trash and left by the side of a road. During the coming days, the FBI revealed that Walker had been the head of a family spy ring and that Walker himself had been spying for the KGB for eighteen years. The media called him the "spy of the decade."

Rick read everything he could about Walker's arrest because he was afraid that someone inside the Soviet embassy had tipped off the FBI. By this time, Sergey Motorin, GAUZE, had been recalled to Moscow and was no longer working in the embassy, but Valery Martynov, GENTILE, still was, and Rick wondered if Martynov had fingered Walker for the FBI. He thought about asking his boss, Rodney Carlson, because he was handling Martynov, but Rick was afraid Carlson might become suspicious of him if he asked too many questions. "The press reports said Walker's wife, Barbara, had turned him in, but that struck me as a cover story at first—something the FBI had ginned up to protect its real source. I immediately thought *Oh God, they are going to find out about me too! What I did.*"

Rick was scared. "My scam was supposed to be a one-time hit. I was just going to get the fifty thousand dollars and be done with it, but now I started to panic. I felt caught, trapped."

On June 13, 1995, Rick met with Chuvakhin at Chadwicks, a popular

Washington restaurant. The KGB had not asked him for any additional information, but Rick had decided on his own to give the Soviets the names of every CIA "human asset" that he knew about, with the exception of two names. Besides the names of U.S. spies, Rick also had decided to tell the KGB about Oleg Gordievsky, the KGB *rezident* in London who was spying for the MI- 6. Rick also had tucked seven *pounds* of CIA intelligence reports into the bottom of a shopping bag for the KGB. He had carried these classified documents out of the agency in a brown bag one night when leaving work. None of the CIA guards stationed at the doorways had asked to look inside the package.

Since Ames's arrest, four books and thousands of articles have been written about him, but none of them has accurately identified all the agents he betrayed. Most accounts have reported that Ames double-crossed ten men. What follows is as complete a list as possible of the agents whose identities he revealed. It is based on my one-on-one interviews with Ames and later discussions with the CIA, FBI, KGB, and several relatives of spies who were executed. I have chosen to identify some of these men only by their CIA cryptonyms, because they have never been arrested by the KGB or GRU, and are still living in Russia. U.S. intelligence officials are not certain why these agents were not punished. It is possible that the KGB felt it needed corroborating evidence before it could arrest them. Some of these agents may have escaped punishment because of family or political connections. It is also possible that a few of them were double agents, actually working for the KGB. The Soviets did use at least one double agent to deflect suspicion away from Ames. This has never before been made public. Even Ames does not know this agent was actually working for the KGB. I will reveal more about him later in this book. Readers should be aware that the KGB insisted during interviews with me that several of the agents on this list already were under investigation when Ames identified them on June 13 at Chadwicks restaurant. In these cases, Ames confirmed what the KGB claimed it had already learned from other sources.

Agents Identified by Aldrich Ames

1. BLIZZARD   Sergey Bokhan

2. VANQUISH   Adolf Tolkachev

3. TICKLE   Oleg Gordievsky

4.	WEIGH	Leonid Poleschuk
5.	MILLION	Gennady Smetanin
6.	FITNESS	Gennady Varenik
7.	VILLAGE	Still Living in Russia
8.	COWL.	Sergey Vorontsov
9.	GENTILE	Valery Martynov
10.	GAUZE	Sergey Motorin
11.	MEDIUM	Vladimir Potashov
12.	TWINE	Boris Yuzhin
13.	JOGGER	Vladimir Piguzov
14.	TOPHAT (also known as ROAM)	Dmitri Polyakov
15.	ACCORD	Vladimir Vasilyev
16.	GLAZING	Still Living in Russia
17.	TAME	Still Living in Russia
18.	BACKBEND	Still Living in Russia
19.	VEST	Still Living in Russia
20.	EASTBOUND	Still Living in Russia

After June 13, Ames would betray: PYRRHIC, BYPLAY, MOTORBOAT, and another Russian volunteer given the cryptonym PROLOGUE. Although it has not been widely reported, a woman would also become one of Ames's victims. Gennady Smetanin's wife, Svetlana, was arrested and later imprisoned for five years because she had helped her husband commit espionage. The CIA never gave her a separate cryptonym, but it considered her one of its agents. This brings the total number of agents betrayed by Ames to *twenty-five*—more than *double* the number that has been previously made public. Five of these agents were never prosecuted, and this is the first time their cryptonyms have been revealed.

When Rick and Chuvakhin finished their lunch on June 13, Ames knew that he had put nearly all of the agents whose names were on the list in mortal danger.*

Ames would later tell federal investigators and two members of Congress, who interviewed him in jail, that he was not certain why he had decided to gave the KGB the names of all the Soviet agents known to him. "My memory is sort of a blur," he said. But he would later confirm in interviews with me that there were two reasons for his decision: *fear and profit*. Ames had been afraid, especially after John Walker, Jr., was arrested, that one of the CIA's sources would somehow learn about what he had done. The best way for Ames to protect himself was by giving the KGB the names of every "U.S. intelligence asset" whom he knew. Their arrests and executions were simply a matter of self-preservation. Greed also played a role. He knew that if he became a KGB spy, the Soviets would pay him "as much money as anyone could ever use."

"All of the people whose names were on my June 13th list knew the risks they were taking when they began spying for the CIA and FBI," Ames told me during our jailhouse sessions. "If one of them had learned about me, he would have told the CIA, and I would have been arrested and thrown in jail. Now that I was working for the KGB, the people on my list could expect nothing less from me. It wasn't personal. It was simply how the game was played."

THE WORDS OF RICK AMES

A lot of the barriers that should have stopped me from betraying my country were gone. The first barrier was [the idea] that political intelligence matters. It doesn't. Our foreign policy is conducted in such a massively internal and political way that there is virtually no chance of any outside influence altering it. On a tactical level, yes, good intelligence matters. If TRIGON had told us that the Kremlin was about to start a war, of course

---

*A few weeks before Ames met with Chuvakhin, Sergey Bokhan, BLIZZARD, defected to the United States at the urging of the CIA's Burton Lee Gerber, then chief of the SE division. The KGB had been investigating Bokhan because of information from sources other than Ames. Obviously, Bokhan was in no danger when Ames gave his name to the KGB, since the Russian already was living in New York City.

*that would have been important. But the truth is that no one in our govern-
ment really pays attention to political intelligence because there are too many
other agendas.*

*Another barrier that collapsed had to do with what others had done. Henry
Kissinger crossed the line when he helped prepare the Soviets for the SALT II
negotiations. TRIGON's cable proved this. Angleton betrayed agents who had
helped us. He used them and sent them back knowing that they would be imprisoned or killed. He held and tortured Nosenko and everyone knew it was
wrong, but no one wanted to tell the emperor that he was not wearing any
clothes. Now I realize these men's actions do not excuse mine, but they did influence my decision making and help grease that slope.*

*I also had come to believe that the CIA was morally corrupt. No, my feel-
ings were more intense than this. I had come to believe that it was a dangerous
institution. The CIA is all about maintaining and expanding American impe-
rial power, which I had come to think was wrong. We have no right to behave as
if we somehow should find an interest in every culture and then pursue our interests in those cultures.*

*By 1985 I also felt I knew more than anyone else about the real Soviet
threat, the real Soviet tiger, and I did not believe that what I was about to do
would harm this country. Look, the Russians love to bluff and bluster, and they
do it all the time. They have to do it. Why? Because they are scared. The only
time they claim to be strong is when they are feeling weak. That is the purpose
of deception and bluster. Telling them the names of their traitors did not risk
putting us at war or threaten our military superiority. And finally, I personally
felt totally alienated from my own culture. I did not feel any sense of loyalty to
what mass culture had become. I did not feel part of our society.*

*All of these things worked against the potential barriers. The truth is that
there was only one barrier left, and that was one of personal loyalty to the people I knew and, unfortunately it was not a very strong one.*

*How does treason fit into all of this? In some ways not at all. I would love
to say that I did what I did out of some moral outrage over our country's acts of
imperialism or as a political statement or out of anger toward the CIA or even
a love for the Soviet Union. But the sad truth is that I did what I did because
of money and I can't get away from that. I can't defend what I did.*

*Now let me explain something else. I was afraid. Falling in love with
Rosario was difficult, conflicted, but it also seemed to me to be a matter of life
and death—really. I am being serious here. My failures with my first wife, my
sense of loneliness and alienation from warmth and humanity, all convinced
me that if I failed in loving Rosario, only a kind of living death or suicide re-*

mained for me. So you see, Rosario herself was not my salvation, but we would be—but only if there could be a we. I could only survive if I could find a way for us to survive. And that is what this really is all about and the real reason why I did what I did.

Why did I do it? I did it for the money. Period. I am not lying. I wanted the cash. But the reason I needed the money was not for the reasons most people want money. I did not want it for a new car or new house, but rather for what it could guarantee. It seemed to be the only way for me to guarantee that the us I desired so desperately would survive. It would make us possible and, therefore, make our love a lasting one. I wanted a future. I wanted what I saw we could have together. Taking the money was essential to the re-creation of myself and the continuance of us as a couple. Do you understand now why I did it for the money but did it really for something else entirely? It all made sense at one point, until I did it, and then the enormity of what I had done sort of settled on my shoulders. I was not worried about the KGB pressuring me after I got its $50,000. They were not going to blackmail me. They would simply wait for me to reappear. I didn't stay away long. People ask why I turned in retired agents no longer spying. You must understand that I was totally alone. I couldn't tell anyone, but even beyond a sense of danger, it was this feeling of tremendous, tremendous, ah, I don't know how to describe it, but of tremendous—my God, I had talked to the KGB! I had sold out! I was suddenly a man with no one to help me. And so I kept saying to myself, What to do? What to do? I thought the cash from the KGB would solve all of my problems, but now I had to worry about security, survival, protecting myself.

[Laughs]

So you see, my turning to the KGB was actually a great act of cowardice. I decided to let the KGB worry about keeping me safe. I decided not to deal with the enormity of what I had done. The way not to deal with it was by giving the KGB everything that I knew in one sitting, not because I wanted millions of dollars, but because it was quick and the easiest way for me to get a sense of re-lief. I told myself, Okay, give them everything, the whole thing, and then let them worry about it. I knew they had to take care of me. Here is where the cow-ardice came in. I had walked away from the protection that the agency gave me and I was in the cold and I didn't like it, so I moved to the other camp and said, 'Okay, guys, now you protect me.'

I was never an admirer of the Soviet system, but I do feel a sense of contin-uing obligation and gratitude to the KGB, and I guess the reason is because the KGB stuck with me, and protected me and I think the men who became my handlers developed a genuine warmth and friendship for me.

You know love has never come easy for me. I am reserved, uncomfortable with small talk and casual sociability, skeptical of others' opinions and motives, with a mix of arrogance and shyness. I've always had difficulty dealing with superiors, had few real friends, etcetera, etcetera. I've always felt alone and a bit unworthy. I'll never forget my sister Nancy's reaction after I returned from Mexico. I stayed with her for a month or so and finally brought myself to tell her about Rosario and our intentions to marry. Her immediate sympathy and support for me—not directed against Nan—was an immense relief. There's no way, I know and knew, it could have been otherwise, but still it was hard to tell her about Rosario, and my relief seemed hardly distinguishable from surprise! This is, I think, characteristic of me. I don't like admitting failure. I was incredibly apprehensive about my first phone call to Nancy [Everly] from jail and her first. Part of this was my shame, but the other was a mistaken, baseless fear that Nancy would withdraw her love. Now I know I'm ranging on psychobabble here, and I know that some will accuse me of simply seeking sympathy and reconstructing history to my liking, but I am being as genuine as I can be. I have always quietly doubted myself, my own self-worth, and I was afraid to risk losing what I had. This is my innermost fear—that those who claim to love me will walk away once they see who I really am. Where does this come from? I don't know. Neither my mother nor father ever seemed to me to condition their love. I know the real answers are in me, but I am afraid that I am blind when it comes to seeing them. All I know is that this fear is real and it often surfaces, and when it does, I reach out for someone, and hope they will be there and not abandon me.

THE WORDS OF OTHERS

Treason is an unnatural act. It's like incest. So, knowing Rick like I do, I know he had to have spent a tremendous amount of time sitting around thinking about what he had done and ways to ease his conscience—you know—to rationalize and justify what he had done. He had to.

—David T. Samson, CIA

CIA Director R. James Woolsey denounced Ames in a speech as a "malignant betrayer of his country" and a "warped, murdering traitor."

—*The Washington Post*, July 19, 1994

I can't think of a more appropriate job than working for the CIA for some-one who wants to cop out of having to show his true feelings.

—David Blake, close friend

Does it really matter why he did it? He killed people, it is as simple as that.
—Relative of Gennady Grigorievich Varenik, CIA *spy executed by KGB*

You know, I read the SAWDUST files. I knew about everything horrible that Angleton did, and so did most of us in senior management, but we didn't go out and sell out our country because of it.

—Paul Redmond, CIA

Nan is to blame. After they came back from Turkey, she decided she didn't want to go anywhere else. He had been offered a great job . . . but he never went. He never was able to make the right choices in that sense, because she wouldn't go, and that was what started him down this pathway. If anyone is to blame, it is her.

—Rosario Ames

I remember Rick telling me once, "Never tell anyone your true feelings." It was weird. We were only seventeen, and I was in one of my periodic mood swings. He had been trying to comfort me, and he suddenly just said it: "Never tell anyone your true feelings. Let them believe an illusion." I didn't know what in the hell he was talking about.

—High school classmate

CHAPTER 13

At about the same time in May 1985 that Ames was making his first contact with the KGB, Vladimir Zaitzev was ordered in Moscow to report to the office of General E. M. Rasshchepov, head of the Seventh Directorate of the KGB, which was responsible for surveillance inside the USSR. Zaitzev was the commander of a special "Group A" team, sometimes called the Alpha unit, which was used by the KGB to make commando-style arrests. Zaitzev usually got his orders from the director of the Alpha unit, not a KGB general, so the young commander was nervous as he waited outside Rasshchepov's office. Sitting there, he quickly reviewed his own recent actions, as he later put it, "looking for possible sins that you can get into trouble for."

An attaché led him in to see Rasschepov, who welcomed him as if they were close friends, beckoned him to sit in an overstuffed chair, and politely asked about his family. After hot tea was served with cookies, the general told Zaitzev that he had been chosen to make an "illegal arrest," a term used by the KGB to describe the abduction of a hostile suspect for interrogation.

"You must not even let a hair fall from the head of this subject," warned Rasschepov, who added that the suspect was "under no circumstances to commit suicide" before he was questioned. Without being told, Zaitzev knew that Rasschepov was referring to the embarrassing suicide of Alexander Ogorodnik, TRIGON, the CIA spy who had swallowed cyanide while under arrest. "You will be told later who you will be sent to bring in," the general concluded. "Meanwhile, pick your very best men and get them prepared."

Zaitzev was worried. "You must remember that this was when the situation in our country was rather complicated," he explained in an article that was published in a KGB internal publication. Mikhail Gorbachev had been elected that March as General Secretary, rumors about reforms filled the Kremlin, and Zaitzev feared he was about to become "embroiled in some high-stakes political game" by being ordered to arrest a member of the Politburo or some other top party official.

A few days later, Zaitzev returned to Rasschepov's office and found a second general waiting to give him orders. This general didn't introduce himself, but Zaitzev deduced from his brisk manner and his comments that he was from the KGB's First Chief Directorate, the organization responsible for foreign intelligence. He clearly outranked Rasschepov, if not militarily then politically. This new general removed a black-and-white photograph from a folder and handed it to Zaitzev.

"This is the man you will arrest. His name is Adolf Tolkachev. He is an American secret intelligence agent," the general said.

Zaitzev was ordered to return in forty-eight hours with an arrest plan for both generals to review. He didn't need that much time. He was back the next afternoon. Tolkachev owned a dacha outside Moscow that he visited every weekend during the summer, and he was reputed to be a heavy drinker. "If our client doesn't like to miss the opportunity to get drunk, it would be logical to suppose that during the weekend at his dacha . . . he will probably drink to relax," Zaitzev explained. Knowing how harshly the Soviet police treat drunk drivers, Zaitzev speculated that Tolkachev's wife would insist on driving them back to Moscow on Sunday afternoon. Zaitzev would have two of his men pose as police officers near the road leading to Tolkachev's dacha. One of his men would be busy scolding the driver of a van that would be stopped by the side of the road. The other police office would order Tolkachev to pull over. As soon as Tolkachev's car stopped, a squad of men would burst from the van, surround the car, and overpower Tolkachev. Two cars filled with additional officers would be nearby in case Tolkachev somehow escaped. The generals nodded their approval.

Shortly after five o'clock on the following Sunday, Tolkachev and his wife began their return trip to Moscow from their dacha. As they approached the main road, a policeman ordered them to stop. Just as Zaitzev had predicted,

Tolkachev's wife was driving, and she obediently pulled her Zhiguli sedan off the road. "Before she even realized what was going on, my team had her husband all tied up and packed away in our vehicle. Handcuffs! Clothes cut off to ensure that he could not take any hidden poisons! . . . He was in shock because of the suddenness of the maneuver." Zaitzev's men videotaped the arrest to show the generals. Tolkachev was taken directly to Lefortovo Prison for interrogation. A few hours later, he signed a full confession.

"Tolkachev was taken to spots where he left secret signs for his people or carried out other previously agreed-upon activities to indicate to them that he was all right," Zaitzev recalled.

On June 13, 1985, Paul M. Stombaugh, Jr., a thirty-three-year-old employee at the U.S. embassy in Moscow, was surrounded by a swarm of KGB agents as he was walking toward a park for a meeting with Tolkachev. The CIA station sent an urgent cable that same night to Burton Lee Gerber, the chief of the SE division, in Langley. Tears formed in Gerber's eyes as he read the message. If Stombaugh had been ambushed, then Gerber correctly assumed that the KGB had already arrested Tolkachev, and Gerber knew what that meant. The KGB would eventually execute him. Gerber had succeeded Gus Hathaway as the station chief in Moscow in 1980 and had personally overseen the Tolkachev case for more than two years. Oftentimes, Tolkachev had sent the agency notes that explained why he was helping the United States. In them, the spy described himself as a "Russian patriot" and wrote that he wanted to help "destroy" the Communist Party because in his opinion, it was ruining his country. Gerber had admired Tolkachev. *How had the KGB found out about him?*

On June 14, the morning after Stombaugh was caught, Gerber telephoned Rick. "We got something going on here we need to talk about right now!" he said. As Rick hustled up the stairs to Gerber's fourth-floor office, he fought back a surge of panic. The day before, June 13, was the day he had met Sergey Chuvakhin at Chadwicks restaurant and given him the roster of Soviet agents working for the CIA. Ames later recalled his feelings that morning. "I wondered, *Did I screw up? Does he know already? Has someone told on me?* I honestly thought I might be greeted by two security officers with handcuffs when I entered Gerber's office." Instead, he found a somber Gerber sitting behind his desk, studying a stack of cables.

"Last night, Stombaugh was arrested and is being expelled," he announced. "There is a problem with Tolkachev. Let's figure out what went wrong, and if we've got a problem, let's get it fixed."

Rick nodded and immediately did some mental calculations. He had given Tolkachev's name to Chuvakhin around noon on June 13, and they had spent more than an hour together. Moscow was eight hours ahead in time from Washington. The soonest that Chuvakhin could have gotten word to Moscow about Tolkachev would have been 9 P.M. That would not have given the KGB enough time to arrest Tolkachev and ambush Stombaugh, and that meant Rick couldn't have been responsible for Tolkachev's arrest.* "I immediately wondered if Tolkachev had done something stupid or if the station had done something stupid, and then I thought to myself, *Is it possible that the KGB has another mole working for it, besides me, in the CIA?*"

Rick spent June and much of July looking for reasons why Tolkachev had been caught. He would later say that he saw nothing ironic about the situation: having a CIA officer, who was a KGB spy, investigating how the KGB had caught a CIA spy. When Rick was doing his job at the agency, he focused on being as good a CIA officer as he could, he said later. When he was working for the KGB, he focused on being as good an agent as he could. It was as if there were two different compartments in his head marked CIA, KGB. "Of course, when I was at work, I would pick up cables to give the KGB, but I never went out of my way to get anything that would not routinely cross my desk. I never sought out information from my colleagues. This compartmentalization was for my own protection. It reduced risks, because I didn't have to invent excuses or remember lies."

Still, there were times that summer when Rick felt overwhelmed, not only at work but home. Rosario left in late June for a six-week seminar in Chicago on literary criticism. Rick's divorce from Nan was scheduled to become final on August 1. He and Rosario planned to get married on August 10. Rosario's mother and brother were arriving from Bogotá in late July for a short vacation and the wedding. Rick's mother was driving up from her home in North Carolina to meet Rosario's family. Besides dealing with the wedding and his job, Rick was still delivering documents to the KGB during his lunch meetings with Chuvakhin. "If we pitched some guy in Greece, I'd make sure the KGB heard about it, or if we were launching some clandestine action against the Soviets, I'd tip them off." Among the cables that Rick delivered to the Russians were reports that he was writing to Gerber about the

---

*The CIA would later determine that Tolkachev was arrested June 9, or four days *before* Rick gave his long list of CIA spies to the KGB.

Tolkachev investigation. Rick never asked Chuvakhin or the KGB for any information, nor did he offer to help the KGB mislead the agency. Such moves would be too risky. "I played everything as straight as I could." He faithfully reported his lunch dates with Chuvakhin to John Murphy, the CIA's station chief in Washington, and to the appropriate FBI intelligence agents. After each lunch, he wrote in his reports that his meetings with Chuvakhin were certainly worth continuing, but that the Soviet had not shown any interest in espionage or weaknesses that could be exploited. "Basically, I just kept saying that I needed more time to work on him."

With each day that passed, Rick's fears about being caught began to lessen. On July 31, however, the KGB shocked him. When he arrived at Chadwicks restaurant, he found Chuvakhin and three *additional* Soviets waiting to have lunch with him. Worse, all of them were sitting at a table in front of the restaurant's picture window! Rick gasped. What if someone saw him there? When he discovered that one of his lunch partners was Viktor I. Cherkashin, the counterintelligence chief at the embassy, he got even more jittery. He knew the FBI routinely tailed Cherkashin. Its agents could be photographing him with them right now! "What was I supposed to say? 'Gosh, guys, guess who I bumped into today, good old Vic Cherkashin. We just sat down and had a bite together.'" Rick was still fretting that afternoon when he returned to his office. He knew the agency and the FBI would expect him to file a report about his lunch, but he didn't know what to write. He was afraid to lie and leave the three additional Russians out of his account. Someone might have seen him with them. Yet if he put them in, the FBI was bound to ask why they had joined him. "I decided to do nothing. I decided to stop writing reports about my lunches. I was hoping no one would notice."

Ames would later tell the FBI and CIA that the KGB never told him why it had decided to have the extra Soviets meet Rick for lunch. But during one of my trips to Moscow, I spoke with Viktor Cherkashin, and he claimed credit for the idea. "We knew the CIA often gave its officers polygraph tests, and one of the questions it always asked was 'Have you recently had any unofficial contacts with KGB or GRU officers?' The lunch was done to give Ames an alibi or excuse if he indicated deception when asked that question. He could honestly say that three Soviets had surprised him while he was eating lunch one day with a potential recruit. We were trying to help protect him."

Shortly after 11:00 A.M. on August 1, a Thursday, Burton Lee Gerber re-

ceived an urgent cable from the CIA station in Rome that contained exciting news: Vitaly Sergeyevich Yurchenko had walked into the U.S. embassy
that morning and had announced that he wanted to defect. Gerber immediately informed Gus Hathaway, who was now the CIA's chief of counterintelligence. Yurchenko was arguably the biggest Soviet catch in the entire
history of the CIA. His most recent assignment had been as deputy chief in
the First Department of the KGB's First Chief Directorate. That meant he
had helped oversee most of the KGB's *clandestine operations* and its *spies* in
the United States and Canada. Gerber and Hathaway were scheduled to attend a retirement luncheon at noon being hosted in the reception area on
the seventh floor by CIA Director William Casey. Both arrived smiling. The
reception was for Edward J. O'Malley, the FBI's counterintelligence chief,
and the room was filled with the nation's top intelligence officers, as well as
FBI director William H. Webster. Hathaway quietly spread the news about
Yurchenko as he made his way across the room, leaving an electrified buzz
behind him. Casey was jubilant. Yurchenko's defection was just the boost
that he needed because Congress had recently rebuffed his efforts to continue supplying U.S. aid to the contras fighting to overthrow the government of Nicaragua.

As soon as Gerber returned to his office that afternoon, he consulted
with his deputy, Milton Bearden, and Rodney Carlson, the head of the SE
division counterintelligence group. The three of them agreed that Rick
would be put in charge of debriefing Yurchenko. He understood how the
KGB worked, had done well handling important and often temperamental
Soviets, and could write reports quickly. Rick was called into Gerber's office
and told about the defector. Yurchenko was scheduled to arrive aboard a
U.S. military airplane early Friday morning at Andrews Air Force Base on the
southeastern edge of Washington. In less than twenty-four hours, Rick was
expected to become the agency's expert on Yurchenko. Others would find a
suitable safe house, arrange security, and make certain that the agency and
the FBI agreed about how the defector would be handled. Rick would be responsible for coming up with a prioritized list of questions. No one had to
tell him what the first was going to be. Were any U.S. citizens working for
the KGB as spies? If so, who?

At 8:30 P.M. on that same Thursday, Gerber received another urgent cable from Rome. Yurchenko had revealed that an American had contacted
the KGB in Vienna during the fall of 1984, and had sold the Soviets the
names of several Russians working for the CIA as spies. The defector had

never met this U.S. traitor, who he called "Robert," but he knew that the spy
had once worked for the CIA and was being groomed for an assignment in
Moscow when he had been abruptly fired. SE division chief Gerber was a de-
vout Roman Catholic and a precise man, who always chose his words wisely
and rarely swore, but when he finished reading the cable, he exclaimed:
"Damn! He's talking about Ed Howard."

Once again Gerber called Rick into his office, this time to brief him
about the Edward Lee Howard fiasco. Gerber wanted to make certain that
Rick was ready to question Yurchenko more thoroughly about Howard as
soon as the defector arrived in the States. Gerber had never met Howard,
but he had heard plenty about him. Howard had been fired in May 1983 for
lying about his previous drug use while serving in the Peace Corps before he
joined the agency. He and his wife, Mary, had moved to Santa Fe, New Mexico, and Howard had found a good job there, but he had been unable to get
over his bitterness toward the agency. He had started drinking heavily, had
made a number of strange telephone calls to CIA employees, and had become despondent. In February 1984, Howard had gotten into an altercation
outside a bar, pulled a pistol, and fired it. The police had arrested him, and
he had eventually been found guilty. But because he had not been in trouble
before, Howard had been placed on probation and ordered to undergo several hours of psychiatric counseling. Howard had blamed the agency for his
mental problems, and in May 1984, he had stopped at the CIA during an
East Coast business trip and had demanded that it reimburse him for his
court-required psychiatric care. On September 24, 1984, the agency had
sent two officers to New Mexico to meet with him. One was a former colleague, the other a CIA psychiatrist. During this meeting, the two officers
slipped Howard an envelope with $200 in it to cover the cost of his therapy.
Howard had accepted the money and had assured them that he had overcome his anger at the CIA.

Howard had then made a shocking disclosure. In the fall of 1983 during
a trip to Washington, Howard had sat on a park bench outside the Soviet
consulate for several minutes, trying to decide whether or not he should go
inside and sell CIA secrets to the KGB. He had decided not to do it, he told
his two stunned CIA visitors. But he had considered it. The officers hurried
back to headquarters, where they repeated Howard's tale to senior agency officials. During questioning, however, both men agreed that they thought
Howard had seemed relaxed and seemed to have overcome his fury at the
agency. He had been clearheaded and chipper. Gerber had been one of the

agency officials briefed about Howard and, at the time, he had decided that this mood change in Howard was a good sign. After reading the Rome cable on August 1 about Yurchenko's description of "Robert," Gerber now suspected that the real reason why Howard had been so cooperative and chipper on September 24 was that he had already exacted his revenge.*

"How much does Howard know about our Moscow operations?" Ames asked.

Gerber said he couldn't be certain, because he had been in Moscow when Howard was hired, trained, and fired. And then, Gerber suddenly felt ill. The pieces had come together. He had just recalled that Howard was being trained to be the "clean slot" officer in Moscow when he was fired.

"Howard's the one who betrayed Tolkachev!" he exclaimed. "I'm sure of it."

In reports published after his arrest, Ames would be described as being absolutely petrified when he arrived at Andrews Air Force Base on August 2 to greet Yurchenko. Several authors and journalists would write that Ames had worked himself into a drunken frenzy the night before because he was terrified that Yurchenko would step from the C-5A cargo plane onto the tarmac and dramatically jab a finger at Ames and declare: *It's you! You are a CIA mole!*

But such conjecture is simply untrue.

"I knew I was safe," said Ames. "It was apparent that he didn't know anything about me. If he had, I would have been one of the first persons he would have identified in Rome."

Walking up to the defector, Rick smiled, stuck out his hand, and repeated several lines that had been written by the agency for just such occasions. "Mr. Yurchenko, welcome to the United States. I bring you greetings and welcome from Director Casey. Do you believe that you are in any imminent danger?"

Yurchenko seemed a bit confused. He glanced around the well-guarded airfield and shook his head, indicating no.

"Good," said Rick. "If you come with us, we have a comfortable area prepared for you."

Rick led Yurchenko into the back seat of a waiting agency car and slipped in beside him. Not wishing to miss anything, two FBI agents crowded into

---

*Gerber apparently was right. The FBI and CIA would later claim that Howard had contacted the KGB during an eight-day trip to Europe in September 1984. He had returned from that trip on September 23, *one day* before he met the two CIA officers!

the back seat of the car with them. Rick introduced himself as Phil. When the car started to pull away, Rick took a card out of his pocket. Once again, this was standard CIA procedure. The card contained a message written in both English and Russian.

> If you have anything extremely important to tell us which you would like to tell only to the director of Central Intelligence or some other senior U.S. government official, tell me now and I will take you directly to him.

Yurchenko studied the card and then said: "Nyet."

The security officer driving the car had been told to spend at least a half hour "dry cleaning," driving evasively to ensure that the KGB was not following. Two other "chase" cars filled with armed officers were part of the escort. Rick thought the delay was a waste of time. Yurchenko had been awake for more than forty-eight hours, and Rick wanted to get him to the safe house in Herndon, Virginia, so he could rest. Although Rick was not supposed to begin interrogating Yurchenko until they got there, he decided to make absolutely certain that the defector didn't know anything about him.

"Are there any other *really* important leads or indications that you know of that may indicate that the CIA has been penetrated by a KGB mole?" he asked. Ames later recalled Yurchenko's reply: "Yurchenko looks at me, and says, 'Well, something strange happened in April.' He told me that he had been in Moscow and had heard through the grapevine that the counterintelligence chief at the Soviet embassy in Washington had made an unexpected trip back to Moscow and had met personally there with the chief of the First Chief Directorate. There had been speculation that something big had happened in Washington, but Yurchenko said he hadn't heard anything more. Of course, I knew what had happened in Washington. April is when I had first volunteered. That meeting had been about me!"

Yurchenko said he was exhausted when they reached the safe house, but he was too excited to sleep, so Rick and an FBI agent began debriefing him. One of his first revelations was that the KGB *resident* in London had been recalled to Moscow and put under house arrest because he was suspected of being a British spy. "I knew instantly that he was talking about Oleg Gordievsky, and my first thought was, *Jesus Christ, we've got to do something to save him! We've got to get a cable to London and tell the Brits.* And then I realized that I had given the KGB Gordievsky's name. I was responsible for his arrest! This is how compartmentalized I was. While talking to Yurchenko, I was consumed by the need to get more information to help save Gordievsky. I genuinely was worried about him. Yet at the same time, I knew I had exposed him."

It was late when Rick got home that night. He wrote his notes in longhand. He planned to drop them off at the agency the next morning for his secretary to type while he was at the safe house debriefing Yurchenko. He would put a copy aside, of course, for the KGB. At this point, Rick knew that the agency had identified Edward Lee Howard as a spy, but he didn't feel any obligation to warn either Howard or the KGB. He would later claim that he hoped the FBI would arrest Howard. "My attitude was: 'Let's catch this bastard before he does more any more damage.' I know that sounds crazy, because I was a KGB agent, too, but that was how I felt."

Yurchenko made a number of dramatic revelations during the coming weeks. He identified another KGB agent, a former employee of the National Security Agency, who had contacted the KGB in 1980. Although Yurchenko didn't know the traitor's actual name, the FBI identified him as Ronald W. Pelton.* Yurchenko also told his debriefers about "spy dust," a chemical which the KGB was squirting inside cars used by employees at the U.S. embassy in Moscow. The chemical was invisible to the naked eye, but could be seen through special glasses. The KGB looked for traces of it on the skin and clothing of Russians whom they suspected of being CIA spies. For example, if a CIA officer ever gave an informant a ride in his car, the passenger would be marked with spy dust.

Rick was mesmerized by Yurchenko. Even though he and Rosario were getting married in less than one week, he was having so much fun that he hated to leave the safe house at night. Yurchenko also liked him. When the Russian learned that Rick would be taking a day off to get married, Yurchenko wrote a message on a five-ruble note and presented it to him as a wedding present. "Dear Phil," it said. "On the day of your wedding I wish you to be happy and lucky." He signed it: "Alex."

Ames would later tell me that he had provided the KGB with copies of all of the notes that he wrote during Yurchenko's debriefings. "I gave the KGB the address of our safe house, too, and the telephone number for the phone there in case they wanted to try calling him direct some night!" Rick met Sergey Chuvakhin about every two weeks with packages of stolen docu-

*Pelton was arrested on November 24, 1985, and later sentenced to life in prison.

ments. In exchange, Chuvakhin gave him bundles of cash. Usually, both men hid their packages in the bottom of shopping bags, which they exchanged after lunch.

Although Rick now had plenty of cash, he did not flaunt it. He did not want to attract attention. His wedding on August 10 was a low-budget affair. Rosario was Roman Catholic, but no local priest would agree to marry them, because Rick was divorced. Rick was an atheist, but his mother had been a member of the Unitarian Church in Oakton, Virginia, so he contacted the minister there, and he agreed to perform the ceremony. About twenty guests attended. Rosario wore a short white party dress that she had bought on sale at Bloomingdale's. Rick bought several bottles of champagne and Rosario served guests pieces of a traditional Colombian wedding cake that she had made herself. The meager refreshments surprised their New York friends David and Angela Blake. "We're Jewish and we kept wondering: *How can you have a wedding without feeding people?*" Angela said later. They decided Rick and Rosario were broke. Only one person at the wedding had noticed that Rick and Rosario seemed to have more money. A few days before the wedding, Diana Worthen had stopped at their apartment and had found Rosario and her mother, Cecilia, laughing about a stupid error that Rick had made. The two women had spent hours one day shopping and had been totally exhausted by the time they finished. Rosario had put all of their purchases into a large plastic garbage bag that she found in the car trunk, because she didn't want to make several trips from the car to her eleventh-floor apartment. As soon as she and her mother stepped inside the apartment, Rosario put down the bag and went to take a nap. Rick came in a few minutes later and assumed the bag was trash. He carried it downstairs and tossed it into a dumpster. By the time Rosario realized what had happened, the trash had been hauled away.

"Oh my God," Worthen said, after hearing the story. "You lost everything?"

"Oh, it wasn't so much, only about seven hundred dollars' worth," Rosario replied.

Her reaction startled Worthen. Only a few months earlier, Rosario had turned down an invitation to go shopping because she and Rick didn't have any extra money. "Now she was acting as if losing seven hundred dollars was funny," Worthen recalled. "Rosario and her mother just went out and bought everything again the next day."

Not long after Rick's wedding, the agency moved Yurchenko from the safe house into a spacious two-story Colonial-style house in a suburb called

Coventry. The agency told him that it would buy him a comparable house after the debriefings ended and he had time to decide where he wanted to live. The CIA also said it would pay him an annual salary of $62,500 per year, and give him $50,000 worth of furnishings. Rick met with Yurchenko more than twenty times during August and September. Sometimes they spoke informally during strolls around a nearby pond and meals. Rick felt sorry for him. Yurchenko was convinced that he was dying of stomach cancer, and he soon developed a reputation as a chronic complainer. Just as Rick had done with Shevchenko, he became the agency's unofficial babysitter. It wasn't an easy task.

"Someone in Rome had promised Yurchenko that the agency would not tell the USSR that he had defected," Ames said later. Under a long established practice, both sides usually required defectors to meet face to face with a representative from their former country to prove that they had not been kidnapped or abducted. Yurchenko was furious when he learned that the CIA was going to tell the KGB that he had defected. He told his debriefers that the KGB could not seize any of his property (primarily his dacha) or his belongings in the USSR unless it had proof that he had changed sides. His family still lived in Moscow and he didn't want them to suffer. "We were shocked because we thought the KGB could do whatever it wanted," Ames said later, "but Yurchenko told us the Soviet system was much more legalistic than we had ever imagined."

One reason Yurchenko had defected was because he had fallen in love with Valentina Yereskovsy, the wife of a Soviet diplomat stationed in Montreal. He was certain that she would leave her husband and join him in the United States once he got settled. Without telling Canadian authorities, the FBI smuggled Yurchenko across the border in September so that he could meet secretly with his girlfriend. He waited outside a high-rise Montreal apartment building with his FBI guards until he saw Yereskovsy's husband leave for work. Then he scampered up to the sixteenth floor and knocked on his lover's apartment door. She was stunned and told him that she never wished to see him again. Yurchenko returned to the States dejected. "Yurchenko was lonely. None of us really would hang around and chat with him much at his house," Ames recalled, "When it came time for us to go home, we'd run off to our wives and families, and he wouldn't have anything to do but listen to the bullfrogs in the pond croak."

One Sunday, Rick decided on his own to brighten up Yurchenko's weekend. The Russian had mentioned that he wanted to meet Rick's new bride, so Rick took Rosario to Yurchenko's house for lunch. Yurchenko was delighted. He cooked his specialty for her: a chicken that was put in a saucepan filled with water and salt and steamed for about an hour. Rosario thought it was half-cooked, the worst-tasting meal that she had ever eaten, but she enjoyed being fawned over by the Russian. SE Division Chief Gerber was irritated when he learned that Rick had thumbed his nose at the agency's security regulations by taking his wife to eat lunch with Yurchenko. When Rick explained why, however, Gerber backed off. Gerber and his deputy, Milton Bearden, began discussing ways to make Yurchenko feel better about his new life. "How about giving him $1 million?" Bearden asked. He had calculated that it cost the U.S. government at least $1 million to support a Soviet defector during his lifetime after he was granted asylum. Rather than paying Yurchenko a yearly salary, Bearden suggested that the agency impress him by issuing him a check for $1 million. Gerber liked the idea. "Defectors often look at how much money they are being paid as a signal of how valuable or important they are in the West," Gerber was later quoted as saying. The agency would be sending Yurchenko an ego-building message, especially when it told him that he was the first defector ever to be paid $1 million. The two men decided to arrange a private dinner for Yurchenko with CIA director Casey, too.

Yurchenko's mood improved, but not for long. Someone told the media about him. He was furious when he read about himself in *The Washington Times*. It would be impossible later to determine who had tipped off the press. Some would claim it was Congress, others would blame Casey.

While Yurchenko's debriefers searched for ways to keep him from falling into another slump, the FBI tried to find sufficient evidence to arrest Edward Lee Howard in New Mexico for espionage. Except for Yurchenko's statements, there was none. The bureau had been watching Howard and it appeared that his contact with the KGB had been a limited-time affair. On September 19, the FBI sent three agents to confront him. Their goal was to get him to break down and confess, but he admitted nothing. Howard seemed unflappable. The next morning, September 20, however, the FBI received help in rattling Howard from an unexpected source. The KGB announced in Tass, the state-controlled news service, that Adolf Tolkachev had been arrested for spying. Howard knew the FBI couldn't tie him to Tolkachev's arrest, at least not yet, but he also knew that he had violated his five-year probation on his earlier assault conviction by traveling to Europe without first getting permission from the court. The FBI was bound to find

out about his overseas trip, and it could play hardball by revoking his probation and putting him in prison for one year. On Saturday afternoon, September 21, Howard and his wife drove from their house, located about
twelve miles outside Santa Fe, to a restaurant for dinner. Howard was certain
that the FBI was shadowing them. He had noticed several men who looked
like FBI agents watching his house earlier that day. Mary was driving their
1979 Oldsmobile when the couple left the restaurant's parking lot after dark
that night. During their trip home, she slowed while turning a curve on an
isolated road, and Howard leaped from the passenger side of the car. Mary
quickly swung a life-sized dummy that Howard had made into place in the
seat next to her, so the FBI agents following them would think Howard was
still in the car. What the Howards had no way of knowing was that the FBI
was not following them. The agent who was supposed to be watching their
house that afternoon had not seen them leave. Howard was safe to flee to
Moscow.

The FBI was badly embarrassed by Howard's escape, and it blamed the
CIA, in part, for contributing to the disaster. The bureau criticized the
agency for not telling it earlier about Howard. It was particularly irked at the
CIA for not telling it in September 1984 that Howard had admitted fanta-
sizing about walking into the Soviet consulate and selling U.S. secrets to the
KGB.

At about this same time, an FBI agent assigned to a special squad inside
the FBI's Washington, D.C., base station noticed that Rick had stopped filing reports about his lunchtime meetings with Chuvakhin. The FBI sent
four inquiries to the CIA asking about the missing reports, but none was answered.

Rick told Yurchenko goodbye in early October. The agency had agreed
to send Rick to Rome as the Soviet branch chief in the station there. He
and Rosario were supposed to report to Italy in mid-1986. Meanwhile,
they were going to study Italian full-time at the CIA's language school.
On Monday, November 4, one of the school's instructors interrupted the
Italian class and told Rick that he had an urgent telephone call. It was Burton Lee Gerber's secretary. The SE division chief wanted Rick to report to
his office immediately. "I felt a true sense of panic," Ames said later. "I
thought about simply running away, because I truly believed that I had been
caught. I thought another defector had come over and had identified me as
a mole."

In fact, just the opposite was true.

"Yurchenko has redefected," Gerber announced. On Saturday, November 2, Yurchenko and a young CIA security officer had driven into Georgetown, a ritzy area of Washington, to eat at Au Pied du Cochon, a French restaurant about one mile from the Soviet residential compound. After they finished, Yurchenko asked: "What would you do if I got up and walked out? Would you shoot me?"

"No, we don't treat defectors that way," the officer replied.

"I'll be back in fifteen or twenty minutes," Yurchenko announced. "If I'm not, it's not your fault."

Yurchenko left. The officer waited several minutes for him to return and then went outside to find him. A nearby movie theater was showing a Russian film, and the officer assumed that Yurchenko had gone inside. The officer showed the theater attendant his credentials and went inside, but he didn't see Yurchenko there. By the time he had called Gerber for advice and had notified the FBI, Yurchenko was already inside the Soviet compound. On Monday afternoon, Yurchenko announced at a press conference that the CIA had abducted and kidnapped him in Rome. He claimed the agency had used drugs to control him for more than three months while it interrogated him. He personally attacked Gerber and criticized all his CIA and FBI debriefers, except for one. The officer he had known as "Phil" was not mentioned. When Yurchenko revealed that the CIA had planned on paying him $1 million to betray his country, a grin appeared on Gerber's face for the first time that Monday. "Thank you, Mr. Yurchenko," he said out loud. Yurchenko had just done the agency a favor, he explained to the other CIA officers watching the news conference on the television in his office. If there were any KGB or GRU officers listening, Gerber figured the $1 million offer was going to make them salivate. "We didn't pay him, did we?" he suddenly asked. The answer was no. The agency had still been processing all the necessary paperwork when Yurchenko fled.

"A couple of officers in SE division really wanted to burn Yurchenko," Ames later recalled, "by releasing the tape recordings that we had made during his debriefings. They would have shown that he hadn't been drugged and that he was having a good time telling us KGB secrets, but Gerber, much to his credit, said, 'No, let him go.' The agency had gotten everything it wanted out of Yurchenko, and we weren't going to pull an Angleton-like trick and betray him with the tapes just because he was heartbroken and wanted to go home. It was a really decent thing to do."

On November 6, Yurchenko boarded a Moscow-bound Aeroflot Ilyushin jet with an escort of four KGB agents, and waved to the media photograph-ing him. About two weeks later, Yurchenko held another news conference in Moscow claiming, among other things, that the zipper on Director Casey's trousers had been open when they had dinner together. Once again, he at-tacked all the agency and bureau officers who had debriefed him, except for Rick. Everyone in the SE division assumed that Rick had escaped criticism because Yurchenko had genuinely liked him. Rick figured there was another reason.

Although Rick was spending most days studying Italian, he still reported to the SE division most nights. No one thought this was odd, because he was expected to keep track of what the division was doing. But he had another reason for the trips. He was stealing classified information for the KGB. The Soviets told him in a written note in late 1985 that it wanted to meet him outside the United States as soon as possible. Rick suggested that the KGB meet him in Bogotá, since he and Rosario were planning on spending Christmas there with Rosario's mother. The KGB sent him a note confirm-ing the "initial contact point" and time for the meeting. They told him to carry a copy of *Time* magazine under his arm and told him what to say when his contact met him. Rick and Rosario flew to Colombia that December, and on a Tuesday night just before Christmas Day, Rick announced that he needed to buy a present for his mother. Rachel Ames was flying to Bogotá to spend part of the holidays with them. Rosario was worried about Rick going out by himself, but he assured her that he would be safe. One of Colombia's largest shopping malls, Uno Centro, was located near Cecilia's apartment, and Rick said he would find something there. Rosario reminded him that they had been invited to eat dinner with several of her relatives at nine o'-clock. "Don't be late," she warned. Unbeknownst to Rosario, Rick had al-ready chosen a present for his mother. It was an emerald, and he raced over to the mall and bought it for $3,000 in cash. He then rushed outside, hailed a cab, and thirty minutes later was at the spot where he was supposed to meet his KGB contact.

"Excuse me, didn't I see you in Paris recently?" he heard a voice say. Rick turned and faced a tall, muscular man in his early fifties with striking silver hair.

"No, perhaps we met in Vienna," he replied, repeating the words that he had been instructed to say.

"I have a car waiting," his KGB contact said. He led Rick to a sedan. "It would be better if we did not speak any more until we reach our destination." They slid into the car's rear seat, and the driver shot out into the traffic. Rick had wondered where they would talk. He knew the KGB detested meeting in restaurants, which could be bugged. Sometimes they spent hours walking the streets with their agents. He had no idea where they were going, until he spotted a flag hanging outside a large, walled compound. It was the Soviet embassy. Rick wondered if it was being watched by Colombian intelligence officers. He began to fidget. His KGB companion seemed to sense his fear. Without being asked, he handed Rick a baseball cap and muffler to help him hide his face. Moments later, they were inside the compound and out of sight of the street. The KGB officer led Rick into a small room in the embassy. The Soviet seemed as excited as Rick was. He suddenly grabbed Rick, gave him a big hug, and kissed him on both cheeks. "You may call me VLAD," he announced, beaming. He poured them each a vodka and offered a toast to Rick and their efforts to bring about "world peace." Rick almost burst out laughing. "He was doing the exact same things that we do whenever we meet one of our spies," Ames recalled later. "He was building a rapport, talking about how our actions were going to benefit both our countries and humankind. It was the same spiel we used on them."

Rick mentioned that he didn't have much time, so they switched to drinking mineral water and got to work.

"Is Mr. Chuvakhin still acceptable to you as a contact?" VLAD asked.

Rick said he was. They spent more than an hour talking about what the KGB wanted him to steal for it and different ways for them to communicate with each other. They both were enjoying themselves. VLAD would suggest an idea, and Rick would tell him that the CIA already had a better way of doing the same thing. Then Rick would make a suggestion, and VLAD would tell him how the KGB had improved on it.

"I'd like you to tell me the name you are using in your internal reports about me," Rick said at one point. "I have a reason for asking. If the CIA gets a cable that mentions my cryptonym, or a defector mentions it, I will be forewarned."

VLAD agreed that it was a good idea. "We are calling you LYUDMILA in our cables," he said. "It is a woman's name." Rick thought that was a good ruse. "What would you like to call yourself in your notes to us?" VLAD asked.

"KOLOKOL," said Rick.

"Why have you chosen the Russian word 'bell?'" VLAD asked.

"It's the name used by Aleksandr Herzen's nineteenth-century reformist journal that had an impact on modernizing Russian thought. He chose it for its cultural resonance—a warning!" Rick replied, showing off his knowledge of Russian history. And then he added, "There's also a bit of irony in using the letter K." James Jesus Angleton had spent his career searching for a KGB mole whose name reportedly began with the letter K. "Out of respect for Angleton," Rick quipped, "I think it is only appropriate that I sign my notes with a K." He smiled, but he wasn't certain if VLAD understood the sarcasm.

It was 9:40 P.M. when Rick returned to his mother-in-law's apartment, and Rosario was fuming. Cecilia asked why he was so late. Rick said he had gotten lost. He told them that he had to put away the present that he had bought for his mother before they could leave to eat dinner with Rosario's relatives. Hurrying into the bedroom, he tucked the $50,000 into the bottom of his suit bag. When they got to dinner, Cecilia made some joke in Spanish about how Americans are always getting lost, and everyone laughed.

Rick was happy to see his mother when she arrived a few days later. He knew how much she enjoyed visiting foreign countries. Cecilia suggested that they drive to Cartagena, a seaside resort, so Rick, Rosario, Rachel, Cecilia, and Rosario's younger brother, Pablo, packed themselves into a van that Rick rented, and drove north. Everyone had such a good time that Rick and Rosario decided to buy a condominium there. He told his mother that they had gotten it cheap because the condominium complex was still under construction and the builder needed cash to finish. Rick, Rosario, and Rachel breezed through U.S. Customs when they returned to the States in January 1986. No one checked the suit bag where the KGB's cash was still hidden.

That spring, Rachel visited them again in Virginia. She had come to see her grandson, one of Nancy Everly's boys, graduate from the U.S. Naval Academy in Annapolis, Maryland. Rachel was staying in the guest bedroom at Rick and Rosario's apartment, and one night she and Rosario decided that they would get up early the next morning and go shopping together. When she didn't get out of bed the next day, Rosario telephoned Rick. He discovered that his mother had suffered a heart attack in her sleep. Rick was overwrought. Rosario was surprised when she saw how emotional he was. Rick always seemed in control. She often joked about how in control he and his sisters were. Every time Rosario called him at work about some emergency, he would assure her in an irritatingly paternalistic voice that everything would be fine if she would just calm down. That was the Ames family way: *Don't betray any emotions, just deal with the problem at hand.*

Rick and Nancy made the funeral arrangements. Only one person from the agency called to offer his condolences. It was Burton Lee Gerber, the SE division chief. Rick and Rosario were scheduled to leave for a brief Club Med vacation the morning after the funeral. Nancy thought Rick might cancel the trip, but Rosario didn't want to do that. Later that night, after Rosario had gone to bed at the hotel, Rick poured himself a vodka and sat alone in the darkness. The last twelve months had been incredible. He had gotten divorced, remarried, become a spy, helped debrief Yurchenko, met his KGB handler in Bogotá, and now had buried his mother. He thought about his parents. They had been so proud of him. He had really straightened out his life after fumbling for a few years when he was living in Chicago. Sitting there, he thought about the nasty letter that he had written to them after he had flunked out of college, telling them to butt out of his life. In a strange way, he decided it was best that they were dead. *Now they will never know the truth*, he later recalled thinking. He felt relieved.

Rick and Rosario completed language school that spring. Rosario got the equivalent of an A plus. Rick got a C, which meant he could handle some basic Italian but wasn't fluent. A short time later, Rick received a notice from the CIA's Office of Security, informing him that it was time for his routine background investigation. Every employee was supposed to undergo a routine investigation and take a polygraph test every five years. Rick had forgotten that he was due for testing. He decided to ask VLAD for advice. He had heard rumors that the KGB had discovered a way to fool the lie detector machine. VLAD told him to "remain calm, get a good night's rest, eat a good breakfast, and convince the examiner that you want to be helpful in answering all questions." Rick was disappointed. He had hoped the KGB had invented some sort of pill that would help a person conceal his reactions. He thought the test had gone well, until the woman giving it announced that the machine had noted that he had reacted slightly to one question, possibly indicating an attempt at deception.

"Which one?" he asked.

"Why don't you tell me which one you think it is?" she replied.

Rick shrugged his shoulders. "Well, I can't imagine."

She read him the question: "Have you ever been approached or pitched by a foreign intelligence service?" She asked Rick if he had any idea why the machine showed he was stumbling over that query.

"I guess it's because, you know, I have been involved in a lot of developmental relationships with Eastern Europeans and I, myself, have pitched them and oftentimes they were probably thinking about pitching me at the same time I was pitching them," he replied. As an afterthought, he added that he was nervous because he was leaving soon for Italy and he thought he might be pitched there.

The examiner said that she would give Rick a few minutes to relax, and then ask him that same question again. As he was sitting there, Rick suddenly realized that he had never been pitched by the KGB. "The question was written incorrectly. It was: 'Have you ever been approached or pitched by a foreign intelligence service?' and I hadn't been! I was the one who *approached* them! I wasn't lying when I said I'd never been pitched."

When the examiner asked Rick the question again, he answered, "No," and this time the machine didn't indicate a reaction.

"I thanked the examiner and walked outside the building and it was a beautiful Friday, and I stopped and took a deep breath and just felt absolutely great about being alive," Ames said later. "I was deeply in love with Rosario, I had just passed my polygraph, I had more money than I could ever spend, and I was on my way to Rome, which was a city that Rosario and I both wanted to live in. It is hard to describe just how much of a high I was on at that moment.

"I said to myself, *You've finally done it, Rick. You're on top of the world.*"

PART THREE

FALSE STARTS

Counterintelligence people are like wolves chewing dry bones—you have to take away the bones and make them find new quarry.

—John leCarre,
The Spy Who Came in from the Cold

CHAPTER 14

THE OTHER SIDE

In 1985, the KGB operated in Washington, D.C., from the top floor of an imposing turn-of-the-century stone mansion built, but never lived in, by Mrs. George M. Pullman, widow of the railroad sleeping-car magnate. The last czarist government, the House of Romanov, bought the rectangular four-story structure from her for an embassy, and the communists later moved in. Located three blocks north of the White House, the Soviet embassy was a forlorn place guarded by a fence of pointed iron bars. Drab gray shutters covered all the windows, which were kept sealed. Some forty KGB officers worked inside four cramped rooms on the fourth floor, and the air captured inside reeked of cigarette smoke so thick it could be seen floating aimlessly under the harsh fluorescent lights, which burned twenty-four hours per day for security reasons. Each office handled a specific task: political intelligence, foreign counterintelligence, scientific and technological intelligence, and technical operations. There was only one entrance to the fourth floor, and it was protected by a thick steel door that could only be opened by punching the correct numbers into a sophisticated digital lock. No one was allowed inside wearing a jacket or suit coat, a security precaution aimed at making it more difficult for a spy to smuggle in a miniature camera. Special screens were built around the offices to shield them from FBI eavesdropping.

The chief *rezident* was Stanislav Andrevich Androsov, a KGB bureaucrat appointed to the Washington post in 1982 largely because of his friendship with Vladimir Aleksandrovich Kryuchkov. At the time, Kryuchkov was in charge of the CIA's chief rival: the First Chief Directorate, the KGB's foreign intelligence operation. He had been in power eleven years by 1985, and during his tenure he had earned a reputation for politicizing the directorate. Kryuchkov had forced several veteran KGB officers, such as General Boris Solomatin, to retire and had replaced them with party hacks loyal to him. Androsov was considered a Kryuchkov lackey, and many of the KGB officers under his command viewed him with contempt, in part because of an embarrassing incident that had occurred shortly after he became the KGB *rezident*. In 1983, Androsov decided to erect a large map of Washington, D.C., outside his office. Every KGB officer was required to use a pin to mark on the map where he was going before he left the embassy. With a quick glance, Androsov could tell from the map where his troops were at any given moment. Viktor Cherkashin, the KGB's counterintelligence chief at the embassy, was horrified when he saw Androsov's map. "If the FBI or CIA has corrupted one of our officers, all this spy has to do is look at this map every morning, and he will know where our men will be that day," he complained.

Androsov scoffed at the warning, so Cherkashin set out to prove his point. It didn't take him long. He found the evidence that he needed in the KGB's own files. "We knew the radio frequencies which the FBI used to communicate with its agents when they were following us," Cherkashin explained years later, during an interview with me in Moscow, "and we could tell from their radio conversations who the FBI was tailing and who it wasn't. We kept very complete records of this." Before May 1982, it was clear that the FBI did not know which employees at the embassy were KGB or GRU officers. On an average day, the FBI might follow ten Soviets, but only six of them were in the KGB or GRU. In May 1982, however, the FBI's accuracy rate dramatically improved. "If ten people left the embassy, the FBI only followed the six who were KGB officers," Cherkashin recalled. Worse, the FBI often showed up at a location where the KGB officer was going before he did! "I immediately asked myself, 'Why is the FBI so brilliant now at identifying our men?' What happened in May 1982?" To him, the answer seemed obvious.

"We have an American spy working in the embassy," Cherkashin told Androsov. "Someone is telling the FBI what our men are doing by looking at your bloody map."

Androsov still didn't believe the counterintelligence chief, so one morning Cherkashin announced that a new pin was being added to the map. It represented a "clean" officer working under disguise inside the embassy. No one except for the ambassador, Androsov, and Cherkashin knew this officer's identity. Cherkashin told everyone that he would personally mark the clean officer's location on the map each day, so other officers would not inadvertently lead any FBI agents following them into the area where the clean officer was working. During the coming week, Cherkashin faithfully moved the clean officer's pin. Of course, there was no clean officer. Cherkashin was simply running a test. Three days into the experiment, the KGB intercepted radio chatter between an FBI surveillance team and its base station. The FBI team was waiting at the spot on the KGB's map where Cherkashin had put the clean officer's pin. It had been sent there to get a photograph of the new KGB officer.

Cherkashin now had the evidence he needed to convince Androsov that his map was a mistake. It also seemed obvious that there was a CIA mole working on the fourth floor. But who? Cherkashin compiled a list of all KGB officers who had worked at the embassy in May 1982 and compared it to his current roster. One name stuck out. "For reasons I cannot go into, I immediately suspected that (Valery) Martynov was the FBI spy."

Cherkashin was right. Although the FBI and the CIA have never revealed the exact date when Martynov was recruited, both agencies have said he started in "early 1982." Cherkashin read Martynov's personnel file and learned that the 38 year-old KGB officer and his wife, Natalya, along with their two small children, had arrived in Washington on November 4, 1980, the day Ronald Reagan was elected president. Martynov claimed to be a cultural affairs attaché, but his real job was to steal scientific and technical information. In late 1982, Martynov had obtained technical drawings of several electronic components used in older U.S. weapons systems. Even though the drawings were of outdated weapons, Martynov was given the Order of the Red Star, a prestigious decoration, for the theft. Cherkashin was suspicious. There was nothing in Martynov's records that revealed how he had stolen the documents. Was it possible, Cherkashin wondered, that the CIA and FBI had provided the information to the spy to help advance his career and make Martynov appear less suspect as a mole?

By April 1984, Cherkashin felt he had enough circumstantial evidence to arrest Martynov. He presented his accusations to his boss. "Androsov was very impressed by my work," Cherkashin recalled, "but he wanted to wait until May, when one of Kryuchkov's most trusted deputies was scheduled to come from Moscow for a routine inspection. Androsov said that exposing Martynov during the inspection would be a very good thing for my career, and his, too."

Cherkashin was elated when the deputy arrived. "I thought he would be appreciative of my discovery, but he began yelling at me. 'Don't you know what is happening in Moscow right now! If word leaks out that our Washington station has been infiltrated by an American spy, Kryuchkov will be humiliated and ruined, and the entire service will be badly embarrassed.'"

Two months earlier, Yuri Vladimirovich Andropov, the general secretary of the USSR and former head of the KGB, had died, and Kryuchkov, who had been one of Andropov's favorites, had lost his strongest patron. A longtime Andropov rival, Konstantin Chernenko, had been elected general secretary, and Kryuchkov was now worried that he was about to be replaced as chief of foreign intelligence. All Chernenko needed was an excuse to oust him. "Kryuchkov's deputy told us to transfer Martynov into a less sensitive job where he had no access, and to eventually send him back to Moscow where he would be dealt with quietly," said Cherkashin. "I was so furious about these political games that I took the special report I had prepared about Martynov and put it in a paper shredder. I said to myself, *The hell with catching this guy*. No one cares."

Eleven months later, Ames boldly walked into the Soviet embassy and volunteered to spy. Because Cherkashin was the counterintelligence chief at the time, he was deeply involved in what happened there after Ames appeared. The interview that Cherkashin gave me is the first he has ever granted an author, and much to my surprise, his account of those key days in early 1985 differ from what Ames has always claimed. During the interview, Cherkashin confirmed that the KGB's first contact with Ames at its embassy was on April 16, 1985, when he handed a guard in the lobby an envelope addressed to Androsov. But Cherkashin insisted that Ames *did not* reveal his true name in that letter, nor did he include a page from the SE division phone list with his name highlighted.

"He told us his name was 'Rick Wells' and said only that he worked for the CIA," Cherkashin recalled.

"How did you know that Ames was a legitimate traitor?" I asked.

"Because in his letter, he told us about two or three important CIA spies."

"Who were these men?"

At this point, I expected Cherkashin to restate what Ames has always said: that the men who he identified in the letter were double agents.

"In his very first letter, Mr. Wells [Ames] told us the names of two traitors: Valery Martynov and Sergey Motorin. He also wrote about other very sensational and important Western spies who had penetrated our service."

Cherkashin's answer startled me. I thought he might be confused. "Are you certain that Ames wrote the names of Martynov and Motorin in that *first* letter in April 1985?" I asked.

"This is not something I will ever forget," Cherkashin replied, "particularly since I was already suspicious of Martynov. Yes, I am sure. Rick Wells [Ames] gave us the names of Martynov and Motorin, and this act, by itself, convinced us that he was a senior CIA officer, because we knew only a few officials would be told the names of spies in our embassy."

What Cherkashin had just told me was significant. I knew the FBI and CIA were not convinced that Ames had told investigators the truth about his first contacts with the KGB. They were particularly suspicious of his story about how he had tried to "scam" the KGB by demanding $50,000 in exchange for useless information about three double agents. The investigators had given Ames several polygraph tests, and all of them had shown that he was being "deceptive" whenever he answered questions about the scam and the contents of his April 16 letter to the KGB.

At this point in my interview with Cherkashin, I made what I now consider to be a tactical blunder by asking him for a third time if he was absolutely certain that Ames had betrayed Martynov and Motorin in his first letter.

"What does Ames say happened?" he asked me.

"He says he didn't tell the KGB the names of any real agents until June 13," I explained.

Now it was Cherkashin who appeared surprised. "Perhaps you should talk to Kobaladze about the exact sequence of events," he stammered, referring to Yuri Kobaladze, the Russian Foreign Intelligence Service's public relations spokesman. "I'm sure he can resolve this question for you. Perhaps I am, well, let's just say that I'm sure whatever Mr. Ames said is the truth."

Clearly, Cherkashin was backpedaling. Before our interview, he had mentioned that he had retired from the KGB in early 1991 and had not been in communication with anyone from it since then. He said he had not read any books written about Ames nor studied any of the Russian newspaper articles published about him. This seemed important to me, because I suspected that Cherkashin would have parroted Ames's original story back to me if he had known about it before we had started our interview.

Which account is accurate? Did the April 16 letter contain the names of three double agents, as Ames insists, or is Cherkashin's version the truth? In interviews with me, Ames has always insisted that he tricked himself into becoming a KGB mole. "My fifty-thousand-dollar scam was supposed to be a one-shot deal," he recalled. "I didn't realize I had crossed the line until it was too late and I couldn't go back." But that is not how Cherkashin remembers the situation. According to him, Ames had demanded fifty thousand dollars and, in return, had identified at least two spies working for the CIA—the equivalent of twenty-five thousand dollars per head.

While I was in Moscow, I tried to find Ames's April 16 letter to Androsov, but the KGB refused to show it to me. Until it surfaces, it will be impossible to know for certain what really happened. What follows, then, is pure speculation. I mention it only because several federal investigators believe it could be what actually happened. There are several reasons why Ames might have done what Cherkashin says that he did. Ames knew the most dangerous time for a spy is when he volunteers, and he also knew that the CIA and FBI had at least one informant working inside the Soviet Embassy in April 1985.* It was impossible for Ames to know beforehand who he might meet when he walked into the embassy. It was also impossible for him to know what rumors might swirl through the building after he left. Ames had to make certain that the KGB knew it had a CIA spy working in the embassy, otherwise Martynov might learn about him. The best way for Ames to protect himself was by fingering Martynov before he could tell the CIA about its newest traitor.

When I told Ames what Cherkashin had said about the April 16 letter, he replied: "Cherkashin is mistaken. The only names I put in my first letter were the names of double agents. I have no reason to lie about this. After all, I have admitted that I later identified Martynov and Motorin in my June letter. My first letter was part of my scam."

---

*After he was arrested, Ames told me that Motorin and Martynov had both been working inside the embassy that April. However, records show that Motorin returned to the USSR in January 1985, and was working in Moscow at the KGB's headquarters when Ames volunteered. The CIA would later find notes that showed Ames had been present during briefings at the agency when Motorin's January departure from the United States was discussed, so its investigators would decide that Ames had known in 1985 that Motorin was gone—a fact he simply had forgotten by the time he spoke to me.

Some federal investigators, however, believe Ames has plenty of reason to put a spin on his story. "Ames wants us to believe he sorta stumbled into becoming a mole, you know, sorta got sucked into it," said an FBI agent familiar with the Ames investigation. "But if he gave Martynov and Motorin's names right off—that's cold, man, like putting a gun to both men's heads."

After my gaffe during our interview, Cherkashin once again picked up his story about what happened when Ames volunteered. "Androsov called me into his office as soon as the lobby guard brought him the letter. We immediately agreed that this Rick Wells was a legitimate and very important CIA source."

"How could you be so certain?" I asked.

"Because he identified Mart— uh, er," Cherkashin answered, stopping before he mentioned Martynov's name. "Let me just say this: the letter contained sufficient information for us to know that it was written by someone who was high-ranking in the CIA and was willing to help us."

Cherkashin and Androsov kept Ames's letter secret from everyone else in the embassy. A short time later, Cherkashin flew to Moscow, where he hand-delivered the letter to Kryuchkov.* One of Kryuchkov's deputies, Lieutenant General Vadim Kirpichenko, was also present. After that meeting, Kryuchkov and Kirpichenko went to see Viktor Chebrikov, the chairman of the KGB. Even though Kryuchkov was the chief of the First Directorate, he was not authorized to withdraw more than $10,000 in U.S. currency from the Military Industrial Commission unless he explained in writing how he intended to use the money. At the time, it was against the law for Soviets to spend any currency except rubles. The military commission was the only entity in Moscow that had access to large amounts of foreign currencies. As KGB chairman, Chebrikov could withdraw $50,000 for Ames without being questioned. I was later told that Chebrikov, Kryuchkov, and Kirpichenko decided that all information about Ames would be kept a closely guarded secret. Only *seven* KGB officers, I was told, were ever told Ames's actual name during the nine years that he was a KGB spy.

It was also decided that Ames would be "run" from Moscow by Kirpichenko, who had experience overseeing sensitive KGB cases. In the early

---

*It is unclear when Cherkashin made this trip. Ames said that KGB defector Vitaly Yurchenko told him that the counterintelligence chief in Washington (Cherkashin) had flown back to Moscow in April, indicating something important had happened at the embassy. Cherkashin told me that he returned to Moscow "immediately after receiving the [April 16] letter." But the U. S. Customs Service and the FBI have no record of Cherkashin leaving the United States until May 20. He returned May 31.

1960s, Kirpichenko had been the case officer who had handled Sami Sharaf, the director of Egypt's intelligence service. Kirpichenko gave Cherkashin explicit instructions about how Ames was to be treated. Moscow would take care of everything. No one at the Soviet embassy would be told anything of importance about Ames. Nor was anyone there authorized to read the contents of any future packages that he might deliver. This included Androsov and Cherkashin, despite their rank. Because Ames already had been in contact with Sergey Chuvakhin, it was decided that he would serve as the KGB's go-between, even though he was not a KGB officer. This would work to the KGB's advantage, Kirpichenko told Cherkashin, because neither side would suspect that Chuvakhin was engaged in a clandestine operation. Chuvakhin was to be prohibited from discussing anything with Ames during their lunches except for normal chitchat about world politics. Cherkashin would be in charge of preparing the KGB's deliveries at the embassy. Money would be sent from Moscow, along with notes, in diplomatic pouches. Cherkashin would be responsible for guarding the money and notes until Chuvakhin was ready to leave the embassy for his lunch exchange with Ames.

As soon as Cherkashin returned to Washington, he called Chuvakhin into his office. "I told Mr. Chuvakhin we wanted him to begin having lunch with Rick Wells, and, much to my shock, he refused. He told me, 'I'm not a KGB man. Let one of your boys do this dirty work.' I was unsure how to proceed." Cherkashin sent a cable to Kirpichenko. A short time later, a humbler Chuvakhin appeared in Cherkashin's office and apologized.

On May 17, Ames returned to the Soviet embassy and was led into a conference room to meet Cherkashin face to face. "There was only one reason why this meeting was necessary," Cherkashin said later. "Kryuchkov was not going to give fifty thousand dollars to an American unless he had someone in the KGB meet that person. I was going to be blamed if this turned out to be some sort of clever trap." After they met, Ames was paid fifty thousand dollars.

On that same day, May 17, a top secret cable was sent from KGB headquarters in Moscow to Oleg Gordievsky, the KGB's *rezident* in London. The message informed Gordievsky that he was to return to Moscow at once to brief Chebrikov and Kryuchkov about "England's foreign policy." Gordievsky had been secretly spying for MI-6 for nine years, and he had never received a cable like this one, ordering him home. "It had been written in a hurry," Gordievsky told me later in London. "Even more suspicious was this premise that Chebrikov wanted to discuss English foreign policy. Che-

The Ames family in Washington, D.C., where Carleton was training for the CIA. Left to right: Rachel, Alison, Rick, Nancy, and Carleton. *(Photo courtesy of Nancy Everly)*

Rick the Boy Scout with his uncle Frank LaBrash, a West Point cadet. *(Photo courtesy of Nancy Everly)*

Rick(left) in high school, shortly after the family returned from Burma in 1955. *(Photo courtesy of Nancy Everly)*

Rick after dropping out of the University of Chicago in 1962. He grew a moustache and took up skydiving. *(Photo courtesy of Nancy Everly)*

Rick and Rosario in Acapulco, April 1983. Shortly after this, he announced that he was in love with her and willing to divorce his wife. *(Photo by Dave Samson)*

Rick and Rosario at their wedding in August 1985, shortly after he became a spy.

Vladimir Kryuchkov. The Ames case helped him rise to head of the KGB.

Viktor Cherkashin, the KGB's counterintelligence chief at the Soviet embassy in Washington.

Stanislav Androsov, chief *rezident* at the Soviet embassy in Washington.

Sergey Chuvakhin, who passed Ames shopping bags of cash in exchange for stacks of CIA documents. (*FBI photo*)

Sergey Divilkovsky, the embassy employee Ames was supposed to recruit.

KGB Lt. Colonel Valery Martynov, codenamed GEN-TILE, and KGB Major Sergey Motorin, codenamed GAUZE. Both were executed when Ames named them. *(FBI photos)*

General Dmitri Polyakov, codenamed TOPHAT, the CIA's greatest Russian asset until Ames betrayed him. His body was dumped in an unmarked grave.

```
                      Dear Friend,
        this is Your balance sheet as on the May 1, 1989.

        * All in all You have been approriated ----  2,705,000 $
        * From the time of oppening of Your
          account in our Bank (December 26,
          1986) Your profit is --------------------  385,077$ 28c
        (including 14,468$ 94c as profit on bonds, which we
        bought for You on the sum of 250,000$)
        * Since December 1986 Your salary is ------  300,000$
        * All in all we have delivered to You -----  1,881,811$ 51c
        * On the above date You have on Your
          account (including 250,000$ in bonds) ---  1,535,077$ 28c


        P.S.  We believe that these pictures would give You some
        idea about the beautiful piece of land on the river bank,
        which from now belongs to You forever, We decided not to take
        pictures of housing in this area with the understanding that
        You have much better idea of how Your country house (dacha)
        should look like.

        Good luck,
```

Ames's "balance sheet" from the KGB in June 1989, indicating he had been paid more than $1.8 million. *(FBI photo)*

Greetings, Our dear Friend,

We are glad that everything is good with You. We should
not hide that Your not showing up at the meeting in April and
then some delaying of our contact in May have given us hard
time. And You could imagine our sincere happiness when You
gave a call to Sam. Having in mind Your letter of May 16, we
feel we share the same understanding that any braking of the
commo plan could be only trough some unforeseen extraordinary
circumstances.

We would like to express some basics on our future
cooperation, the heart of which - we stress it - is Your
personal security.
We believe that our first personal contact should be in
six month s after You returned to Washington DC. That will
give You some time to get settled.
In the base of our commo concept are personal meetings
in Bogota and Vienna and deaddrops in Washington, which we
consider to be reliable and tested means of impersonal communications. In accordance with our previous arrangements our
personal meetings in Bogota and Vienna will be on the third
tuesday of a certain month.

I. Our first meeting in Bogota we plan to arrange in
December 1989. How will it look like in detailes?
a) The fixed meeting will take place on the third Tuesday
of December 1989 at 7 p.m.
b) Alternate meetings:
= the same day at 8 p.m.
= next day at 7 p.m. and 8 p.m.
= in a week time at 7 p.m. and 8 p.m.
= next day at 7 p.m. and 8 p.m.
For December 1989 in dates it will look like this:
a) Fixed meeting - December 19 at 7 p.m.

First page of a nine-page
KGB letter to Ames in
June 1989, explaining
future procedures and
meetings. *(FBI photo)*

A note from Ames to the
KGB, September 1992,
reconstructed from a print-
er ribbon recovered from
Ames's trash a year later.
(FBI photo)

My dear friends:

I write this in some haste on Tues evening, 1 September. I
am afraid that the signal HILL is not well-thought-out;
the wooden post is often damp and mildewed -- discolored --
and the pencil mark I made on the morning of 19 August does not
appear to have been observed. After making the signal at HILL with
pencil at about 0700 on 19 August, I placed the drop at GROUND
about 1600 that same day. I was worried about the visibility of
the signal and waited until daylight of 20 August to check to see
if it had been erased -- it did not appear to have been erased,
and I retrieved my package (which included documents!) later that
day. Unfortunately, I left Washington for a vacation trip
to California on 21 August, returning on 30 August. I will signal
HILL on Weds morning, 2 September, but this time using chalk
instead of pencil. If my package is not retrieved during the
evening of 2 September, I will return to the old, SMILE, signal
site to mark it on 4 September and put my package down
that afternoon. In any case, I'll keep trying until you get it.
Given the shortness of time before our next meeting, I am putting
a note on the package which I hope will cause the people here to
send you a telegram confirming my intent to make our scheduled
meeting on 5/6 October. Best regards, K

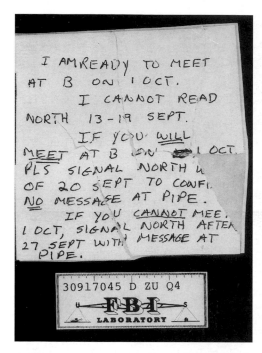

I AM READY TO MEET
AT B ON 1 OCT.
        I CANNOT READ
NORTH 13-19 SEPT.
        IF YOU WILL
MEET AT B ON 1 OCT.
PLS SIGNAL NORTH L
OF 20 SEPT TO CONFI.
NO MESSAGE AT PIPE.
        IF YOU CANNOT MEE.
1 OCT, SIGNAL NORTH AFTER
27 SEPT WITH MESSAGE AT
PIPE.

30917045 D ZU Q4
FBI
LABORATORY

The mailbox codenamed SMILE at 37th and R streets. Ames's chalk mark signaled the Russians that he could meet ANDRE in Bogotá on November 1, 1993. *(FBI photo)*

A torn note recovered from Ames's trash, September 15, 1993—the first definite evidence that he was a spy. *(FBI photo)*

Ames photographed by an FBI camera as he waited to meet ANDRE in a Bogotá shopping mall. *(FBI photo)*

The CIA mole-hunting team. Left to right: Sandy Grimes, Paul Redmond, Jeanne Vertefeuille, Diana Worthen, Dan Payne

Special Agent Leslie G. Wiser led the FBI team. *(FBI photo)*

The happy couple. Rick and Rosario shortly before the arrest.

FBI agents swarming around Ames on February 21, 1994. Handcuffed and put in the back of a car, Ames was heard admonishing himself, "Think, think, think." *(FBI photo)*

brikov was a man who knew nothing about foreign policy and never cared about it. I asked myself, *What is the real meaning of this telegram?*" The next day, another telegram from Moscow arrived. It was more polished, and it listed several topics that Chebrikov wanted to discuss. "There was no mention in this telegram of English foreign policy."

Gordievsky contacted his MI-6 handler. "Do you think they are on to me?" he asked.

"My controller agreed that the telegram was suspicious, but he assured me that there was no way I could have been compromised by a mole inside MI-6," Gordievsky said. "Only a few top people in the British government knew I even existed."

On Sunday morning, May 19, Gordievsky landed at Sheremetyevo airport outside Moscow, and immediately sensed something was wrong. He saw a customs officer telephone someone and report his arrival. That had never happened before. When Gordievsky reached his apartment, he knew before he opened the door that it had been searched. He and his wife, Leila, used only two of the three locks, but someone had bolted all three. The next morning, Gordievsky was taken to Yasenevo, the headquarters of the First Chief Directorate on the outskirts of Moscow. He was escorted to an empty office and told that his rushed meetings with Chebrikov and Kryuchkov were being indefinitely delayed. A week went by. No one spoke to him. He was being watched constantly and assumed the KGB was waiting for him to contact his British handlers. On Saturday, one of Kryuchkov's deputies, KGB general Viktor Grushko, invited Gordievsky to his dacha for lunch. While they were eating sandwiches and drinking Armenian brandy, two KGB officers from Directorate K, the office responsible for hunting down moles, arrived with a second bottle. "This brandy had been drugged, because when I drank from it, I became almost a different man and began talking without being able to even control my own words." Gordievsky's two interrogators pelted him with questions and accused him of being a British spy. He was given a piece of paper.

"Confess now," he was ordered. When he refused, he was told, "Don't you remember? You confessed a moment ago. Confess again!" In his drugged state, Gordievsky wasn't certain what he had said, but he didn't believe he had confessed. "I kept telling myself, they must not have any evidence, otherwise they would not need me to confess." Gordievsky woke up the next morning in one of the dacha's bedrooms, with a splitting headache. He was taken back to his apartment in Moscow, and for the next three days, he was left alone. On May 30, he was called before Grushko again. "General Grushko told me that my family had been called back to Moscow from London and that they were being held under guard. Then he said: 'We have known for a very long time that you have been deceiving us and are a traitor, but if you confess, you can continue to work for the KGB and you will only be reprimanded.' I thought, *How stupid do you think I am? You will shoot me if I confess.* I said nothing, and as I was being taken out, General Grushko turned and said, '*Mr. Gordievsky, if you only knew from what a peculiar source we learned about you, you would not be so proud.*' I kept thinking, *What does he mean—a peculiar source?* I decided someone had identified me as a spy, but it couldn't have been anyone who was British, otherwise it would not be a peculiar source."

Gordievsky was taken to a KGB "sanatorium," a resort outside Moscow, where he was held for several weeks. On two occasions, he was allowed to visit his wife and two daughters in Moscow, and it was during one of these visits that he sent a message to the MI- 6. In July 1985, Gordievsky was released from the sanatorium and taken back to his apartment. On July 19, he went for an afternoon jog along Leninsky Prospekt, a major thoroughfare in Moscow. It was part of a routine that he had intentionally established. The KGB team watching him did not pay much attention as he ran down the busy street, and when he turned a corner and jumped into the back of a waiting van, Gordievsky felt certain that no one had seen him. Gordievsky was smuggled across the Soviet border into a friendly European country. MI-6 had successfully snatched him out of the USSR. His wife and daughters, however, remained behind. "The first thing I did in England was tell the MI-6 about General Grushko's 'peculiar source' comment. None of us could figure out who had betrayed me," Gordievsky recalled later.

To this day, there is an ongoing debate within the CIA, the FBI, and the MI-6 about the identity of the "peculiar source." Ames continues to insist that he is not to blame for identifying one of England's more valuable spies. Several CIA officials, who spoke to me about the Gordievsky case on the condition that they not be quoted by name, also believe that Ames was not the first agent to betray Gordievsky to the KGB.

"The dates don't match," Ames told me. The first telegram that Gordievsky received ordering him to return to Moscow was sent to London on May 17. Ames insists that he didn't tell the KGB that Gordievsky was a traitor until June 13. "There is no way that I can be held responsible for what happened to Gordievsky, and since I am not the one, then that can mean only one thing," Ames excitedly told me. "The Brits have a problem! They got a mole of their own in MI-6 who gave up Gordievsky before I did! They have a penetration! That's what I will tell MI-6 when they come here to see me."

There is another possible explanation. Ames could be lying. I asked Viktor Cherkashin during our interview if Ames had identified Gordievsky in his April 16 letter. But Cherkashin balked at telling me anything more about the letter, and instead suggested that I ask the Russian intelligence service's public relations man.

Did Ames tell the KGB about Gordievsky in his April 16 letter? Initially, Cherkashin had told me during our interview that the April 16 letter contained the names of two or three spies and information about *"other very sensational and important Western spies who had penetrated our service."* Had he been referring to Gordievsky?

Once again, we can only speculate. As the KGB's *resident* agent in London, Gordievsky could be viewed as the most important agent, after Tolkachev, who Rick knew about. Telling the KGB that its *resident* in England was an MI-6 spy was certain to alarm the Kremlin. It would also be an easy way for Ames to prove to the KGB that he had access to extremely valuable information. Because of Gordievsky's position within the KGB, it was also possible that he might hear gossip or learn about Rick in some way. His rank and his access, some federal investigators suspect, made him a prime target for Ames. "He would have wanted to get rid of Gordievsky as soon as possible in order to protect his own neck," an FBI agent close to the investigation said later.

When I asked Ames about this theory, that he had identified Gordievsky in April 1985, he again insisted that he was not responsible for Gordievsky's recall on May 17 to Moscow. "Listen, I didn't give up Martynov, Motorin— or Gordievsky—until I gave the KGB my complete list of names on June 13," he said. "You cannot blame me for Gordievsky. The Brits have a mole. It is as simple as that."

There are other possible explanations for Gordievsky's arrest besides a mole. The KGB could have unmasked him on its own. The CIA had identified Gordievsky in early 1985. The detective work had been done by an officer in the SE division, who had used two clues to identify the British spy. The officer knew from classified KGB documents that MI-6 was sharing with the CIA, that the British had someone inside Soviet intelligence working for them and that spy was privy to information about England, which suggested that he worked at the Soviet embassy there. The SE division officer also knew that a Danish intelligence officer had once let slip that the MI-6 had recruited a KGB officer in 1974 while he was stationed in Copenhagen. Using those two clues, the SE division officer had compiled a list of KGB officers who had worked in Copenhagen in 1974, and a list of KGB officers currently stationed in London. When he compared them, Gordievsky's name jumped out. Of course, no one in the CIA suspected that Ames would use this detective work as he did.

When I asked the KGB how it had learned that Gordievsky was a traitor, I was told a rather unbelievable story. In March 1985, a telephone operator at the Soviet embassy in London was waiting for a bus, when she saw Gordievsky leave an apartment with a group of "British-looking men." She thought this was odd and reported it. Gordievsky was put under surveillance and later photographed meeting with MI-6 officers, the KGB told me. The KGB said the woman was later poisoned by MI-6, because the British were afraid she would identify Gordievsky as a spy. This story seems absurd. If the KGB had photographic evidence, it would have confronted Gordievsky with it when he was recalled to Moscow. Still, this was the KGB's official explanation. Unofficially, one of Kryuchkov's former aides told me that the story about the telephone operator was disinformation. Gordievsky was identified by a paid KGB source, he said, "and it wasn't Ames."

During our interview in England, Gordievsky told me that he still does not believe anyone in British intelligence betrayed him. "Mr. Ames is responsible for what happened to me," Gordievsky said. "It cannot be a coincidence that on the day I received my telegram calling me back to Moscow, the KGB paid Mr. Ames fifty thousand in blood money."

Who identified Gordievsky? The debate continues, but few disagree about what fate awaited him if he had not been rescued. Prime Minister Margaret Thatcher ordered MI-6 to keep Gordievsky's escape a secret in July 1985. This is why the CIA did not know that he had been recalled to Moscow and put under house arrest, until Vitaly Yurchenko defected in August and told Rick and other debriefers about Gordievsky. The main reason why Thatcher kept Gordievsky's flight a secret, according to accounts published later in the British press, was that she did not want to embarrass the USSR. Mikhail Gorbachev had been elected general secretary only five months earlier, and Thatcher did not want to hamper his efforts at reform. Her willingness to keep mum, however, did not lessen KGB Chairman Chebrikov's outrage over the escape. He demanded to know how the MI-6 had been able to snatch a KGB *rezident* off a busy street in the center of Moscow in broad daylight when he was under suspicion of being a British spy! Chebrikov asked Kryuchkov for an explanation, and the chief of the First Chief Directorate, in turn, vented his anger at General Grushko. What happened next tells much about how politics work inside the Kremlin. It has never been made public before. It is based on interviews with two retired KGB officers who worked for Kryuchkov. For their own safety, neither will be named.

When the Politburo asked how Gordievsky had escaped, Chairman Chebrikov and Kryuchkov blamed the Second Chief Directorate, the branch of the KGB responsible for maintaining internal security and conducting counterintelligence investigations. The fact that *no one* in the First Chief Directorate had ever told the Second Chief Directorate that Gordievsky was a suspected spy and needed to be investigated was not mentioned. Nor did anyone reveal that it was Grushko's men in the First Chief Directorate who were watching Gordievsky when he escaped.* Politics were at play. In late 1984, it had become obvious in Moscow that Konstantin Chernenko was in failing health and would not be able to continue as the party's general secretary. This had set off a scramble. Even though KGB chairman Chebrikov was a longtime Communist hard-liner, he had correctly recognized that the reform-minded Gorbachev was going to be elected the next general secretary. The KGB threw its weight behind Gorbachev, a fact noted in several newspaper articles at the time and later in books. After Gorbachev was elected, he made Chebrikov a voting member of the Politburo, something he had long wanted. Chebrikov had a total of sixteen directorates and various departments under his supervision as KGB chairman. Each was headed by an ambitious man eager to be his successor. Although Kryuchkov was one of the least popular of all these KGB managers, Gorbachev liked him and Chebrikov was grooming Kryuchkov to succeed him as KGB chairman. It was these connections that saved Kryuchkov and General Grushko from being reprimanded for Gordievsky's flight. In an official report, the Politburo was told that it was the *Second Chief Directorate* whose sloppiness allowed Gordievsky to slip away, even though it had had nothing to do with it.

"Gordievsky's escape was a terrible embarrassment, and it was decided that no other spies would ever be given another opportunity to escape," a retired Kryuchkov aide told me later. Chebrikov and Kryuchkov briefed

---

*At the time, the Seventh Directorate was responsible for surveillance inside the USSR. However, the First Chief Directorate did not tell it about Gordievsky or ask for its help, either.

Gorbachev about Ames. "They did not tell him the real name of Ames. Gorbachev was told that the KGB had successfully planted a mole inside the CIA, and this mole had identified a number of traitors," a former aide to Kryuchkov explained. "The discovery of Mr. Ames showed the CIA and FBI were still continuing to infiltrate and undermine our government."

During the summer of 1985, Vladimir Zaitzev and his fellow Alpha Team members, who had successfully snatched Adolf Tolkachev from his car on June 9, received orders to prepare for a new round of sensitive arrests. It was in the midst of this stewpot that Vitaly Yurchenko defected in Rome.

At least two books have been written about the Yurchenko defection, yet even today FBI and CIA investigators are still debating whether or not he was a genuine defector or part of some clever double agent plot intended to fool the United States and cast suspicion away from Ames. What has always been missing from these debates is the KGB's side. Here is the Soviet version, as told to me by Cherkashin.

On August 1, Cherkashin received an urgent message at the Soviet embassy in Washington, signed personally by Kryuchkov. "He told me Yurchenko had disappeared in Rome and was presumed to have defected." The rest of the cable, Cherkashin recalled, was about possible ways to help protect Ames. Even though Yurchenko had recently helped oversee KGB clandestine operations targeted at the United States and Canada, Kryuchkov wrote in the cable that the defector had not been included in the tightly controlled loop of KGB officers handling Ames. Still, it was possible that Yurchenko might have overheard gossip about him. "Kryuchkov gave me two instructions in the cable," said Cherkashin. "I was to let Ames know that the KGB was ready to help him escape from the United States if he wished. We were prepared to do in Washington what the British had done in Moscow with Gordievsky! Mr. Kryuchkov also instructed me to determine if it was necessary for us to have a special team flown into the U.S. to silence Yurchenko. I understood this message to mean that Kryuchkov was willing to authorize the immediate execution of Yurchenko, even though he was under the protection of the CIA and the United States."

Cherkashin was supposed to contact Ames as quickly as possible, but Ames was busy debriefing Yurchenko and did not meet his KGB contact for lunch until three or four days had passed. "When Ames told us he had been chosen to debrief Yurchenko, it was clear that he [Ames] did not feel in any danger from the defector, so we did not discuss Mr. Kryuchkov's offers of escape and other proposals with him."

Cherkashin said Kryuchkov was badly embarrassed by Yurchenko's defection and that morale in the KGB had slumped. A few weeks later, Yurchenko called Cherkashin on the telephone. "Yurchenko asked me what would happen if he came home to the Soviet Union," Cherkashin recalled. "I contacted Kryuchkov, who told me that we were to tell Yurchenko whatever he wanted to hear. We were to do everything to get him back." Yurchenko's decision on November 2 to redefect was not a spur-of-the-moment act, as it has often been portrayed in the U.S. media, Cherkashin said. "We spoke more than once on the telephone." It was during these calls that Yurchenko first mentioned that he had been kidnapped and drugged by the CIA. "I told him that we understood how evil the CIA could be and that he would receive a hero's welcome if he came back to his motherland. All would be forgiven."

A car was waiting to whisk Yurchenko to the Soviet residential compound as soon as he finished eating with his CIA guard in a Georgetown restaurant. "Androsov and I both kissed and hugged Yurchenko and greeted him as a great hero. Kryuchkov, himself, had approved of this charade." Meanwhile, Yurchenko was surrounded by armed guards. "I said, 'Vitaly Sergeyevich [Yurchenko], these men are here to protect you, because you and I both know the FBI is capable of doing anything—even breaking into our compound or our embassy to try to kidnap you back again.' He thanked me, but Yurchenko knew exactly what was going on," Cherkashin said. "I will now tell you a great secret. On the night that Yurchenko came back to us, I had an order signed by Kryuchkov, himself, giving me the power to have Yurchenko 'commit suicide' if I felt there was any chance that he might try to escape again. He would not have left us alive for a second time."

According to Cherkashin, Yurchenko announced that he was not "returning home with empty hands." Yurchenko told Androsov and Cherkashin that he had learned the name of a KGB traitor. An FBI agent had accidentally revealed that the bureau had recruited a new source who worked in the Soviet embassy.

"I remember thinking: 'What a perfect traitor this man Yurchenko is,'" Cherkashin recalled. "Before he defected, he learned as much valuable information as he could, so he could betray the KGB to his new comrades in the U.S. Now he wishes to come back, so he learns as much as he can about the CIA and FBI and betrays them to us. He made me want to vomit."

I later asked federal investigators if Yurchenko had inadvertently been told during his debriefings the name of a Soviet source. I was told that he had. An FBI agent mistakenly let slip that the bureau had recently recruited an agent known as GLAZING. After Yurchenko returned to Moscow, GLAZING was summoned home, arrested, and interrogated for several days. However, he was eventually released without explanation. He still lives in Moscow, and neither the FBI nor the CIA have any idea why he escaped without being punished. This foul-up during the debriefings has never before been made public. I was told that the FBI agent who endangered GLAZING was not reprimanded. By the time Yurchenko redefected in November 1985, the KGB already knew about GLAZING. Ames had included GLAZING's name on the June 13 list that he provided the KGB.

Cherkashin said he received another urgent cable from Kryuchkov a few hours after Yurchenko voluntarily returned. "I was instructed to pick one officer from each of our four departments to serve as an honor guard for Yurchenko." Cherkashin thought the order was one of the stupidest that he had ever read, until he finished reading the entire message. "It was brilliant. The purpose of the honor guard was to get the CIA spy, Valery Martynov, out of the U.S. without arousing the suspicion of the FBI or CIA. He was going to be one of the honor guards." Kryuchkov was worried that Martynov would defect if he were ordered to return to Moscow. "We did not want to have another Gordievsky-style escape," said Cherkashin. The night before Yurchenko was scheduled to return to the USSR, Cherkashin didn't sleep. "I wasn't worried about Yurchenko. I was worried the FBI would see through our ploy to get Martynov out of the U.S. and back to Moscow. I was afraid they would grab him."

Martynov followed Yurchenko up the portable stairs leading to the Aeroflot flight on November 6. "Martynov had no idea that he would be arrested as soon as the airplane landed at Sheremetyevo airport. We later heard that Kryuchkov was so pleased that he actually gave the other honor guards decorations, even though they didn't do anything!"

According to Cherkashin, Yurchenko was a genuine defector. It is doubtful, however, that his comments will sway those diehards inside the CIA and FBI who continue to believe that Yurchenko was part of some resourceful KGB ruse to protect Ames. "Vitaly Yurchenko . . . is a typical son-of-a-bitch," General Boris Solomatin replied when I asked his opinion. "I don't know of a single proved case of kidnapping of the Soviet people by Americans. . . . It doesn't happen, and not because the American special services consist of only righteous people who would not do such a thing. They simply are afraid that we will retaliate, and they are afraid rightly."

According to Oleg Gordievsky, "The idea that Yurchenko was sent to protect Ames is total nonsense. The KGB would never have let Yurchenko ruin the information that he did in order to protect someone like Ames who, at that point, was in no serious danger."

Yuri Shvets, a former KGB major who worked at the Soviet embassy in Washington when Yurchenko returned to the USSR, told me during an interview, and later wrote in his 1994 book, *Washington Station: My Life As a KGB Spy in America*, that he was told by the KGB officer who interrogated Yurchenko in Moscow that the defector had broken down, confessed, and begged Kryuchkov for forgiveness after he returned home. "Yurchenko's confession was hidden because Kryuchkov wanted the Politburo to believe that Yurchenko was part of some KGB master plot—not that he had fled to the West like so many were doing at the time," Shvets said.

Finally, Ames himself is convinced that Yurchenko was a legitimate defector. "He didn't know anything about me. There was never a knowing wink or comment. The KGB never bragged about how they had sent him to protect me."

If Yurchenko was part of some brilliant plot, he certainly has never been rewarded for the ingenious role he played. Today he lives in a rundown apartment, where he receives a KGB pension that barely provides him with enough rubles to buy food. He refuses interview requests and turns away when approached by Westerners. His neighbors claim that he suffers from depression.

In August 1986, Cherkashin was awarded the prestigious and, up to that point, rarely given Order of Lenin, the second highest award in the Soviet Union. No one was told why, but Cherkashin said later it was because of his role in the Ames case. "Kryuchkov gave out ten Orders of Lenin that day, and minor awards to dozens of other KGB officers," Cherkashin said. Such awards had always been given in private before, because the KGB did not want Western intelligence services wondering why the decorations were being given. "Kryuchkov put on a big show. He wanted everyone in the Kremlin to think the KGB was doing a great job under his leadership." After the ceremony, Cherkashin was informed that he was being reassigned to a desk job in Moscow. He also learned that he would never again be permitted to travel outside the USSR for fear that he might say something that would expose Ames. "I was the first KGB officer to meet this man. It was a high point of my career, and it also destroyed it."

CHAPTER 15

Federal investigators would later look back and try to pinpoint when the CIA should have first realized that something terribly wrong was happening to its Soviet spies. Some would claim that Adolf Tolkachev's arrest in June 1985 should have set off an alarm. Others would argue that the first hint had come when Vitaly Yurchenko announced in August that Oleg Gordievsky had been mysteriously recalled to Moscow. But Ames himself would name September 1985 as the pivotal month. It was when the KGB first tipped its bloody hand.

The first clue surfaced on September 14, during a briefing in SE division chief Burton Lee Gerber's office. Rodney W. Carlson, the head of the SE division's counterintelligence staff, was recounting what he and an FBI agent had learned the night before during a secret meeting with Valery Martynov, GENTILE, the CIA spy operating inside the Soviet embassy. Martynov had told them troubling news. The KGB's *rezident*, Stanislav Androsov, had just returned from a trip to Moscow and had disclosed that a KGB officer had been caught picking up a package left for him by the CIA. Martynov wasn't certain who the officer was, nor where he had been arrested, but Androsov had said the spy had shown up drunk at the dead drop site.

"You're describing WEIGH," Gerber declared suddenly, using the cryptonym given Leonid Poleschuk. "I'm sure of it." Gerber knew Poleschuk liked to drink, and that the CIA had left a package for him on August 2 in Izmaylovskiy Park in Moscow. Gerber called Sandy Grimes into his office. She was Poleschuk's case officer. He told her that Poleschuk might be in trouble. "Damn," she said. Leaving the dead drop had been her idea. She felt sick. She felt responsible. She told herself that her decision had been the right one at the time. She reminded herself that Gerber had made the final call. He had agreed that leaving a dead drop for Poleschuk was the right thing to do. She had merely suggested the drop. But those rationalizations didn't quiet her conscience. "I kept wondering," she said later, "Did I do something wrong? Is it my fault?"

Grimes, blonde and attractive, had joined the agency in 1967 directly out of college, and had risen up the ranks of the male-dominated CIA bureaucracy into a top management slot by working harder, and oftentimes smarter, than many of her male counterparts. Her first contact with Poleschuk had been in the early 1970s, when he was a KGB political intelligence officer stationed in Nepal. Roguishly handsome and a playboy, Poleschuk had provided a few useful tidbits to the agency in return for spending money. Back then, Grimes had been the desk officer in Langley responsible for making certain that the CIA station in Katmandu had enough cash to pay him and that he was issued a package of CIA spy gear when his overseas tour ended. Poleschuk had promised that he would stay in contact, but as soon as he returned to Moscow, he had ditched his spy gear. For more than a decade, the agency had not heard from him, and then in early 1985, he had resurfaced as the head of the KR Line (counterintelligence) at the Soviet embassy in Lagos, Nigeria. As brash as ever, he had walked into the U.S. embassy and volunteered to resume spying. By this time, Grimes was in charge of Soviet–Eastern European operations in Africa, and she had been thrilled by Poleschuk's return. In Katmandu, he had not really had access to many secrets, but his job in counterintelligence made him a highly desired source. The CIA didn't have many sources in Soviet counterintelligence, and Grimes knew Poleschuk's real value was in his potential. After his African tour ended, he undoubtedly would be reassigned to a counterintelligence job in Moscow, where he would be able to provide the agency with vital information.

In May 1985, Poleschuk announced that he was being recalled to Moscow for his annual home leave. Each year the KGB brought its officers back to the USSR for a short vacation. Poleschuk wanted the CIA to pay him some money, but he was nervous about trying to smuggle it into the country. That was when Grimes had suggested delivering $20,000 in rubles to him at a dead drop in Moscow. "Eventually, WEIGH is going to be recalled," she had told Gerber, "and he could really help us there, but not if he dumps all of his gear and we lose contact for another ten years." The dead drop would give the CIA a chance to prove it could operate safely in the Kremlin's back-yard without putting him at risk.

Rick Ames had disagreed with Grimes. He had claimed that leaving a dead drop for Poleschuk was too risky. Grimes had not said anything, but she suspected that Rick was just being petty. In April, she had been promoted to the GS-15 pay grade level, bypassing Rick, whose last promotion had come four years earlier. The move between the GS-14 and GS-15 pay levels was viewed as a critical career step in the agency. Employees who were in their forties, such as Rick, and still stuck at the GS-14 level, understood that their careers had peaked. Grimes had bumped into Rick after her promotion was announced, and he hadn't even whispered a polite congratulations. "Rick, to me, did not have good operational sense," Grimes said later, "and our dis-agreement about Poleschuk was just one more instance where he didn't un-derstand our business. My promotion added fuel to the fire."

SE division chief Gerber and his deputy, Milton Bearden, had agreed with Grimes, and she had instructed an officer in Moscow to go ahead with a dead drop. A ruble-filled fake rock had been left for Poleschuk at a pre-arranged site in Izmaylovskiy Park. As an extra precaution, Grimes had told the Moscow station not to put a message in the delivery. If Poleschuk were caught, she wanted him to be able to argue that he had found the rock by ac-cident or claim that the money was from some other illegal enterprise be-sides espionage. She also told the station not to send anyone to make sure that the rock had been picked up. That simply doubled the chances of a CIA officer getting caught. If Poleschuk didn't get the rock, the $20,000 would stay sitting on the ground.

On October 2, Grimes was given a cable from Moscow that confirmed her worst fears. Poleschuk had been arrested by the KGB while picking up the fake rock. Grimes needed to notify Poleschuk's handler in Africa. "How do you tell someone in writing that your friend, and theirs, has been arrested and is about to face a firing squad?"

SE division chief Gerber reviewed the case alone in his sixth-floor office. *How had the KGB known?* Gerber was fifty-two, tall, thin, reserved, academic in manner, deeply religious. On the walls near his desk were photographs of wolves. He was fascinated by them. The return address labels that he attached to his personal letters had wolves printed on them. So did his favorite necktie. He read about them, took vacation trips to nature preserves to study them, admired their cunning, courage, and resiliency. As a boy growing up in Ohio, Gerber had delivered newspapers and had gotten into the habit of rising early to read the news, although the word "read" really didn't adequately describe what Gerber did: devour. Every story, every detail, every typograpical error, was noted. After baseball, world events were his favorite. At age ten, he decided that he would join the foreign service and live abroad after he grew up. World War II had started when he was thirteen, and Gerber had gone to the library and carefully noted the dates when the United States had gone to war. He deduced that his country called upon its young to fight about every twenty-five years, and he was disappointed because his calculations showed that he would reach draftable age during a period of peace. The CIA gave him what he had wanted: foreign travel and an ongoing battle against communism. He took the loss of Poleschuk personally. The Russian had been one of his troops.

Gerber replayed the last few months in his mind. He was certain that Tolkachev had been betrayed by Edward Lee Howard. He was certain that Operation TAW, the agency's taping of the KGB and GRU's communication lines at Troitsk, also had been betrayed by Howard, because he had been trained to sneak into the communication tunnel and remove the tapes that were used to record conversations. TAW had recently stopped working. But Howard could not have been responsible for Poleschuk's arrest. Howard had been fired in 1983. Poleschuk had reappeared in Africa in early 1985. There was a slim chance that Howard might have learned that Poleschuk had been a spy in the 1970s, but that was unlikely. Old files were kept locked in a vault, and Howard hadn't been authorized to go inside it. If Howard wasn't behind Poleschuk's capture, what, or who, was? The KGB *rezident* had said that Poleschuk had shown up drunk at the dead drop. But Gerber didn't know if that was true. It could be KGB disinformation. Of course, if the KGB *rezident* was intentionally spreading disinformation to his own men, that meant something, too. Surrounded by his photographs of wolves, Gerber considered the whys and pondered the what-ifs.

In October 1985, the SE division received a cable from its station in Lisbon, Portugal, with more bad news. A CIA case officer there had been scheduled to meet, on October 4, with Gennady Smetanin, known by the cryptonym MILLION, but he hadn't shown up. At their last meeting on August 6, Smetanin had said that he was being recalled to Moscow on home leave, but he expected to return in plenty of time for their October 4 rendezvous. Smetanin and his wife, Svetlana, had been spying for the agency since 1983. The agency had dubbed the GRU officer MILLION, because that was how much money he had asked for when he volunteered. When the agency balked, he'd dropped the figure to $360,000. He claimed he needed it because he had embezzled that much from a GRU account and was about to be caught. The agency had paid him the money, but had been suspicious of his story. No one believed that a GRU officer stationed in a small post such as Lisbon could steal $360,000 without it being noticed. Smetanin later admitted that he had been lying. He hadn't stolen any money, he was just trying to get the best price he could for his services.

Again, Gerber studied the case. What had happened to Smetanin? Was the fact that he and Poleschuk had both disappeared during home leaves significant?

In mid-November, another spy vanished, this time in Germany. Gennady Varenik, a KGB officer known as FITNESS, had been seen last by his case officer, Charles Leven, on November 4. They had agreed to meet again later, but Varenik had missed that meeting, and when Leven checked, he had discovered that Varenik's wife and children were gone, too. Leven had met Varenik in April 1985, shortly after the young KGB officer had volunteered to spy. Varenik had embezzled seven thousand dollars and was scared. He had used the money to buy a dress for his wife, new furniture for their apartment, clothes for his daughters, and books for himself. The CIA gave him enough cash to pay back the KGB.

"Varenik told me that the KGB had drawn up contingency plans for a covert operation that, in essence, called for the murder of American soldiers and their families," Leven later recalled. The KGB had sent Varenik to find restaurants near U.S. military bases where it could hide "minibombs." The KGB planned on exploding these bombs when the restaurants were busy, and then blaming the carnage on German terrorists. The Soviets hoped the bombings would upset U.S.–German relations, make it appear as if the U.S. military was no longer welcome in Germany, and remind Germans that they were not safe from terrorist acts. "The idea of killing innocent Americans made Gennady sick," Leven said later. "It wasn't that he was pro-American. He was simply outraged that the KGB was planning on killing innocent men, women, and children."

Leven's reports about the minibomb plot caused a stir in Langley. Several veteran SE division officers doubted the KGB would ever carry out such a "cowboyish covert action." But others argued that the minibomb plot was an example of just how monstrous the KGB could be. "We told the White House about the minibomb plot, and you can imagine how President Reagan and his advisers reacted to it," Ames said later. "It was proof that the Evil Empire still existed."

Leven believed the minibomb plot was real. The CIA had sent officers to several of the restaurants where Varenik claimed the bombs would be placed. "All of the information he had told us was accurate," Leven said.

Besides the minibomb plot, Varenik claimed that three top members of the West German government were actually KGB moles. "Gennady gave us a wealth of information about the KGB operations in Germany. He wanted to do as much damage as he could to the KGB," Leven said. "He had come to hate it."

In October, Varenik had contacted Leven in a panic. He felt certain the KGB was about to activate its minibomb operation. "Gennady said, 'I don't know what to do. We have to stop this.' He said, 'If you want me to defect, I'll do that and go public.' But I told him not to do that just yet, to sit tight, and let us monitor the situation," Leven later recalled. On November 4, Leven met Varenik at a hastily called meeting in a CIA safe house. "Gennady said he was being sent to East Berlin to be briefed about the minibomb plot. We were both really nervous about what might happen next." The two men agreed to meet as soon as Varenik returned from East Berlin and felt it was safe. Leven had waited for a signal, but none ever came. Now he was afraid Varenik had been arrested and his family hustled back to Moscow.

In a cable to Leven, Gerber asked if Varenik had noticed anything odd happening at the KGB *rezidency*. Leven recalled that Varenik had told him that the KGB *rezident* in Bonn had been called to Moscow unexpectedly in September, but that Varenik did not notice any change in him when he returned.

Gerber made himself a note. The KGB's *rezident* in Washington had told his men about Poleschuk after returning in *September* from Moscow. The KGB's *rezident* in Bonn had been called back to Moscow in *September*, too. Was this significant or a meaningless coincidence? Gerber had three missing agents. He was absolutely certain now that Howard could not be blamed for all of them. Varenik had only been a spy for eight months. Howard couldn't have known about him. *There had to be another explanation.*

In another area of the CIA's complex, Gardner "Gus" Hathaway, head of the CIA's counterintelligence division, was reaching the same conclusion as Gerber about Varenik's disappearance. He was also asking himself the same question: *If not Howard, then who, or what was to blame?* At age sixty, Hathaway had spent nearly forty years working exclusively in Soviet–Eastern European operations. He'd never been interested in any other area. It was Hathaway who had insisted that the agency meet Tolkachev, and he had been the station chief in Moscow who had warned FEDORA that he was in danger. Inside the agency, Hathaway was famous for single-handedly stopping a squad of KGB officers, posing as firemen, from entering the CIA's most sensitive communication area in the U.S. embassy in Moscow during a 1970s fire. Everyone else had run to safety, but Hathaway had blocked the doorway and refused to move when the ax-carrying fake firemen appeared. Hathaway never spoke to the media. Still, his name had surfaced periodically over the years in articles and books. He was always described as having an "aristocratic" presence, an "acerbic" wit.

Hathaway and Gerber began comparing notes, exchanging ideas. The Christmas holidays and the new year brought both men more bad news. In mid-December, the agency confirmed that Gennady Smetanin, MILLION, and his wife, Svetlana, had been arrested. They had been dragged off a train in handcuffs while returning to Moscow from a relative's house. The KGB would later claim that it had found forty-four diamonds sewn inside the leather belt that Svetlana was wearing. In January 1986, the agency confirmed that Varenik also had been arrested on November 4 when he had crossed into East Berlin.

Hathaway and Gerber agreed that it was time for action. In January 1986, Gerber told Sandy Grimes about the losses. He also told her that the agency had just recruited two new agents in Eastern Europe. "I'm putting you in charge of keeping these two men alive," he said. Gerber explained that he wanted her to handle the new spies personally. She would deal directly with the case officers in Eastern Europe who were meeting the agents face to face. She would report directly to Gerber. There was no need to tell anyone else in the division about the new recruits. She could choose one person to help her. Without hesitating, Grimes said she wanted Diana Worthen to work with her. Gerber wasn't surprised. He knew the two women had been part of a similar "back room" operation in the 1970s, run out of a corner office on the fifth floor. Employees were told the office was just another secretarial pool where clerks typed, filed, and shuffled paperwork, but its real function had been to support TOPHAT, Dmitri Polyakov. The GRU general was sending the agency so many Soviet military secrets that it couldn't keep up. Gerber liked the idea of pairing Grimes and Worthen. If word leaked out inside the agency that Grimes was handling a new spy, everyone would assume the agent was someone in Africa, not Eastern Europe, because Grimes was the African branch chief. Worthen worked in counterintelligence (CI), and CI employees rarely handled spies in the field. "The security that Gerber, Grimes, and Worthen put in place was really draconian," one of their bosses later recalled. "There was no way that those two women were going to let anyone find out the names of the new recruits."

Director Casey also was briefed in January. Hathaway, Gerber and his deputy, Milton Bearden, and Clair George, the chief of covert operations, told him that agents were disappearing and being arrested and no one was sure why. "What the hell are you doing about it?" he demanded. They were investigating to see if the KGB had found a way to intercept CIA communications, Casey was told. It seemed like a logical step. After all, the CIA had managed to tap into the KGB and GRU's communications lines in Operation TAW. Said a CIA officer later: "The thinking was, 'Hey, if we did it, then they probably have, too.'"

Casey decided to launch his own investigation. He asked John H. Stein to look into the losses. Stein was an old hand when it came to Soviet–Eastern European operations. He had been the SE division chief and the deputy director of operations, and was just completing a stint as the CIA's inspector general, an appointment that had put him in charge of ferreting out waste, fraud, and abuse in the agency. Stein asked Casey when he expected him to finish his investigation. "Yesterday," Casey replied.

A series of key events unfolded with breathtaking speed during the next few months.

- In February 1986, the agency learned that the KGB had stopped a westbound train on the Trans-Siberian railroad on January 24, and seized a cargo container filled with electronic sensors. Operation ABSORB had been exposed.*

*The KGB would later tell me that it had profited handsomely from ABSORB. Not only did it seize the CIA's advanced technology, but it managed to extort $500,000 from the Japanese company that had agreed to ship the CIA's fake cargo container to Hamburg, Germany. The KGB threatened to accuse the Japanese company of being a CIA front unless it paid it $500,000 in hush money, which it did, according to the KGB.

- On March 10, the KGB ambushed CIA case officer Michael Sellers while he was en route to a meeting with a spy known as COWL. The CIA did not know COWL's name, because he had never told it to Sellers, but it later learned that COWL was Sergey Vorontsov, a KGB officer assigned to the local Moscow KGB office. Ironically, it was the Soviets who revealed Vorontsov's true name. After Sellers was declared persona non grata and expelled, the Soviet government sent a letter of protest to the State Department and identified Vorontsov as the spy Sellers had been going to meet. Vorontsov had been a spy since 1984, and had told the CIA about how the local KGB watched the U.S. embassy in Moscow. In a meeting in 1985, Vorontsov gave Sellers samples of spy dust, the chemical that the KGB was spraying into U.S. embassy cars to help the KGB keep track of its occupants.
- In mid-March, a spy known as VILLAGE was ordered to return to Moscow from his station in Surabaja, Indonesia. Once he crossed the border, he was not heard from again.

In late March, an anonymous letter writer contacted the CIA with an offer to help. A CIA case officer in Bonn, Germany, found a letter tucked in his mail box written by someone who claimed he could tell the CIA why Gennady Varenik had been caught—in return for $50,000. The writer identified himself as a KGB officer and said he had been friends with Varenik. To prove that he was telling the truth, he wrote in his letter that Charles Leven was the CIA officer who had been handling Varenik. Leven was working undercover as a State Department employee at the time, and no one was supposed to know about him and Varenik. The writer also hinted that the KGB had found a way to intercept CIA's messages. Under *no* circumstances, he wrote, should his letter be mentioned or sent to CIA headquarters "by electronic means."

The Bonn case officer sent the letter by courier to CIA headquarters, where it was studied by Hathaway, Gerber, and Paul Redmond, Jr., who had replaced Rodney Carlson as the head of the counterintelligence group inside the SE division.* The three men dubbed the letter writer Mr. X, and quickly agreed to pay him $50,000. A case officer in Berlin was told to deliver the cash to a site in East Berlin that was described in the letter. A few days later,

---

*Hathaway was in charge of the CIA's counterintelligence staff. Redmond was chief of the counterintelligence staff *within* the SE division. Although their interests regularly overlapped, these were two separate staffs.

another letter arrived. This time, Mr. X gave them specifics. He said the KGB was electronically intercepting CIA cables that were being sent overseas through the agency's secret communications center in Warrenton, Virginia. He also accused Charles Leven of pocketing money that the agency had given him for Varenik. Once again, Mr. X asked for $50,000 and offered in the future to tell them more specifics. There was a mole at the Warrenton facility, Mr. X added, as a teaser.

Mr. X's claim that the KGB was electronically intercepting CIA cables sounded real to Gerber, Hathaway, and Redmond. Most of the agency's messages went through the Warrenton center, and if the KGB had found a way to read those messages, then it could have learned the identities of the spies. But Mr. X's accusations against Leven seemed absurd. Leven had worked for Gerber in Moscow, and Gerber trusted him. So did Hathaway. The accusation made Redmond suspicious of Mr. X. "The KGB had sent us similar notes in previous cases, and it always put something nasty about our case officers in them," Redmond said later. Mr. X's accusation against Leven had done more damage to Mr. X's credibility than to Leven's reputation. Even so, the three men agreed that Leven should be questioned and Mr. X paid.

While they were waiting for Mr. X to respond, Redmond decided to run a test of the Warrenton communications center. He arranged for two messages to be sent overseas. The first cable was sent through the communications center to the CIA station chief in Nairobi. It said that Gerber's deputy, Milton Bearden, would be arriving there soon to recruit a specific KGB officer. Several weeks later, a cable was sent from Nairobi to CIA headquarters, announcing that Bearden had successfully recruited the KGB officer as a CIA spy. Redmond's second cable was sent from headquarters through the Warrenton facility to the Moscow station. It disclosed that the CIA had successfully recruited a KGB officer stationed in Bangkok. Redmond's cables were untrue. The agency had not recruited either KGB officer. But if the KGB was intercepting the CIA's messages, Redmond figured that both KGB officers would be immediately recalled to Moscow for interrogation. He sat back and waited. "I had chosen two KGB officers who were not nice guys at all, and I hoped, quite frankly, that if the KGB was reading our mail, that it would arrest these guys and their careers would be ruined," said Redmond. Nothing happened. The officers were not called back to Moscow.

Mr. X sent the agency a total of six letters during 1986, and in each, he would repeat his claim that the KGB was reading the agency's cables. But by the fall of 1986, Redmond's test was complete, and Gerber and Hathaway were convinced that Mr. X was a fraud, albeit an expensive one.

Meanwhile, the agency had received more bad news. On May 7, Erik Sites, who was identified as a U.S. embassy attaché, was arrested while trying to meet a CIA spy whose cryptonym was EASTBOUND. The CIA would not learn until several years later that EASTBOUND had been a "dangle," a KGB officer who had volunteered to spy specifically to entrap a CIA officer and pass along bad information.

"What the hell is going on in Moscow?" an angry Casey demanded, after Sites was declared persona non grata and booted out of the USSR. It had been four months since he had been told about the 1985 losses, and no one seemed to know any more now than in January. Casey pushed John Stein to hurry up his investigation. A short time later, Stein delivered his ten-page study. He concluded that each of the cases that he had reviewed had contained "the seeds of its own destruction." The losses, he said, did not appear to be related. Some were caused by Edward Lee Howard, others by mistakes made by CIA case handlers or the spies themselves. There was no evidence of any electronic penetration of the agency, or of a much feared mole, Stein wrote.

Stein's report didn't convince Hathaway, Gerber, or Redmond. In May, Hathaway sent a cable to Jeanne Vertefeuille, the station chief in Libreville, the capitol of Gabon in West Africa. Her tour there was scheduled to end in June, and he informed her that he had a special assignment waiting as soon as she returned. Vertefeuille liked and admired Hathaway, and she immediately agreed to accept whatever job he wished, but a number of problems forced her to extend her tour until late October.

Federal investigators would later criticize Hathaway and the agency for waiting for Vertefeuille before launching a formal investigation of the losses. The five months between Hathaway's cable to Vertefeuille and her arrival at Langley, however, were not the main reason the CIA's top managers did not pay as much attention to the 1985 losses as they should have. A few weeks before Vertefeuille's return to headquarters, a Nicaraguan soldier fired a surface-to-air missile at a low flying C-123 cargo airplane. It was a direct hit. The airplane crashed. The lone survivor, Eugene Hasenfus, appeared at a press conference four days later in Managua, and revealed that he had been delivering weapons to contra rebels trying to overthrow the Sandinista government. His flight had been financed, he said, by the CIA. Congress was outraged. It had imposed a two-year ban on supplying aid to the rebels, and it immediately suspected that the White House and Director Casey had circumvented the law. The agency came under siege. This event immediately pushed all other emergencies off Director Casey's desk.

Meanwhile, Hathaway, Gerber, Redmond, and Vertefeuille, who had recently arrived, continued to monitor the KGB's actions in Moscow. On October 22, Tass announced grim news: "The CIA spy, Adolf G. Tolkachev, has been executed." The killing of the agency's human assets in Moscow had begun.

That same month, the CIA learned that Sergey Motorin, GAUZE, and Valery F. Martynov, GENTILE, both were in prison. They had been arrested in August 1985—*more than one year earlier*. Motorin was the KGB officer whom the FBI had blackmailed into becoming a spy; Martynov was the CIA's spy inside the Soviet embassy who had returned to Moscow as part of an honor guard chosen to accompany Vitaly Yurchenko home. *Why had the KGB kept their arrests secret?* At one point, the KGB had arranged for Motorin to telephone his girlfriend in Washington, D.C., from Moscow. The FBI had been monitoring that call and had heard Motorin assure her that he was fine. Obviously, the telephone call had been part of a KGB ruse. "The KGB was clearly trying to keep us from learning about something that had happened in 1985," Redmond said later.

In November 1986, Vertefeuille began meeting with the members of her special task force. All of them had been chosen by Hathaway. His choices were: Fran Smith, Benjamin Franklin Pepper, and Daniel R. Niesciur. Smith was a veteran SE officer. Pepper had retired several years earlier and was best known for being the leading opponent in the 1960s to James Angleton's paranoid theories. Niesciur, who had recently retired, was the author of a comprehensive study of Larry Wu-Tai Chin, a CIA mole who had spied for the communists for nearly thirty years.

Paul Redmond, Jr., was delighted that Hathaway had appointed a task force to investigate what were now being called "the 1985 losses," but he was frustrated with the pace at which the agency was moving. He was also worried that Casey and his top lieutenants were so preoccupied with the developing Iran-Contra scandal that they were not paying enough attention to the bloodletting in Moscow. "Redmond is not a detail person," a former CIA colleague said later. "His contribution to the agency has been and always will be his willingness to stand up and demand that something be done. He's not afraid of anyone, and he loves to lead charges." Redmond decided it was time to lead a charge. He drafted a memo for Casey. "The KGB is wrapping up our cases with reckless abandon," he declared. "Forty-five Soviet and East European cases" have been jeopardized.

Redmond's memo didn't contain any new information. It simply recapitulated and highlighted what he, Gerber, and Hathaway had been discussing for months. But Redmond infused it with the fire and outrage of a Bible-beating evangelist. He also went on record saying that he suspected the agency had been penetrated by a mole. Redmond sent his memo to SE division chief Gerber for his approval and comments. Gerber told Redmond to tone it down. Redmond had cited several old cases in his memo, dating back to the 1970s and TRIGON. Gerber suggested that he focus only on agents who had been compromised since 1985. Redmond made himself a list.

1. SPHERE   Adolf Tolkachev

2. TICKLE   Oleg Gordievsky

3. WEIGH   Leonid Poleschuk

4. MILLION   Gennady and Svetlana Smetanin

5. Operation TAW

6. FITNESS   Gennady Varenik

7. Operation ABSORB

8. COWL   Sergey Vorontsov

9. VILLAGE

10. EASTBOUND

11. GENTILE   Valery Martynov

12. GAUZE   Sergey Motorin

By his count, ten agents had been arrested and, he assumed, would soon be executed. That was outrageous! He didn't know of another case in agency history where so many agents had been caught. He sent a revised memo to Gerber and in it he once again warned that there could be a mole burrowed in the CIA.

Gerber read and reread Redmond's memo. He agreed with what Redmond was saying. That was part of the reason why he had instituted stringent safeguards to protect the SE division's new agents. But talk about a mole also made Gerber nervous. He did not want the CIA to become engulfed in another agency-wrecking, James Jesus Angleton witch hunt. This time if there was going to be a mole hunt, Gerber was determined to make certain that the mole was identified without the reputations of innocent employees being destroyed. Gerber suggested a few minor changes to Redmond's memo and then forwarded it up the chain of command. Both men waited for a reaction. None came.

In December, Casey suffered a scizure while working in his office and collapsed. Doctors discovered a malignant tumor in his brain and hospitalized him. His deputy, Robert M. Gates, was appointed acting director. He would later testify that he was never told how serious the 1985 losses were.

THE WORDS OF RICK AMES

[CIA Director R. James] *Woolsey has called me a "serial killer" and compared me to Benedict Arnold. First let me address the "serial killer" charge. I did not execute anyone, did I? And if our courts had retained capital punishment for espionage, a number of the agents whom I betrayed would have had blood on their hands, too! Would Woolsey have called Polyakov a serial killer?*

His comments about Benedict Arnold are more fascinating. As someone who tries to distinguish history from legend, folklore and official myth, let me comment, knowing, of course, that I have read both of Kenneth Roberts's excellent novels, Arundel *and* Rabble in Arms, *which have long been taken as the definitive portraits of Arnold. I can only assume that Woolsey no doubt heard something about Arnold somewhere and rushed to make the comparison, because it doesn't fit.*

Arnold promised to betray West Point for money and position, and although the betrayal of West Point failed, he did profit handsomely. I also profited handsomely, though temporarily. This analogy ultimately fails, however, on several levels.

Arnold was fed up [and] embittered, and dissented from the bulk of his political and military leaders. In fact, he felt persecuted, and probably was. In those circumstances, in those times, national and institutional loyalties had not hardened into law, tradition, myth, and orthodoxy. A man who dissented from the Revolution could see himself morally and ethically free to choose sides, even to change them, though perhaps not for personal gain. The cause of independence had become the War of Independence and Arnold had come to believe that those conducting the revolution did not deserve to win it and that he would no longer support them, so he chose to switch sides.

Now let's look at my case. My immediate motivation to con the Soviets was purely financial, but my choice in mid-June showed and foreshadowed a more complex mixture of motives. The fact that I could even conceive of the con game that I implemented demonstrates a striking inhibition, and one must wonder: what were some of the elements—beyond a midlife crisis and a new wife— which prompted such eagerness? Obviously I did not feel persecuted, as Arnold did, but I had come to believe that most of my leaders were engaged in folly and were carrying out this folly in spectacularly incompetent ways. The basic folly, of course, was the demagoguery of the Cold War and the corruption or misuse of the intelligence process. In some strange way, I, just like Arnold, came to believe that I had the personal right to make these judgments—that I understood these things better than my leaders—and having reached this point, I acted upon those feelings and accepted the risk—just as he had. The quality of my betrayal was fundamentally more radical than Arnold's. Arnold took up arms against the government and nascent country, which trusted him, and plotted to turn over the strategic West Point to help the British win the war and crush the Revolution, with surely great loss of life among his soldiers. In my case, I am convinced that American autonomy, safety, and interests were not at hazard, nor were American lives. Tremendous harm was inflicted upon a relatively few people, a responsibility I cannot deny or evade, and many felt great pain and anguish over it all. But to put it starkly, we were not at war, despite the decades of hype and lies.

I'd like to go off on a sidelight here. Nathan Hale is the official patron saint of the CIA. It is his statue that stands out front. But within the culture, dating back to the earliest days in the agency, the true fascination and admiration is not for Hale but for Major John Andre—the British officer who handled Benedict Arnold. He was later captured and hanged after Arnold's escape. Within the agency, Hale is considered to be a bit of a wimp, but admiration for Andre—the case officer rather than the spy—is almost unbounded. The fact that he was an English gentleman helped, but I think there are deeper and more significant roots for this adulation. Having been both a case officer and a spy, I can tell you clearly that there is a difference in attitudes toward both roles. The agency's leadership, as opposed to the rank and file, has consistently denigrated and despised the spy. One of Allen Dulles's favorite lines was Sir Francis Walsingham's line about how he had gone out and "hired a low fellow" to spy. Meanwhile, Andre is described as the model of professionalism.

To me, this is a comment about the inherent depravity of espionage. All of us, in truth, detest a traitor, no matter how he sugarcoats his treason or justifies his betrayal or—in the case of those who help us as agents—how our coun-

try glorifies him. The truth is that the man whom we really admire is the one who convinces another to betray his own country—not the one who actually commits the treason.

THE WORDS OF OTHERS

My husband was a good father; honest, kind, strong. We met in a theater and fell in love at first sight. He was handsome. Our wedding took place in the summer of 1970. I was a teacher. He was an officer of that special agency. Unlike so many in his service, he did not drink, smoke, or go out with other women. He loved to read adventure stories—Jack London. In 1980 we had our first daughter. Our life was beautiful. There was so much love. We were excited when the KGB said he was being sent to Germany in January 1982. His father was an important man in the KGB, and he wanted to please him. In Bonn, my husband worked himself to exhaustion each day but the others in his secret group—hah—they goofed off and laughed at him. Our second daughter was born there, but things were extremely difficult. There was not much money for clothing, even for food. I didn't mind, but he was worried that he was not providing enough for his family, and he became depressed. He found a German who agreed to help him with information, but this man was really a German spy, and my husband was afraid that we would all be sent back to Moscow in disgrace. He told me he was going to an important meeting in East Berlin in November 1985, and later that day, one of his coworkers came to me with a note from my husband saying I should take our children and come immediately to Moscow. We grabbed a few things and left, but I had forgotten my passport, and when I returned to our apartment, the KGB officers were searching it and wouldn't let me in. In Moscow, they told me he had been arrested for smuggling, but that I didn't need to worry because his father would protect him.

—Gennady Varenik's wife

My son did not betray our motherland. Yes, he told the agents of the CIA about the plot to put bombs in the places frequented by Americans, but I do not believe he gave them anything that damaged our nation. I retired from the KGB. I was decorated in the Great Patriotic War. Later, I was responsible for suppressing dissidents and interrogating spies. I did my job well, and my conscience is clear. My son said to me before he left for Germany, "I will take re-

venge on the fascists for the twenty million people who perished in the war!" But I never wanted him to follow in my footsteps. He was always too trusting, too sincere, too scrupulous. He romanticized about it too much from reading too many novels. Romantics are the first to fail in the line of duty. You must be a hard man to work in intelligence, and my son was a dreamer. Once he told me about problems with his boss in Germany—how this man sent him to take his wife shopping and running errands. He told me that his colleagues were drunks. I told him that he should not talk about such things. The people must always believe the KGB is filled with strong men. Yes, these men can sometimes be hard, but the people will only respect men if they fear them. He was wrong to turn to the wolves of the CIA. They used him. He was a boy, really, a good boy who made a mistake. Had he been in any other profession, the penalty would not have been so great. A few years in prison, and he would have been free. But in the KGB? They had to show they were strong men.

—Gennady Varenik's father

His father was in the KGB, and he had wanted to please him, but he had become disillusioned. Many of his colleagues were promoted because of reports they wrote based on what they saw on television or made up. We were the same age, but his life was completely different from mine. We had long talks, trusted each other, became friends. My wife and I had tried for a long time to have a baby, and when we finally did and he heard about it, he gave me a gold medallion. "This is for your son," he said. "Someday tell him who it is from." When I heard about his arrest, I couldn't sleep for three months. I kept thinking, Did I do something wrong? I wondered about his daughters and wife, but I was afraid to contact them. I came back to CIA headquarters after he was executed, and I remember Rick Ames coming into my office and the two of us talking about the losses. He could tell how upset I was. I told him that I would never find any peace until I knew what had happened to Gennady—who had betrayed him. I remember Rick just looking at me. He didn't say a word.

—Gennady Varenik's CIA handler

This man was a traitor. Why romanticize him? He was a nobody. We did not find any real basis to suppose that he had committed this treason for ideological reasons. Of course at the trial, he spoke about this alleged plot to kill U.S. servicemen and about corruption in the KGB. What would you expect him to say? The law was very clear about his fate. I am proud of the job that I did and shed no tears for this traitor.

—KGB investigator

They would not give him the packages I took with me to Lefortovo prison. He looked like a dead man when I was allowed to see him. His face was pale and he mumbled. I tried to fight back the tears, but I couldn't. I told the children that their father had died in an airplane crash. I told them that he was a soldier and that he had jumped out of the plane with a parachute. I said, "Maybe he did not die and is in a faraway country where he misses us, writes letters every day, but for some reason, the letters don't reach us." During our last visit, he told me that he never did harm to his homeland, only the KGB. They didn't let us attend the trial. We received a letter saying he had been executed on February 25, 1987, but it is possible he is still alive. Isn't it? This has happened in some cases before. I can never marry another man. I am a Russian woman, and once we fall in love it cannot happen again. I want to believe he will come home. So much has changed. Our daughters are grown. He missed those years but I will tell him about them. I will tell him how difficult it was to live here without him. How good it is to have him back with me. We will laugh about our sorrows. Once he returns, we will be able to go on with our lives. We will still have our final years together—once he comes home.

—Gennady Varenik's wife

(written with help from Ilya Milstein,

editor of *Ogoniok* magazine)

CHAPTER 16

IN ROME, 1986–1987

How did Rick Ames explain the money? By July 1986, he had spent the $50,000 that "Robert from Chicago" had "loaned" him, yet he still had plenty of cash. "I told Rosario that my friend, Robert, and his associates were going to invest lots of money in Europe, and since we were about to leave for Rome, they had decided to pay me a commission to watch their investments," Ames said.

Years later, Rosario would repeat the same story as her husband about the generous Robert from Chicago. "Rick's explanation didn't sound weird at all. .... I know tons of people in Colombia who make their living from investments and making commissions," she said.

The Ameses insisted in interviews with me that Rosario had never showed any curiosity during their marriage about the source of Rick's cash. She had never asked for details about Robert from Chicago, had never asked Rick to tell her Robert's last name, had never wondered why Robert had never visited, had never sent a Christmas card, a letter, or even telephoned. Nor had Rosario ever questioned why her husband did not report his "commissions" on their joint income tax returns, which she signed, even though these earnings exceeded his CIA salary by tens of thousands of dollars. The federal agents who interrogated Rick and Rosario thought their story about Robert was concocted and that both of them were lying about how much Rosario knew. So did most of their close friends and even members of their own families when I interviewed them. By July 1986, a new side of Rosario's personality had started to emerge. Gone was the sweet innocence. She was more demanding, more dominating. The idea that she would blindly accept the Robert from Chicago explanation seemed preposterous to those who knew them well. It seemed equally preposterous that anyone would hire Ames to oversee millions of dollars of foreign investments, since he had no experience, had never shown any previous interest in investments, and had managed his own finances so poorly that he had gotten himself heavily in debt.

None of this, of course, means that Ames told Rosario the truth about his income. But few would later believe that she was as naive as she claimed. Diana Worthen, who was still close friends with Rick and Rosario in 1986, would later offer this explanation. "I think Rosario probably asked Rick about the money, and he brushed her off in such a way that she knew not to ask anything more. Rather than pushing for the truth and possibly hearing something that she didn't want to hear, she just decided to keep quiet, and started spending and enjoying the money."

Spend and enjoy they did.

Once they landed in Rome on July 22, 1986, neither Rick nor Rosario made any attempt to hide their affluence. Rosario replaced her entire wardrobe. She charged such large amounts during one all-day shopping spree that the bank which had issued the Ameses a credit card called Rome to ask Rick if someone had stolen his charge plate and was trying to steal as much as possible before the account was closed. Rosario's closets overflowed with designer dresses from Rome's best boutiques. The most dramatic transformation, however, was in Rick's appearance. Gone were the tattered J. C. Penney navy blazers, the polyester gray slacks and socks bought at half price. Now Rick favored $1,500 custom tailored Italian silk suits with monogrammed shirts and hand-sewn leather shoes. His teeth, which were yellow from years of smoking, were capped. His old thick black glasses frames were discarded. He began wearing his hair cut stylishly. He drove an Alfa Romeo sports car, wore a Rolex. He and Rosario dined in Rome's finest restaurants; their telephone bills alone topped $5,000 per month, because of Rosario's daily chats with her mother in Bogotá. They spent their weekends sightseeing, always traveling first class, staying only in Europe's most elegant hotels.

From the start in Rome, Rosario alienated most of Rick's coworkers. She had taken one look at the apartment their predecessor had rented and had declared: "I'm not going to live here!" It was located on the outskirts of the city in an apartment complex similar to those found in the States, and it was where most other embassy employees lived. "This is so typical of Americans," she complained, after inspecting the unit. "They move to a foreign country and immediately find a place that is as close as possible to what they left behind." Rosario rented an apartment in Velabro, a chic older section of downtown Rome near the Roman Forum. The CIA paid for new carpet and had all the rooms painted. Rosario finished the decorating. It looked elegant, expensive.

Rick and Rosario were invited to a station party one night. Rosario didn't think much of the other women there. Several were working as secretaries at the embassy because they couldn't work anywhere else in Rome.

"Are you interested in a secretarial position?" someone asked.

"Certainly not!" Rosario snapped. "I was the cultural attaché and assistant to the ambassador in Mexico City. I'm used to having secretaries, not being one." It was one of several icy remarks she made that night. Afterward, Rick gently chided her for being "haughty."

"I'm not haughty," she fired back. "My friends come from all sorts of social levels, but what do I have in common with these American women?" Most of them were mothers, she said. She didn't have children. Most of them "get their thrills shopping at the U.S. commissary for frozen American pizza." She was a gourmet cook. Years later, Rosario would complain that she had never been accepted by the wives of other embassy employees in Italy because, in her own words, "I didn't wear sneakers or dress in a sweat suit all day. I knew I didn't fit into the U.S. embassy community in Rome, and quite frankly I didn't want to." Rosario had not come to Italy to live like an American or worry about promoting her husband's career. "In Rome, I found out that I was *just* the wife of somebody," she said later, "and that was not me! The American wives don't really participate in anything, especially at the first secretary rank where Rick was working—he never got invitations to go anywhere."

Rosario set out to find her own social circle. "I just got into a taxi and told the driver to take me to the Italian foreign ministry, and I walked in and told them I wanted to join the club for diplomats' wives." The women in charge were shocked. "They said, 'Oh you must be from the Colombian embassy,' and I said, 'No, my husband is an American diplomat,' and they couldn't believe it—first because I spoke Italian, and no other American wives had bothered to learn the language—and because no one from my husband's rank had ever joined before." Rosario soon became a regular at the club meetings, and friends with the wives of several ambassadors. "What social life we had in Rome was because of me, not Rick," she bragged. "He never wanted to do anything." The fact that her husband held a much lower job than most of the husbands of the other women in the club didn't bother Rosario. "His job was *his* problem. His rank was funny to most of them. Of course, their normal mixing would be with people who were further up in the diplomatic ranks, but these were the educated and wealthy people with whom I'd always associated, and, of course, they accepted me without any question."

Rosario began hosting lunches at her apartment, and she rekindled her Colombian contacts. When Julio Cesar Turbay Ayala arrived in Italy as Colombia's new ambassador to the Vatican, it was Rosario who hosted a reception at her apartment welcoming him. Turbay was the former Colombian president who had appointed her to be cultural attaché. She felt indebted. "He asked me if I would teach him Italian, so I began going to the ambassador's residence very often in the afternoons on the pretext of teaching him Italian, but really just to have tea with him and his wife."

The whirlwind that Rosario was causing in Rome's diplomatic circles didn't go unnoticed. One night a jealous wife of a top aide to U.S. ambassador Maxwell M. Rabb confronted Rosario at a reception held in the New Zealand embassy. "This woman comes running over to me and says, 'What the hell are you doing here?'" Rosario later claimed. "So I told her the name of my friend from New Zealand, and explained that she had invited me. I said, 'Is that so hard for you to understand?' Later this same woman comes over and says to me, 'Are you enjoying yourself being around all these blond Anglo-Saxons?' She was terribly offensive and racist, but there was nothing she could do about me being there."

Rick thought it might help Rosario's image if they gave a party for his coworkers and their spouses. He also wanted her to meet Alan D. Wolfe, the CIA chief of station, and his deputy chief, John P. Gower. The party was a disaster. Wolfe liked to swear and he told several raucous jokes that night.

"I don't think there is anyone more coarse and uncivilized in all of Rome than Alan Wolfe," Rosario complained to Rick, after their guests had gone. "He came here, got drunk, and spilled stuff all over my carpet. He was disgusting." Rosario thought Rick's coworkers were drab and vulgar. "CIA employees fit a certain mold," she said later. "They all had really bad taste, they dressed badly, and they fit the stereotype of the ugly American. . . . Rick accused me of intimidating the people he worked with. I guess I came across as being too snobbish or too intellectual at these little parties that I had to go to with him—his branch or whatever it was called—but so what? One of his coworkers asked me if there were any horses in Colombia? I mean, really. We're in the middle of the Amazon. Yes, there are horses. I can't be blamed for not finding much to discuss with such people."

Rosario began whining. "The myth that Rick was going to take care of me quickly began to crumble in Rome," she said. "If I wanted something, I had to find it. If I wanted to have a party, I had to do it. . . . I had to prod him to do the least little things." She began to think of him as "someone who was turning into an old man."

When David Samson visited them in Rome, he noticed uncomfortable silences and flashes of anger. "At times, Rosario would treat Rick with complete contempt, and it was unpleasant to be around them." Rick and Rosario's friends from New York, David and Angela Blake, also were startled during a 1986 visit. "Our first surprise was the obvious wealth. It was staggering. We both assumed Rosario had money," David Blake said, "either that or the CIA was paying for all this as some sort of cover story for Rick." The Blakes noticed something else. "When they were first married, there had been a certain puppy-dog quality to Rick's relationship with Rosario," Angela Blake said. "He was constantly lighting her cigarettes, bringing her drinks, waiting on her. Rosario also was attentive to him, and seemed to want to do things for Rick, but in Rome, she was constantly belittling and criticizing him. We began to notice that she was forever talking about herself, and she had a real disdain for other people. It was an aspect of her character that we simply hadn't seen before."

Rick always defended Rosario. "She's a bit high-strung," he'd say at a party whenever she was rude, or he would joke about how she was a "hot-blooded Latin." For her birthday that year, he organized a surprise party at her favorite restaurant. He invited the Colombian ambassador and his wife, and four other couples. Rick paid cash when he was brought the bill. Rosario told him the surprise party was the most romantic thing that he had ever done for her. But her admiration didn't last. A few days later, she accused him of caring more about his job than he did about her, when an emergency at the embassy made him fifteen minutes late for dinner.

"You're always apologizing," she told him, "but you don't mean it or you'd stop doing these things that irritate me."

The next day, he brought her flowers. He hated confrontations. Besides, he had more pressing problems. Before they moved to Rome, he had heard about the 1985 losses. "Unlike everyone else, I knew what was going on and I thought, *What the hell is the KGB doing? It's going to get me caught.*" The KGB had given Rick a note in Washington, D.C., telling him that VLAD would meet him in Rome on October 20, outside a pharmacy near the Piazza Re di Roma. Rick got there early and was upset. He had spotted blood in his urine about an hour before their meeting. His father had died of cancer, and Rick was sure he had it, too. He didn't mention his problem to VLAD, but he kept thinking about it, and he didn't pay as close attention as usual to what VLAD was saying.

VLAD showed Rick a photograph of Aleksey Khrenkov, the officer from the Soviet ministry of foreign affairs who was assigned to the Soviet embassy in Rome. He had been chosen to be Rick's new go-between. VLAD suggested that Rick and Khrenkov begin meeting for lunch. "Perhaps you will tell your CIA bosses that you are trying to recruit him," VLAD said. Rick nodded. Khrenkov would introduce himself to Rick at an upcoming diplomatic association. They both were members.

"My friend, I have some unfortunate news to share with you," VLAD continued. "We have been forced to close everyone down on the list that you provided us."

Rick was stunned. "Everyone? You've arrested everyone on the list? All of the spies?"

VLAD shrugged. "Most of them. This is being done as we speak."

"Jesus Christ!" Rick exclaimed. "You're going to get me arrested! Why not just put up a big neon sign over the agency with the word *mole* written on it?"

"You must understand this is not what we wanted to do," Ames would later recall VLAD assuring him. "VLAD told me that the decision was out of the KGB's control. It had been made at a much, much higher level. He said to me: 'You may rest assured that we will not do this again precipitously. If you give us such leads in the future, you can trust us to protect you, and we are trying everything that we can to deflect suspicion away from you.'"

Rick felt overwhelmed. "From that date on, I knew, deep down I knew, I was doomed. There was no question that I was living on borrowed time."

The KGB was trying to make it appear as if it had learned about the spies by tapping into the agency's communication system in Warrenton, Virginia, VLAD said. "We are also blaming [Edward Lee] Howard, of course, and we are open to any of your suggestions."

Rick mentioned money. The KGB had told him that it had put aside $2 million for him. He wanted as much of it as he could get—now. "Unfortunately, it is difficult to deliver such sums in shopping bags," VLAD replied. Rick suggested the KGB transfer it electronically into a Swiss bank account, but VLAD said that was impossible. It could be traced. "How about German bearer bonds?" Rick asked. "You can buy them and then give them to me. They're as good as cash." VLAD said no. Rick assumed VLAD was stalling. He knew the KGB didn't want to pay him everything at once, because it would lose control of him. "Just get me as much cash as you can," Rick said. When Rick got home that night, he checked his urine. It was bloodier than before. He couldn't sleep. He got up and had several drinks. Suddenly, he realized that he hadn't been paying attention when he and VLAD had agreed on a time for their next meeting. Rick thought they were supposed to meet the very next night at the same place, but he couldn't remember. VLAD was supposed to give him more cash. The following evening, Rick waited outside the pharmacy, but VLAD never came.

Rick told a nurse at the embassy about his urine. She sent him to a doctor for tests, who told him he had a urinary infection. Rick was relieved. A few days later, he received a cable from headquarters, asking him to return to Langley. The agency wanted him to brief two Canadian intelligence agents who were investigating claims that Vitaly Yurchenko had made about KGB moles working in their government. "Someone had screwed up. All the stuff Yurchenko had told us about Canada hadn't been tape-recorded for some reason," Ames said later. The only notes about Canada were the ones he had taken. He returned to the States on November 12. "I learned that we didn't have a single asset left in Moscow, not a single one. The whole network had been arrested. I couldn't believe the KGB had done that to me." Rick was told that Jeanne Vertefeuille had been put in charge of a task force investigating the losses. He also heard that Paul Redmond, Jr., thought the agency had been penetrated by a mole.

Rick knew both of them. He liked Vertefeuille, but not Redmond. Although Rick and Redmond were about the same age, they had little in common. Short and energetic, Redmond was the son of a well-to-do Massachusetts insurance executive and the product of elite prep schools and Harvard College. But it was Redmond's impertinence, not his pedigree, that made him something of a legend in the SE division. Redmond didn't always play by the rules, and he didn't let anyone bully him. Typical was an incident that happened after Redmond received an order from Director Casey that he thought was stupid. A wealthy businessman, who had been a major contributor to President Reagan's election campaign, had read a newspaper article about Vitaly Yurchenko's defection and had written a personal letter to Casey asking for help. The businessman wanted to know if the CIA had questioned Yurchenko about the disappearance of Raoul Wallenberg, the Swedish businessman who had helped nearly 100,000 Hungarian Jews escape deportation to Nazi death camps during World War II. The Soviets had arrested Wallenberg in 1945 on trumped-up charges of espionage, and even though the KGB later admitted the arrest had been a mistake, Wallenberg was never seen again. The Soviets later claimed he had died of a heart attack in a Moscow prison in 1947, but periodically reports would surface about how he was still being held somewhere in Russia. Casey had sent the letter to Burton Lee Gerber, who, in turn, had sent a copy down the line to Redmond. The letter irritated him. He didn't want a campaign contributor telling him how to interrogate Yurchenko, nor did he think chasing Wallenberg's ghost was a good use of his men's time. He tossed Casey's request into a file drawer and forgot about it.

"Do you have an answer for Director Casey?" Gerber asked a few days later.

"Yes, I have dealt with his request in an appropriate manner," Redmond replied.

Gerber, who was familiar with Redmond's frequent insubordinations, asked him to explain.

"I've not done a damn thing, because it's a waste of time and a stupid question."

Gerber ordered Redmond to get an answer for Casey. A short time later, he sent his reply to Gerber. "Yurchenko says he doesn't know anything about Raoul Wallenberg," he wrote, and then he added: "He also doesn't know where Jimmy Hoffa is buried." It was classic Redmond.

Rick returned to Rome on November 15 and wrote a memo about his trip for VLAD. He gave it to Aleksey Khrenkov, his new KGB contact, when they met for lunch. Khrenkov was much livelier than the stone-faced Sergey Chuvakhin in Washington. The Russian told him that he was thrilled to be working with him. Khrenkov added that his grandfather had been one of the Bolsheviks who had marched with Lenin during the great October Revolution. "He'd be proud of me now if he could see me sitting here talking to someone important like you," Khrenkov said. Rick beamed. Khrenkov handed Rick a shopping bag with $60,000 in cash hidden inside. Rick was worried about depositing it in Rome, because he wasn't familiar with Italian banking laws and had no idea how a clerk might react when given that much cash. He decided to open a Swiss bank account. It was the first of two checking accounts that he would open in Zurich. The second account was for his mother-in-law, but Rick controlled it. Running the KGB's cash through Cecilia's account helped substantiate the cover story he was spreading among his coworkers—that his wealth was coming from Rosario's side of the family. Rick didn't have any trouble getting Cecilia to sign all the necessary papers. He had started sending her money each month, at Rosario's request, and he always paid for her airline tickets whenever Cecilia wanted to visit them in Rome. She owed him.

Rick got along with his mother-in-law, better than Rosario did, he claimed. Cecilia acted as if she were a queen. She was totally self-absorbed, and she talked endlessly about how wealthy and socially important her ancestors had been. Rick thought she put tremendous pressure on Rosario to live up to impossible standards. She was constantly picking at her for the way she dressed, cooked, ran her house. Rosario would eventually revolt, and the two women would start screaming at one another. But as soon as Cecilia returned to Bogotá, Rosario would be on the telephone, asking her for advice.

Rosario was particularly lonely during Christmas in 1986. Rick was, too. It was the first time either of them had been away from their relatives over the holidays, and without children around, Christmas morning seemed no different from any other. Rosario had always wanted to have children, and she decided now was a perfect time to start. Rick agreed. He was forty-five. "I didn't even think about how being a KGB spy might ultimately affect all of this. I just wanted a child."

That spring, doctors told Rick that his younger sister, Alison, had advanced breast cancer. Rick and Rosario flew to see her. She was in worse condition than Rick had thought. Doctors told him that Alison's prognosis was not good. Rick had never liked hospitals. He began to worry about his own health. He and Rosario flew to Bogotá after visiting Alison. They stayed with Cecilia for a few days, and then drove to their condo in Cartagena. From there they drove north to La Guajira, where they had bought several acres of beachfront property from one of Cecilia's friends. She had arranged the deal. Their 150 meters of beachfront property was Rick's favorite place to go. There was a rustic bungalow there but little else, only coconut trees and sand. When they returned to Rome, Rosario decided that she was tired of

Rome. It hadn't been as much fun as she thought it would be. She wanted to spend all of July in Bogotá with her mother. Rick obediently drove her to the airport.

VLAD arrived in Rome a few days later. With Rosario gone, Rick had started drinking heavily at night. He met Aleksey Khrenkov in front of a restaurant, and the two of them slipped into the back of a nearby sedan. Rick crouched down in the rear seat while the driver spent at least a half hour weaving through Rome. When the car stopped, Rick discovered he was inside the Soviets' residential compound. VLAD was waiting inside. He led Rick up a staircase into the attic.

"We built this room just for you," VLAD said, opening a door. The room was enclosed by two walls with a five-inch gap between them. Music was piped into the gap to prevent anyone from using electronic devices to listen in on what was being said inside. As was his practice, Rick had brought along copies of secret cables that he had stolen from the embassy. The stack was about fifteen inches high. VLAD seemed depressed when Rick handed him the stack of cables.

"I could tell he wanted to say something, but he didn't want to offend me," Ames recalled later. "Finally, he says, 'You know, there's an awful lot of the information that you give us, even though it is very valuable and very interesting, that we simply can't handle.' VLAD told me that Moscow couldn't keep up with processing all the documents I was passing! I was told that I was too much of a good thing!"

VLAD suddenly stood up from the table where they were sitting and began pacing. "There is something I must ask, as one professional intelligence officer to another," he said after a few moments. "Please do not be offended."

Rick said that he wouldn't.

"Oftentimes we have found that people who come to us do not tell us everything they know, especially about people who are special to them," VLAD continued. "I am certain this is true among your agents, too. There is always a reluctance among sources to reveal the names of people who, for instance, they personally recruited."

Rick understood where VLAD was going. The KGB had correctly guessed that he was holding back the names of spies he had handled personally. A face flashed before Rick's eyes. It was his friend from their days in New York: Sergey Fedorenko, PYRRHIC. Another face followed Fedorenko's. It was BYPLAY, the Soviet scientist whom he had befriended ten years earlier.

"Tell me, my friend," VLAD continued. "Are there others who you would now like to mention?"

For a second, Rick sat quietly, thinking about Fedorenko and BYPLAY. He knew the KGB had arrested and was executing nearly everyone whose name he had already revealed.

"You're right, of course," Rick replied. "There are two more spies." Rick told VLAD about Fedorenko and BYPLAY. After they finished talking, VLAD handed Rick another thick bundle of one-hundred-dollar bills. When he got home, he drank himself to sleep. The next night, Rick got drunk at a reception in the garden of Ambassador Rabb's residence. He began arguing with another guest and then walked outside and passed out in the street. The police took him to a hospital. The next day, he couldn't remember a thing. When he reported to work, Rick bumped into his station chief, Alan Wolfe. "He told me that I needed to be more careful. I gave him a kind of a hangdog and apologetic look and said . . . that he was right. I knew people were suckers if you told them right off that you were really, really sorry and were embarrassed about how you had acted. They'd feel sorry for you." That night, Rick got drunk alone in his apartment.

About a week after his meeting with VLAD, one of Rick's coworkers gave him a folder filled with documents and photographs from the Italian intelligence service. "The Italians are trying to figure out who this big shot is who came to Rome a few days back, and why he was here," Rick's coworker explained. Rick opened the file and saw VLAD's face looking back at him from a photograph. The pictures showed VLAD arriving at Leonardo da Vinci International Airport, where he had been met by the Soviet embassy's counterintelligence chief. Rick fought an urge to panic. "Of course, I knew why VLAD had been in Rome—to meet me," he recalled. Had the Italians seen or photographed him meeting with VLAD or Khrenkov? He quickly scanned the photographs. He wasn't in any of them. Rick decided not to tell VLAD about the photographs. He was afraid that VLAD would insist that they begin meeting in Vienna. The KGB felt safe meeting foreigners there, but Rick didn't want to be bothered. It was more convenient having VLAD come to Rome.

Rosario extended her stay in Bogotá for another month, and when she did finally get home, she broke into tears as soon as she walked off the airplane. She had suffered a miscarriage, she said. "It's okay," he assured her. "You can get pregnant again." Rosario wasn't so sure. She was worried that she was getting too old. She decided to begin taking large amounts of vitamins. She didn't like any of the brands that were sold in Rome, so she called Diana Worthen and asked her to begin buying and sending her vitamins.

"After the miscarriage, Rick wouldn't touch me for a long time," Rosario claimed later. "He said he didn't want to harm me and all this, but it was more than that. It was a lack of interest. It was like he couldn't be bothered with sex any more." When a month passed without them making love, Rosario started to fuss. One night she told Rick that she wanted to make love, but he couldn't perform. The next night she tried again, and he was impotent. She was insulted, and suggested that he visit a doctor to find out what was wrong. An examination showed there was nothing physically wrong. Rosario decided Rick didn't find her attractive anymore. He swore that he did. He was just tired from working so hard. Rosario decided he was having a sexual affair with another woman. But when she confronted him, he laughed. They both avoided making love for a while, and then Rick suggested that they get away for a short vacation. They decided to drive to Frankfurt, Germany, where one of Rosario's friends from Colombia lived. They made all the necessary arrangements, but just before they were scheduled to leave, Rick's sister, Nancy Everly, called. Alison had died of breast cancer. Nancy assumed Rick was coming home for the funeral. "I can't," he mumbled. "It's impossible for me right now." Rick didn't tell her why: He didn't want to irritate Rosario by canceling their vacation.

When they first left Rome for Frankfurt, Rick felt guilty about missing Alison's funeral, but he soon began feeling better. He had bought a Jaguar sports car from a British diplomat, and the 1983 silver-gray XJ-6 moved effortlessly through the Alps. When Rick reached the German autobahn, where there was no posted speed limit, he accelerated and soon was holding the car steady at the equivalent of 130 miles per hour. "I know it sounds a bit silly, but I must admit at that moment, I felt as if I was living one of my childhood fantasies," he said later. He felt like Simon Templar, the Saint, a British agent driving in his Jaguar across Europe.

CHAPTER 17

INSIDE THE CIA

On December 14, 1986, a young Marine guard sauntered up to the CIA's chief of station in Vienna, Austria, during a Christmas party for U.S. embassy employees, and whispered: "I'm into something over my head. I need to talk to you about it."

The station chief led Sergeant Clayton John Lonetree by the arm into a hallway and asked what the matter was. In a voice cracking with emotion, Lonetree revealed that he had been recruited by the KGB as a spy at his previous duty station.

"Where were you stationed before coming to Vienna?"

"Moscow," Lonetree replied. "The U.S. embassy in Moscow."

During the next nine days, a CIA counterintelligence officer interrogated Lonetree in a room at the Intercontinental Hotel in Vienna. After every session, the officer sent detailed cables to Langley. Jeanne Vertefeuille and her task force greeted the news about Lonetree with guarded optimism. At first glance, it appeared that the Marine could have been the reason why the KGB had been able to identify the CIA's spies. But Vertefeuille and her team knew that in their profession, first appearances often were deceiving. Judging from the cables, it appeared that Lonetree had been entrapped in a classic KGB sex trap.

Lonely and emotionally insecure, Lonetree had been the only

Native American assigned to the Marine guard force in Moscow in late 1984. In his first letter home to his father, Lonetree had written that he was an oddity in Moscow because of his Indian ancestry. The first time Lonetree attended a diplomatic reception, he was surrounded by a group of Warsaw Pact generals who wanted to know how American Indians were treated in the United States. At first, Lonetree was leery of the two hundred Soviet employees who worked at the U.S. embassy, but eventually he fell in love with one. Violetta Sanni was a Ukrainian Jew who worked as an interpreter at the embassy. Shortly after they became lovers, Sanni introduced Lonetree to her "Uncle Sasha," who she claimed was interested in Native Americans. Uncle Sasha would later be identified in the media as Aleksey Yefimov, a KGB officer. That, however, was an alias. His real name, which has not been made public before, is Aleksey Yegorov. No one would later be able to prove for certain whether Sanni had actually loved Lonetree or was a KGB pawn used simply to seduce him. No matter, Lonetree soon found himself being pressured by Yegorov for information about his job and coworkers.

On March 10, 1986, Lonetree's eighteen-month assignment at the embassy ended and he was reassigned to Vienna. Uncle Sasha came to visit him there, and gave Lonetree a teary-eyed letter from his much-missed lover. Lonetree gave Yegorov a discarded U.S. embassy telephone book that he had recovered from a trash can, and a fire drill poster that showed the floor plan of the CIA station in Vienna. Yegorov paid him $1,800 for each item. Lonetree spent the money on gifts for his Soviet sweetheart. The next time Lonetree met Yegorov, the KGB agent showed him several photographs of embassy employees who the KGB suspected were CIA officers. Lonetree recognized three of them and pointed them out.

At this point Lonetree began to panic. He was scheduled to meet Yegorov again on December 27, 1986, to finalize plans for a secret trip back to Moscow to meet Sanni. In his own mind, he didn't think the information that he had given Yegorov was significant, but he knew that if he returned to Moscow with Yegorov's help, he would be viewed by both sides as a full-fledged KGB spy. He decided to tell the CIA what he had done and volunteer to help them run a double-agent ploy against the KGB. Ironically, Lonetree didn't know who the CIA station chief in Vienna was, so Lonetree asked Yegorov.

After Lonetree confessed on December 14, he told the CIA counterintelligence officer debriefing him at the Interconential Hotel that he wanted to atone for his sins. He offered to kill Edward Lee Howard for the CIA.

Howard had surfaced in Moscow on August 7, 1986, nearly one year after he had jumped from his car into the New Mexico desert and vanished. In an interview on Russian television conducted by a KGB agent, Howard insisted that he had never done anything illegal, nor had he, in his words, "inflicted damage on any Americans or jeopardized the security of my country." No one in the CIA or FBI had believed him.

Lonetree said he was willing to continue meeting with Yegorov and return with him to Moscow. Once there, Lonetree would convince Yegorov to introduce him to Howard. He would then draw Howard out into the open, so the CIA could grab him, or he could kill Howard with his bare hands.

It is impossible to tell now if the CIA ever took Lonetree's offer seriously during his debriefings. But what is now known is that the agency let Lonetree *believe* that it was going to use him in some sort of clandestine operation. It wanted to keep him talking, and talk he did. After the CIA had learned everything that it could from him, Lonetree was asked if he would mind repeating his story to some other intelligence officers, described by the CIA officer as "my colleagues." Lonetree immediately agreed, without knowing that the men he was about to meet were not CIA officers, but criminal investigators from the Naval Investigative Service (NIS) sent to build a case against him. The CIA cannot make arrests. Within minutes, a gullible Lonetree was blabbing away.

Vertefeuille and her task force pored over Lonetree's statements, looking for evidence that he was to blame for the 1985 losses. The more they looked, the more convinced they became that he wasn't responsible. They began to focus on other clues. Meanwhile, the NIS charged Lonetree with espionage on January 27. On its own, it also began looking at other Marines who had been stationed with him in Moscow.

Vertefeuille and her task force decided that there were three possible explanations for the 1985 losses:

1. Leaks by Edward Lee Howard

2. Human errors, such as poor "tradecraft" by a CIA officer or the spy himself

3. Something unknown or, as Vertefeuille liked to put it, "the question-mark factor." This included a technical or human penetration of the CIA.

This did not mean that the task force believed all the losses had been caused by one of the above. "Burton Gerber continually warned me not to look for a 'monocausal' explanation," Vertefeuille said later, "so none of us saw these three as mutually exclusive." The breakdown simply gave the team a place to get started.

On paper, it looked as if investigating those three explanations would be easy. Surely Howard's bosses would be able to tell the task force what he had been trained to do and what spies he had been told about. The task force, however, discovered that determining what Howard knew and didn't know was not nearly so simple. For example, there was no reason for Howard to have been told about Operation ABSORB, and no one at the agency thought he had been. But when the CIA went through a number of personal papers that Howard had left behind in his desk, it discovered several notes in his handwriting about the secret Trans-Siberian rail operation. *How had he found out about ABSORB?* No one knew.

Trying to figure out how many of the CIA's spies had been caught because of mistakes made by the agency or by the spies themselves also proved difficult. For example, after the agency confirmed that Poleschuk, WEIGH, had been arrested at a dead drop delivery in Izmaylovskiy Park, it heard at least three different explanations for his arrest from sources in Moscow. The first was that Poleschuk had been drunk when he went to pick up the fake rock that had been left there for him. The second was that he'd been spotted by the KGB because a youth conference was being held in the park, and there were more KGB officers patrolling the area than usual. Finally, the agency was told that the KGB had followed a CIA case officer to the park and seen him put the fake rock there. The KGB had arrested Poleschuk when he had showed up to claim it. *Which was true?* No one knew.

The third possible explanation for the losses, the so-called question-mark factor, proved the most maddening for the task force. During its first month together, the task force identified forty-four different "links" that the doomed spies had in common. For example, nearly all of them had been paid in rubles at some point. Because only the Soviet Union used rubles as its currency, the U.S. government had to buy them from the Soviet treasury. *Had the KGB discovered a way to mark the rubles being bought by the CIA so that they could be traced once they were spent in Moscow?* No one knew. Another link was the CIA's pouch system. Most of the spies had given documents to the CIA at one time or another. The CIA depended on the military and State Department courier networks to hand-carry sensitive materials back and forth between Langley and its stations overseas. *Had the KGB found some way to examine the contents of diplomatic pouches during international transit?* No one knew.

The most obvious link shared by the spies was that they all worked for the CIA. And that proved to be the most complicated link of all. For example, Tolkachev had worked as a spy for eight years. *How many departments in the agency had received cables about him? How many secretaries had handled intelligence reports emanating from Tolkachev? How many of those departments and those secretaries had received information about the other spies? How many had received information about Tolkachev and Poleschuk, but not about Varenik?* No one knew.

Years later, the task force would be criticized for "wasting time" collecting minutiae and "looking at individual trees while missing the forest." Critics would claim that Vertefeuille and her team had been reluctant to see what was painfully obvious—that the agency had been *penetrated* by a mole. It was suggested that Vertefeuille and her task force had not wanted to admit that someone in the CIA was a traitor. That charge would outrage Vertefeuille and her cohorts. "I always knew that we could have a traitor in our midst," she said later. "I was not an ostrich with my head in the sand. Nor, I believe, were the people I was working with. The problem was to decide if there *was* a mole at this point."

Vertefeuille and the other team members all knew the damage Angleton had done looking for a mole. "We *all* agreed that we would not act in any Angletonian fashion," she said later. That meant letting the evidence lead them to a mole—if there was one—not picking a suspect and then trying to prove that he or she was a traitor.

The problem was that no one had ever found a mole based purely on detective work. Every spy caught by a U.S. intelligence service in recent history had been nabbed because of a snitch. Vitaly Yurchenko had told the CIA about Edward Lee Howard. Howard had told the KGB about Adolf Tolkachev. Traitors betraying traitors. That's how moles were exposed. What Vertefeuille and her task force were trying to do had never been done before.

At fifty-four, Vertefeuille did not fit the stereotypical image of a CIA case officer, particularly Hollywood's version. She looked more like someone's grandmother or fifth-grade English teacher than a James Bond heroine. Short, unassuming, gray-haired, Vertefeuille had worked for the agency for thirty-two years, having joined it in 1954 directly from college. In those days, women were automatically assigned to the secretarial pool at the CIA. Few were ever offered career training. The fact that Vertefeuille had graduated with a degree in European history and spoke German didn't matter. Verte-feuille was assigned the task of typing letters for the agency's senior managers. Back then there was no way to correct a typing mistake on the original, and nine carbon copies that had to be made. If she hit a wrong key, the entire page had to be redone. Vertefeuille's meticulous personality paid off. She was one of the first to be issued an electric typewriter, and in less than a year, she was sent to Senegal to handle the station's administrative duties. Her boss there soon recognized that her talents were being wasted on clerical work. He quietly began sending her out on more exotic assignments. In the early 1960s, Vertefeuille became one of the first women in the agency to be sent to the Farm for career training. Out of sixty-six trainees, seven were women. They were not allowed to take the same courses as men—the agency didn't believe women could endure the physical training—nor were they taught how to use weapons. In the 1970s, she was chosen to head the Biographic Branch in the SE division. If a KGB officer appeared in Athens and no one was certain who he was, they called Vertefeuille. Most of the time she knew from memory the officer's name, last post, and what sort of cases he had been involved in. If not, she knew where to find that information. She had a knack for making connections when others simply saw random dots. In a study that she wrote in the 1970s, Vertefeuille described several common-sense ways for CIA officers to identify their opponents. One typical tip: at Soviet embassies abroad, the ambassador was supplied with a chauffeur and a limousine. Mid-level employees and "straight" (non-KGB) officers rode in car pools or bought used cars if they could afford them. However, KGB officers always drove brand-new Western-made cars. Inside the agency, Vertefeuille was known for being a stickler for details, someone not afraid to correct her bosses whenever they made a mistake.

In mid-March 1987, a ghost returned to haunt Vertefeuille and her team. The NIS announced that it had found evidence of widespread spying by the Marine guard force in Moscow. The key piece of evidence, the NIS said, was a confession by Marine corporal Arnold Bracy, who had served in Moscow with Lonetree and had been disciplined there for unauthorized contact with a Soviet woman. The NIS said that Bracy had admitted allowing KGB officers to roam through the U.S. embassy in Moscow at night. Within days, the NIS arrested several other Marines and charged them with helping the KGB sneak into the embassy at night to photograph documents and plant bugs in the Communications Program Unit, where the embassy's most important cipher machines were kept.

The NIS's accusations caused an international panic. The embassy in

Moscow was ordered to cease all classified communication with the outside world and to stop using all computer terminals, electric typewriters, and even manual typewriters, for fear they might be bugged. Embassy officers were told to whisper, and to write all their reports in longhand. All correspondence was hand-carried out of the Soviet Union by couriers. The State Department spent $30 million replacing sophisticated communications gear and shoring up embassy security. Caspar W. Weinberger, then secretary of defense, compared the damage to Iran's "seizing our embassy in Tehran. . . . We're very, very distressed. It is a very great loss." For the first time in history, the entire twenty-eight-man Marine guard force was replaced. In a special appearance before the news media, President Ronald Reagan condemned the security breach and added that he had long suspected that the KGB was planting listening devices in the trouble-plagued new U.S. embassy, which was still being constructed in Moscow. In April 1987, a specially equipped communications van was flown to Russia so Secretary of State George P. Shultz could feel comfortable sending messages back to the White House about the tense, ongoing intermediate range nuclear forces (INF) negotiations. During a news conference, Shultz complained: "We didn't break into their embassy, they broke into our embassy. They invaded our sovereign territory and we're damned upset about it."

Lawyers for the accused Marines, meanwhile, claimed the entire NIS investigation was a fraud. Overzealous NIS investigators had fabricated evidence, lied, and threatened young Marines, they charged.

Vertefeuille and her task force didn't know what to make of the charges. Based on what the NIS was now telling the agency, it suddenly looked as if Lonetree and the other Marine guards could have been responsible for the 1985 losses. "We thought that they might have let KGB technicians into sensitive areas of the embassy, including the CIA station," said Vertefeuille. The task force immediately put aside the other leads that it was pursuing and began investigating whether Lonetree, Bracy, and their fellow guards could have done what the NIS claimed they had. Daniel Niesciur led the task force's probe by examining stacks of "watch logs," lists that showed when and where Lonetree and Bracy had been while standing guard at the embassy.

In the midst of this national brouhaha, Paul Redmond called on Sandy Grimes for help. "You are going to hate me for giving you this assignment," he warned, "but I need you to inventory every scrap of paper that is in the CIA station in Moscow. We have to assume a worst-case scenario here. If the

KGB did get inside the embassy, we need to know what it might have seen there." Grimes asked Diana Worthen to help her.

It would take months for Grimes to collect, copy, and inventory more than 60,000 pages of cables, reports, and other classified papers that the CIA found atop desks, in files, and tucked away on shelves in its Moscow station. Reading, filing, and inventorying the paperwork was a daunting task. One afternoon, while Grimes was sorting through a large bundle of intelligence reports, Worthen walked into the office wearing a brightly colored Italian scarf.

"Where did you get that beautiful scarf?" Grimes asked.

"Rick and Rosario sent it to me," Worthen replied. Rosario had asked her to send several packages of vitamins to Rome, and Worthen had received several scarfs in return as thank-you gifts.

"You're kidding!" Grimes replied. "That's a Salvatore Ferragamo scarf. It must have cost several hundred dollars."

Both women were surprised. They had never heard of Rick being so generous. "Maybe I should start sending Rosario vitamins," Grimes quipped.

While the task force was preoccupied with the Marine guard scandal, and Grimes and Worthen were spending months digging through mountains of embassy papers, the agency learned that two more of its spies had been arrested. Once again, the KGB had done its best to keep the arrests a secret. Vladimir Potashov, known as MEDIAN, had been arrested in July 1986. He had worked at the Institute of U.S.A. and Canada, and had been a spy since 1981, when he had surprised Harold Brown, then secretary of defense, at a strategic arms meeting by asking if he would arrange for him to talk privately with a CIA officer. It was the first time that anyone in the agency could remember a defense secretary recruiting a Soviet spy. The agency also heard rumors that the KGB had arrested Vladimir Piguzov, whose cryptonym was JOGGER. He had been recruited during the 1970s in Indonesia, but had not been in contact with the agency since 1979, when he returned to Moscow. His arrest surprised the agency. It now knew that the KGB had arrested spies who had worked for it as recently as eight months ago and as long ago as eight years!

With the arrest of Potashov and Piguzov, the agency now knew that twelve of its spies had been arrested. Vertefeuille already was familiar with all of the cases that had been compromised, but others on her team were not. Each arrest meant the task force members had to study a new case. It meant they had to learn as much as they could about each individual spy, his fam-

ily, his job assignments, his career moves, his reason for spying. None of the
spies remained a stranger. Each file wore a human face.

One of the ironies of espionage is that the CIA and KGB frequently mir-
rored one another. Each time one of the CIA's spies was arrested, Vertefeuille
and her task force knew their counterparts in Department Five of Directorate K would be studying the same case, but from a completely different
angle. The CIA would try to learn why its spy had been caught. The KGB
would try to assess how much damage the spy had done. The task force knew
that Piguzov's case was going to be particularly difficult for the KGB to assess. His most recent assignment had been at the KGB's training academy,
the equivalent of the CIA's Farm, where he had had access to the true identities of all new KGB recruits and detailed psychological profiles of two gen-
erations of KGB officers. The KGB usually was able to force detailed
confessions out of the spies it captured. Still, its investigators would have to
wonder if Piguzov was telling the truth when he claimed that he had not
spied for the agency since 1979.

The CIA was not the only federal agency investigating the 1985 losses.
The FBI had formed its own six-person team to determine why Valery Martynov, GENTILE, and Sergey Motorin, GAUZE, had been caught. Tim
Caruso, a counterintelligence supervisor at the FBI's Washington, D.C.,
base station, was put in charge of the probe. He called the investigation AN-
LACE, the name for a menacing medieval dagger, the sort used to stab
someone in the back. It seemed appropriate. When the CIA's Gus Hathaway
heard about ANLACE, he suggested that the FBI and CIA begin sharing information. Several joint meetings took place, and the two teams met twice
for overnight conferences out of town. "We had somewhat different missions," Vertefeuille said later. "The FBI was worried that there might be a
mole in the bureau, while we were investigating what might have gone
wrong in the agency."

On June 12, 1987, the Marine Corps dismissed all charges against Corporal Bracy. "He is innocent not because of any technicality or lack of evidence," his Marine Corps attorney, Michael L. Powell, declared at a press
conference. "He is innocent because the things they said he did, didn't oc-
cur. They did not happen. They were fantasy in the minds of [NIS agents].
Fantasy." The Corps had dropped all charges against Bracy, after questions
were raised about how the NIS had interrogated him and the other young
Marines it had charged. Bracy's so-called confession, in particular, had
caused the Corps to question the validity of the NIS's evidence. The two
NIS investigators who had interrogated Bracy on March 17, had received a

message from their headquarters that had set a " seventy-two-hour reporting deadline." The agents took this to mean that they had seventy-two hours to find Bracy, interrogate him, and wrap up their entire investigation. In fact, the message meant only that they were supposed to file a report within seventy-two hours after they finished interviewing Bracy. Because of this miscommunication, the two agents interrogated Bracy for more than sixteen hours, during which they administered five lie detector tests. At the end of the interrogation, Bracy had signed a confession. But within seconds, even before he had left the interview room, Bracy was recanting his statement. "We've got ourselves a spy!" Bracy would later recall one of the agents gushing.

That summer, the Marine Corps dropped the charges it had filed against the other Marine guards. It went ahead with Lonetree's court-martial, however, based on his initial statements about his Soviet lover and Uncle Sasha. On August 13, Lonetree was found guilty by a jury of eight Marine officers and sentenced to twenty-five years in prison.* Lonetree submitted to several lengthy debriefing sessions with FBI, CIA, NSA, and other US intelligence services after his court-martial, and by early 1988, nearly all of them had reached the same conclusion: The NIS had badly bungled its investigation and dramatically overdramatized the entire Marine guard scare. After spending nearly a year studying the charges against the Marine guards, Vertefeuille and her task force were reaching much the same conclusion. Niesciur's review showed that Lonetree and Bracy had only been together on duty twice in positions at the embassy where they could have let the KGB inside. "Opinions changed over time," Vertefeuille said later, "but we eventually became more and more convinced that it would have been impossible [for the Marines to have done what the NIS claimed]."

The State Department agreed in early 1988. "Our judgment today is . . . there were no Russians in the secure parts of the embassy," Robert E. Lamb, a State Department spokesman, announced at a press conference.

In early 1988, Grimes and Worthen also finished their mind-numbing inventory of the CIA station in Moscow. They reported that the KGB could have learned the names of all the spies who had been arrested, except for one, if it had somehow gotten into the CIA station. Division Chief Burton Gerber, Gus Hathaway, and Paul Redmond were surprised. No one had realized how many sensitive documents were being stored in Moscow.

Grimes and Redmond went to lunch not long after she completed that study. It was his way of apologizing for giving her such a dreadful assignment.

*His sentence was later reduced to twenty years.

"Tell me something, Paul," Grimes said. "Why would the KGB recruit a Marine guard in Moscow, but never ask him to steal anything from the embassy there?" She was referring to Lonetree, and his claim that he had never provided any information to the KGB until he was sent to Vienna. Without waiting, Grimes answered her own question. "Either they figured Lonetree didn't really have access to anything of value, or they didn't need his help because they already had someone else giving them information."

By the spring of 1988, Vertefeuille and her task force had eliminated Lonetree and his fellow Marines as a reason for the 1985 losses. The task force also had decided that there didn't appear to be any leaks at the CIA's communication center in Warrenton. Meanwhile, the agency had heard that another of its spies had been arrested. KGB lieutenant colonel Boris Yuzhin, known as TWINE, had volunteered in the mid-1970s while stationed in San Francisco. Once again the KGB had kept Yuzhin's arrest on December 23, 1986, a secret for more than one year. That brought the total number of spies to thirteen.

As always, Redmond was ready to lead a charge. He contacted a friend of his who worked in the FBI's counterintelligence division, and they agreed to launch a joint CIA/FBI operation. The FBI called it BUCKLURE, as in the lure of big bucks. The CIA called it RACKETEER, simply because Redmond liked the sound of it. Each agency began spreading the word: The U.S. government was willing to pay a reward of $1 million in cash to anyone who could tell it how the KGB had identified the thirteen agents who had been arrested. Redmond was going back to the fundamentals. "What we need to solve this case," he told his colleagues at the agency, "is a source—someone in the KGB who can tell us what happened."

Once word spread about the $1 million bounty, Redmond assumed it would only be a matter of time before someone in the KGB or GRU came forward.

He was right.

CHAPTER 18

IN MOSCOW

It was a warm Friday afternoon on July 4, 1986, when retired GRU general Dmitri Fedorovich Polyakov received word at his dacha that he was to report at ten o'clock on Monday morning to GRU head-quarters in Moscow for a special presentation. He was not told why, only that a car would be sent to take him there. His first thought was that the GRU was having a surprise retirement party for one of his former colleagues, but after his youngest son, Peter, arrived at the dacha later that night, Polyakov became suspicious. Peter, who had followed in his father's footsteps by joining the GRU, had spot-ted two ambulances lingering near the road that led to his father's dacha. Their appearance seemed odd, because the closest town was too tiny to have its own ambulance service, and there was no appar-ent reason for ambulances from Moscow to be parked by the rural road. Peter and his father both knew that the KGB and GRU some-times used ambulances as cover when they made arrests. An Alpha Team could hide in the rear of the vehicles, and the sight of an am-bulance was not as alarming in an area as the arrival of police cars.

Peter mentioned that he had been told to report at 10:00 A.M. on Monday to GRU headquarters for an important meeting—just like his father. The senior Polyakov did not want to upset his wife. Sun-day was his sixty-fifth birthday, and she had invited their sons and neighbors to a party at the dacha. He told Peter not to say anything about the ambulances or the Monday meeting. Despite their outward demeanor, both men were worried. In June 1980, Polyakov had been recalled to Moscow from New Delhi on what was supposed to be a routine home leave. However, he had been told during that vacation that his tour in India was being aborted, and he had been reassigned to a desk job at GRU headquarters. Polyakov had made some discreet inquiries, and had learned that he was suspected of being a U.S. spy. He had come under suspicion because of the 1978 book *Legend: The Secret World of Lee Harvey Oswald*, but that, by itself, wasn't enough. One of his rivals at the GRU had become convinced that he was a traitor, and it had been this man who had continually questioned his loyalty.

Polyakov had retired a short time later and had assumed that, once he had left the GRU, his rival's hatred of him would dissipate. Now he wondered if he had underestimated his opponent. Polyakov had spent the last several years working on his dacha. He had built it completely with his own hands. To relax, he had played with his granddaughters and, occasionally, written articles for gun magazines about hunting rifles. He and his wife had two adult sons. A third boy had died in the early 1960s, when the family had been stationed in New York. Polyakov had asked for permission to have his son undergo an operation in a New York hospital, which could have saved the boy's life, but the GRU had said no. It was about this same time that Polyakov had approached a U.S. military official about working for the United States. That had marked the start of his extraordinary *eighteen* years as a U.S. spy. Inside the CIA, Polyakov was considered the most productive Soviet spy in U.S. history. He had provided the CIA with more than one hundred issues of the classified version of *Military Thought*, a document that revealed what the Soviet's high command was thinking and planning. He had given the agency thousands of pages of documents about Russian weapons, including technical data about Soviet-made antitank missiles, which allowed U.S. forces to defeat those same weapons years later when they were deployed by Iraq during the 1991 Gulf War. More than twenty-seven file drawers at the agency were stuffed with stolen Russian secrets provided single-handedly by Polyakov. During the Vietnam War, he had provided the CIA with important information about the size, structure, and capabilities of North Vietnam's troops. In the early 1970s, he had revealed that China was about to end its close ties with the Soviet empire—information that helped Henry Kissinger, then U.S. national security adviser, and President Nixon forge their 1972 opening into China.

Over the years, Polyakov had helped the CIA identify at least six Americans and one British officer who were KGB spies. Although the British case had taken place in the early 1960s, it was still being discussed inside the CIA twenty years later because of the clever way it had been solved. Polyakov had given the CIA *photographs* he had taken of *photographs* that a KGB spy had taken of secret documents that described U.S. guided weapon systems. By studying Polyakov's photographs of the KGB spy's photographs, the CIA was able to trace the secret documents to the missile guidance branch of the aviation ministry in London where Frank Bossard worked. He had been arrested and sentenced to twenty-one years in prison. One of the very first bits of information that Polyakov had given the FBI in the 1960s resulted in the exposé and expulsion of several Soviet "illegals," spies who had come to the United States as immigrants and had wormed their way into sensitive government jobs.

On Sunday, Polyakov's second son, Alexander, arrived at the dacha, and he, too, mentioned that he had been instructed to report on Monday to GRU headquarters for a meeting at 10:00 A.M. Surrounded by his granddaughters and two sons, Polyakov celebrated his sixty-fifth birthday that night as if he had no worries about the future. The next morning, he rose early and dressed in his finest GRU uniform. No one had told him to wear it. After carefully adding all the decorations he had been awarded during his career, he kissed his wife goodbye and stepped outside, where a car was waiting. When he arrived at GRU headquarters, he was immediately arrested and accused of being a spy. Without flinching, Polyakov announced that he would not speak to anyone except for KGB chairman Chebrikov. Polyakov was driven to Lubyanka, where he met privately with Chebrikov for more than an hour. During that session, the two men negotiated the terms of his arrest. Polyakov agreed to sign a full confession and submit to several months of debriefings by the GRU and KGB. In return, Chebrikov agreed that no one else in the general's family would be arrested, and that his wife would be permitted to keep the dacha that he had built. Everything else that he and his wife owned would be confiscated. In August, his wife and two sons were allowed to visit him briefly in prison. Even though he had not been in custody long, Polyakov already was a changed man. His ruddy complexion was gone, his natural cheerfulness replaced by a haggard mix of exhaustion and depression. Without ever asking, his family knew what his fate would be once the interrogations ended: *bratskaya mogila*—a common, unmarked grave.

Yasenevo, the headquarters of the KGB's powerful First Chief Directorate, rises from flat pastures southeast of Moscow. From the windows of the upper floors in what is known as the main building, you can see modern-day peasants working in oat fields. From those same windows, if you cast your gaze downward, you will find a granite bust of Lenin staring back at you across a pond and carefully landscaped grounds. The main office building is connected to smaller structures: an auditorium, library, clinic, sports complex, and swimming pool. There is a newer twenty-two-story building next to the old one, and a separate dacha complex. A passerby might mistake Yasenevo for a private college, were it not for the double row of chain link fences, the guard dogs, armed sentries, motion detectors, and other modern gizmos used to detect and deter unwanted guests. Vladimir Kryuchkov had worked hard to become the master of Yasenevo. Bald, humorless, in his mid-fifties, he had started out his professional life as a factory worker, but had studied correspondence courses at night and become a prosecutor and then a diplomat. His mentor, Yuri Andropov, had brought him into the KGB and helped hone his political skills. Kryuchkov was a hard-driving workaholic. Behind his back, his aides said Kryuchkov was a KGB officer *twenty-five* hours a day. He was a formal man, even with his own children. He ruled Yasenevo and his home with a disciplined hand. In a country where vodka flowed freely as the unofficial national drink, Kryuchkov was a teetotaler. He constantly fretted over his health, frequently squeezed a tennis ball during meetings to tighten his grip, disliked small talk.

Kryuchkov had never looked kindly on those who had dared question his judgment, even when he was later proven wrong. He had sacked several up-and-coming officers, most notably Oleg Kalugin, who later became well known in the West. Despite his position, Kryuchkov knew little about his main adversary. One of his pet theories, according to Oleg Gordievsky, was that Jews in New York City, and not Watergate, were behind the ouster of Richard Nixon as president.

Kryuchkov had depended heavily on Lieutenant General Vadim Kirpichenko for advice. Together they had chosen Vladimir Ivanovitch Mechulayev, the KGB officer who Ames knew as VLAD, to handle their most important spy. Inside the KGB, Mechulayev was known as a "tough guy." The students at the KGB's training academy had given him that tag because of his lectures. Others often complained in their speeches about how difficult it was for the KGB to compete against the CIA, which had more money and better technology. Not Mechulayev. Odds meant nothing to him. "He honestly believed in the superiority of the Soviet system," recalled retired KGB major Yuri Shvets. "That's why he was considered tough. He never doubted communism. He was a perfectionist too. He paid close attention to all details." Mechulayev had been *rezident* in Ottawa, Canada, and he had served in New York City. He felt comfortable around Americans.

One of Kryuchkov's former aides told me during an interview in Moscow that Kryuchkov had introduced Mechulayev to Edward Lee Howard in October 1985 when the CIA turncoat was secretly brought to Moscow by the KGB. Howard had made his way from the United States to Europe, where he had contacted the KGB at a Soviet embassy. He had been smuggled into the USSR on September 24, 1985, and eventually taken to a dacha outside Moscow. Kryuchkov had taken a personal interest in Howard, and had gone to the KGB dacha where Howard was being debriefed to welcome him. A short time after that, Kryuchkov had introduced Mechulayev to Howard. I was told that during October through December, Mechulayev met repeatedly with Howard, quizzing him about the CIA. All of this was in preparation for Mechulayev's first meeting with Ames over the Christmas holidays in 1985 in Bogotá—although Mechulayev certainly never mentioned anything about Ames to Howard. Even though he was welcomed as a defector, Howard was not trusted by the KGB.

In July 1987, Mechulayev returned to Yasenevo from meeting Rick in Rome and went immediately to brief Kryuchkov and Kirpichenko. Kryuchkov led his two officers from his office through his private gymnasium and into a sauna that he had ordered built with KGB funds. The walls of his sauna were lined with wood imported from Finland, the sinks were marble, the fixtures imported. He often talked to his senior generals while relaxing naked in the sauna. Even if the CIA found a way to bug his office, he was certain it could not listen to conversations here. Nor was there a way for anyone to secretly tape-record his comments if they were sitting nude next to him.

Mechulayev told his bosses that he had warned Ames that the spies he had identified were in the process of being arrested, and he told Kryuchkov and Kirpichenko of Ames's stunned reaction. Mechulayev assured them that he had told Ames that the KGB was doing everything it could to keep the arrests secret. Mechulayev then told his two sauna-mates that Ames had suggested that the KGB exploit the Marine guard embassy scandal that was making headlines in the United States and in Moscow. I would later be told by one of Kryuchkov's former aides that Ames's suggestion had struck Kryuchkov and Kirpichenko as funny. Why had it taken Ames so long to think of it? they joked.

According to Kryuchkov's former aide, the First Chief Directorate had not been told about Lonetree when he was first recruited by the KGB. This was because Lonetree had been approached by the KGB's Second Directorate, and its director was still angry about the way that Kryuchkov had blamed him for Oleg Gordievsky's escape from Moscow. Kryuchkov had learned about Lonetree later, when KGB Chairman Chebrikov decided to tell him about TYULPAN (Russian for "tulip"), the codename for the Lonetree case. Kryuchkov's former aide told me this about the Lonetree case. The KGB had never seriously discussed using Lonetree to sneak a KGB officer into the U.S. embassy at night. The reason: It was too risky. Getting inside was only the first step. The rooms used by the CIA were filled with safes, detection devices, and surveillance cameras. But the main reason the KGB did not try to sneak into the embassy was politics. "We would not have dared to undertake such a foolhardy operation in 1986," the aide told me. At the time, Gorbachev was desperately trying to convince the West that it needed to finance perestroika with hard currency and favorable trade terms if it wanted his reforms to succeed. "You Americans give us in the KGB credit for being much more daring than we often are. Can you imagine the political repercussions if one of our agents had been caught inside your embassy? Gorbachev would have had Chebrikov's head." There was another reason why Chebrikov would not have used Lonetree to sneak a KGB officer into the embassy. The KGB already had several KGB informants working inside the U.S. embassy as interpreters and other staff personnel. They had more access than Lonetree did and were better trained, better motivated, and more reliable.

It was *not* Lonetree's access as a spy that interested Chebrikov, but his value as a propaganda tool. No Native American had ever defected, and Chebrikov was convinced that the United States would be badly embarrassed if Lonetree defected, and denounced the government that had murdered and robbed his tribal ancestors.

Shortly after Lonetree had been reassigned to Vienna, Chebrikov had ordered the Second Directorate to turn him over to Kryuchkov, since his department handled all KGB spies in foreign countries. Chebrikov had wanted

Kryuchkov to find a way to get Lonetree to defect, and Kryuchkov had been working on a plan to woo the Marine back to Moscow, when he had confessed to being a spy.

As it turned out, Lonetree's confession and the NIS's overzealous investigation of the Marine guards had resulted in creating an effective smokescreen for Ames. "To tell you the truth, we never did anything to promote this scandal in your country about the Marines and the embassy," the former aide to Kryuchkov told me. "We simply sat back and celebrated what you were doing for our favorite hero [Ames]."

During the coming months, Mechulayev met repeatedly with Kryuchkov and Kirpichenko. They often talked about ways to protect Ames. In early 1988, they heard that the CIA and FBI were offering a $1 million reward to anyone who could help them explain why so many of their spies were being arrested. After conferring with Kirpichenko, Kryuchkov decided it was time to send the CIA someone who could answer their questions.

CHAPTER 19

The CIA was under new management.

Director Casey died on May 6, 1987, and President Reagan nominated acting director Robert M. Gates for Senate confirmation. But Gates was forced to withdraw his name after Congress began raising questions about his possible involvement in the Iran-Contra scandal. Reagan's next choice was FBI director William H. Webster, and on May 26, he became the agency's fourteenth director. At the CIA, he was respectfully addressed as "judge," even though it had been nearly a decade since he had sat on a federal court bench. The title fit the sixty-two-year-old administrator. In a capital city where duplicity and doublespeak were often seen as regrettable but perfectly acceptable behavior, Webster had earned a reputation for honesty and straightforwardness. President Jimmy Carter had brought him to Washington to run the FBI after it had been sullied by Watergate and other scandals, and during his nine-year tenure, Webster had worked wonders there. Now he was being dispatched to do the same at the CIA. Its top DO officials were spending much of 1987 testifying before Congress about "The Enterprise," the codename that Lieutenant Colonel Oliver North had used to describe his convoluted effort to keep money and weapons flowing to the contra rebels in Nicaragua.

Webster arrived at the CIA with a broom in hand. Clair George, the director of covert operations, resigned because of his role in the Iran-Contra affair. Webster disciplined seven others, including Dewey Clarridge, who had written the scalding fitness evaluation of Rick Ames in Turkey in 1972. Several months later, Webster began instituting several reforms aimed at improving relations between the agency and the FBI.

Webster knew that the bureau and CIA often were reluctant to share information and help each other when it came to espionage investigations. He wanted to put an end to the petty jealousies and turf wars that had caused friction in the past. In April 1988, he announced the formation of a Counterintelligence Center (CIC) at Langley. It was going to be a joint FBI and CIA operation, he said. The purpose of the center would be to serve as a clearinghouse for counterintelligence information gathered by both agencies. According to a press release issued at the time, Webster planned to force the FBI and CIA to begin cooperating by physically "putting people in each other's offices." The FBI, Webster said, would immediately send two special agents to Langley to work in the center alongside counterintelligence investigators from the CIA. This forced cooperation would ensure that each of the two bureaucracies would know what the other was doing at all times. Webster named Gus Hathaway as the CIC's director. Congress hailed Webster's announcement and he was praised in newspaper editorials. But what Webster, Congress, and the media didn't know was that Webster's grand plan was never implemented. The FBI didn't send anyone to Langley in 1988 to work at the CIC as ordered. It didn't send anyone in 1989 or 1990, either. It wasn't until 1991, when the CIA asked for help in the Ames investigation, that the FBI finally sent two agents to work at the CIC.

Besides creating the CIC, Webster, and his successor at the FBI, William Sessions, also signed a written pledge that said the CIA would notify the FBI whenever it learned that a CIA employee might be a foreign spy. This "Memorandum of Understanding" was in direct response to Edward Lee Howard's embarrassing escape from the FBI. An investigation of the Howard case had showed that Gus Hathaway and Burton Gerber had not told the FBI in 1984 that Howard had admitted to the agency that he had fantasized about contacting the Soviets during his 1983 trip to Washington. The bureau accused the two men of hiding this information because it was embarrassing. Hathaway and Gerber said that they hadn't known it was their responsibility to tell the FBI that an ex-agency employee was having adjustment problems. The memorandum was written to clarify the issue.

One reason the FBI and CIA frequently bumped heads when it came to tracking spies and preventing the loss of U.S. intelligence was because the two organizations had different goals. The differences were perhaps best described by Gerber when he gave lectures to new employees. "FBI agents are trained to think like bank guards," Gerber said. "CIA officers are trained to think like bank robbers." The FBI was responsible for arresting spies and protecting secrets. The CIA's main function was to gather intelligence. Tempers flared when both agencies were asked to do the same job, and there was one area that often brought them together: mole hunts.

The creation of the CIC, in effect, put Jeanne Vertefeuille and her task force out of business. She was named deputy chief of the Security Group, and chief of the Investigations Branch within the Security Group. That typically confusing bureaucratic title basically meant that she was given a number of new jobs, each of which was considered more important than finding the cause of the 1985 losses. Although no one in the CIA would later admit it, the bloodletting in Moscow was simply not much of a priority any more. Years later, Congress would demand to know why. There would be lots of finger-pointing. Webster would testify that he was never made aware of just how serious the 1985 losses were. His deputy, Robert Gates, would make the same claims, although Vertefeuille would later produce records that showed she had briefed Gates about the losses in July 1988. Hathaway, Gerber, Redmond, and Vertefeuille would later insist that they had remained committed to finding the cause of the 1985 losses. They were simply preoccupied with tasks that seemed more important at the time. It is difficult now to judge what did and didn't seem important in 1988, but a glance at how the new CIC allocated its time, money, and workforce raises questions about some of the CIA's priorities. One month after it opened, CIC staffers launched an intense investigation to learn if the KGB was tapping telephone calls from Nancy Reagan to her astrologer in San Francisco. The CIC was worried that the first lady might inadvertently reveal some White House secret by asking the astrologer a question about world affairs.

Part of the reason why the 1985 losses were not a priority by 1988 was because the CIA mistakenly thought the damage was over. As far as the CIA knew, the wave of arrests had petered out. There was a growing feeling that whatever had caused the losses was no longer a threat. None of the new agents who had been recruited since mid-1985 had been arrested. Even more important, the devastation in Moscow had happened during Director Casey's watch. A new management team was now in place, and it wanted to look toward the future, not dwell on the past. The CIA's top managers hoped to impress their new bosses with new ideas, not by dredging up bad memories.

There was one person assigned to the new CIC, however, who still wanted to explore the 1985 losses. Dan Payne was a twenty-nine-year-old investigator employed by the CIA's Office of Security. Within the agency, the security office was not held in high regard. It was responsible for performing background investigations of employees, providing bodyguards for defectors and visiting dignitaries, and safeguarding the agency's buildings and grounds. Oftentimes, other employees looked upon security officers as glorified night watchmen, whose chief job was making sure office doors were locked at night. Payne had worked hard to dispel that image. He had joined the CIA in 1984 and had been assigned a number of grunt jobs. One of them was helping protect Vitaly Yurchenko. Payne was the security officer who had driven Rick and Yurchenko from Andrews Air Force base to the CIA safe house when the KGB defector had first arrived in the United States. Payne had risen rapidly up the ranks since then, and when the CIC was formed, Gus Hathaway had specifically asked the Office of Security to loan Payne to the CIC for two years. Hathaway needed good investigators, and he liked Payne's enthusiasm.

He assigned Payne to work for Vertefeuille. They already knew each other. In 1986, Vertefeuille's task force had asked Payne and two other investigators to compile a list of every CIA officer who had traveled to Moscow during 1985. The task force thought that one of these officers might have stolen information from the Moscow station about the CIA's agents and sold it to the KGB. Payne had interviewed several CIA officers, and it was during these interviews that his easygoing manner and boyish charm paid off. People tended to underestimate him. He was easy to talk to. During an interview, Payne would get his subjects to relax and then ask them to tell him about their coworkers. His subjects would tell him which of their coworkers were disgruntled and who was having financial problems, sexual affairs, drinking problems. Once they finished, Payne would turn the tables. "Just as you have provided information to me about your coworkers," Payne would say, "I will be asking them about you. It might be a good idea if we discuss some of the things that are likely to come up, so I can hear them from you first." Few left the interview room without revealing their innermost secrets.

The task force never got anywhere with its theory about a possible leak in Moscow, but the exercise had gotten Payne hooked on finding an explanation for the 1985 losses. When he reported to his new assignment at the CIC, Payne told Vertefeuille that he wanted to continue the probe on his own. He also told her that he had a new idea for how to investigate the losses.

"Let's hear it," Vertefeuille said.

"The Office of Security spends most of its time investigating employees who are considered security risks," Payne said. "These are usually employees who are alcoholics, disgruntled, heavily in debt, or suffering from some other personal problem. This has always been a good way to identify a problem employee, but not necessarily a spy." Payne had noticed that the KGB had paid John Walker more than $1 million. Despite repeated warnings from the KGB to keep a low profile, Walker had spent his cash on a sports car, an airplane, a posh apartment, and a houseboat, even though it would have been impossible for him to have afforded these niceties on his Navy pay. "The Drug Enforcement Administration and Internal Revenue Service have used financial investigations for years to track down drug dealers and tax evaders," Payne continued. "Why can't we track down spies by looking at people who are spending lots of unexplained cash?"

Vertefeuille's task force had talked about looking for someone in the agency who was living beyond his income, but no one had known how to do it. Payne did. He had taken several courses on his own that showed investigators how to identify money-laundering schemes and find hidden assets.

Payne even had a "target." He'd identified a CIA employee who had been spending more cash than usual. This employee had known about some of the spies who had been caught, and he'd also been having trouble passing recent polygraph tests. Vertefeuille was impressed by Payne's initiative. She told him to "go for it."

Rick drank a champagne toast. Rosario was pregnant. Life was good. Even at work. Alan D. Wolfe, the CIA's chief of station in Rome, was being replaced by Jack Devine. Rick considered him an old friend. They'd started out working in the CIA's Records Integration Division in the early 1960s, and Devine had come to his wedding when he'd married Rosario. Rick assumed they would get along better than he had with Wolfe. Rick had been irritated by the last performance evaluation Wolfe had given him. "Ames handles no ongoing cases," Wolfe had written. "Ames's efforts to initiate new developmental activity of any consequence have been desultory."

Wolfe wasn't the only officer who thought Rick was lazy. Rick had developed a reputation as someone who was quick to spout off opinions and complain, but slow to really do much. The only Soviet who Rick showed any interest in was Aleksey Khrenkov, and Rick kept telling Wolfe that the chances of recruiting Khrenkov were minimal. After a while, Rick stopped writing reports about his lunches with Khrenkov. Wolfe noticed and asked why he wasn't turning them in. "Our lunchtime conversations are not really worth writing about." If that was the case, Wolfe replied, then why was Rick wasting his time and the CIA's money taking Khrenkov to lunch? Wolfe suggested that he stop meeting the Soviet. "No," Rick replied, "I think I'd better keep meeting him. One never knows what might happen." Wolfe said he wanted Rick to stop meeting Khrenkov. Rick said he would begin paying for his lunches with Khrenkov out of his own pocket. Incredibly, no one found that odd.

"I encouraged everyone to think that Rosario was rich and I was living off her," Ames later recalled, "and in some ways that backfired, because people thought less of me because of that. The truth is that in Rome I simply began losing interest in my job. Part of it was age, part of it was my disillusionment. I mean, I kept asking myself, *Why are we bothering to do this?* And then, of course, the ultimate devaluer was that I was working for the KGB and it was hard for me to continue going through the motions at the station."

Some of Rick's colleagues would later claim that Rosario was partly to blame for Rick's mediocre performance. Rosario called him three or four times a day, always in a panic about some emergency. Rick had told everyone that she was pregnant and that she had suffered a miscarriage the summer before. Still, her daily calls became an office joke. After a while, Rosario's daily harangues began to bother Rick, too. "Rick told me I didn't have any consideration for his work and this-and-that," Rosario said later. "The truth was, he didn't have any consideration for me and what I was going through!" Their son, Paul, was born in November 1988. Rick enjoyed being a father. Rosario liked that at first, but soon began to resent how much time he spent fussing over the baby. One night she made it obvious that she wanted to make love, but he didn't respond. She got angry. The next day, he bought her a small gift. That made her feel better.

Rick paid for Cecilia to fly from Bogotá to Rome. Rosario said she needed her mother there to help with the baby, even though they already had an older married couple as live-in servants. After Cecilia arrived, Rick made a trip to Zurich. He had gotten $125,000 in cash from the KGB. That brought the total in his Zurich accounts to $1.5 million. It wasn't enough. "I knew I needed to retire and get away from the agency, to move to Bogotá, but I kept thinking, *Well, it looks as if I'm still safe and the Soviets are still holding lots of money for me in Moscow,* so I would decide to stick around and get just a little more."

Christmas came and went, and during the spring of 1989, Rick and Rosario began making plans for their return to the States at the end of July. Neither of them spoke seriously about him retiring. One morning, Rick got a telephone call from the Marine guard in the lobby at the embassy.

"A Mr. Clean is here to see you, sir," the guard said. That was what the guards had been told to say whenever someone walked in and said they wanted to see a CIA officer. Rick grabbed a packet of language cards and hurried downstairs. The cards contained simple instructions, such as "Please write down your full name" and "Please tell me your occupation." On one side, the phrases were printed in English, and on the other, they were written in the major languages spoken around the world. No matter where someone was from, a CIA officer was supposed to be able to use the cards to communicate with him. Luckily, the man waiting downstairs spoke enough English that they could understand each other.

The volunteer was given the codename MOTORBOAT by the agency.

After Ames was arrested, MOTORBOAT would be identified in the media as an intelligence officer from Czechoslovakia. A few stories would list him among the agents who were executed. This is incorrect. MOTORBOAT was from Bulgaria. In 1989, he was a government employee, and he was secretly working with a group that would later help topple the communist government of President Todor Zhivkov. MOTORBOAT told Rick that he was offering his services as a spy because he wanted the CIA to help finance and organize demonstrations against Zhivkov.

During our private interviews in the Alexandria jail, Ames told me that MOTORBOAT had provided the CIA with information about a U.S. government employee who was under the control of the KGB.

"MOTORBOAT told me about a penetration in the United States government," Ames said. "This person is a U.S. citizen. He was recruited by the Bulgarians, and they later turned him over to the KGB to run."

"Did MOTORBOAT identify this American?"

"MOTORBOAT said he knew the guy who did the recruitment and this guy told him that he had recruited an American who did such and such, in such and such a place, and that the case was turned over to the KGB, so it was a real recruitment," Ames said.

"Did MOTORBOAT fill in those 'such and such's, I mean, did he tell you where this government employee worked?"

"Yes, but I'd better not say anything more."

"Why, this is an old case, right?"

"As far as I know, the agency has never been able to track this person down. It has several suspects who are being watched, and it knows that this was a real recruitment, but it is still an open case, so I can't say anything more, really."

"Are you saying that as we speak, here, in 1994, that to the best of your knowledge, there is a U.S. government employee out there somewhere still under the control of the Russian government? Another spy besides you, you know, who is working in the CIA, FBI, White House, or God knows where?"

"I have to be careful here, uh, look, MOTORBOAT identified a U.S. citizen. He said this person had been recruited by Bulgarian intelligence. He said the Bulgarians had turned this person over to the KGB when this person left Eastern Europe and returned to the United States. I know this is still an active lead. I don't want to say anything more."

In early 1996, I met with several CIA officials and told them what I had learned about MOTORBOAT. At that point, the CIA asked me informally not to publish any information that would reveal the identity of MOTOR-BOAT. I was asked to describe him as being from Czechoslovakia. I was told that if I published any details about MOTORBOAT and his meetings with Ames, I would be putting MOTORBOAT's life in danger. This struck me as odd, because Ames had told me that he had already identified MOTOR-BOAT to the Russians. I mentioned this. "It is possible that the KGB, for a variety of reasons, never told the Bulgarians about him," I was told. Obviously, if the CIA was worried about me identifying him, MOTORBOAT was still alive and had never been exposed. I told the CIA that I would not publish any detailed information about MOTORBOAT, but I said that I would identify him as being from Bulgaria. I also said I would print that he had provided valuable information to the agency during the toppling of the Bulgarian communist government. I then explained why. If I were to mislead readers intentionally by saying MOTORBOAT was from Czechoslovakia, and the truth about MOTORBOAT was eventually made public, then readers would wonder how many other facts I had changed in this book. It was then suggested that I describe him as being from Eastern Europe. I declined. The fact that the CIA had a key source in Bulgaria and that this source wanted the CIA's help in overthrowing the communist government was worth noting. I then asked the CIA if what Ames had told me about a "penetration of the U.S. government" was true. The CIA declined to comment on this question.

Ames told me that after he met with MOTORBOAT, Jack Devine asked him to arrange for MOTORBOAT to be taken to a safe house so that he could be debriefed.

"I was dead set against it," Ames said, "because I thought it would put MOTORBOAT at risk. . . . I said, 'Well, Jack, you are just going to have to order me to meet with him, because I don't think it is safe.' And Devine told me, 'Well, I think it is worth the risk,' and he sat down and wrote a memo to the file, saying that I didn't want to do it but he was ordering me to do it."

Ames told me that he was required to meet MOTORBOAT at a safe house. "I must admit it was a very strange situation for me to be in," Ames said. "Here I was, I mean, I was working for the KGB, right, and here I am interviewing a Bulgarian who is telling me about a penetration of our government by a U.S. citizen, someone who the KGB had under its control. It was a rather weird sensation."

Ames told me that he later passed everything that he had learned about MOTORBOAT to the KGB. "Only a few days earlier, I was arguing strenuously with Jack Devine about putting MOTORBOAT in danger. Now, I was telling the KGB all about MOTORBOAT. All I can say is that I had been genuinely worried about protecting MOTORBOAT at the moment when I was arguing with Devine. It is just another sign of how compartmentalized I was."

During their final meeting together in Rome, Aleksey Khrenkov gave Rick a nine-page letter. In it, the KGB explained how it would contact him after he returned to the States. The KGB also gave Rick a shopping list. It asked him for the identities of any CIA or FBI spies who had managed to penetrate the KGB, the GRU, or the Soviet government. It then asked him for the names of CIA or FBI employees who Ames thought could be recruited. It also gave him a tally of his money. "Dear Friend. . . . all in all, you have been appropriated: $2,705,000." Of that sum, Ames had been paid: $1,081,811.51. The remainder was being held in a bank in Moscow. The KGB said it had decided to pay Rick an annual salary of $300,000, in addition to what already had been put aside for him. The KGB also gave him three Polaroid color photographs. "These pictures show the beautiful piece of land on a river bank which now belongs to you forever," the note said. It explained that the land was a prime spot for a dacha if he decided to defect and live in Russia. "Good luck!" the note ended.

Khrenkov told Rick to destroy the note and photographs as soon as he had looked at them, but he didn't do it. "I kept the damn note and the pictures. Don't ask me why. . . . I felt the KGB was being genuinely nice to me and I just didn't want to destroy the letter or pictures."

Before returning to the States, Rick made another hurried trip to Zurich to deposit his first year's salary of $300,000. When he, Rosario, and Paul returned on July 20, 1989, to Washington, Diana Worthen was waiting at the airport to welcome them. They had asked her if they could leave several suitcases at her house. They were only going to stay in town for a few days at a hotel, before leaving for a month-long vacation in Bogotá. Worthen had gladly taken in their extra luggage and had invited them over for dinner one night. Rick was dressed better than she had ever seen him, and Rosario wore a chic dress. They still seemed like the same old Rick and Rosario to her, however, despite the expensive clothing. It wasn't until after they returned from Bogotá in September 1989 that Worthen began to notice their new wealth. Rosario had stopped by Worthen's apartment one afternoon with a list of houses that she and Rick were thinking about buying. Rosario showed it to Worthen. Every house on the list cost more than a half million dollars. "I just assumed they had managed to save up quite a bit of money while they were overseas, because they didn't have to make a house payment," she said later.

Rosario began complaining about what a hassle it had been for them to bring their servants from Italy to the United States. They were an older Filipino couple who had lived with them in Rome, Rosario said. "They are on vacation in the Philippines now while we work out our problems with immigration. They needed a holiday and so did we."

"I hope you didn't have to pay for them to go home," Worthen said, joking.

"Of course we did," Rosario replied. "That's how these things are done."

Rick and Rosario took Worthen to see the house they had bought. It was a five-bedroom, two-story house on North Randolph Street in Arlington that had been owned by a lawyer. It had cost $540,000.

"Geez," said Worthen, who thought the split-level house was huge, "what are you going to do? Have a family of ten move in the downstairs with you?"

Rosario wasn't amused.

Despite Rick's lackluster performance in Rome, he was given another plum assignment when he returned to work at headquarters. Memories would later differ about who was responsible for appointing Rick as the new chief of the Western European branch of the SE division. By the time Rick returned, Burton Lee Gerber had been named chief of the Europe division and his former deputy, Milton Bearden, had become the SE division chief.

Bearden would later tell reporters that he had tried to kick Rick out of the SE division and had done everything that he could to get rid of him. His statements would dumbfound many of the people who worked with both men. "It was Bearden who took Rick back," said one. Said another: "I always thought Bearden and Rick got along really well." Regardless, Rick's new assignment gave him access to virtually all of the SE division's clandestine operations. His appointment could have unleashed another round of KGB arrests and executions, had it not been for the compartmentalization that Gerber had implemented earlier; the so-called back room operation being run by Sandy Grimes and Diana Worthen. Ames would later acknowledge that his new job had given him access to a slew of CIA intelligence reports and secret studies. Before leaving his office at the end of a typical workday, Rick would stuff handfuls of classified material into his briefcase and simply walk past the guards stationed at the doorways.

In November 1989, not long after Rick had returned to work, his telephone rang, and a voice said: "You'll never guess who has reappeared." It took Rick a moment to recognize the voice. It was R. Patrick Watson, the FBI agent Rick had worked with in New York City twelve years earlier. Although they hadn't kept in close contact, Rick had heard that Watson was now a deputy assistant director in the FBI's national security division, which meant he helped oversee the FBI's entire counterintelligence operation.

"So who's resurfaced, Pat?" Rick asked.

"It's Sergey, Sergey Fedorenko! He's been spotted in town, and I understand he will be having dinner tonight at the Madison Hotel around seven o'clock," Watson replied. "I was thinking we should join him."

Fedorenko was already eating with another Soviet in the hotel's restaurant when Rick and Pat Watson arrived. They sat across the room from him. Fedorenko noticed them come in, but did not acknowledge that he had seen them. He simply continued eating, and after several minutes, he excused himself, and walked into the men's room. Rick casually walked across the room and stepped into the men's room, too. Fedorenko had already checked to make sure no one else was there. The Russian hugged him.

"Rick! Rick! It's so great to see you!" he said.

"We've got a room upstairs," Rick replied, pushing an extra hotel key into Fedorenko's hand. "Can you join us later?"

"I must go back to our hotel first and get rid of my dinner guest, but then I'll sneak out. Yes, it can be done," Fedorenko answered. He was still holding Rick in his arms. "I wasn't sure we would ever see each other again, my friend."

Rick grinned. "We were afraid that Howard had betrayed you and that you had been arrested," he said.

"Who's Howard?" Fedorenko asked. Rick quickly told him about Edward Lee Howard, and then Fedorenko returned to his table. Rick waited a few minutes before rejoining Watson.

"It's all set," Rick said. "He'll meet us as soon as he dumps his dinner partner."

Just before 10:00 P.M., Fedorenko tapped on the door of the hotel room. Now it was Watson's turn for a hug. Fedorenko was excited to see them both.

"I was afraid they'd arrested you," Watson said.

"Yes, this business about Howard," Fedorenko replied. "It's terrible."

Years later, when Fedorenko recalled his meeting with Ames and Watson at the hotel, he would wonder if Ames had shrewdly manipulated him. "There was a reason why Rick mentioned Howard's name to me when we were alone in the men's room. I could tell he was nervous, but I didn't know why. Now I know that he was the one who had betrayed me and that is why he was trying to put this idea in my mind that Howard was responsible. He wanted Howard's name to be on my tongue, and it worked. When I mentioned Howard's name to Pat, I was confirming that Howard was the traitor. From that point on, the conversation always centered on Howard. Rick was very smart doing this."

Fedorenko announced that he had been appointed to a special team in Moscow that was advising Mikhail Gorbachev on some of the reforms that he was implementing. "Life is full of delicious ironies," Fedorenko beamed. "Can you guess what branch of Soviet government I am now helping write regulations for?" Rick and Watson didn't have a clue. "The KGB! I'm on a team advising Gorbachev on how to restructure the KGB!"

Although Rick and Watson wanted to ask intelligence-related questions, they spent the first hour listening to Fedorenko recount what had happened to him after he left New York City in late 1977. He told them that he had buried his spy gear in a park when he learned that TRIGON (Alexander Ogorodnik) had been arrested at the foreign ministry. He recalled how he had gone to work at the Institute of U.S.A. and Canada Studies. "The KGB watched everything I did." His apartment was repeatedly searched. "They tried to trap me." No Soviet was allowed to be alone with foreigners during the early 1980s, he explained. "We always had to be in twos when we met foreigners." But the KGB had told Fedorenko that he could meet with foreigners by himself. "They wanted to catch me slipping them a note." Fedorenko had not been permitted to leave the country, but he managed to slip into Hungary in the mid-1980s. "I had written Rick a letter, but when I approached the U.S. embassy, I saw that the KGB had the place surrounded. It was too dangerous." Fedorenko destroyed the letter and returned home.

There were several times during the past twelve years when Fedorenko thought he would be arrested. He was once in a meeting at the institute arguing about Soviet–U.S. arms negotiations, when a colleague had accused him of being "pro-American." The accusation had badly embarrassed him, and he and his accuser had become bitter enemies. Not long after that squabble, Fedorenko learned that his accuser had been arrested by the KGB and charged with being a CIA spy. He was Vladimir Potashov, MEDIAN. "The entire time Potashov was attacking me and acting like he hated America, he was actually helping your side."

The incident had scared Fedorenko, because he did not know how the KGB had learned that Potashov was a spy. "I thought I would be next." Strangely, the KGB began backing away from him, and it recently had told him that he could travel outside the country once more. "The only reason I can imagine for this is because I am now advising Gorbachev. The KGB knows it would have to have extremely strong evidence to arrest one of Gorbachev's advisers."

Watson asked the Russian if he were still willing to help the United States. "Of course," said Fedorenko. He had been excited when Gorbachev had first come into power, but now he was worried that Gorbachev was backing away from some of his reforms, especially when it came to muzzling the KGB. In 1988, Gorbachev had replaced KGB director Viktor Chebrikov with Vladimir Kryuchkov, who had been chief of the First Directorate. Because Chebrikov had been a Communist hard-liner, Fedorenko had been happy to see him go and, at first, it appeared that Kryuchkov was eager to support Gorbachev's new vision. But now there were rumors that he was advising Gorbachev to slow down and adopt a more conservative tack. "I'm worried about where this is leading," Fedorenko said.

The three men's reunion ended that night with Fedorenko promising to contact them again in a few months, when he was scheduled to attend a conference in Canada.

Watson suggested that Fedorenko keep his eyes open for any "interesting material" that he might come across when he got back to Moscow.

"Yes, it will be just like the old days," Fedorenko said.

"Yes," Rick replied. "Just like the old days."

One afternoon, Rosario invited Diana Worthen over for coffee. She wanted to show her some fabric samples. Worthen had just had new drapes put in her living room, and Rosario was about to buy drapes, too.

"Help me choose," said Rosario.

"Okay," replied Worthen, "which room are you going to do first?"

"What?"

"Well, it's so expensive, I figured you'd want to do one room at a time, so we need to pick which one you want to do first," Worthen explained.

Rosario laughed. "Diana, don't worry about the price. I'm going to have the whole house done at once." Now, let's choose fabrics."

It was the draperies that had done it, Worthen said later. When she was driving home that night, she started adding up the price of buying and installing all the drapes in the Ames house. "I thought, *Where the hell did they suddenly get all of this money?*" By the time she reached home, Worthen was so upset that she couldn't sleep. For at least one week, she didn't say a word to anyone, and then finally one afternoon in late November, she went to see Sandy Grimes. Closing the office door behind her, Worthen said, "Sandy, I really need to talk to you in private about something."

Grimes could tell that Worthen was upset.

"I know this sounds terrible, and I feel like I'm being a real rat doing this," Worthen continued. "I mean, these people are two of my closest friends, but I think there is something that you need to know about them. I'm talking about Rick Ames and his wife, Rosario."

THE WORDS OF RICK AMES

The easy answer is to blame Rosario, to say that I was afraid that I would lose her unless I had enough money to keep her happy, and that is what I told myself at first. That she was to blame. That I really had no choice after the divorce, because of Nan. That I would have lost Rosario unless I had the cash.

But the truth is that Rosario hadn't demanded that I have great sums of money when we met. I was the one who was convinced it was necessary.

Why? Why did I do this? I had never cared about or been interested in money or even accumulating things before I met her. Even after I began getting these large amounts, I never controlled the money well. I mean, I like comfort, good food, toys such as the Jaguar, but I proved to be too generous with my friends, indulgent with Rosario, and even careless about the money I was paid. There was still a part of me that didn't really care about the wealth. Why then did I think it was so necessary to have it?

Why?

I have come to believe that blaming Rosario is a very superficial reason. The real blame lies in my self-doubt and my own fears. I was convinced that I had to have lots and lots of money because not having it was a public confession of weakness and inadequacy on my part. Deep down, I knew Rosario wasn't going to leave me because I didn't have large sums of money. She had never been rich. It was me! I didn't want her to think less of me, especially after she learned that I wasn't who she thought I was in Mexico City. I wasn't a diplomat. I didn't want to look like a failure in her eyes. Nor did I want to admit to myself that I was weak, that I was inadequate. After Rome, having the money became more important, not because of what I could buy with it, but because of what it said about me.

What did it say?

It said Rick Ames was not a failure.

THE WORDS OF OTHERS

What did Rick Ames ever achieve? What was he successful at? Was there anything? Was he a successful husband? A successful father? We know he wasn't successful at his job. So how did he get the recognition that he wanted so desperately? He was only successful in one area—betraying other people.

—Sandy Grimes, CIA

Rick always had this problem and it shows in Ankara, Mexico City, and in Rome. He just didn't do well when he had to get out in the streets, where it was illegal to do what he was doing and he didn't have anyone to protect him if he got caught.

—Jeanne Vertefeuille, CIA

My brother never cared about money. He never worried about it, and then when he comes home from Rome, he shocks us all by his spending. It wasn't just that he bought nice things. It was really gluttony. One Gucci watch wasn't enough. They had to have four or five Gucci watches.

—Nancy Ames Everly, Rick's sister

He was upset because he didn't feel he was being appreciated at work and he wasn't getting any promotions. He said, "Tell me what I'm doing wrong." So Rosario and I sat there in the kitchen, and we spent several hours telling him what he needed to do to improve as a manager and to impress the people he worked with. He just didn't get it, though.

—Diana Worthen, CIA

As far as I was concerned, Alan Wolfe, the chief of station in Rome, had a bantam rooster complex. He was a short guy and really, really nasty. Rick was really intelligent, and yet he always ended up working for some prick who knew how to get ahead in the agency. It had to grate on him.

—David T. Samson, CIA

Rick doesn't think anyone can get close to him. . . . It's his arrogance, really. He doesn't think anyone is as smart as he is. He figures he can manipulate everyone.

—Rosario Ames

Rick's first wife, Nan, told me during the divorce: "The thing you must remember about Rick is that he is an actor first. He feels much more comfortable playing a role than himself."

—David Blake, close friend

PART FOUR

NOT A CARE
IN THE WORLD

The surest way to be deceived is
to think one's self more clever than
others.

—La Rochefoucauld
Maximes 127

CHAPTER 20

Diana Worthen had no trouble convincing Sandy Grimes that the source of Rick and Rosario's newfound wealth needed to be investigated. Secretly, Grimes had always suspected that the 1985 losses in Moscow were the handiwork of a KGB mole, and Rick seemed to her to be a likely suspect. Early on in her career, Grimes had felt sorry for Rick. They had ridden together in a car pool in the 1970s when both of them lived in Reston, and Rick had struck her as being a good-hearted but inept case officer. She could still picture those days. He was never ready when the car pool arrived. Its members would wait for five or ten minutes, and then someone would finally suggest that they leave without him. As if on cue, Rick would come running outside, his hair uncombed, his shirt untucked, his pants pockets sticking out. He'd be holding his tie in one hand and a crumpled jacket in the other. His hair never looked as if he washed it, his fingernails were always dirty.

Although Rick hadn't cared much about his looks back then, Grimes had liked his enthusiasm for his job. Everyone in the car pool worked at the CIA, and Rick had talked about how much fun he was having. That changed. After Rick was passed over for promotion to the GS-15 level in 1985, he developed a reputation for being argumentative, resentful. Grimes had been stunned by the "new" Rick Ames who had returned from Rome. It just wasn't the expensive Italian suits, newly capped teeth, erect posture, or improved grooming. "Rick had undergone an almost complete personality change," Grimes later noted. "There was an air of confidence that I'd never seen before. He exuded it, and I couldn't believe it, because he certainly wasn't getting his ego stroked professionally by the agency." There was another difference. "The gentleness was gone."

Grimes popped up from her chair as soon as Worthen finished telling her about Rick and Rosario's new lifestyle. "We have to tell Paul," she said, referring to Paul Redmond.

"Are you sure?" Worthen replied. "I mean, what if I'm wrong? I feel like such a rat already, but I don't want to be right about this either, you know, because they are two of my closest friends, and all."

"Paul needs to hear this. If there's nothing to it, Rick will never find out, and if there is, then Rick's not really a friend, is he?"

As soon as the two women entered Redmond's office, Grimes warned him. "You aren't going to like this, but Diana has something important to say that you need to hear."

After Worthen recounted her story, Grimes added: "You know Rick had access to every case we lost."

Redmond listened, but was preoccupied. "Why don't you tell Jeanne about this?" he suggested.

Worthen went to see Jeanne Vertefeuille at the CIC. She was busy, too, so she sent Worthen to talk to Dan Payne. By this time, Worthen was beginning to wish that she had never mentioned her suspicions to anyone. Still, she told Payne about Rick and Rosario's unexplained wealth. Payne had just finished investigating the finances of another CIA employee, the target he had chosen for his first financial investigation. His research had shown that the employee's spouse had inherited $100,000, and that was why he was able to spend more money than he was earning. There was no evidence that showed the employee was a spy. Payne did not know Worthen well, and some of what she was telling him sounded minor, but he promised to look into Rick's finances.

The telephone was ringing when Worthen got home. It was Rosario inviting her over for dinner that weekend. Worthen tried to act as if nothing were the matter, but she was upset when she put down the receiver. "I had no other life than my work," she said later. "My job meant everything to me, so I felt I had to tell the agency about Rick and Rosario, and yet, I hated myself for even thinking that Rick could be a traitor, because he had been my boss in Mexico City and he and Rosario were probably my closest friends."

Paul Redmond would later candidly admit that he could not remember what Worthen and Grimes had told him about Rick during their rushed meeting in November 1989. He was now the deputy director of the SE division and he was swamped with work. The Berlin Wall had just come down. Demands for democratic reforms were sweeping across Eastern Europe. Countries that had been difficult for the CIA to penetrate were suddenly opening their borders. A new generation of political leaders was taking power, and many of them were more afraid of the old KGB than the CIA. But there was another reason why Redmond had not paid much attention to the two women. His $1 million reward for information had flushed out a new source in Moscow, and it now looked as if the 1985 losses had not been caused by a mole.

Vladimir Smetanin, who was given the codename PROLOGUE, was a high-ranking KGB intelligence officer with access to KGB files about the arrest of the CIA's spies. Smetanin had been exactly the sort of source that Redmond had hoped to attract.* Unlike other informants in Moscow, who were simply repeating gossip, Smetanin had given the CIA internal KGB documents. These records showed the spies had been caught because of good detective work, good luck, and errors by the CIA and the spies themselves. According to the secret KGB reports, several CIA case officers thought they had managed to slip out of the U.S. embassy without being followed when, in fact, the KGB had been watching them. Other documents cited errors that the spies had made that made the KGB suspect them. The agency had analyzed the documents that Smetanin had given it, and they appeared genuine. Even more important, the names of each agent's case officer, the dates that the case officers were spotted outside the embassy, and the locations where they were seen, all matched information that the CIA had in its files.

While Smetanin's evidence was important, it was not the only reason why Redmond was beginning to have doubts about a mole being burrowed inside the agency. The 1985 losses seemed to be a one-shot event. None of the agency's new spies had been arrested. Nor had the Soviets uncovered any of the agency's recent clandestine operations. It was as if the KGB had been able to peek through a window into the CIA for one brief moment in 1985, before someone closed the blinds. If the KGB had a mole operating in the CIA, why wasn't he still giving them information?

*The CIA declined to say how much it paid PROLOGUE for his cooperation.

Unlike Redmond, Jeanne Vertefeuille would later remember exactly why she had been busy in November 1989, when Worthen came to see her. She was embroiled in an investigation that has never been made public until now. At the time, it had seemed more important than questioning Rick and Rosario about their spending. During the fall of 1989, a stranger had approached a young CIA officer stationed in Latin America and had identified himself as an investigator from the CIA inspector general's office. He had shown the employee his diplomatic passport, and a letter supposedly written by the director of the CIA asking all agency employees to answer any questions asked by the stranger. He said that he was investigating everyone at the local CIA station and he quizzed the young officer about her coworkers there. The young officer had started feeling uneasy about the stranger a few days later and had reported the incident. The agency had sent a package of photographs to the station, and the young officer had picked out a picture of the stranger. She claimed it was Philip Agee, a renegade former CIA officer who had resigned in the mid-1970s and had written a book called *Inside the Company: CIA Diary*, which had infuriated the agency. In his book, Agee had revealed the names of dozens of CIA officers working undercover. If the agency had a hate list, Agee's name would have been printed right under Edward Lee Howard's at the top.

When Worthen came to see her, Vertefeuille had been getting ready to leave for Latin America to question the young employee. The agency was worried about what Agee might do with the information if, indeed, he were the stranger. It was also afraid the stranger might have used his ploy elsewhere. Vertefeuille would later send a worldwide cable to all of the CIA's stations describing what had happened and warning employees to be careful. The fact that she did not have time to check on Worthen's claims didn't hamper the investigation, Vertefeuille later said. "I would have sent Diana to talk to Dan Payne in any event, because it was his job to carry out the investigation of the 1985 losses."

Dan Payne began his investigation by pulling three files: Rick's personnel file contained his job performance evaluations; a file kept by the Office of Security held summaries of the polygraph tests he had been given and the results of background investigations into his past; and a "201 file" contained information about Rosario. A 201 file was what the agency opened whenever it identified someone as a potential "asset." The CIA had started keeping a file on Rosario when David Samson recruited her as a source in Mexico City. Payne had read hundreds of personnel files, and although Rick's drinking was mentioned, the investigator did not consider anything in Rick's record particularly shocking. "Heavy drinking is not uncommon among some employees in the DO," Payne said later. "While performance often suffers, most do not go out and commit espionage." The file on Rosario contained ten pages of comments by Samson and some newspaper articles about her father. The clippings identified Rosario's father as a political-party big shot, governor of a Colombian province, and rector of a large university. Worthen had told Payne that Rosario hadn't had much money in Mexico City, but Payne thought she might have inherited a large sum after her father died. That was what had happened in the case he had just finished investigating. So Payne called several Latin American experts at the CIA, and all of them agreed that Rosario's father had probably been wealthy based on his social standing. "I was told that in Latin America, prominent positions go hand in hand with money—lots of it!"

Worthen had said that Rick and Rosario had recently bought a half-million-dollar house, so Payne drove to the Arlington County courthouse to examine the property records housed there. Within a matter of minutes, he had found a deed that confirmed that Rick and Rosario had paid $540,000 for their new home. But Payne couldn't find any record of them taking out a mortgage on the property. He spent several hours looking through record books, but there was no mortgage on file. When he got back to the agency, he went to see Vertefeuille.

"This is really odd, Jeanne," he said. "Rick bought this half-million-dollar house, but there's no record he took a mortgage out."

"You must have missed the papers," she said. "Why don't you look again tomorrow?"

The next day, Payne returned to the courthouse to search again, but he couldn't find a mortgage.

"It's not there," he told Vertefeuille that afternoon. "I checked again."

"Someone has made a mistake somewhere," she said. "Maybe they misfiled it or put it in the wrong book. Go back tomorrow and look again."

Payne spent a third day scouring the record books, but again couldn't find a mortgage. This time, Vertefeuille believed him. Both thought it strange. *Who buys a half-million-dollar house without borrowing money?* Payne told

Vertefeuille that he was going to request information about Rick's bank deposits. He wanted to see if Rick had ever deposited $10,000 or more in cash at one time at his bank. Payne knew the KGB always paid in cash, and he figured that a mole in Rick's position would be worth at least $1 million to the KGB. That was a lot of cash to bury in the backyard. By this time, the Christmas holidays were approaching, and Payne was scheduled to report on January 5, 1990, to the Farm for training. The agency had decided to put him through the same training classes it gave its case officers. It had already sent one of Payne's fellow investigators through the course. The agency wanted Payne to know the same tricks that its case officers were taught at the Farm, since he was responsible for doing internal investigations. Otherwise, a dishonest case officer could use information that he had learned at the Farm to fool Payne. The United States Customs Service, a branch of the Department of the Treasury, kept track of large cash deposits made at banks. Payne hand-carried his request to the Customs Service during the last week of December 1989. Then he returned to his office and began packing for the Farm. His training was supposed to end in March. He figured that would be plenty of time for the Customs Service to check on Rick's records.

The KGB did its best to keep the execution of GRU general Dmitri Polyakov a secret, but news eventually filtered back to the agency. After the KGB had finished debriefing him, Polyakov had been led into a room, ordered to kneel down with his back to his executioner, and shot in the back of the head so that the blast would make his face unrecognizable. His body had been taken to a secret location, where it had been buried in an unmarked grave. A form letter had been sent to his wife and two sons. It said that Polyakov's sentence had been carried out. A box marked "execution" had been checked.

At about this same time, the CIA learned that another spy, Vladimir Vasilev, known by the cryptonym ACCORD, also had been arrested and executed. He had helped the CIA catch Clyde Lee Conrad, a U.S. army sergeant, in 1988. The agency had led the media to believe that there were other explanations for Conrad's arrest in order to protect Vasilev, but he had provided the CIA with proof that Conrad was a spy. Although the case did not spark many headlines in the United States, the agency considered Conrad a major spy. He had sold the KGB the defense plans that the NATO alliance would have used if Europe were attacked by the Soviets. He'd also provided the Soviets with crypto, the secret codes that NATO countries used to encipher and decipher messages.

Diana Worthen and Sandy Grimes had worked closely with Polyakov, and both were distraught by his execution. In the mid-1970s, Worthen had been sent to New Delhi, solely to help the CIA case officer there take care of the prolific GRU spy. "Polyakov asked us for some fish hooks once, because he loved to fish," Worthen said later. "I mistakenly ordered some that were twenty times larger than what he wanted, and he told his handler to tell me that he wasn't trying to catch whales. He had a good sense of humor." Grimes had helped handle the Polyakov case from headquarters during that same time period. "I felt like he was part of my family because I knew so much about him and his family, even his father-in-law's pants size. He had a forty-two-inch waist," she said. "I had to schedule my vacations to correspond with his home leave back to Moscow, because I couldn't be gone unless he was taking a break." She had always admired him. "He had fought in World War II and was aware of the great human sacrifices that had been made by his country—all for nothing—because only a handful of people in Moscow were benefiting. He was worried that the United States really didn't understand the Soviet mind or what a dangerous threat communism was." Grimes had always told herself that she would resign from the CIA if anything ever happened to Polyakov. "That's how strongly I felt about him and our obligation to protect him. When someone you work that closely with is caught and executed, it really destroys you." Now, she told Worthen that she would never quit until she knew why Polyakov had been caught.

One afternoon, Rick strolled into the office that Worthen and Grimes shared without bothering to knock. Worthen immediately covered several papers on her desk and Grimes shot him an angry look. Word had spread inside the SE division that the two women were running a "back room operation," and no one was supposed to enter their office without knocking, even when the door was open. Rick ignored Grimes's stare.

"Diana, how would you like to take a ride in my new car?" Rick said cheerfully.

"Sure, Rick, what'd you buy?" Worthen replied, as she diplomatically maneuvered Rick back into the hallway away from Grimes.

"A Jag," he replied, referring to his new Jaguar XJ-6 sedan. "You know I loved the one I had in Italy."

Worthen had never ridden in a Jaguar. "Gosh, Rick," she gushed. "What'd you do, rob a bank?"

Rick grinned.

In late 1989, Rick had no idea that Worthen had raised questions about his spending. He felt confident that he had covered his tracks. "I was never worried about the CIA catching me. I knew how inept the organization was." Rick opened eight separate bank and brokerage accounts in the United States. He shuffled his money between them. He also "laundered" it through his mother-in-law's Zurich account before transferring it by wire into his various accounts. He had paid for his house with money from Cecilia's account to make it look as if she had bought the house for them. To further the ruse, Rick contacted William Bruce Gair, a Virginia attorney and friend, and told him that Cecilia was buying the house as a present. Gair recommended that Rick get his mother-in-law to sign a "gift letter," just in case someone at the IRS or the agency questioned the purchase. Rick got Cecilia to sign one. "Cecilia never felt it was her place to ask any questions about money. I had bought the apartment in Bogotá where she was living, and I was supporting her each month, so she just went along with whatever I told her to do," Ames said later.

Records would later show that Rick transferred $652,080 from Switzerland into his various U.S. accounts during late 1989. In 1990, he transferred another $199,990 by wire into the States. Rosario would later insist that she thought all of the money came from commissions that Robert from Chicago had paid her husband.

Rick's job as chief of Western European SE operations didn't last long. With all the changes taking place in Europe, Milton Bearden decided to reorganize the SE division. Rick was put in charge of Czech operations. For a KGB mole, it was a lousy assignment, and Rick soon began to fuss. When he heard that the deputy chief's job in Moscow was about to become vacant, Rick began lobbying Bearden for it. Serving in Moscow would be a "fitting finale" to his career, he said. But Bearden chose someone else, so Rick came up with another proposal. He asked Bearden to create a task force that would be responsible for investigating the credentials of all Eastern Europeans who were now volunteering to work as CIA spies. The KGB would probably try to slip a few double agents into that crowd, Rick warned. He could help the agency separate the legitimate sources from the false ones. Bearden turned him down. Rick was worried. There was always a chance that a former Eastern European intelligence officer, who had somehow learned about him, would step forward. "I just hoped like hell that the KGB was protecting me."

In early 1990, Rick's ego got a boost at work. With Bearden's approval, Rick was chosen to serve on a promotion panel. He helped decide which CIA case officers were promoted to the GS-12 pay level. After Ames was arrested, there would be speculation in the press that he had divulged information about these up-and-coming employees to the KGB. But Ames denied it. "I'd already told the KGB who I thought it might approach," he said later. "There was nothing in those records that was worth noting." Still, being on the panel gave him a thrill. Always before, he had been the one begging for a promotion. Now he was helping make those decisions.

In interviews, Rosario would later claim that she no longer loved Rick when they returned to the States from Italy in 1989. She would insist that they were on the verge of a divorce. Those statements shocked her close friends. None of them could remember Rosario ever talking in 1989 about filing for a divorce, although there were signs that her relationship with Rick had visibly become less affectionate. "I still felt they loved each other, but the relationship had really, really changed," said David Samson, who stayed with them three different times at their house during late 1989 and early 1990. "I mean, Rosario just dominated Rick. She was the queen of the house. I used to look at him and think, *God, here's a guy who probably wishes he could just go out and drink a few beers and relax*, but he didn't dare because he knew Rosario was going to tear his head off the next day if he ever did. She was just picking at him all the time."

Samson was astounded the first time he saw Rick and Rosario's new house.

"How did you pull off buying this place?" he stammered.

"Cecilia popped for it," Rick replied.

Samson thought that was strange. "I asked myself, *How could Cecilia pay for this?* because I didn't think Rosario's family had any money. I mean, I was the one who had loaned Rosario money in Mexico City and I was the one who was paying her to use her apartment as a safe house. Then I remembered that her father had been a politician and there are plenty of examples where Latin American politicians steal millions. I thought, *Well, maybe Cecilia figures this is a solid marriage and now that she has a grandson, she is letting go of some of her cash.*"

Samson asked: "Did the Office of Security buy your explanation about Cecilia?"

"Yeah," Rick replied. "I got a gift letter from her, and as soon as I showed it to them, they knew it was legitimate." He was lying. He had never shown anyone at the CIA the gift letter that Cecilia had signed.

Rick showed Samson the Jaguar. It had cost close to $50,000. "Rick told me that he had planned on buying a used one, but the salesman convinced him that the price for a new one wasn't that much more and he had just decided to go for it."

One night, Samson and Rick started drinking vodka and arguing about politics in the kitchen after dinner. Samson was a Reagan supporter. Rosario got tired and marched upstairs, but an hour later she reappeared and demanded to know when Rick was coming to bed. Samson noticed that whenever the conversation wasn't about her, Rosario seemed to lose interest. By this time, Rick and Samson had finished a bottle of vodka and were drinking wine. Rick told Rosario to go to sleep without him but an hour later she reappeared in the kitchen and this time, she really told him off, but he was drunk and he didn't care that she was angry. That made her even more upset. She announced that she was going to sleep in a spare bedroom. "I don't think Rick even noticed I wasn't in our bed," she later complained. "The next morning, Rick says, 'Why are you mad at me? What did I do?' I was so furious I could barely speak to him."

That night Rosario found a bouquet of red roses waiting for her when she came in from shopping. There was a letter of apology attached to the flowers. "Rick used to write me a letter every time he got drunk as a skunk or we had a fight. . . . It was his way of saying he was sorry. . . . That's what made it hard. . . . The next day he was back to the same lovable person. He'd write 'Don't leave me. I can't live without you,' and being the stupid person that I am, I would feel sorry for him. Looking back on it, I now see that he really knew how to manipulate me . . . and in a strange way, I became totally dependent on him."

Rick suggested that Rosario go back to school. She suspected he wanted to get her out of the house, "so I would lay off and leave him alone for awhile," in her words. Still, she liked the idea. She began visiting the numerous universities in the D.C. area, but none suited her. "Washington may be full of universities," she complained, "but I really think the only one that's worth anything is Georgetown." Even it didn't have the classes that she wanted. "Your universities are not as good as what we have in Colombia," she said. Just the same, she enrolled in three philosophy classes at Georgetown University and Rick hired a nanny to take care of Paul during the day so that Rosario could attend classes and study. The Filipino couple who had come with them from Rome had quit as soon as they had received the documents that they needed to work in the United States. They said later that they had grown tired of Rosario's tirades.

Midway through his training course at the Farm, Dan Payne heard that Karl Koecher had been spotted traveling in Western Europe. Koecher and his wife, Hana, were the Czech "illegals" who had worked at the agency in the mid-1970s and were responsible for telling the KGB about TRIGON. Payne knew that Koecher had provided the Czechs with personal information about his coworkers while he was working in an operation known as SCREEN. Most of the employees involved in SCREEN were native Russians or Eastern Europeans, hired to translate tape recordings of conversations overheard by the CIA through wiretaps and other electronic bugs. Most of these employees had moved to better jobs inside the CIA after SCREEN ended, and during the late 1980s, several of them received letters from long-forgotten relatives living in the Soviet Union asking for help; others had been approached by KGB officers who knew intimate details about their lives. It was clear to the agency that Koecher had given the KGB a list of employees he thought might be vulnerable. That was why the KGB had started contacting them. Payne had been assigned in the 1980s to interview these employees.

"I had tried to 'see through Koecher's eyes' when I did these interviews," Payne later recalled. "I was trying to figure out why he had chosen these people. What was it about them that made him think they were vulnerable?" Payne had always wondered if Koecher had recruited someone in the agency to be a mole. Perhaps he had blackmailed a case officer who had slept with his wife during one of their wild sex parties. "I knew Koecher's only loyalty was to money," said Payne, "so while I was at the Farm I proposed that the agency offer him fifty thousand dollars in return for a series of face-to-face interviews." Payne thought that he could get Koecher to tell him if the KGB had recruited a mole. Koecher had a huge ego, Payne said later. The key would be appealing to his vanity. The agency contacted Koecher, and Payne was told during the last week of his training at the Farm that the Czech spy had agreed to meet him in Bonn, Germany.

Payne hurried back to Langley to prepare for his interviews with Koecher. The agency had already booked a flight for him. When he returned to his office, Payne found a report about Rick's finances waiting on his desk. The Customs Service had found three "hits." A Virginia bank reported that Rick had deposited $13,000 in cash on October 18, 1985. He'd deposited another $15,660 on February 18, 1986. More recently, he had converted Italian lire into $22,107 at a bank on August 1, 1989, after returning from Rome. While those cash deposits were large enough to be reported, they were not stagger-ing figures. Payne left for Bonn.

"It is nice to finally meet someone I know so well," Payne told Koecher when they met in a hotel lobby in March 1990. Koecher's response: "Files don't tell you everything."

At the same time Payne was meeting with Koecher in Bonn, Vertefeuille was sorting through reams of intelligence files the CIA had received from the new reunified German government. These documents were copies of files that had been kept by the much-feared East German intelligence ser-vice, known as STASI, considered by many to be the best of the communist world's spy operations. Under the direction of the infamous spy-master, Markus Wolf, STASI had successfully infiltrated several foreign govern-ments. The CIA station chief in Bonn had reviewed some of the STASI files before they were shipped to Langley, and he had made an alarming discov-ery that he referred to Vertefeuille for further investigation.

The STASI files showed that during the early 1980s the East Germans had not known which employees at the U.S. embassy in West Berlin were diplomats and which were CIA officers. But in 1985, STASI had suddenly been able to positively identify everyone in the CIA station in West Berlin, except for one man. *What had happened?* The station chief in Bonn thought the answer was obvious: STASI had penetrated the station with a mole. If that were true, then it was possible that the STASI mole had returned to the agency, learned the names of the CIA's agents in the SE division, and passed them to the KGB.

Vertefeuille sent a cable to Payne in Bonn, suggesting that he meet with the Bonn station chief as soon as possible about the STASI files. Payne got that message during his second day of interviews with Koecher. The two of them were playing mental chess. The Czech agent would hint that he knew about the 1985 losses and then pull back. Payne suspected that Koecher was baiting him, trying to get Payne to tell him what the agency knew. It was frustrating. Payne had told Koecher that he wanted to interview him at least three times, with breaks in between. That would give Payne a chance to check out what Koecher was telling him, to see if he were lying. They agreed to end their first session after three days and meet again in a few weeks. Payne hurried over to the Bonn station once Koecher left.

During the next several months, Payne would jet back and forth between Germany and the United States to interview Koecher and investigate the STASI files. Eventually, he and the Bonn station chief were able to reconstruct how the East Germans had identified all of the CIA officers except for one in West Berlin. *It had nothing to do with a mole.* "Whenever an American diplomat crossed into East Berlin, he was required to show the border guards a 'flag card,'" Payne later explained. Flag cards were issued to diplomats who frequently crossed between West and East Berlin. They contained the card-holder's photograph, his or her name, a description, and an identification number. Payne learned that a clerk working in the CIA station had decided that it was a waste of time to send all the CIA officers to the military office that issued flag cards, so she had requested a large block of blank flag cards, which she had filled out and distributed to the CIA officers. These cards were numbered consecutively, and a STASI officer noticed one day, when two well-known CIA officers crossed the border, that they had flag cards whose numbers were only a few digits apart. This same officer was able to identify another CIA employee a few days later. He noticed that the number on the CIA officer's flag card fell in between the digits of the other two. The STASI officer deduced that all of the CIA officers had been given flag cards from the same block of numbers. "After that, it was simple for them to fill in the blanks," said Payne. The only CIA employee who was never identified was an officer who had never crossed into East Berlin.

In the fall of 1990, Payne returned to Langley, tired and disappointed. By this time, he had finished with Koecher and had decided that the Czech had not known anything about a mole. He'd also plowed through most of the STASI files, although he still had a few more translated copies to read. Then he could get back to checking on Rick's finances. It was tedious work, but Payne returned to the STASI files, and as he neared the last of the records, he hit pay dirt. He discovered a file filled with intimate information about a CIA employee who had been stationed in Germany during the early 1980s. It was obvious that STASI had been trying to recruit the employee. Payne recognized the name. The case officer still worked for the agency, and during 1985, he had been in a job where he would have known the names of the CIA's agents in the SE division. It looked as if Payne had finally found a mole.

CHAPTER 21

In June 1990, Rick announced that Robert from Chicago needed him to fly to Zurich to take care of some investments. Rick told Rosario that he didn't want anyone to know he had left the country. "If anyone asks, tell them I'm in New York," he said. Rick was required by CIA regulations to inform the agency whenever he traveled abroad. Rosario promised that she would lie for him. Of course, Rick was lying to her. He was going to meet VLAD in Vienna. He flew to New York first, and then to Zurich, to cover his tracks in case Rosario called the airlines. There he bought with cash a ticket for Austria.

Rick was drunk when he met VLAD. The Soviet hustled Rick into a waiting car and gave him a hat to pull over his head. Their sedan darted down several streets and then turned into the Soviet embassy grounds. Rick would later claim that he had been so groggy during their meeting that he couldn't remember much about their conversation, although he knew that they discussed the collapse of communism in Eastern Europe.

"I remember asking him what the hell was going on, because I was sure that we were being overrun with agents wanting to sell the agency information about KGB operations," Ames said later. VLAD assured him that his identity was being kept secret in Moscow. "You have no reason to fear," Ames would later quote VLAD as saying. VLAD mentioned that Vladimir Kryuchkov was now the director of the KGB and that Kryuchkov was indebted to Rick. "You have helped this man's career immeasurably," VLAD said. "He will always protect you."

Rick told VLAD that Sergey Fedorenko had resurfaced. "He volunteered to begin helping us again." This was the second time that Rick had betrayed his "close personal friend." On the way back to his hotel, Rick bought a bottle of vodka. He began drinking it as soon as he entered his room. Suddenly, he realized he hadn't telephoned Rosario as he had promised.

"Where are you?" she asked.

"I'm here in Zurich at the Hotel Savoy where we always stay," he replied.

"No, you're not! I tried to call you, and the receptionist at the Savoy's front desk said you weren't registered there as a guest."

Rick struggled to free his mind from the vodka. He later remembered how scared he was. "Rosario had me! She knew I was lying and probably thought I was meeting some babe somewhere. She always had this fantasy that I was cheating on her. I guess I shouldn't have been so disturbed that she thought it, because it kept her from thinking other things, like the fact that I was spying, but it was always very painful to me that she thought I was betraying her."

Rick assured Rosario that the Hotel Savoy's front desk clerk had made a mistake. "I'm going downstairs right now and clear this up! You call the hotel first thing tomorrow and you'll see. I'm not letting them humiliate my wife like this."

As soon as he put down the receiver, Rick raced to the airport. He caught the next flight to Zurich, and was in the hotel when Rosario called the next morning.

"I really gave the clerk hell," he assured her. "There was some sort of mistake, a new person was working when I checked in or something."

Rosario was fooled. "You know they really should be more careful," she said. "They could really cause a person a lot of embarrassment doing dumb things like this."

Rosario told him that his boss at the agency had called about an emergency. He needed to call Langley.

What happened next is disputed. Ames would later claim that he had telephoned the agency over a regular telephone line from Zurich, and that his boss had told him that Fedorenko was in Canada and needed to speak to him. "I asked them where he was staying and then telephoned the hotel," Ames said. "It wasn't dangerous. The KGB can't listen to every telephone call that is placed across the Atlantic!"

The CIA would later insist that this did not happen. "Rick's boss would never have given an agent's true name over an open, international line!" Vertefeuille said later.

What no one disputes is that Fedorenko did receive a telephone call from Rick at some point. The Russian did not know where Rick was calling from. Fedorenko said he wanted to defect. "I'm not sure Gorbachev is going to survive. I'm tired. I want to live in the United States." Rick passed the word up the chain of command, and the agency arranged for Fedorenko and his wife to cross the border into the United States. The agency brought them to Washington, D.C., where they moved into a CIA safe house. Fedorenko had never asked for any money when he was a spy in New York, but Rick had assured him during the 1970s that the agency was putting aside an annual salary for him. "Everyone had forgotten about this until Sergey resurfaced," Ames said later. "It turned out that the entire time Fedorenko was in Moscow, his salary had been automatically deposited." The CIA was holding $330,000 for him, but when Rick tried to withdraw it, Paul Redmond objected.

"Fedorenko is a double agent," Redmond said.

Rick was furious. "What proof do you have?"

Redmond showed him a memo that his deputy, Paul Stombaugh, Jr., had written about Fedorenko. According to the memo, a KGB officer —identified in the memo only by the cryptonym PROLOGUE—had told the agency that a double agent had managed to pass false information to the CIA and FBI in New York during the 1970s. Redmond and Stombaugh were convinced that PROLOGUE was describing Fedorenko.

Rick had never heard of PROLOGUE. "This guy isn't describing Sergey," he said. "He's lying. Sergey is not a double agent."

Redmond refused to budge. He insisted that Fedorenko be given a polygraph test. "I couldn't believe it," Fedorenko said later. "At first, I thought it was a joke. Why were they suspicious of me after all of those years?" When the polygraph operator asked him if he were a double agent, Fedorenko indignantly replied, "No!" The machine recorded a nervous reaction. The operator told Fedorenko that the test indicated that he was being "deceptive." Fedorenko began cursing, and demanded to be taken back to the safe house. Now Redmond and his deputy were certain Fedorenko was a fraud. Redmond said that he was going to recommend that the agency send Fedorenko back to Moscow. Fedorenko pleaded with Rick. Even his politically powerful in-laws wouldn't be able to save him if he were deported. "I will be put in prison and executed!" Fedorenko said. Rick tried to go above Redmond. "Rick really stuck his neck out to help Fedorenko," Vertefeuille recalled. Although several veteran SE officers, including Vertefeuille, did not believe that Fedorenko was the double agent being described by PROLOGUE, Redmond and Stombaugh won out. Desperate, Rick telephoned R. Patrick Watson at the FBI and asked him to intervene. A few days later, Redmond, Stombaugh, and Rick met with Watson at FBI headquarters. Redmond was blunt: Fedorenko was dirty. "Every one of our assets except for this guy was busted in Moscow from 1985 to 1986," Redmond said. "Why wasn't Fedorenko arrested?" He told Watson that Fedorenko matched the description of a double agent that had been provided to the agency by a reliable source.

Watson was unconvinced. He had always liked Fedorenko, but he would later claim that it was more than his personal affection that had made him disagree with Redmond. Watson had asked the FBI's top Soviet analyst, Jim Milburn, to review the information that Fedorenko had provided the bureau in the 1970s. Every statement that the Russian had ever made was compared to what the bureau had learned later from other sources. "In every case, the significant information Sergey gave us checked out," Watson said later. "I can't explain why the KGB did not arrest him, but there is nothing in our files that suggests Fedorenko is or ever was a double agent."

Watson told Redmond about Milburn's research. "Our position is that Fedorenko was a legitimate spy for the United States," Watson said.

Redmond mentioned that Fedorenko had failed a polygraph test, but Watson brushed that aside. Although he didn't say anything, Watson suspected the CIA had rigged the test to intimidate Fedorenko. "The FBI's policy always has been that if you put your life on the line for the bureau, we owe you big-time," Watson explained later. "We are not going to walk away from you. I don't feel the CIA always felt this way about the people it had used."

Watson told Redmond that the FBI would take responsibility for Fedorenko. It would arrange for him and his wife to stay in the United States permanently, and would support them financially until they could find jobs.

"You're making a mistake," Redmond said.

"Then it's my mistake, not yours," Watson replied.

As soon as Rick got back to his office, he filed the necessary paperwork to collect the $330,000 for Fedorenko. The agency issued the check, and Rick hand-carried it to him. "The only reason you aren't on an airplane heading back to Moscow is because Pat Watson saved your ass," Rick said.

A sad look came over Fedorenko's face. "The reason I'm staying here is because the KGB is regaining its power. I'm afraid it is going to take control of all foreign travel outside Russia again, and if I go home, the KGB will never let me out." For a moment, Fedorenko didn't speak, and then he added: "You know, I thought you guys were different, but the truth is you are all the same."

Rick learned later that the FBI had arranged for Fedorenko to work as a senior research fellow and visiting professor at the Naval War College in Newport, Rhode Island.

In August 1990, SE division chief Milton Bearden told Rick about a new long-range planning directorate the agency was creating. "Milt says to me, 'Rick, you're always talking about changes you would make in the agency, maybe you should join this new fancy plans directorate.' I didn't think Milt was trying to get rid of me, but I went to see the person in charge." Rick liked the idea of helping shape the CIA's future, but the chief of the new office didn't think much of Rick's views. "I told him it was time to really cut back the size of the agency, and he told me he thought the CIA was going to need at least three hundred more employees within five years," Ames recalled. "Needless to say, I didn't get the job." A short time later, Bearden mentioned for a second time that Rick should look for another job. "I began to think Bearden wanted me out, but I thought it was because I was unhappy with my assignment, not because he suspected me of being a mole."

Rick decided to apply for a job in the CIC. Gus Hathaway had retired in March, so Rick talked to his replacement, and in October 1990, Rick became an analyst there. He was now a member of the *very department* that was responsible for protecting the agency from KGB moles. Jeanne Vertefeuille and Dan Payne worked in offices right down the corridor from him. Rick began writing papers about his speciality: the KGB. He announced in a paper that the CIA had never really understood its chief rival. While the KGB exercised tremendous power, it was still a "huge Soviet bureaucracy" plagued with all the same weaknesses that other Russian agencies shared. "I wrote a long paper about how the KGB was not some monolithic organization, but was regionalized. Sometimes the KGB in Moscow had no idea what a regional KGB outpost was doing." Not everyone agreed with Rick, and he soon began arguing with his supervisor, Kay Oliver. "She was afraid to say anything too controversial," Ames later complained. "I began slipping copies of my papers to Milt Bearden, and even Paul Redmond, and they really, really liked my stuff—at least that is what they told me."

Rick was supposed to meet VLAD in Vienna in October, but he flew to Zurich first. After his last experience with Rosario calling the Hotel Savoy, he liked spending at least one day in Switzerland before continuing on to Vienna. He also had some banking to do. VLAD had given him the home telephone number of a KGB officer stationed in Vienna and had told Rick to call the officer at precisely 8:00 A.M. on the day *before* their meeting. Rick was supposed to wait ten seconds after the officer said "Hello," and then hang up without saying a word. The call would be his signal to the KGB that he was in Vienna and ready for their meeting. The KGB had told Rick to make the telephone call from a public pay phone in Vienna, but he used the phone in his hotel room instead. He caught a flight to Vienna that afternoon and checked into the Intercontinental Hotel. The KGB had warned him not to stay there because it was the most popular hotel in Vienna for U.S. tourists, but he didn't care.*

The next morning, Rick looked in a directory for the address of the Cafe Palermo, the site VLAD had chosen for their meeting at 7 P.M., but he couldn't find it. He searched for the address in a local restaurant guide. It wasn't listed. Rick asked the hotel's concierge if he knew where it was. He had never heard of it. The concierge took Rick outside, where a taxi was waiting, and asked the driver if he knew the address of the Cafe Palermo. He didn't. Rick began to worry, but the concierge said he would call a taxi dispatcher and get directions. When Rick returned from lunch, the concierge handed him a slip of paper with the cafe's address written on it. A taxi took him there just before seven o'clock. The sign outside read: *Pizzeria Palermo*. Rick thought it was odd that VLAD would choose a pizza joint for a spy meeting, but he assumed the Russian had his reasons. He waited two hours. VLAD didn't show up. VLAD had told him that if they ever missed connections, they should try to meet the next night at the same time and same location. The next morning, Rick checked with the concierge again and was assured that the Pizzeria Palermo was the only restaurant in Vienna with Palermo in its name. Rick returned to the pizzeria. Once again, VLAD didn't show up. He left Vienna empty-handed. After Ames was arrested, the FBI would show him photographs of the Cafe Palermo in Vienna. "It was this huge restaurant in the center of the city with a big neon sign with palm trees on it," he said later. "I think I spoke to the only concierge and taxi driver in the city who didn't know where it was!"

*It was also the hotel where the CIA had spent nine days interrogating Sergeant Clayton Lonetree.

Rick was irritated during the flight home from Vienna. He had been expecting to be paid at least $100,000. He decided to deliver VLAD a message through a dead drop. He wanted to apologize for missing their meeting and he wanted the KGB to pay him some money. Early one weekday morning, Rick drove into Washington and turned north onto Connecticut Avenue, a major city thoroughfare. His destination was St. Thomas Apostle Church on Woodley Road, a residential street that was popular with the KGB because many of its officers used it as a shortcut when driving between the Soviet residential compound in northwest Washington and the Soviet embassy located downtown. Rick turned left from Connecticut Avenue onto Woodley Road and parked his Jaguar directly in front of the Roman Catholic church. There was a brick wall in front of the building, and Rick used a piece of white chalk to draw on it a horizontal mark about five inches long. VLAD had told him that whenever he wished to arrange a dead drop, all he needed to do was mark the wall before 8 A.M. on any day except Saturday and Sunday. Rick correctly assumed that the KGB had ordered one of its officers to drive past the church each morning on his way to work to check for his signal. In keeping with the KGB's philosophy of making dead drops as simple as possible, the Soviets called Rick's signal site "church."

Then Rick drove west to Massachusetts Avenue, another major route through the city. He turned north, passing Washington National Cathedral as the morning sunlight danced across its stone towers. He crossed into Maryland and turned onto Little Falls Parkway. Minutes later, he entered Little Falls Branch Park. Rick had been instructed to walk along an asphalt footpath. After about five minutes, he came to a pedestrian bridge that spanned a creek. In his instructions, VLAD had called this "bridge." Rick was carrying a four-inch thick package of stolen CIA documents in a shopping bag. He had wrapped them inside a black plastic garbage bag to keep out moisture and hide the contents. He looked around. Earlier, he had encountered a woman walking her dog, but he didn't see anyone now, so he stepped off the path and reached underneath the bridge. Its beams were supported at each end by slabs of concrete, and Rick had been told to leave his package on top of the slab at the southeastern end. The only way anyone would know a package was hidden between the beams was if they had seen Rick hiding it. Rick walked back to his car and left. He had been told the KGB would "unload bridge" between 7:00 and 10:00 P.M.

In a note he had put in his package, Rick told VLAD that the CIA had recruited a new KGB spy known as PROLOGUE. Rick also suggested that they stop writing messages on paper and begin communicating by exchanging computer disks.

Shortly after 9:30 that night, Rick told Rosario that he needed to go into CIA headquarters to handle a minor problem. He promised to be home before midnight. He drove to "church" to see if the chalk mark was still there. VLAD had told him that the KGB would erase it after one of its officers picked up his package at "bridge." If the mark was on the wall, Rick would know something had gone wrong. It was so dark he couldn't tell, so he parked and stepped out of his car to inspect the wall. It had been wiped clean. Rick drove to Little Falls Branch Park and started down the asphalt footpath. Just before he reached the bridge, he heard footsteps coming up fast behind him. He spun around, not knowing what to expect, and almost collided with a jogger just as alarmed as he was. Rick waited until the runner had disappeared in the blackness. He took a deep breath, stepped off the path and reached under the bridge. A parcel was there. He could tell from its weight and dimensions that it contained several bundles of bills wrapped tightly inside a garbage bag. He dropped it into the shopping bag he was carrying and started walking back to his car. Suddenly he realized how crazy this was. He was carrying several thousand dollars in cash while walking alone in a park late at night. *Wouldn't a mugger be surprised when he opened the trash bag? And there would be nothing Rick could do if he were robbed. He couldn't report the theft to the police.*

The package contained $37,000 in hundred-dollar bills and a message. The note said the KGB was sending someone new to meet him in Bogotá in December, which was when he was scheduled to meet VLAD again. Rick wondered if he had gotten VLAD into trouble by showing up drunk in June and then missing the October meeting. He'd liked VLAD. The KGB hadn't put as much cash in the dead drop as Rick had wanted. He made a mental note: *Got to find a way to get more cash at dead drops!* Rick took $30,000, divided it into thirds, and deposited it at three different branches of his bank. He had decided that making deposits of $10,000 or more really wasn't dangerous, since everyone knew he had money. What he was trying to hide was its source, not that he had plenty of cash.

In early December, Rick flew to Bogotá. He told Kay Oliver, his supervisor, that his mother-in-law needed his help. "I filed the necessary paperwork to travel and told Kay that I was willing to stop by the CIA station there and brief our people about what was happening in Eastern Europe," Ames said later. "I wanted to make my trip to Bogotá look more normal. I mean, what sort of mole tells the CIA when he is going to meet the KGB? Besides, making contact with the CIA station gave me a reason to leave Cecilia's apartment at night without arousing suspicion. Rosario and Cecilia always wanted to know where I was going because they were afraid I'd get lost. This way, I could tell them I needed to stop at the embassy."

Rick waited outside Bolicentro, a bowling alley in the Unicentro mall near Cecilia's apartment. A stranger walked up to him.

"Haven't we met in Vienna?" he asked.

"No, but perhaps we met in Paris," Rick replied, repeating the exchange that the KGB had mentioned in its dead drop message. They shook hands and stepped outside, where a car was waiting.

"Where's VLAD?" Rick whispered.

"He has retired and is now enjoying an easy life," the Russian said. "You may call me ANDRE." He opened the back door of the sedan. "It would be better if we do not talk while we are in the car." They rode in silence to the Soviet residency. Rick eyed his new contact. He was taller than VLAD, in good physical shape, and in his late fifties. He was nearly bald. What black hair he had was slicked back. There was an odd-shaped bump on one side of his skull, some sort of growth, Rick imagined. When they got inside the residency, ANDRE poured two shots from a bottle of vodka and offered a toast. "To you and our continued success!"

Rick downed the shot and noticed that ANDRE did the same. He was waiting for ANDRE to pour him another, but he didn't. VLAD had always been generous with vodka.

"I want to talk to you about money," Rick said. "Why can't you put more in the dead drops? If you squeeze it together, you could easily get a hundred thousand in each one."

ANDRE frowned. "That is too much to put into a package, I think." But he promised to investigate. ANDRE took a card out of his coat pocket and began reading from his notes. He asked about Rick's new job at the CIC. Even though Rick was an analyst, he worked inside what was known as a "vaulted area." No one could enter the office where he worked unless they punched a secret code into an electronic lock on the entryway door. The entire area was thought to be secure, as if it were one big safe, and that meant the file cabinets were kept unlocked. Because Rick was studying the KGB, no one thought it was strange for him to root through the files. Although he couldn't find out the names of any current CIA agents, he could look through old Soviet case files that the KGB was curious about. He also had access to cables that described double agent cases the CIA was currently running against the KGB.

Rick asked ANDRE what the KGB was doing to protect him from being identified by a KGB traitor. "How about this new agent, PROLOGUE?" he asked. As far as Rick knew, PROLOGUE was still providing information to the CIA. "Can he find out about me?"

ANDRE smiled. "You have nothing to fear from this man. Of this you can be absolutely certain."

In August 1990, Dan Payne decided to run a routine credit check on Rick and Rosario. He wanted to see if they were running up large bills each month. The credit check showed that Rick and Rosario had charged about $3,000 during August 1990. Payne didn't consider that an outrageous amount. The report said the couple had a good credit rating.

Payne returned to his investigation of the mole suspect whom he had read about in the STASI files. That probe was taking most of his time. The only reason he had bothered to check on Rick and Rosario's credit was because of their house. He didn't like loose ends and he was still trying to figure out how they had bought it without taking out a mortgage.

Payne's investigation based on the STASI records had taken a curious turn. He knew from the STASI files that the KGB had paid money to a source in Germany, and it appeared, at first, that this money had been paid to the suspected mole. But when Payne began investigating the mole suspect's personal finances, he couldn't find any cash that wasn't accounted for. Nor had he found any examples of extravagant spending. How was it possible, he kept asking himself, that the STASI records could show that several thousand dollars had been paid to an informant and yet there were no records of the suspect ever receiving any extra cash?

At about this same time, Payne received a tip from the SE division. A KGB source in Moscow claimed that the KGB had successfully recruited a CIA employee in the 1970s. The source didn't know the employee's name, but the description he gave was similar to one that a different KGB source had provided to the agency several months earlier. Payne decided to compare the two tips. Maybe he could identify a suspect if he combined the two descriptions.

In late November, Payne noticed that it was about time for Rick to undergo a mandatory security review. Every CIA employee was supposed to be given a polygraph test and undergo a background examination every five years. These were done by the Office of Security. Rick had passed his last polygraph test on May 2, 1986. Payne met with Vertefeuille and her boss at the CIC, Raymond Reardon, to discuss Rick's upcoming review. "We didn't want to do anything at this point to tip our hands to Rick," Vertefeuille said later, "so we decided that we couldn't bore in on the financial questions more than usual, but we decided that a well-briefed polygraph examiner could lead the conversation in the right direction." On December 5, 1990, Payne typed a two-page, single-spaced memo that raised questions about "Ames's lavish spending habits over the past five years." As examples, Payne mentioned Rick's $540,000 house, how Rosario had recently renovated the kitchen of their house "sparing no expense," and Rick's Jaguar sports car. He also noted that Rick had made three cash deposits of more than $10,000. But Payne did not want to be accused later of using Angleton tactics to smear Rick, especially if he weren't the mole. "There may be a logical explanation for Ames's spending," he wrote. Rick's mother had died and she could have left him an inheritance. "Ames's in-laws are well-connected politically in Colombia," he added. "The money could have come from [them]."

"There is a degree of urgency involved in our request," Payne concluded in his memo. ". . . We are quickly running out of things for Ames to do without granting him greater access."

On January 22, 1991, the security office sent Ames the forms he needed to fill out so that it could give him a polygraph test. Rick had until March 4 to return them, but he missed that deadline. The security office began pestering him and he turned them in on March 10. Rick's polygraph was scheduled for April 12—some four months after Payne had written his memo.

On the same day that Rick was scheduled to take his test, Payne received a copy of a background report about Rick that had been done by a security officer. She had interviewed twelve people, including Rick's bosses and neighbors. After Ames was arrested, investigators for the Senate, House, and even the CIA inspector general's office would make public three shocking statements from Rick's background report:

- One coworker says Ames was assigned to CIC "under a cloud." Another says the SE division did not trust Ames.
- In Rome . . . Ames routinely left his safe open. . . . at least once a week there was evidence that Ames had been drinking during his lunch hour. . . . Ames could not be expected into the office before nine or ten o'clock.

- One of Ames's coworkers said he didn't think Ames was a spy, but wouldn't be surprised if that someday came to light. When asked to explain his remark, the person retracted it . . . but said he didn't trust Ames as a colleague.

On the basis of these statements, the CIA would be hotly criticized for not immediately identifying Rick as a mole. While the CIA deserves criticism for the errors that it made during its mole hunt, it is unfair to claim that Payne should have known from reading the background investigation that Rick was a mole. The lengthy report contains many positive, even laudatory statements about Ames that were never made public, and *everyone* who was interviewed said that they would recommend Ames for continued access to classified information. The person who said that he thought Ames was a spy, and then retracted that statement, explained that he did not trust Ames because they had tangled over the Fedorenko case. Nearly everyone who was interviewed said they were aware that Ames had lots of money. But none of them thought that was alarming because they had heard that Rick had gotten his money from his wife's family. Even Ames's drinking habits did not worry any of the people who were interviewed. "I didn't flinch after reading the background investigation about Rick," Payne said later, "because we already knew about his lavish lifestyle and drinking."

What the CIA should have been hotly criticized for is how the Office of Security handled Dan Payne's December 5 memo that had raised questions about Rick's finances. Someone—the CIA has refused to reveal who is responsible—decided that Payne's memo contained too much detailed information about Rick. So *all* mention of Rick's expensive house, remodeled kitchen, sports car, and cash deposits were deleted from the memo before it was given to the background investigator and polygraph examiner. As a result, Rick was *never* asked any of the tough financial questions that Payne had wanted asked during the polygraph test.

Rick was not worried about taking another polygraph. He had passed his first one less than one year after he had given the KGB the names of nearly all the SE division's agents. If he had made it through that test, he figured he wouldn't have any trouble with this one.

"Are you trying to hide anything from the CIA?" the examiner asked him during the test.

"No," said Ames.

The machine showed no nervous reaction.

"Are you or have you ever been in contact with a foreign intelligence service without the agency's knowledge or approval?"

"No," said Ames.

The machine did not show any reaction. It didn't on any of the other questions either, until near the end of the exam, when the examiner asked:

"Are there any contacts you have had with foreign nationals that you wish to hide from the CIA?"

"No," Rick replied, but this time the machine noticed that Rick had a nervous reaction, indicating possible deception.

The examiner asked Rick why he had reacted to that question.

"I really have no idea."

Rick was told to think about it and return for a second test in four days. When he did, he was tested by a different polygraph operator. Before he was hooked up to the machine, Rick tried to establish a rapport with the operator. "I wanted to seem really, really concerned and helpful." This time, Rick would be asked only one question—the one about his contact with foreign nationals.

"Have you thought about this?" the examiner asked before posing the question.

"Absolutely, and all I can think of is that my wife is Colombian, and I've met dozens of her friends and colleagues in Bogotá. I guess the machine is picking up on the fact that I really don't know anything about most of these people." Just in case that lie didn't work, Rick offered another. He was thinking about retiring, he said, and opening a business in Colombia. He'd talked to a number of foreigners, and some of them could have had ties with foreign intelligence services without him ever being told.

The examiner asked him the question. Rick answered. The machine showed that he was being deceptive. The examiner told him not to worry. He had passed.

THE WORDS OF RICK AMES

QUESTION: You didn't know most of the agents personally, but you knew Sergey Fedorenko. He was your friend, yet you turned him over to the KGB, knowing that the Russians had been arresting and executing the others. How could you do this?

I told VLAD about Sergey for the first time in Rome in late 1986. VLAD had just apologized to me about how the KGB had lost control of the situation and had been forced by others, the Politburo, I presume, to arrest all of the agents whose names I had given them. There's no question I was nervous and tense when I learned this, but I didn't have steam coming out of my ears. I did tell VLAD that his government's actions had put me in grave danger. But I did not react strongly or panic, because the truth is that I knew the sensational impact of my reporting would have been extremely difficult to contain within the confines of the KGB. What did I expect would happen? Did they have a choice? At the same time, I had no interest in pressing VLAD for details about why they had done what they did. I was trying to bury my feelings of guilt and dismay over the executions, I think. In any case, VLAD was quick to tell me what had happened in the most reassuring terms he could find, and he assured me, and of course I was looking for reassurance, that it would not happen again, implying quite plausibly and reasonably that after the initial shock, the KGB had itself been assured that it would decide how to do things in the future and the executions would stop. This made sense to me, and I was also affected by what I believe was the frankness of VLAD's statements. After all, it is not normal to tell an agent about the loss of control over operational security back in headquarters! Now this may be a small point, but it was small points like this which accumulated to shape and retain the respect and confidence I had in VLAD. So it was in this context that I told him about Sergey—knowing and feeling comfortable that Sergey would not be executed, and maybe not even arrested.

You must understand that I had felt all along that I shouldn't hold anything back from VLAD. Sergey was literally burning a hole in my pocket. I wanted to tell VLAD about him and, in a sense, I was looking for the right opportunity to unload his name, and this meeting with VLAD was the right time. Why? Because I did not want to lose the trust and confidence I felt that I had begun to establish with VLAD, and I felt that VLAD now would feel obligated to prove to me that the KGB could control those who had demanded blood. So I described for VLAD the nature of Sergey's past reporting on classified military research, and I must admit that the stakes were high for Sergey. I was clearly putting him at risk. My revelations certainly made him vulnerable. But I also told VLAD why I thought Sergey should be spared. VLAD gave me no explicit commitment, and I expected none. Yet he indicated by his reaction that there would be "no problems," and I took that to be an implicit commitment that nothing would happen to Sergey. I admit that I am rationalizing here. There is no doubt I put Sergey's life in danger, and I am eager to find some excuse that absolves me of this. But Sergey was not punished, and it is a comfort to me to have learned over time that my judgment and confidence in VLAD was not misplaced.

Now you may ask: How could I condemn the others and spare him? That is obvious. He was a friend. The others weren't. But let's be frank. The men I betrayed knew what they were doing. They knew the risks. Do you believe any of them would have hesitated to have reported me if they had learned my name? So their deaths, while sad to me, are not really my responsibility. They have no one to blame but themselves for putting their lives in danger. This does not mean that I don't feel some guilt. Of course I do. But these were not innocent men.

I just thought of a story which I haven't thought of for years. I'm not sure why or what it means. Shortly after I arrived in Mexico City, I had several drinks too many at a TGIF [Thank God It's Friday] office party. I've forgotten now how the conversation between me and a couple of others went, but I haven't forgotten how I turned maudlin. I described how agents I'd worked with had lost their lives, and the burden of responsibility I felt—not because I or others were somehow to blame—but simply that this was a burden we all should feel and share. I was emotional, and tears came to my eyes. Also, I exaggerated for effect the facts of some generally described assets. I had the suicides of TRIGON and Shevchenko's wife in mind. I don't know what the others thought, but I knew I was trying to impress them, both with the point I was making and with my own, tragic self. You can imagine the contempt I felt for myself afterwards. I put it out of my mind, and no one ever referred to it. But I've often wondered why I felt compelled to do that in Mexico. Why did I feel the need to identify or proclaim our joint responsibility for these people's tragedies? I guess the reason I thought of that story is because there was a time when I felt strongly about our agents. I felt that all of us had a commonness.

There's something I'd like to mention here. My father's career, my agency employment in high school, my sense of belonging to the agency and my life-long fascination and study of what it's all about, led to an irrational, mostly unconscious, feeling that the CIA belonged to me. Of course, this is not reasonable, and I've always scorned the talk of the good old days when the agency "really" cared about and took care of its people. My semiconscious feelings were not so much that of being a member of a strange sort of family, but of a much more personal feeling of being possessed and possessing. This is an important component, I think, of what I and others have called my arrogance, my delusion or belief that I could not only think as I thought, but, out of anxiety and other motives, act as I did.

It's interesting to think how different not only my career but my own feelings and thoughts, too, might have been had I not encountered such a rogues' gallery of incompetent and sometimes vicious [in the sense of behavior and habits] superiors in my field assignments. In Turkey, New York City, Mexico City, and to a lesser extent in Rome, I worked for a collection of men who were almost universally despised, pitied, or condemned. This bred a very casual contempt for authority, I suppose, and probably magnified my admiration for those who resisted such low values. It's very odd, but my experiences working at headquarters were rather different. I wonder how my attitudes would have been affected had I worked, for example, for Milt Bearden in Africa, who I greatly admired.

I had better make something clear here. I am not exaggerating about the nearly dozen men I say were incompetent and generally contemptible, mostly professionally but often personally as well. Some of my bosses were disgusting men who took great joy in seducing the wives of their own employees and viciously destroying officers' careers.

Now back to my possessiveness. I felt a personal alienation in the mideighties, almost as if "they" had taken the agency from me. And my feelings of alienation certainly intensified once I began my relationship with the Russians. Did I feel cast loose from a personal commitment to the agency? Yes, I . . . felt a sense of not only independence, but perhaps abandonment, and with that abandonment, my belief in the struggle between the light and darkness evaporated. I became a mercenary, beholden only to myself. My own wants became paramount.

THE WORDS OF OTHERS

Rick could have gotten millions from the KGB without telling them anyone's name. He could have just told them about technical operations. He didn't have to do what he did, and he did it completely on his own. The KGB didn't have to pry information out of him. Look at Polyakov. The guy was a grandfather! He was retired! He wasn't even spying anymore! He was living in his dacha playing with his grandchildren! Why did Rick have to tell the KGB about him? Why?

—Sandy Grimes, CIA

Traitors are not all the same. Sure, some of the Russians we recruited were doing it for money. Some of them were despicable characters. But others were not. We in the United States have so many outlets if we don't like what our government is doing. You can write a letter to the president, run for Congress, join some protest group or organizations to fight for change. They didn't have these outlets, particularly Eastern Europeans who didn't like what the Soviets were doing to their countries. For many of them, espionage became a way of protesting the injustices which they saw.

—Jeanne Vertefeuille, CIA

I used to tell Rick when we had fights—Why don't you hit me? It would be better than saying or doing the type of thing you're putting me through, which is psychological torture.

—Rosario Ames

I don't think Rick perceives himself as being a bad American. I mean somone like John Walker, why, he hurt his country, but Rick, he was doing a spy-versus-spy thing. The nation was never at risk because of Rickie.

—Chuck Windley, high school friend

A number of times when we went to lunch, Rick would get wasted, and then he would say, "Please don't tell your wife that you were out with me, because I don't want her to tell Rosario because of all of the trouble it will cause at home."

—Richard Thurman, State Department

Rick loved acting, better than anything in the world.

—High school friend

Not too many people are real men. They don't have the guts, the courage, the honor to be called a man, and I thought he was. He was not man enough to stop this from happening to me, to protect me.

—Rosario Ames

CHAPTER 22

After their December 1990 meeting in Bogotá, the KGB officer known to Rick only as ANDRE returned to Moscow with exciting news. ANDRE, whose real name was Yuri Karetkin, presented Lieutenant general Leonid Shebarshin, the new head of the First Chief Directorate, with a note Rick had written.

"I have learned that PROLOGUE is a cryptonym for the Second Chief Directorate officer I provided you information about earlier . . . ," it read.

Shebarshin grinned as he listened to Karetkin recite how the CIA's Paul Redmond had accused Sergey Fedorenko of being a double agent, based on information provided by PROLOGUE. Obviously, the CIA believed PROLOGUE was a legitimate agent.

PROLOGUE was a fraud. All the KGB documents that Vladimir Smetanin (PROLOGUE) had provided to the CIA about the 1985 losses were KGB disinformation. The details in those records—about the spies, their CIA handlers, and the dead drops in Moscow—had been gleaned by the KGB when it had interrogated the CIA spies after their arrests. The documents had been carefully fabricated with one purpose: protecting Rick.

Shebarshin went to tell Kryuchkov. The new KGB chairman was in dire need of hearing good news. The Soviet economy had plummeted since Gorbachev had come to power. The entire USSR seemed to be unraveling. Nationalists in Russia's fifteen republics were demanding independence, especially in the Baltic states, where a million people had formed a human chain four hundred miles long one day as a demonstration of solidarity in support of breaking free from the Kremlin. At first, Kryuchkov had backed Gorbachev's policies. He had promised that the KGB would become a more open, kinder, and gentler intelligence service. But when Lithuania and Latvia began challenging Moscow's authority in late 1990, Kryuchkov convinced Gorbachev to send in troops, and on January 13, 1991, Soviet solders killed fifteen demonstrators in Lithuania's capital. Seven days later in Latvia, four more protesters were shot.

Most Americans paid little attention to the turmoil in the USSR because on January 16, 1991, President Bush launched an air attack on Baghdad. The Persian Gulf War was underway. But not everyone in the U.S. government was focused on Iraq. Inside the CIA, the Soviet-watchers were hearing reports that Gorbachev was in deep political trouble. In late April 1991, the agency's Office of Soviet Analysis sent President Bush a still-classified report entitled "The Soviet Cauldron," which warned that a coup d'état was in the works. One of the plotters, it said, was Kryuchkov.

Rick flooded SE division chief Milton Bearden's office with unsolicited opinion papers about the discord there. He also secretly flew to Austria that spring to meet ANDRE.

The CIA's Office of Security sent Dan Payne and Jeanne Vertefeuille a memo. As far as it was concerned, Rick had successfully passed his five-year security clearance. It planned on giving him a clean bill of health. Payne and Vertefeuille were not so sure. The "missing" house mortgage still bothered them.

"We need to find out once and for all if Rosario's family is rich," Payne said. Vertefeuille agreed and decided to send a CIA officer to Bogotá to investigate. When the officer returned about a week later, he told them that Rick's in-laws were indeed wealthy. They owned vast amounts of real estate and operated a successful import-export business and part of a chain of ice cream stores. The officer said Rosario's family had once donated land worth several million dollars to the city for a soccer field and sports arena. The officer's report convinced the Office of Security that Rick was not a risk. It announced that it was closing its investigation of him.

Payne and Vertefeuille reviewed what they knew. Rick had passed two polygraph tests; his relatives were rich. Still, both of them felt uneasy. "I'm not convinced that we should take him off our suspect list," Vertefeuille said. Payne agreed. They would simply move him down a few pegs.

Payne went back to investigating the CIA employee whom the STASI records suggested was a mole.

Payne and Vertefeuille would not learn until months later that they had been misled. The officer sent to Bogotá had not done any investigation on his own. Instead, the Bogotá station had asked one of its paid informants to tell it about Rosario's family. No financial reports were ever checked, no property records examined. The entire report about Rosario's family had been based on a *single* informant, who had based his opinion on gossip and hearsay. Even more incredible, a few weeks after this informant gave the station incorrect information about Rosario, the station discovered that he had provided it with inaccurate information in another, unrelated case. It fired him. But no one told headquarters that the man who had only a few weeks ago vouched for Rick's rich relatives had been deemed an unreliable source.

Diana Worthen was miserable. She had heard that Rick had passed his security clearance and she took that to mean that her suspicions had been proven wrong. "I really felt bad about accusing him," she said later. "But then something would happen with Rosario or Rick, and I'd think, *Wait a minute. This just doesn't make sense.* And I'd get suspicious again. It was driving me nuts!" Worthen talked to Sandy Grimes about it. They were still working together in SE division. Grimes assured Worthen that she had done the right thing in raising questions about Rick. Grimes didn't care what the Office of Security had decided. She remained convinced that Rick was the mole. She just didn't have any proof. Worthen decided to ease out of her relationship with Rick and Rosario. She thought that they spoiled Paul, and she really didn't enjoy being around the toddler. It was a good excuse to let the friendship die.

In early 1991, Vertefeuille applied for the job of chief of the counterespionage group at the CIC. She had been the deputy of the group for three years and her boss, Raymond Reardon, was leaving. The agency picked someone else. It also chose Paul Redmond, Jr., to become the new number-two official at the CIC. He was now Vertefeuille's boss. She was less than two years away from the CIA's mandatory retirement age. Redmond asked her what she wanted to do.

"I'd really like to take a fresh look at the 1985 losses," she said. "Our agents who were executed deserve someone giving it one more 'good old college try.'"

Redmond liked the idea. It had been five years since he had written his fiery memo demanding that then-director Casey investigate the losses, and he agreed. She planned on working alone, but a few days later, she and Redmond were briefing two FBI special agents about another matter at FBI headquarters, when someone asked Vertefeuille what she was going to do now that she was so close to retirement.

"Jeanne's going to take another look at the 1985 losses," said Redmond.

"Hey, we'd like to buy into that," replied Robert Wade, the FBI's liaison with the CIA. The FBI's ANLACE task force, which had been created to investigate why Valery Martynov (GENTILE) and Sergey Motorin (GAUZE) had been arrested, had disbanded in 1987 after concluding that the bureau did not have enough information to know why the two spies had been caught. Redmond and Wade cut a deal. The FBI would send James P. Milburn, its Soviet expert, and Jim Holt, a veteran FBI agent, to the CIC to work with Vertefeuille.

On the drive back to the CIA, Redmond asked Vertefeuille if she wanted someone from the agency to help her, too.

"You have someone in mind?" she asked.

He did.

"Who?"

"Sandy Grimes."

Grimes had recently told Redmond that she was going to resign because she didn't like her new boss in the SE division and she was still upset about Polyakov's death. Redmond didn't want to lose her.

"Sandy would be great," Vertefeuille said, "but under one condition."

"What's that?" Redmond asked, surprised that she had a requirement for taking Grimes.

Vertefeuille pointed out that she outranked Grimes. "I'll only take her on the task force if she agrees to work with me as an *equal*."

Redmond laughed, and when they got to the agency, he asked Grimes if she wanted to help Vertefeuille investigate the 1985 losses.

"You've just made me the one offer that will keep me from resigning," she replied.

In June 1991, Vertefeuille and Grimes moved into their new fourth-floor quarters. Vertefeuille had been assigned an office that was barely big enough for a desk. If more than three people wanted to talk to her, one of them would have to sit on the safe because there wasn't enough room for three chairs. Grimes didn't get an office. She was assigned a cubicle outside Vertefeuille's office. Judging from the appearance of their new surroundings, their task force was not a high priority. In fact, some employees thought that Redmond was playing favorites. No one had known what to do with Vertefeuille after she was passed over for the chief's job, and Grimes was clearly unhappy at her job. The task force's codename was JOYRIDE.

Not long after the two women moved in, Rick stopped by and spoke to Grimes. His office was only a few steps away. "Hey, what's going on here?" he asked.

"We've formed another task force to look at the 1985 losses," Grimes said, watching to see his reaction. She was still convinced that he was a mole. Rick didn't flinch. Instead, he offered to give the task force advice if it wanted to tap into his expertise on the KGB.

Later, Vertefeuille mused over Rick's offer to help. Although she was not convinced that he was a mole, Vertefeuille still considered him a prime candidate. "Rick thinks we're just a couple of dumb broads, doesn't he?" she said.

Grimes nodded. Rick was acting as if he didn't have a care in the world.

On June 17, 1991, during a closed session of the USSR's Supreme Soviet, KGB chairman Vladimir Kryuchkov declared that he had uncovered evidence that "sleeper agents" planted by the CIA in the 1970s had moved into key positions in the Gorbachev government. These CIA-controlled spies were undermining the Soviet economy and encouraging the Soviet republics to break free. Kryuchkov said he had shown Gorbachev evidence of this conspiracy, but the general secretary had refused to take action. (One of the names Kryuchkov had shown Gorbachev was Sergey Fedorenko.) Kryuchkov's attack was part of a carefully coordinated attempt to strip Gorbachev of his authority, but the Supreme Soviet refused to go along.

Three days later, Jack Matlock, the U.S. ambassador to the Soviet Union, sent a top secret message to Secretary of State James Baker: the mayor of Moscow had warned him that Kryuchkov and three others were about to oust Gorbachev in a military coup. Baker personally warned Soviet foreign minister Alexander Bessmertnykh, but in a telephone conversation later that same day with President Bush, Gorbachev brushed off the plot. There had been rumors about a coup for months and nothing had ever happened.

The reason for this new round of Soviet unrest was a treaty Gorbachev was about to sign which would allow the Soviet republics to begin governing themselves. Hard-liners in Moscow were correctly afraid that once this so-called Union Treaty went into effect, the USSR would be dissolved. On August 18, a Sunday, two days before the treaty was scheduled to be signed, Gorbachev and his family were vacationing at a retreat on the Black Sea, when one of his bodyguards announced that a "special" delegation from Moscow was at the main door. Suspicious, Gorbachev reached for a telephone and discovered the line was dead. Seconds later, the delegation pushed its way into Gorbachev's office and put him under house arrest.

Analysts in the U.S. intelligence community began suspecting that a coup was underway when they examined images beamed to them from a spy satellite orbiting over Gorbachev's retreat. *The satellite shots were so precise that analysts could tell by looking at them that Gorbachev's Volga limousine had not left the compound for the airport and his return trip to Moscow as scheduled.* They also showed that an unusually high number of armed guards had surrounded the building. A short time later, Tass announced that the Soviet Union's vice president was taking charge because Gorbachev had become "ill." A "state of emergency" was being imposed by a junta that included Kryuchkov. As news of the coup swept across Moscow, tens of thousands of Russians mobbed the Russian parliament building where Boris Yeltsin and his band of supporters were opposing the junta. At the CIA, Rick watched live broadcasts of Soviet tanks and armored personnel carriers moving into position to attack Yeltsin and his stubborn supporters. If the Soviet military were going to attack Yeltsin, the CIA was certain it would do so at dawn on Wednesday morning.

When the sun rose that morning, however, it was the putsch that had fallen. Kryuchkov and two other coup leaders were arrested that afternoon after they commandeered an Aeroflot jetliner and flew to the Crimea to beg Gorbachev for mercy. By nightfall, Yeltsin loyalists had rounded up the other plotters. One shot himself.

On August 22, 1991, a mob formed outside Lubyanka, the KGB headquarters on Dzerzhinsky Square. As television cameras recorded the event, a man scaled a towering black statue of Felix Dzerzhinsky, the founder of the Soviet secret police. The statue overlooked the square, and as the mob watched, the man looped a rope around the statue's neck and tossed the rope into the crowd. Within seconds, the mob was trying to topple "Iron Felix," but it refused to fall. Afraid that there would be a riot, city officials sent a crane to help, and within minutes Dzerzhinsky had fallen. The Soviet parliament chose Vadim Bakatin, an outspoken KGB critic, to take charge of the service. He accepted the job after setting one condition: that he could dismantle the KGB.

Rick was scared. As long as Kryuchkov had been in control, he knew he was safe. Now he wasn't sure. Three days after the failed coup, Milton Bearden's secretary asked Rick to report immediately to the SE division chief's office.

"My first thought was that someone in the KGB had defected and identified me as a traitor," Ames later said.

Bearden told Rick to sit down. "I thought he was going to tell me that he knew I was a mole. Instead, Milt says he is putting me in charge of a special group that he is creating to destroy the KGB. Milt says, 'Rick, I want you to drive a stake into the KGB's heart.'"

Rick couldn't help himself. He broke into a huge grin.

Dan Payne solved the mystery. STASI had recruited a German in the early 1980s, but it wasn't a CIA employee. It was a *friend* of a CIA employee. STASI had been paying the friend to get close to the employee, learn everything that he could about the officer, and then try to get him to discuss classified information. That was why there were records of STASI payments yet no record of the employee being paid. He went to tell Vertefeuille and Grimes. Although he was not a member of their task force, he was still trying to solve the 1985 losses.

Vertefeuille and Grimes were now teamed with the FBI's Milburn and Holt. The two G-men hadn't known about some of the CIA agents who had been caught in 1985 because the FBI hadn't been told about them. Vertefeuille told Milburn and Holt that they could read any of the files they wished, except for CIA medical/psychological records. She hadn't asked anyone for permission to show the two FBI men the CIA files, nor was she about to. She knew that if she did, her request would get bogged down as it made its way up the CIA's chain of command. Someone would worry about the precedent being set. One advantage of being close to mandatory retirement, she joked, was that she could take risks that someone who was worried about their career would never dare. No one would later be able to recall when there had been such good cooperation between the FBI and CIA.

By the fall of 1991, the task force had compiled a list of eighty KGB officers who were likely to have known about the 1985 losses because of their rank or position or because they were hotshot KGB investigators. The task force used a computer to identify where the KGB officers had been stationed and where they had traveled during 1985. They were looking for some sort of pattern that might reveal that one of the KGB officers was meeting a CIA mole somewhere. They didn't find one. The task force members turned to bribery. *The CIA and FBI agreed to pay as much as $5 million to any KGB official willing to identify a CIA mole.* The task force picked four KGB officers from their list to approach. None accepted the offer.

The task force had also identified 198 CIA employees who at one time or another had had access to one or more of the compromised cases. Vertefeuille and Grimes felt the list was too big. "We need to trim it to twenty or so names," Grimes said.

Milburn asked how the two women planned to do that.

Vertefeuille suggested that they vote. They would give the list of 198 names to a total of ten people, six others besides the four of them. Those ten would pick the twenty people on the list who they thought were most likely to be a Russian mole.

Milburn and Holt didn't like the idea. Relying on a poll to whittle down a suspect list ran against everything they had been trained to do in the FBI. There was nothing scientific about "gut reactions."

"We don't have a choice," said Grimes. "We've got to cull this list."

The FBI agents skeptically agreed to go along with the poll. Besides the four of them, the task force asked Dan Payne, Paul Redmond, and four FBI officials to rank the "candidates"—Redmond insisted that they not be called "suspects" because he did not want to be accused later of smearing anyone's reputation. Ironically, Redmond was one of the 198 names because he had known about the cases.

Names at the top of each person's list were awarded five points. Second choices were given four points. When all the lists were turned in, Vertefeuille tallied the results. Rick had the most votes: twenty-one points. The next "candidate" had seventeen points. Although Sandy Grimes was the only person who had listed Rick as her first choice, his name was on *everyone's* list—all ten.

Vertefeuille and Grimes arranged for the CIA's medical department to have two of its psychiatrists review the list of "candidates" that had been identified by the ten voters. They asked the psychiatrists to pick out the persons who best fit the psychological profile of a mole based on exhaustive studies done by the government. The psychiatrists chose five people who seemed to fit that profile. Rick was not one of them.

Now that it had its list narrowed down, the task force decided to begin interviewing the "candidates," including Rick. It didn't want to tip off him or the other suspects by interviewing just them, so it chose forty CIA officers to question. In order to further hide who was and wasn't a suspect, the task force agreed that it would ask everyone the same basic questions. Despite these precautions, Milburn and Holt were nervous about using the word "interview" to describe the sessions. If Rick or anyone else said something incriminating, his lawyer might later claim that his constitutional rights had been violated because he had been "interviewed" by two FBI agents without first being read his rights. The team agreed that if anyone admitted any wrongdoing, Vertefeuille and Grimes would immediately leave the room so that the two FBI agents could take charge and read the suspect his constitutional rights. The team interviewed nearly a dozen employees before calling Rick into the interview room on November 12, 1991.

Rick immediately announced that he had made a foolish mistake in early 1985 that might have caused the losses. "I left a safe unlocked overnight," he said, doing his best to sound embarrassed. "I thought it was locked, but it was open when I came in the next day." After pausing for dramatic effect, he added, "What really bothers me is that safe had a sheet inside it with the combinations for all of the other safes written on it. If someone had seen that sheet, he could have opened all of the other safes and learned about our agents."

Ames later told me that he had intentionally mentioned the safe incident to "misdirect" its investigation. "I wanted them to worry about who might have come in and gotten into all of the other safes." He thought his trick had worked. "When I walked out of the interview room, I felt I had answered all of their questions without saying anything incriminating. I honestly, still had no idea that they were looking at me as a suspect."

The members of the task force discussed Rick when they were certain that he was out of earshot. Vertefeuille thought Rick's comments about the safe were overkill. "He mentioned it at the beginning of the interview and then brought it up again out of the blue," she noted.

Grimes agreed. She accused Rick of performing. "He was way too slick," she said. Rick seemed to have a ready answer for every question. "How come he is the only one who didn't say, 'Oh gosh, let me think, what was I doing back then, it was so long ago, I can't remember? He knew instantly everything that he was doing and when he was doing it.'"

At one point, Vertefeuille had asked Rick what he thought had gone wrong in 1985, adding, "Some people think the agency might have a mole working in it."

Without hesitating, Rick had replied that if there was a mole, he had to be someone who had died or left the agency. Otherwise, why hadn't any of the agency's newest sources been arrested. And then Rick had said that the losses that couldn't be blamed on Edward Howard could have been caused by other problems. "How long is the arm of coincidence?" he asked rhetorically.

Grimes thought Rick had memorized his answers in advance. Just the same, she and Vertefeuille agreed that Rick had stumbled over the final question.

If you were going to contact the Soviets, how would you do it? Vertefeuille had asked.

Later, Grimes would recall that Rick had been caught-off guard. "Here is a guy who loves to play intelligence games, who thinks of himself as an actor and who really gets off on role-playing, and suddenly he falls completely out of character when he is asked that question." Other employees had described elaborate ways to contact the KGB without being caught. Rick said he would walk into the Soviet embassy and volunteer.

The next morning, Diana Worthen came to talk to the task force. After Rick was interviewed, he had talked to her. He had asked her if she had been interviewed by the task force. "Not yet, Rick," she had replied, lying. "Was it difficult?"

"Well, the last question was sort of puzzling," she quoted Rick as saying. "They asked me 'If I was a spy, how would I contact the KGB?' and I was just wondering if they had asked everyone that or just me?"

"Oh, thanks a lot, Rick!" Worthen had replied. "Now I know one of the questions, and when they ask me, they'll think I'm the mole because I'll have an answer ready!"

Rick had chuckled, and then had said, "Oh, I never thought about that. I guess someone who was worried might figure out some answers in advance."

A few days later, Rick was called before Milton Bearden. Rick thought he was going to be congratulated because of the work he had been doing. "When

[Vadim] Bakatin was put in charge of the KGB, the agency went all out to congratulate him and tell him that we supported his efforts to reform the KGB," Ames told me later. "Now here is something no one has ever made public. *I was the one who was writing all of Milt's telegrams to Bakatin!* Can you imagine? But wait, it gets even juicier. Bearden is getting ready to go to Moscow to discuss ways we can cooperate with the KGB, you know, exchange information about terrorists and narcotics and stuff like that, and we are giving Bakatin so much information that Milt decides we need to ask Bakatin for something in return, but he can't decide what. That's when I wrote Milt a note, suggesting that Bakatin give us the plans that the KGB had used to plant listening devices in our new embassy building in Moscow. I mean, Bakatin is telling everyone that he is reforming the old KGB and we are now all friends, so anyway, Milt does, and you know what? *Bakatin gave us the blueprints! He tells us exactly where the KGB had put every one of its bugs in the new embassy!* The CIA will never admit that, but it's true! We know where all those bugs are! So I thought Milt was going to pat me on the back."

Instead, Bearden told Rick that he was being transferred to the agency's Counternarcotics Center (CNC). "Milt said he was reorganizing the entire division and he really didn't have a place for me, which was true. He said, 'Rick, you could really be an asset in the CNC.'"

As 1991 came to a close, the four members of the task force still remained divided on whether the 1985 losses had been caused by a mole and, if so, who that traitor was. Only one person was absolutely convinced that Rick was a traitor. Just before Christmas, Sandy Grimes decided to make a list of important dates in Rick's life and career. She began with the day that he first reported to work at the agency. Grimes reviewed Rick's overseas travel reports, vacation dates, even his sick days, and put all those dates into the time line she was creating. It was mind-numbing work, but Grimes didn't complain. She was going to catch a mole.

CHAPTER 23

Sometime in 1992, Rosario discovered that Rick was working for the KGB. At least that is what both of them claimed after they were arrested. Federal investigators, however, noticed numerous inconsistencies in their stories, especially when they were questioned before they had a chance to write letters to each other in jail. These investigators wonder how much of what follows, if any, actually happened.

In interviews, Rosario said she needed a wallet to use in her purse, and she remembered that Rick had a red one that she had given him in Rome, which he no longer used. She found it in a dresser drawer, and when she looked inside it, she found a note. "The KGB had given it to me," Ames said later, "and it mentioned something about my mother-in-law and a meeting in Bogotá. Rosario called me at work in a panic."

"None of my friends or family knew that Rick really worked for the agency," Rosario said later, "so I wanted to know: Why was someone mentioning my mother in a note?" Ames said he brushed aside her questions for several days. Finally, he took Rosario to Germaine's, a Vietnamese restaurant in Washington, and during dinner announced: "I'm working for the Russians." He told her that there was no Robert from Chicago, there were no million-dollar commissions. It was the KGB that was paying him for information.

"Her first reaction was pure horror," Ames claimed later. "She wanted to know if she and Paul were in danger, and I assured her that the Russians were being super-careful on their side and we had to do the same."

Said Rosario, "I can't describe the panic, the shock. . . . I didn't want to believe it. Why was this happening to me? I tried to shut it out. It's not possible, I told myself. Then Rick told me the Russians had asked for my photograph and Paul's. I was scared to death. . . . He knew the effect it was going to have on me."

Rick was scheduled to meet ANDRE in Caracas, Venezuela, in October 1992, and he would later claim that before he left, Rosario made him promise he would tell the KGB that he was going to retire. "Rosario and I agreed it would be better if she didn't know too much, so I never really told her much about what I was doing. We never really ever talked about it, but the anxiety would build up and she would fly off the handle. When that happened, I knew the reason."

When he met ANDRE, Rick never mentioned retirement. He was worried about KGB security. There had been at least five separate government investigations of the KGB, and one of Bakatin's first actions as its new director had been to fire two of Kryuchkov's most trusted deputies.

"How do I know Bakatin isn't going to tell the CIA about me?" Rick asked.

"Because we have not told Bakatin about you," ANDRE replied.

Rick was stunned. The KGB had not told its new director about its most important spy.

Under Bakatin, the KGB had been dismembered. Each directorate had become a separate organization in order to dilute the KGB's strength. Yevgeniy Primakov, a career journalist and academician, had been appointed head of Russia's foreign intelligence. Primakov, a Middle Eastern scholar, had first come to the CIA's attention because of anti-American stories that he published in *Pravda* in support of the Palestine Liberation Organization. ANDRE said that Primakov had been briefed about Rick, and so had Yeltsin, but Russia's new president had not been told Rick's real name.

"Mr. Primakov wants to thank you for your continued help," ANDRE said. He gave Rick a bag. There were five "bricks" of brand-new hundred-dollar bills tucked inside. They totaled $130,000. It was the largest individual cash payment that the KGB had given Rick at a meeting.

In late March 1992, Paul Redmond paused one afternoon while walking past Dan Payne's desk at the CIC and suggested that he take another look at

Rick's finances. Payne was busy writing up his report about the STASI mole case. He and Vertefeuille had already agreed that he would focus on Rick in about three weeks. "Redmond was always bitching about something," Payne said later. So Payne ignored him.

About a week later, Redmond paused as he was walking by Payne's desk again. "Have you started on Ames yet?" he asked good-naturedly. Payne hadn't.

Another week went by, and this time when Redmond walked past Payne's desk, he said: "Dan, I'm getting pissed off! Get on Ames!"

Payne was still finishing his reports. Two days later, Redmond called Payne into his office.

"You have really pissed me off now," Redmond said. "I want you to drop everything else you are doing and get on the Ames investigation."

This time, Payne did. He knew that the federal Right to Financial Privacy Act prohibited government agencies from examining someone's personal financial records, but the law contained a special provision regarding foreign counterintelligence. The CIA had never used this provision. Payne decided that now was a good time. He wrote several National Security Inquiry Letters, which he personally delivered to the banks and credit card companies used by Rick and Rosario. The letters demanded copies of all the information in Rick's accounts and they required the institutions to keep silent about the search. The documents in the first batch Payne received were copies of Rick and Rosario's American Express card receipts. Payne opened the package.

"Holy shit!" Payne gasped.

Rick and Rosario routinely charged $18,000 to $30,000 per month. One year, Rick had been charged an extra $18,000 in finance charges because he had forgotten to pay his monthly statements on time! Payne was dumbfounded. Almost a year earlier, he'd asked for a routine credit check, and had not found anything unusual when he asked about their charges during August. "Entirely by chance, I had chosen the one month in the entire year when they only charged $3,000," Payne said later. "If I had requested July or September or any other month, I would have learned about the huge bills they were charging." Rick's salary was $69,843 per year. Obviously, he couldn't afford to pay $200,000 per year in credit card bills. Rick's records from the Diner's Club charge card arrived the next day. "He was charging thousands of dollars per month on that card, too!"

The individual charge slips from hotels enabled investigators to track Rick's secret trips overseas. One showed he had stayed in Caracas, another proved he had been in Vienna. Sandy Grimes faithfully entered the dates of Rick's trips into her computer.

The next financial records Payne received were from Rick's checking account. The agency had requested a copy of every check that Rick had written since 1984. Redmond came by to see how Payne was doing. "Dan was sitting there with his coat off, his shirt collar unbuttoned, completely surrounded by these huge stacks of checks, with about fifty feet of adding machine tape overflowing onto the floor," Redmond said later. "He kept saying, 'This is impossible! No one spends this much money!'"

The canceled checks showed that Rick and Rosario were spending thousands of dollars each month on clothing and gourmet meals. Rosario had run up huge bills at Nordstrom, an upscale department store, and Victoria's Secret, a store that sells mostly lingerie. (The FBI would later reveal that Rosario owned more than 500 pairs of shoes and had 150 boxes of pantyhose in her bedroom that she had never opened, along with dozens of dresses with their price tags still attached, that she had never worn.) Still, Payne kept reminding the group that none of this meant Rick was a spy. According to the Bogotá station, Rosario's relatives were rich. "To them, this might be pocket change," Payne said.

It was Grimes who found the first link. She was entering the dates of Rick's checks and bank deposits into her time line one afternoon, when she noticed a pattern.

May 17, 1985: Ames reports having lunch with Sergey Chuvakhin.

May 18, 1985: Ames deposits $9,000 into checking account.

July 5, 1985: Ames reports lunch with Chuvakhin.

July 5, 1985: Ames deposits $5,000 in checking account.

July 31, 1985: Ames reports lunch with Chuvakhin.

July 31, 1985: Ames deposits $8,500 into checking account.

Grimes hurried down to Redmond's office. She showed him what she had discovered. "It doesn't take a rocket scientist to tell what is going on here," Grimes said. "Rick is a goddamn Russian spy!"

PART FIVE

A FINAL PERFORMANCE

It is said that men condemned to death
are subject to sudden moments of elation,
as if, like moths in the fire, their destruction were coincidental with attainment.

—John leCarre
The Spy Who Came In from the Cold

CHAPTER 24

In October 1992, Dan Payne discovered Rick's Swiss bank accounts. Payne charted Rick's deposits. At the start of 1985, Rick had less than $2,000 in his checking account. His only regular deposits were from his paychecks—$1,068 per week. On May 18, 1985, that began to change. He deposited $9,000 in cash after meeting with Sergey Chuvakhin. In the next nine months, he deposited another $62,700, all in cash.

Deposits from Unidentified Sources

1986: 11 deposits for a total of $82,399

1987: 15 deposits for a total of $117,269

1988: 4 wire transfers for a total of $109,617

1989: 4 wire transfers for a total of $544,688

1990: 7 wire transfers for a total of $228,514

1991: 13 deposits for a total of $177,783

According to Payne's calculations, Rick had received $1.3 *million* between 1985 and 1991 from unidentified sources, but the task force still had no proof that the money was from the KGB. What would a good defense attorney say in court, that Rick had been

lucky playing craps in some European casino? The task force knew Rick often made cash deposits on the same days that he ate lunch with Sergey Chuvakhin. So what? No one had ever seen the Russian give him money, and
Chuvakhin was certainly not going to testify. Courts required hard evidence
and the team hardly had any. Even the four team members were divided
about whether or not Rick was guilty. Sandy Grimes was the only one of the
four who was absolutely convinced that he was a mole. Everyone else
thought he still might be getting money from his rich relatives in Colombia.

Jim Milburn was assigned to write a report about what the task force had
found, and the quiet, meticulous FBI agent worked on his summary well
into the New Year, finishing the eighty-page document on March 15, 1993.
The task force was "virtually certain" that the KGB had penetrated the CIA,
Milburn concluded, but he did not identify Rick as the mole. Instead, he attached a "short list" of prime suspects to his report. It identified five people,
including Rick. Milburn then attached another list that identified *thirty-five*
others as possible moles!

Milburn's report ended up in the hands of Robert Bryant, the head of the
FBI's Metropolitan Field Office in Washington, and John F. Lewis, a veteran
FBI counterintelligence officer. Both knew most of the CIA officers identified in the report and it seemed obvious to them that Rick was the traitor.
On May 12, 1993, the FBI formally began a Counterintelligence investigation of Rick, codenamed NIGHTMOVER, a tag suggested by Milburn, who
said that a mole was someone who "moved clandestinely at night." Bryant
called Leslie G. Wiser, Jr., a thirty-eight-year-old special agent, into his office. Wiser had worked for the FBI's intelligence division for seven of his
nine years at the bureau. Before that he had served a stint in the navy, where
he had worked as both a prosecutor and defense attorney. Having experience
on both sides gave him an edge: Not only did he know what was needed to
prosecute a criminal, he could switch roles and see what holes a defense
would exploit. The "Bear," as the husky Bryant was called, was blunt. The
bureau was about to begin "one of the most important" spy cases in its entire history, he said. "I was wondering, Les, if you might be interested in running it?"

"Are you kidding?" Wiser replied. This was the sort of opportunity that
he had dreamed about.

The CIA sent Dan Payne over to work with the team of special agents
whom Wiser had handpicked to help him. Wiser knew that the most convincing evidence that he could obtain would be photographs of Rick giving
documents to a Russian or leaving stolen papers at a dead drop. On June 3,

1993, he ordered round-the-clock surveillance of Rick by the bureau's Special Surveillance Group, known simply as the Gs, men and women taught to blend into the scenery when shadowing suspects. Tracking Rick proved to be tough. He lived on a residential street without much traffic. Neighbors noticed outsiders. Even though the Gs posed as trash collectors, yard workers, and door-to-door sales agents, one of Rick's neighbors called the police. Watching Rick at work was equally tricky. How could the FBI get inside Langley without informing the hundreds of CIA security officers guarding the complex? It was the CIA's Payne who later offered Wiser a solution. Payne and the CIA's chief of security announced in a memo that the FBI and CIA were running a surveillance training exercise at Langley. If a carload of strangers was spotted, the CIA guards were supposed to ask for identification and, if shown FBI credentials, immediately leave the area. Otherwise they might ruin the training exercise.

After one week of round-the-clock surveillance, Wiser called off the Gs. Rick hadn't done anything suspicious and Wiser was worried that he might realize that he was being tailed. "We were dealing with an experienced CIA officer who had been taught how to spot tails," Wiser said later. The FBI started depending on two video cameras to keep track of Rick. The first camera was placed on a telephone pole across the street from Rick's house. Its pictures were fed to a monitor located in the bedroom of a nearby vacant house rented by the bureau. The camera was never turned off and videotape recorders were used to make a record of everyone who came and went. A second camera was hidden in the ceiling of Rick's basement office at the CNC.

The FBI also began listening to and recording Rick's telephone conversations. Getting access to his home telephone line was simple. The FBI notified the telephone company and it made the necessary connections at its central office. But the bureau had to plant a bug in Rick's phone at work because of various safeguards that the CIA takes to prevent its lines from being tapped by outsiders. Payne helped sneak a technician into Rick's office to install it. The bug worked, but only for a few days. After that, the FBI began hearing someone else talking on the phone. It notified Payne. As soon as he was certain that Rick had gone home for the night, Payne crept into Rick's office. The phone that the FBI had bugged wasn't on Rick's desk. He had needed to place several calls overseas, so he had swapped his phone with a "secure telephone," one that the agency uses to scramble conversations. Payne began scouring the CNC for the missing unit. He found it on someone else's desk and returned it to Rick's.

On June 25, Payne took a team of FBI crime-scene specialists into Rick's office late at night. They photographed the entire room so that they would know later where everything had been located before they started their search. If they put one note pad or pen somewhere different, Rick might suspect someone had been in his office. Rick was a packrat. His desk was littered with papers, reports, books, empty coffee cups, old notepads. The technicians photographed every document, even the pages of his desk calendar. It took hours but Wiser felt the effort was worth it. Rick had 144 documents marked Secret and 10 marked Top Secret in his office. Top Secret documents were never supposed to be left unguarded. Even more interesting to the FBI was the fact that much of the classified material on Rick's desk had nothing whatsoever to do with his counternarcotics job. One CIA study was about tricks Soviet nuclear submarine commanders played to avoid detection when trailing U.S. subs. Wiser wondered: *How did he get access to reports that seemed to have nothing to do with his job? Was it possible he had an accomplice?*

During the afternoon of July 1, Special Agent Julie Johnson overheard a troubling call. It was Rick calling Rosario from the car phone in his Jaguar. No one in the bureau had known Rick owned a car phone because his Jaguar didn't have a telltale antenna. Obviously, the bureau hadn't tapped his cellular line. Rick said he was on "Massachusetts Avenue" and, "all's well." Only after Rick was arrested did the FBI confirm what it had immediately suspected: Rick had made a dead drop. His mention of Massachusetts Avenue was a reference to a new signal site that the KGB had given him. It was a mailbox codenamed ROSE. Wiser's team had missed a chance at catching him at a dead drop. Wiser ordered his squad to put a tap on Rick's car phone and make certain there were no other lines that had been overlooked. Wiser also decided that he needed some way of tracking Rick without having him under twenty-four-hour-a-day surveillance by the Gs. Wiser decided to turn to technology for help.

Rick didn't know he was being watched. He was too busy having fun at his new job. He had been disappointed at first about being stuck in the CNC, but by mid-May, at just about the same time the FBI was launching NIGHTMOVER, Rick was sent to Moscow with several other CNC employees to discuss ways the CIA and Russians could share information about drug trafficking. Rick had never been to Moscow. The delegation stayed in a special guest house that Rick was certain was bugged. After he was arrested, the media would speculate that Rick had met with one of his handlers during his Moscow trip but he would laugh at such reporting. "That would have been too obvious, too problematic. We were being watched by what had been the KGB's Seventh Directorate and I am quite certain that no one in that directorate had ever been told anything about me." Besides, what was the point? It was safer for Rick and ANDRE to meet in Bogotá. The only reason for them to meet in Moscow would be to save money on travel expenses, and that was not something either of them were worried about.

In Moscow on May 26, Rick turned fifty-two and his coworkers gave him a Russian souvenir. When he was alone that night, Rick gazed out the window of the guest house at the city lights. He could see spotlights a few blocks away, illuminating the ornate towers of an apartment building constructed during the Stalin era. He had been drinking but was not drunk, and in a rare moment of self-reflection the compartmentalization that he had maintained so carefully in his mind melted away. How strange it all was, he thought. He *felt* as if he were both a CIA and KGB officer, serving each organization with equal fervor. He had come a long way from River Falls, he decided. How many men had really ever influenced two superpowers?

The Russians hosted a farewell dinner for their CIA guests on the last night of the visit and when it came time for toasts, Rick gave what his colleagues later jokingly dubbed the "Three Great Nations speech."

"I had had too much to drink, and I remember talking about how everyone knows that the U.S. has two great neighbors—Canada and Mexico—but we have a third neighbor across from Alaska and that is Russia. I went on and on and on about how we had a long history of friendship and how important it was for us to get along, and it turned into a really gushy speech, with me talking quite passionately about the need for us to be friends."

When he returned home, Rick came up with what he thought was a sensational idea called the Black Sea Initiative. He suggested that the CNC host a conference for intelligence officers from countries that border the Black Sea, so that they could develop ways to share information about drug traffickers. Much of the heroin being sold in Western Europe and the U.S. came from Afghanistan and Turkey after it was smuggled across the Black Sea into the newly liberated former Soviet republics. If the Black Sea countries could be persuaded to work together, Rick was certain they could reduce the smuggling. CNC deputy director David Edger had been warned that Rick was suspected of being a KGB agent, but he thought Rick's idea was worthwhile, and he told him to go ahead with it.

▬▬▬

The FBI's Wiser wanted to hide a homing beacon in Rick's Jaguar. The only questions were: how and when? Rick drove to work every morning, so Wiser thought about having his technicians break into Rick's car, drive it to a safe spot on the CIA's grounds, install a transmitter in it, and then return the Jaguar to where Rick had parked it. But that was dangerous. Rick's wine-red Jaguar was designed to be flashy. What if one of Rick's coworkers saw a stranger driving it out of the parking lot? Wiser, Payne, and Redmond discussed their options. "You've got to stop thinking like a bureaucrat if you want to catch Rick," Redmond told Payne and Wiser, "and start thinking operationally, just as if you were running a clandestine mission against the KGB." Payne and Wiser came up with an idea.

A few days later, David Edger told Rick that the FBI was interested in learning more about his Black Sea Initiative. He wanted Rick to brief the agency. Rick was thrilled. Shortly after 10:00 A.M. on July 20, he and Edger left their offices and started toward the CIA parking lot.

"Oh shoot," Edger announced. "My wife has my car. I forgot that I didn't drive today."

"No problem," Rick volunteered. "We'll take mine."

Rick drove into Washington and pulled into the narrow driveway that goes under the massive J. Edgar Hoover Building, the FBI headquarters on Pennsylvania Avenue. An FBI agent stepped forward. "Just park it right over there," he said, pointing to a spot near the cobblestone courtyard in the center of the rectangular building. Rick locked his Jaguar and went inside with Edger. As soon as the elevator doors closed in front of them, an FBI technician opened the Jaguar's door with a key that he had made a few days earlier. He drove the car into the FBI's underground parking garage, where a team quickly installed a transmitting device that emitted a faint signal whenever the car was running. Moments later, the Jaguar was returned to where Rick had left it. On their ride back to Langley, Rick mentioned that he felt the briefing had gone exceptionally well. Edger agreed.

A few weeks later, Rick left for the Black Sea region to meet with various intelligence services and politicians. He had decided that Eduard Shevardnadze, the beleaguered pro-Western leader of the former Soviet republic of Georgia, was the key to getting all the countries to work together to combat drugs. If Shevardnadze would host the first meeting in Georgia's capital of Tbilisi, Rick was certain the other countries would send delegates. Rick arrived in Georgia about a month after Freddie Woodruff, another CIA officer, was sent there to help train Shevardnadze's security forces. Woodruff and Rick had known each other for several years and Woodruff spent one afternoon taking Rick sightseeing. As Rick had hoped, Shevardnadze agreed to host the drug conference and Rick returned home feeling satisfied. He was riding to work a few days later when he heard over the radio that Woodruff and Edar Guguladze, director of the Georgian intelligence service, had been attacked while returning from a sightseeing trip. An unidentified gunman had fired into their car, killing Woodruff with a single shot to the head. Rick began to cry. "Freddie and I had been traveling on the very same road where he was shot!" he said later. The government refused to acknowledge that Woodruff was a CIA officer but R. James Woolsey, the new head of the CIA under President Clinton, flew to Georgia to escort the body back to Andrews Air Force Base.

Rick was one of about forty CIA officers waiting in the airport's VIP lounge for the aircraft. He noticed Burton Lee Gerber coming into the lobby and hurried over to greet him. Gerber was unusually standoffish. Rick decided it was because of Woodruff's murder, but that was only part of the reason. Gerber knew Rick was under investigation. "It must have been as difficult and strange a moment for Burton then as my recollection of it is to me now," Ames said later. "For some reason I was one of the first to sign the memorial book for Freddie at the airport, and typical of me, I hadn't given any thought to such an occasion and wrote some lame and trite words in it. It must be painful for his wife to see my signature there now, knowing I was a traitor."

By the end of that summer, the bureau had been tracking Rick for nearly four months, and still had no evidence. Every day, the chances of Rick learning that he was being watched increased. At the CIA, Sandy Grimes was growing impatient. She frequently bumped into Rick at work and it was becoming difficult for her to hide her anger. One day, Grimes marched into Redmond's office. "Rick is a spy, why don't they just arrest him?" Redmond and David Edger came up with an idea. They decided to arrange for a juicy Top Secret document to be shown to Rick. They figured he would either steal or copy it for the Russians. If the FBI caught Rick outside the CIA grounds with a Top Secret, it could arrest him for spying and seek a maximum sentence of life in prison without parole. The trick was to arrest him with a Top Secret. If the document was classified as Secret or Confidential, then the FBI couldn't seek the maximum sentence. It had to be a Top Secret, and that made Redmond and Edger's plan dangerous. If the FBI didn't stop him in time, Rick might actually pass the document to the Russians. Worse, if word leaked out that the CIA had intentionally sent the document to Rick so that he could steal it, his defense attorney would later claim that the agency had entrapped him. Redmond and Edger checked with Wiser. The FBI agent agreed to risk it. Edger scoured the agency until he found a Top Secret document that he felt would be tempting enough for Rick to steal, but not so dangerous that if it were released to the Russians, it would cause the United States permanent harm. It took several days to get it routed to Rick in a way that wouldn't make him suspicious. The FBI later watched the videotape that had been made by the camera hidden above Rick's desk on the day when the Top Secret document was delivered. The tape showed Rick read it and then toss it into an OUT box on his desk. That done, he had leaned back in his chair, propped his feet on his desk, and had taken a nap. He had shown no interest in the CIA's bait.

Wiser wanted to look through Rick's garbage but Bear Bryant said it was too risky. Bryant said he often woke up during the night and looked outside to see if anyone else in his neighborhood was awake or roaming the street. "If anyone took my trash, I'd know about it," Bryant said. Wiser took that as a challenge. He decided to have his squad members snatch Bryant's trash one night, just to prove that it could be done. Wiser's cohorts, however, balked at the idea. Stealing their boss's trash could prove to be embarrassing. There was also a chance that Bryant might catch them. Wiser dropped the idea and his team set out to learn everything it could about Rick's sleeping habits. What time did he go to bed? Where was his bedroom located? Did he have neighbors who stayed up late or took their dogs out on walks at night? The Gs got a trash container that was identical to the one Rick owned and Wiser had his team practice driving up to a curb at night and switching it with another container. Once Wiser was confident that his squad could pull off a trash pickup without getting caught, he went back and asked Bryant to reconsider. This time, Bryant reluctantly approved the request.

The plan was to grab Rick's trash in the middle of the night, leave the substitute container, and take Rick's garbage to a nearby spot codenamed HILL STREET, after the popular television police drama *Hill Street Blues*. All the trash would be photographed so the agents could put it back into the same bags after they sorted through it. Once the garbage had been inspected, Rick's trash would be returned to the curb in front of his house before the trash collectors arrived. Beginning in late August 1993, the FBI grabbed Rick's garbage three times, but it didn't find anything incriminating.

In late August, the FBI overheard Rosario on the telephone making a hotel reservation in Miami Beach. Wiser thought Rick might be taking his family on a vacation as a cover for a meeting with his Russian handler. The FBI sent seven agents to the Doral Resort Hotel, where they planted bugs inside the room that had been reserved for the Ames family. When Rick checked in, however, the desk clerk unwittingly offered him a better room at the same price. The FBI agents had to slip into the new room and plant bugs when Rick, Rosario, and Paul were sightseeing. But all they heard that weekend was Rosario complaining about how much she disliked Miami, and Rick reading a bedtime story to Paul to help him fall asleep. He read him stories from the hotel's copy of the Holy Bible.

The family returned home September 6, Labor Day. The next morning, a Tuesday, Wiser's squad overheard Rick calling an automated recording that gave up-to-the-minute weather forecasts. Rosario telephoned him later that same day at work and reminded him that he needed to drive Paul to his preschool on Thursday morning because she would be busy.

"I have to go out really early first," he told her.

"What for?" she asked.

"I have that, uh, errand I have to do," he replied.

"*Oh, one of those?*" she replied.

"Yes. Don't worry, though, I'll be back in plenty of time."

Obviously, Rick was up to something. Wiser told the Gs that he wanted them to begin human surveillance of Rick. He ordered them to report to their "stations" before 6:00 A.M. on Thursday. Wiser's use of the word "stations," however, was misunderstood. In his mind, report to "stations" meant that the Gs were supposed to be in place outside Rick's house before 6:00 A.M. in case he went out. But the Gs thought that report to "stations" meant that they were supposed to report to a neighborhood coffeeshop where they had gathered in the past to discuss how they would handle surveillance before leaving for Rick's house. Consequently, the first G to check on Ames arrived outside his house at 6:30 A.M., a half hour later than Wiser had ordered. The G noticed that Rick's car was already parked outside the garage, and it looked as if Rick had already been out that morning. The agent checked the "eye," which is what the bureau called the video camera that it had trained on the Ames house. The videotape showed that Rick had left his house that morning at 6:03 A.M. The Gs had missed him!

Wiser was upset but he figured his squad would get another chance to nab Rick later that day. The FBI's Soviet expert, Jim Milburn, was fairly certain that Rick had left his house that morning to leave a signal for the Russians. Milburn guessed that Rick was telling the Russians that he was going to leave a package at their prearranged dead drop site later that same day. Rick hadn't been away from his house long enough that morning to have done much else. That meant the FBI still had a chance to catch Rick driving to the dead drop site to leave the Russians a package. Wiser ordered the Gs to stick with Rick. If they could catch him at a dead drop, they would have all the evidence they needed.

The Gs were ready this time when Rick left his house for work. En route to the CIA, however, the FBI made a disappointing discovery. The tracking beacon hidden in Rick's Jaguar had malfunctioned. It had stopped emitting a signal. Wiser immediately asked for an FBI reconnaissance airplane to be flown into the area to help the surveillance teams on the ground. At four o'clock, David Edger called the FBI command post and told Wiser that Rick had just left the CNC office and was about to exit the CIA's grounds. The Gs got ready for his Jaguar to appear. When Rick pulled out onto a public road, an FBI surveillance car fell in behind him. But he sped up and the FBI lost him. Wiser called the surveillance airplane. To his horror, he was told the aircraft had been grounded. Air traffic controllers at nearby National Airport had decided to route commercial air traffic over the CIA grounds. As a result, the FBI airplane had been told to stay clear of the area. Rick had slipped away once again!

It was after 5:00 P.M. when Rick returned home. The surveillance team was waiting for him. He parked his car in his driveway and the Gs took that to be a good sign because he hadn't put the Jaguar into the garage for the night. At seven o'clock, Rick and Rosario both left their house and rode in the Jaguar to Paul's preschool for a meeting. Two hours later, they returned to their car and it looked as if they were going home. Suddenly, Rick turned off the street that led to their house.

"He's going into the city!" one of the agents radioed to Wiser. This time the bureau's surveillance team didn't lose Rick. It followed the Jaguar into Washington and watched as Rick and Rosario drove into a residential area and turned into a dead-end street. The couple then drove home. The next morning, the FBI videotaped the dead-end street. Jim Milburn figured that Rick had been looking for some sort of signal left there by the Russians. The most logical spot to leave a signal, he decided, was on the side of a bright blue U.S. Postal Service letter box on the curb of the dead-end street. But there was no mark there. He looked at other possible signal sites, but kept returning to the mailbox. Finally, Milburn figured out what had happened. The Russians had erased a chalk mark on the box that Rick had made earlier that same morning. Milburn had been looking for a signal that no longer existed. "The fact that it had been erased *was* the signal!" he later recalled. Judging from Rick's actions during the previous twenty-four hours, Milburn deduced that Rick had left a signal on the mailbox for the Russians during his morning outing, had dropped off a package somewhere that afternoon when the Gs had lost him, and had driven to the dead-end street and had seen that his signal had been erased, which meant the Russians had gotten his package.

The FBI's new director, Louis Freeh, and CIA Director Woolsey were furious. Wiser's team had allowed Rick to make at least *two* dead drop deliveries to his handlers *while under FBI surveillance*. Without anyone saying anything to him, Wiser knew that he needed to make something happen or he was going to be taken off the case.

Even though Eduard Shevardnadze had agreed to host Rick's Black Sea Initiative conference, the CIA felt that Georgia was too politically unstable in the fall of 1993 to hold a meeting there. Rick switched the site of the conference to a posh Black Sea resort in Turkey. Several CNC officials attended, including Rick and David Edger. "It was absolutely the bizarrest meeting anyone had ever seen," Ames said later. "There were intelligence officers there from countries which despised each other and yet we were able to get them to talk about ways we could all cooperate to combat drug trafficking. I wrote the agenda and was the person responsible for making this happen, even down to deciding who sat next to whom." The delegates included intelligence officers from Armenia, Azerbaijan, Bulgaria, Georgia, Romania, Russia, Turkey, the Ukraine, and the United States. At the end of the conference, the delegates agreed to meet again in March 1994 in Romania. Rick was ecstatic. On the final night, there was a party, and Rick danced with a CIA secretary whom he had known for years. "I remember telling her that of all the things I had done and had happened to me during my career, this was the absolute best moment, the one I would treasure. I felt a tremendous sense of accomplishment. For a few sweet moments, I felt good about the agency and myself."

During the early hours of September 15, the same day that Rick was dancing in Turkey, a black FBI van with its lights off slowly pulled alongside the
curb outside the Ames house. Two men jumped out and switched a duplicate trash container for the one that held the Ameses' garbage. Bear Bryant
had personally ordered Wiser to stop collecting Rick and Rosario's trash, but
Wiser had decided to try at least one more pickup without telling his boss.
The refuse was taken to HILL STREET, where it was spread out on plywood
boards resting atop two-by-four sawhorses. At first, no one spotted anything
unusual, and then one of the Gs noticed a tiny piece of a yellow Post-it note
with the words "Meet at" printed in Rick's handwriting on it. The Gs kept
digging and soon found five more pieces, which they quickly reconnected. "I
am ready to meet at B on 1 Oct," it said. Everyone cheered. They had found
their first clue.

Wiser was waiting to show Bryant the jigsaw note when the Bear arrived
at work the next morning. Bryant later told reporters that Wiser's decision
to go behind his back and collect Rick's trash was "a marvelous piece of in-
subordination." Because of the note, Wiser's team knew Rick was scheduled
to meet his handler on October 1, in B, which everyone assumed was Bogotá. Wiser and several agents left for Colombia a few days before October
1, but on September 29, the FBI overheard Rick calling Rosario on his car
phone.

> RICK: There's news. No travel. . . . My visit was canceled.
> ROSARIO: Uh-huh. And does that mean you retrieved something?
> RICK: Yeah. Uh-huh. Yeah.

Obviously, Rick had just gotten a package and message from the Russians at
another dead drop. The Russians had changed the October 1 meeting date.
Wiser was told to come home. A short time later, the FBI overheard Rick
calling Rosario again on his cellular car telephone to assure her that "All is
well."

> ROSARIO: Financially, too?
> RICK: Ah yeah, ah. Wait till I get there.

It sounded as if Rick had just picked up a package of cash from the Russians. Wiser was frustrated. He had not had the Gs following Rick because

he was afraid that they might spook him, but this was the fourth time that Rick had made contact with the Russians while he was under the FBI's watch.

On October 6, Wiser's squad scooped up Rick's trash once again, and this time they recovered a ribbon from a computer printer. From it, the agents were able to reconstruct several long letters Rick had written to the Russians. In one, he described how he was becoming desperate for cash. In another, he talked about how frustrating it was at the CNC because of his "lack of access." But it was a sentence near the beginning of his second note that jumped out. "My wife has accomodated [sic] herself to understanding what I am doing in a very supportive way," he had written.

A few days later, the FBI learned from its wiretaps that Rick, Rosario, and Paul were planning on attending a wedding in Florida during an upcoming weekend. Wiser asked Attorney General Janet Reno for permission to search Ames's house. Wiser also asked the Foreign Intelligence Surveillance Court, a special court established by the Justice Department to review wiretap requests, to let the FBI hide microphones in the house. A special FBI team dressed completely in black entered the house through a side door at 1:45 A.M. on October 9, a Saturday, while the Ameses were in Florida. Inside the house, the search team found a jackpot of evidence. One of the scraps of paper that it discovered had a telephone number scribbled on it in Rick's handwriting. When the FBI checked, it learned that the number rang at the home of a KGB officer stationed in Vienna. (This was the KGB officer who Rick had called at 8:00 A.M. on the morning before his failed meeting at the Cafe Palermo.) For the first time, the FBI had evidence that tied Rick to the Russians. In an upstairs drawer, the search team found another note, this one scribbled on a piece of newspaper torn from *The Washington Times*. It indicated that Rick's trip to Bogotá had been rescheduled for November 1. The most damaging information, however, came from Rick's computer. An FBI computer expert, Tom Murray, was able to recover from the computer's hard disk several detailed messages that Rick had written to ANDRE. Ames told me later that he had thought that those messages had been destroyed. At first, the KGB and Rick had written their messages on a computer disk using the software program WordPerfect 4.2, he explained. One day, however, Rick couldn't get his computer to read the disk that the Russians had given him. He discovered that the KGB had upgraded its software program. It was now using WordPerfect 5.1. "What I didn't realize was that this new version automatically backed up my files. I thought I had wiped all of the notes off my computer's hard drive. I had no idea these backup files existed, until the FBI found them there."

Wiser now had plenty of evidence that showed Rick was a mole, but the Justice Department wanted to catch Rick actually passing documents to the Russians so that prosecutors could seek the maximum punishment. Wiser and his team left for Bogotá once again. They weren't planning on arresting Rick when he showed up on November 1 to meet his handler. That could present extradition problems because the meeting was in Colombia. Instead, they planned to videotape him there. As the date for Rick's trip drew closer, Rosario could be overheard on the microphones hidden in their house fretting about the meeting.

> ROSARIO: Do you have to lay something [deliver a package] down in the afternoon?
> RICK: No. Uh-uh. Just mark the signal.
> ROSARIO: Why didn't you do it today, for God's sakes?
> RICK: I should have, except it was raining like crazy.
> ROSARIO: . . . Well, honey, I hope you didn't screw up.

The next morning, Rosario began questioning Rick about how he planned on bringing back the cash that the Russians would give him. He usually hid it in the bottom of a suitcase and she was afraid the airlines might lose it.

> ROSARIO: It's happening more and more and you know exactly what I mean. You cannot afford to lose your suitcase and so perhaps you should use a carry-on.
> RICK: I am going to use a carry-on.
> ROSARIO: Well, yeah, you're putting the bulk of the stuff in that suitcase, right?
> RICK: Sometimes, yeah, but I think I'm going to use the carry-on.
> ROSARIO: You are going to have to be a little more imaginative about it—you always have this envelope with this big hunk—I mean really!

Four days later, she mentioned the cash again.

> ROSARIO: . . . I don't want you to bring back anything that will make them look in your luggage.

Rick left for Bogotá on October 30, and called Rosario shortly after he landed. He told her that the airlines had lost his garment bag.

ROSARIO: They what!?

RICK: The airline lost it. They said a bunch of bags got delayed and didn't make the flight in the Miami airport.

ROSARIO: Oh, my God, I am very, very nervous!

A few seconds later she asked Rick what he had been carrying in the bag. She was afraid that he had hidden some documents for ANDRE in it.

ROSARIO: You didn't have anything, uh . . .

RICK: What?

ROSARIO: You didn't have anything that shouldn't have been in that bag?

RICK: No, honey.

Wiser's crew arrived at the Unicentro mall at 5:30 P.M. on November 1. He stayed at a hotel in a makeshift command post. The FBI knew from the notes it had found on Rick's computer that he was supposed to meet his handler at 6:00 P.M. in front of Bolicentro, the bowling alley there. The agents turned on a video camera that was hidden inside a briefcase. But Rick didn't show up at 6:00 P.M. A man in his 50s arrived and stood in front of the bowling alley for several minutes, but Rick was nowhere to be seen. Finally, at 6:30 P.M., the man waiting outside the bowling alley left. Fifteen minutes later, the FBI spotted Rick. He was wearing a raincoat and looked relaxed as he made his way to the front of the bowling alley. Ten, fifteen, twenty minutes passed. Finally, after thirty minutes, Rick left.

The agents hurried back to their hotel to brief Wiser. None of them was certain what had happened. It looked to them as if Rick had arrived at the meeting forty-five minutes late, by which time his Russian contact had already come and gone. Mike Anderson, the FBI supervisor, who was monitoring Rosario back in Virginia, called Wiser in Bogotá later that night with even more confusing news. The FBI had overheard a telephone call that Rosario had made to Rick after he had returned to her mother's apartment from the bowling alley. Anderson reported that Rick had assured Rosario that "the meeting" had taken place. The FBI would later release a transcript of that telephone call.

ROSARIO: Did you really meet?

RICK: Uh-huh.

ROSARIO: When did you get back?

Rick could be overheard asking Cecilia what time he had returned to her apartment.

ROSARIO: What's wrong with you? Why do you have to ask my mother
   when you got back? Don't be an asshole. Have you been drinking?
RICK: No, honest, honey. Not a drop . . .
ROSARIO: Well, the only reason I was upset was because I thought it
   had all been for nothing and that, you know, you hadn't gotten
   the . . . the . . .
RICK: No, no . . .
ROSARIO: You're sure?
RICK: Believe me . . .
ROSARIO: Just be careful. You swear to me that nothing went wrong?
RICK: Yeah, uh-uh.
ROSARIO: Well, you don't sound too sure. . . . You wouldn't lie to me,
   would you?
RICK: No. No. . . .

Rick could then be heard telling Rosario in cryptic language that he was going to meet his Russian contact for a second time the following night, November 2, but he didn't say where.

Wiser wasn't sure what to do. If he and his team tried to follow Rick on November 2, they might be spotted by the Russians. Worse, they could run into problems with the Bogotá authorities. Cecilia's apartment was protected by shotgun-carrying guards who were quick to question anyone lingering outside the building. Wiser decided to send his agents to various key spots in Bogotá where he thought Rick might meet his Russian handler. He sent one of his agents back to the Unicentro mall to wait outside the bowling alley just in case Rick returned there.

The next evening, Wiser waited anxiously at the hotel while his agents watched for Rick to appear. He didn't. No one saw him. Frustrated, Wiser and his troops returned home without any video of Rick meeting his handler.

What Wiser would not learn until later was that Rick had been lying to Rosario during their telephone call. He had not met ANDRE on November 1. He had misread his own notes and had arrived one hour late outside the bowling alley. Rick hadn't realized his mistake until it was too late. "I didn't want to tell Rosario the truth because she was already upset about my luggage being lost." On November 2, Rick returned to the mall and bowling alley where he met ANDRE. *What has never been revealed until now is that Rick and the Russian should have been spotted by one of Wiser's agents—the one assigned to watch the front of the bowling alley. For reasons that the FBI has never revealed, the agent missed seeing Rick and the Russian.*

When Rick got home, he told Rosario that the Russians had promised to increase the amount of cash they were leaving for him in dead drops. Lowering his voice, he whispered: "They're holding . . . one million nine hundred thousand dollars for me in Moscow."

The FBI waited for Rick to contact the Russians. All of November and December, they watched. Nothing happened. In mid-January 1994, the bureau found itself facing a deadline. Rick was scheduled to go overseas on another trip, first to Turkey, then to Germany, and finally to Russia. The CIA already had postponed Rick's trip three times in order to give the bureau additional time to catch him. The agency was afraid that if it postponed the trip once again, Rick would get suspicious. The bureau, meanwhile, was worried about letting Rick travel to Moscow. If he had figured out that he was a suspect, he might just stay there. Wiser came up with a ruse. He suggested that the agency tell Rick that President Clinton wanted to be briefed about the Black Sea Initiative. The White House agreed to play along, but it said that Clinton was not going to get dragged into the mole hunt. The White House said that National Security Adviser Anthony Lake would request a briefing, and to make it appear authentic, several other CIA officers would also be asked to prepare statements. The topic: *cooperation between the former KGB and the United States.*

Rick worked hard on his presentation. He still didn't have a clue about what was really happening. Wiser's ploy bought the bureau a few extra weeks but Rick didn't do anything suspicious, and by mid-February, Bear Bryant decided it was time to arrest Rick *and* Rosario as spies. His decision to go after Rosario sparked a debate inside the Justice Department. Jo Ann Harris, the assistant U.S. attorney general in charge of the department's criminal division, didn't understand why the FBI wanted to charge Rosario, since she had never met any Russians, stolen any classified documents, or done anything other than help spend Rick's blood money and sign fraudulent joint income tax returns. Bryant and Wiser came up with a slew of reasons. Later, however, some involved in the case would quietly suggest that Rosario's personality had played a key role in the bureau's decision to prosecute her. After listening over the hidden microphones for months to

Rosario verbally reprimanding her son and whining, complaining, and hen-pecking her husband, most of Wiser's squad had come to utterly despise her. Simply put, they wanted her punished. "If we felt sorry for anyone in that family, after listening to those tapes, it was Rick Ames," an FBI agent said later.

Shortly before 7:00 A.M. on February 21, 1994, some twenty-five FBI agents began to congregate at a parking lot about a half-mile from the Ameses' house. Because it was Presidents' Day, a federal holiday, the roads were empty. Once Wiser was certain that everyone was there and knew their assign-ments, he drove to the U.S. attorney's office in Alexandria, Virginia, where Mark J. Hulkower, an assistant prosecutor, was waiting. Together, they pre-sented a federal magistrate, who had been called into work specifically to meet them, with a detailed affidavit that outlined the evidence the FBI had gathered against Rick and Rosario. The magistrate signed warrants for their arrest, the search of their house and a safety deposit box, and the seizure of Rick's Jaguar and Rosario's Honda.

"Okay, go ahead," Wiser said in a telephone call to a special command post. The CIA's Dan Payne, who was waiting for Wiser's go-ahead, tele-phoned David Edger at the agency. Rick was getting ready to shave, when Edger called him at home. "I just got a cable in here," Edger said. "It's about your trip. There's a problem. Can you come into the office and send some-thing out about this?" Rick was scheduled to leave the next morning on his long-delayed trip overseas.

"I have to go into the office," he told Rosario, who was just getting dressed, "but it shouldn't take long." He glanced at his wristwatch. It was 9:30 A.M. Rick backed the Jaguar out of the garage and drove down the street. At the corner, he turned right and then made another right turn one block later. He was lighting a cigarette when he noticed a car with a flashing red light on its dash speeding up behind him. "I thought *What on earth*—and then another car came pulling in front of me—and all of a sudden, I knew. I told myself, *It's done.*"

Special Agent Mike Donner, who had designed the arrest scenario, and fellow agents Rudy Guerin and Dell Spry bolted from their cars and raced toward Rick, who was lowering the Jaguar's window. Spry ordered him to keep his hands in sight and get out of the car. "You're under arrest for espi-onage," Donner snarled.

Back at the house, Yolanda Larson, a Spanish-speaking FBI agent, and Special Agent John Hosinski knocked on the front door. Rosario came downstairs after the maid let them in. "Your husband has just been arrested for espionage," Hosinski said. "You need to come with us." A crew of specialists was waiting to search and inventory the house.

Pushed into the back seat of an FBI car, Rick tried to compose himself. "Think," he whispered out loud, "think, think."

CHAPTER 25

Rick was driven to a fake command post that the bureau had constructed in a suburban office. Surveillance photographs of him and Rosario were tacked on the walls. There were aerial shots of their house. Boxes marked "AMES" were stacked in a corner. Wiser's squad wanted the couple to believe that it had such overwhelming evidence against them that they had no choice but to confess. But Rick didn't fall for the scam. He refused to answer any questions, so the FBI drove him to the Alexandria Detention Center.

A terrified Rosario was hustled into the same mock command post moments later. Julie Johnson, the FBI agent who had spent months listening to the couple's conversations, had predicted that Rosario would turn against Rick if she were given a chance to save her own neck. The trick was to treat Rosario kindly and sympathetically and to remember that she thought she was smarter than nearly everyone else. Any attempt to browbeat her would simply push Rosario into an uncontrollable rage. Based on that advice, Agent John Hosinski gently began asking about Rick's finances. Rosario said she didn't know anything about them. She wasn't even sure how much he earned at the CIA. Hosinski asked about Rick's seemingly endless supply of cash. Rosario mentioned Robert from Chicago. Neither Hosinski nor Yolanda Larson, who was also in the room, challenged Rosario's answers. Instead, they politely poked holes in them. *"And you say you never met this Robert from Chicago? He never came to your house or called or wrote Rick any letters?"*

Rosario began tripping over her own lies. The agents pinpointed the inconsistencies. With a sigh, Rosario announced that she was tired of playing games. "Rick works for the Russians," she blurted.

What happened during the next few hours remains disputed. Rosario would later claim that Hosinski and Larson lied to her. "They kept saying the important thing is for you to get back to your son. As soon as you finish this, it's going to be fine, you can go back to him. And I believed them! I thought they would let me go. I didn't think they would charge me if I helped them." The FBI would insist that its agents never promised Rosario any special treatment. Because none of the interrogation was tape-recorded, there would be no independent record of what was said. The only notes were taken by the two FBI agents, who later submitted polished versions to the court. Rosario would argue that her words had been twisted in those notes. "He [Hosinski] starts asking me questions, but the way that he asks them was very exasperating, because he asked questions in a way in which he's already answering them himself, and then he writes down his own answer, not mine." At one point, Rosario told the agents that she had first learned Rick was a spy in 1991. Then she said 1992. "He [Hosinski] writes down 1991, because that sounds better to him because it's an earlier date. I told him, 'No!' and then he writes down 1992, but he makes it look as if I'm lying, instead of having trouble remembering.'" According to Rosario, the agents began treating her differently around midafternoon, after they received a telephone call from the FBI team searching the house. The search team had found so much damaging evidence that federal prosecutors no longer needed Rosario's cooperation to convict Rick. "Suddenly they told me I was going to meet the prosecutor [Mark Hulkower]," Rosario recalled bitterly. "They said, 'This is going to be very important.' I said, 'Why?' They said, 'Because he's the guy who's going to decide your case.' . . . Then this repugnant-looking Hulkower walks in. He's very smooth, he tries to be very charming. . . . But I see him for what he is, a nasty, ill-bred creature who thinks he's great." Hulkower told Rosario that he was going to prosecute her for helping Rick spy. "You can't do that!" she snapped. "I've not done anything!"

The government's version of what happened that Monday in the mock command post differs from Rosario's. The decision to prosecute her was made long before her arrest. There is no mention in the FBI's notes about a telephone call from the search team or a blunt exchange between Rosario and Hulkower. In the FBI's notes, Rosario is quoted thanking the two FBI agents for the "kind way" they treated her during the interview.

Regardless, shortly after five o'clock, Rosario was driven to the same jail as Rick. She immediately clashed with the guards there. "One of the deputies was this blond fat woman who looks like a cow and talks like she's out of the sewer," Rosario complained later. "There were a lot of horrible-looking, dirty, scary-looking people who had been drinking, and they were sitting around waiting to be put in jail and. . . . This woman tells me to go sit there in the midst of all these men who are giving me horrible looks. I said, 'I don't want to sit there.' She said, 'I didn't ask you if you did. Go sit there.' Well, they had me wait there for over two hours! Two and a half hours, really, with these men giving me all sorts of looks!"

Rick was in a nearby isolation cell and could hear Rosario complaining. He began to cry. "I kept thinking, *How could I have been so dumb that I didn't see this coming?* In retrospect, there were so many signals. I just kept going over and over in my mind what I should have done. The only thing that kept me from killing myself was that I kept thinking, *No, you got to help Rosario and Paul. Then you can kill yourself, but not now, not yet.*"

Aleksandr Iosovich Lysenko, the *rezident* at the Russian embassy in Washington, heard about the arrests early Tuesday and immediately sent an urgent cable to Yevgeniy Primakov, who was the director of Russia's External Intelligence Service (SVR) in Moscow. Lysenko had suspected the day before that something strange was in the works. One of his officers had reported seeing a chalk mark at a signal site which the Russians had used previously to communicate with LYUDMILA, the KGB's original cryptonym for Rick. LYUDMILA had been told to change his signal. He had been drawing a horizontal line on the side of the outdoor mailbox whenever he wanted to schedule a dead drop. But the SVR had recently told him to begin drawing a vertical line. The chalk mark the SVR officer had spotted while driving to work was horizontal. Lysenko knew LYUDMILA had a reputation for making foolish mistakes. Once the spy had used a white crayon to make his signal, instead of an easy-to-erase piece of chalk. An SVR officer had been forced to spend several minutes using cleaning fluid and paper towels to wipe away the crayon. It was possible that LYUDMILA had simply goofed up again. It was also possible that this was a trap. The FBI could be waiting to photograph and detain whoever showed up. The SVR was supposed to reply to signals left by LYUDMILA on the same day it saw them, but Lysenko had been uncertain about what he should do, so he hadn't done anything.

When he learned on Tuesday about Rick's arrest, Lysenko knew he had made the right decision. Although he had never been told Rick's actual name, he was certain that the spy who had been caught was LYUDMILA.

The horizontal mark had been part of a trap. The FBI's Jim Milburn knew the mailbox was an SVR signal site, but Milburn did not know that the SVR had told Ames to begin using a vertical chalk mark. Consequently, the FBI had marked the box on Monday morning, and had kept Rick's arrest secret for nearly twenty-four hours in a final attempt to catch a Russian communicating with Rick.

News of Rick's arrest jolted Moscow. Director Primakov immediately called Lieutenant General Vadim Kirpichenko, who was now the chief of the Council of Advisers to the SVR. The two men shared a unique history. When Kirpichenko had been the KGB *rezident* in Cairo, he had recruited Primakov, then a Russian journalist. In the early 1970s, Primakov had warned Kirpichenko that Egypt was about to break its close ties to the USSR, but Kirpichenko had not believed him. When Primakov was appointed director of the SVR, he had jokingly reminded Kirpichenko of the incident in private. It was Kirpichenko who former KGB director Vladimir Kryuchkov had assigned to oversee the handling of Rick when he had first volunteered to spy in 1985. Both men knew the discovery of a KGB mole inside the CIA was bound to rupture U.S.-Russia relations. They went to the Kremlin to brief Russian president Boris N. Yeltsin. He was locked in a nasty dispute with the Russian parliament about whether it would grant amnesty to several of his archenemies—the men who had led an armed insurrection against his government only four months earlier. Yeltsin was angry. He didn't need another crisis. A short while later, Yeltsin was told that President Clinton was lodging a formal complaint and sending two CIA officers to Moscow to question SVR officials about their relationship with the man the U.S. media was calling "America's most damaging traitor." On their ride back to SVR headquarters, Primakov turned to his trusted friend and adviser.

"What now?" he asked.

"We search," Kirpichenko replied. It was now the SVR's turn to investigate why one of its spies had been caught.

Early Tuesday morning, Rick and Rosario were hustled into the backseat of a U.S. marshal's car and driven from the jail to the federal courthouse in Alexandria for arraignment. It was the first time they had been together since their arrests the day before. "We were hysterical," Ames recalled. "I kept saying, 'I'm sorry. I'm so sorry.' Rosario told me she had been tricked by the FBI into making some sort of statement. I said, 'It doesn't matter. It will be okay.'" A horde of reporters and television crews were waiting for them. Inside the tiny courtroom, Hulkower briefly outlined the government's case for U.S. magistrate Barry R. Poretz. Rick felt compelled to say something, but he didn't know what. The arraignment lasted only a few minutes, and then Rick and Rosario were whisked back to jail. At seven o'clock that night, a deputy told Rick that his attorney had come to see him. The government had frozen all Rick and Rosario's assets, so they couldn't afford to hire their own lawyers. They had to settle for court-appointed ones, and Rick was worried that he and Rosario were going to be stuck with a couple of inexperienced public defenders. When he saw the face of his visitor, those worries vanished.

"I'm Plato Cacheris," the attorney said.

"I was wondering what I was going to do for a lawyer, and I get Plato Cacheris!" a grinning Rick replied. He recognized Cacheris from television newscasts and photographs in newspapers and magazines. The sixty-four-year-old defense attorney was considered one of the best in the D.C. area. He had represented former U.S. attorney general John Mitchell during the Watergate scandal; Oliver North's secretary, Fawn Hall, during the Irangate uproar; and many of the rich and famous, including the wife of Jack Kent Cooke, the owner of the Washington Redskins football team. Cacheris charged $400 per hour. As Rick's court-appointed attorney, he would be paid $65 per hour. But Cacheris had agreed to represent Rick as soon as he was asked by Magistrate Poretz. Free publicity was only part of the reason. Cacheris loved fighting for underdogs. He'd spent nearly forty years practicing law, and his happiest courthouse memories were of cases when he had beaten the odds.

Cacheris had stopped at the courthouse earlier that day to read the government's charges against his newest client. The case looked bleak for Rick, just the sort of scrap that Cacheris liked. He studied his client as they shook hands, and was surprised at how calm Rick seemed. Most defendants, even ones who were lawyers, usually showed signs of jailhouse shock after they were arrested. "Rick was in total control of his emotions," Cacheris said later. "His attitude was, 'I expected this to happen. It happened and I'll deal with it.' He did not care about himself. He was absolutely consumed with the notion that he had to do the best that he could to save Rosario." Without being asked, Rick admitted he was a KGB mole. "I'm going to be in prison for the rest of my life," he said, "but we can't let them punish Rosario for my mistakes."

That same Tuesday, Rosario met her court-appointed attorney, William B. Cummings. Even though he was not as well known or as flashy as Cacheris, he had a solid reputation. Cummings, fifty-four, had been the U.S. attorney in northern Virginia during the late 1970s, and he and Cacheris had both handled spy cases before. Cummings was the only attorney in recent history who had won an acquittal for a defendant accused of espionage. He had successfully defended Richard Craig Smith, a retired army intelligence officer, accused in 1984 of spying for the Russians.

In 1967, Cacheris had defended Herbert W. Boeckenhaupt, an Air Force sergeant convicted of selling military secrets to the Soviets. The FBI had caught him because of tips it had received from GRU general Dmitri Polyakov, TOPHAT. Now Cacheris was defending the KGB mole responsible for telling the Soviets about Polyakov and getting him killed.

During the next few days, Cacheris and Cummings began sifting through the evidence. The search of Rick's house had turned up dozens of incriminating records. Two documents in particular worried Cacheris. The first was the nine-page letter VLAD had given Rick in Rome that contained a breakdown of the $2.7 million that the KGB either had paid or was holding for him in Moscow. That same letter contained photographs of land that had been put aside for Rick's future dacha. The second damning document was a copy of the December 17, 1990, note that Rick had written to the KGB, warning it that PROLOGUE was working as a CIA mole. Together, these two documents were prima facie evidence that Rick was a spy. The first showed the Russians were paying Rick huge sums of cash. The second revealed why. What Cacheris didn't know, of course, was that PROLOGUE was a double agent. *Had Cacheris known this, he could have argued that Rick's note about PROLOGUE meant nothing.* How could Rick be accused of betraying a double agent? No one in the government, however, told Cacheris or the media about PROLOGUE. Some FBI agents went so far as to suggest that PROLOGUE had been arrested and executed. Based on what he had learned, Cacheris told Rick that he didn't have much of a defense. Still, he recommended that Rick force the government to put him on trial. Cacheris had a few legal maneuvers he could try, and he knew the CIA would be reluctant to have its inner workings discussed in open court.

Rick balked. He was afraid the Justice Department would punish Rosario if he didn't agree to plead guilty and cooperate.

"You're making a huge mistake," Cacheris warned. If he wanted to help Rosario, he needed to play hardball with the government and act as if he didn't care what it did to her. Rick looked sheepish. When he and Rosario were being escorted out of the courthouse after their arraignment, Rick had talked briefly to an FBI agent. "I had to say something to help Rosario," he told Cacheris, "so I said to this guy, 'Hey, I'm really looking forward to cooperating fully with you guys and your investigation. I want to do anything I can to help my wife.'"

Cacheris grimaced.

While Rick and Cacheris plotted their strategy, Rosario and Cummings met in a different room at the jail. Unlike Rick, Rosario was so distraught that the jail had been forced to call in a psychiatrist to counsel her. Cummings spent much of his time trying to educate her about what was happening. Rosario insisted that she had not done anything wrong. She claimed she was being persecuted because she was from Colombia, and because Hulkower and the FBI agents didn't like her. "Our joint meetings—between Cummings, Plato, Rosario, and me—were, in retrospect, disastrous," Ames said later. "Rosario's confusion, anger, and fears only triggered my own guilt and passivity. Because everything revolved around the issue of Rosario's fate, Plato had little he could contribute. . . . This left the main role to Cummings, and he spent most of his time trying to show Rosario the reality of our situation and the apparent strength of the government's charges against her. The reality was that she was going to have to answer these charges, and not merely keep protesting her innocence—which is what she wanted to do."

Rosario was accused of entering into a "conspiracy to commit espionage." The prosecution claimed she had broken the law because she had offered Rick "advice and support" which had helped him as a KGB spy. The most damning evidence against her were the tape recordings the FBI had made with the microphones it had hidden in the house. The FBI already had made public verbatim transcripts of some conversations which it felt were incriminating. In them, Rosario was quoted talking to Rick about dead drops and his meetings in Bogotá with the KGB. Rosario insisted that her comments to Rick had not been intended to help him spy. Rather, she was trying to protect her son and herself from being dragged into a disaster by her reckless husband. Who knew better than she did how careless and absentminded Rick could be?

Rick suggested that Cacheris and Cummings demand transcripts of every tape recording. "If you listen to all of those tapes, you will hear Rosario complaining about what I was doing," Rick assured them. When the two defense attorneys asked the FBI about the tapes, they were told that the bureau had recorded more than 2,000 hours of conversations. Before Cacheris and Cummings demanded transcripts, Prosecutor Hulkower suggested that they listen to the snippets of tape he planned to play in court. This would allow them to hear exactly what jurors were going to hear. Cacheris and Cummings knew written transcripts could be misleading. There was no way to know what tone of voice was being spoken or if someone was terrified or snickering. Both attorneys listened to the bits and pieces that Hulkower intended to use. Within a few minutes, both understood why the government planned to use these specific passages. On the tapes, Rosario could be heard sniveling about money, griping at Paul, belittling her friends, and constantly degrading and chiding Rick. She sounded arrogant, contemptuous, totally self-absorbed, and, worst of all, greedy. Cummings decided to let Rosario choose for herself if she wanted a jury to hear her words. He arranged for a tape recorder to be set up in the attorney/client room and then switched on the machine. After only five minutes, Rosario told Cummings to turn it off. Cummings asked her for a decision. Did she want to risk going to trial and a possible thirty-year prison sentence, or negotiate a plea bargain? Rosario didn't hesitate. There was no way, she said, that she wanted those tapes to be heard in public.

On April 5, Cacheris and Cummings presented a five-page confidential offer to Jo Ann Harris, the assistant U.S. attorney general at the Justice Department. John Martin, the department's internal security chief; Helen Fahey, the U.S. attorney for northern Virginia; Prosecutor Hulkower; and several other assistant U.S. attorneys were in the room. Both sides had been negotiating for weeks. The government was demanding that Rick plead guilty, accept a life prison sentence without any chance of parole, submit to a comprehensive debriefing by the CIA and FBI, and forfeit all his cash and property, except for the land in Colombia, which the United States could not legally seize. In return, the government would recommend that Rosario get a *five-year* prison sentence.

In his counteroffer, Cacheris asked that Rosario be sentenced to a maximum of *two years*. If the government didn't agree, Rick would get tough, Cacheris warned. He would never tell anyone about the damage that he had done as a spy, and he would force the government to make him stand trial.

Cacheris would also raise several legal issues at the trial about how the FBI had conducted its investigation. Rather than getting its search warrants from a federal judge, as was the normal procedure, it had gotten its search warrants directly from Attorney General Janet Reno and from the Foreign Intelligence Surveillance Court. "The constitutionality of searches authorized by the Attorney General . . . has not been addressed by the courts," Cacheris warned in his letter. If Cacheris could prove that the search warrant had been invalid, then most of the government's evidence would be inadmissible. Rick might even be found not guilty. Harris listened politely, but wasn't scared. A few days later, she told Cacheris and Cummings that the government was sticking to its earlier offer: nothing less than five years for Rosario.

"Rosario was angry," Cacheris later recalled. "She was bitching. She kept saying, 'I didn't do anything. I shouldn't have to plead guilty to this.' Cummings would tell her that if she went to trial, she ran the risk of getting thirty years. We went over it again and again." On April 28, Rick and Rosario appeared before Judge Claude M. Hilton at the Alexandria courthouse and announced that they wished to change their earlier pleas. Cacheris had insisted that Rosario go first. "It was so touch-and-go that I didn't want Rick to plead guilty and then have Rosario back out, and, as I sat there in the courtroom watching her, I would not have been surprised if she had stood up and announced: 'Hey, I'm not guilty, and I'm not going through with this deal.'"

Clutching a huge crucifix on her necklace in one hand, Rosario announced in a voice shaking with emotion that she wished to plead guilty. Rick stood next and, without any show of emotion, declared that he wished to plead guilty, too. Judge Hilton said he would delay sentencing Rosario until after the government had finished debriefing Rick. If he stopped cooperating or was caught lying, the court could set aside the plea agreement and sentence Rosario to a longer prison term. The judge asked Hulkower if he wished to say anything before Rick was sentenced. Hulkower reminded the packed courtroom that Rick had not only sold U.S. secrets to the Russians, but had "caused people to die as surely as if [he] had pulled the trigger." Without mentioning TOPHAT (Dmitri Polyakov]) by name, Hulkower described how the GRU general had provided invaluable help to the United States, only to be betrayed and executed because "Rick Ames . . . wanted to live in a half-million-dollar house and drive a Jaguar." Rick glanced at Rosario. She was crying. "Rosario never really knew that people had been executed because of me until after we were arrested," Ames claimed later.

Judge Hilton asked Rick if he had anything to say, and Rick rose slowly in a dignified manner. He attacked the government for how it had treated Rosario. He didn't know of a single case, he declared, where the Soviets had put a spy's wife in prison because of what her husband had done. He then turned his rancor toward the CIA. "The espionage business, as carried out by the CIA . . . is a self-serving sham, carried out by careerist bureaucrats," he declared.

When Rick finished his fifteen-minute speech, Judge Hilton sentenced him to life in prison without parole.

Diana Worthen was in the courtroom. Rick had assumed she had come to support Rosario and him. He didn't know that she was the one who had told Sandy Grimes, Paul Redmond, Jeanne Vertefeuille, and Dan Payne that Rosario's family wasn't wealthy. Worthen had felt guilty when her two former best friends had been brought into the courtroom. But after hearing Rick's lecture, she was angry. "I needed to hear him say he was guilty, to apologize," Worthen said later. "I was still waiting for an explanation. *Why, Rick, why?*" She decided that the Rick in the courtroom was not the same Rick who had been her boss and a close friend. "The voice I heard speaking sounded as if it was coming from a stranger, a man without a soul."

The SVR said it had never heard of Aldrich Ames. The two CIA officers naively sent by President Clinton to Moscow returned empty-handed. Congress and the media attacked. Some called for ending all U.S. aid to Russia. Others demanded the dismantling of the CIA. An embarrassed Clinton expelled SVR *rezident* Lysenko. Moscow kicked out a CIA officer. To help fend off criticism, CIA director Woolsey ordered three independent investigations. The biggest was done by the CIA's own inspector general, Frederick P. Hitz, who had been in the same career training program as Ames in 1967 when both were novice employees. Hitz's team of twelve investigators, whom he likened to a jury, reviewed 45,000 pages of documents, conducted more than 300 interviews, and issued a 486-page classified report that blistered the agency for "sleeping on the job" and failing to catch Ames much earlier. Hitz recommended that twenty-three current and former CIA employees be reprimanded. When Woolsey issued mild reprimands to only eleven officers and refused to fire any of them, the House and Senate intelligence committees expressed shock. "It looks like business as usual at the CIA. You don't lose your job or get demoted," Senator Dennis DeConcini (D-Arizona), chairman of the Senate Select Committee on Intelligence, complained on the front page of *The Washington Post*. The agency came under even more criticism when, unbeknownst to Woolsey, two senior CIA managers decided to honor Milton Bearden, one of the eleven employees whom Woolsey had just censured. John MacGaffin and Frank Anderson flew to Bonn, Germany, where Bearden was finishing a stint as chief of station, and presented him with a plaque at his going-away party, honoring him for the three years he had spent waging the CIA's successful covert war in Afghanistan. Woolsey was furious, because he had issued a reprimand to Bearden only *two days* earlier for his role in selecting Ames to be the Western European branch chief in 1989. The media accused the CIA of thumbing its nose at the outside world. Woolsey demanded that MacGaffin and Anderson step down from their jobs, a punishment worse than anything he had ordered in the Ames case. Both men refused, and retired instead.

Congress decided to launch its own investigations. Senator DeConcini and Representative Dan Glickman (D-Kansas), chairman of the House Permanent Select Committee on Intelligence, both interviewed Ames in jail. Although Ames acknowledged that some might question his motives, he said he wanted to play a role in the ongoing debate "over the value, future, or the functions of American intelligence." Now it was Woolsey's turn to be outraged. Asking Ames for advice about the CIA was "a little bit like taking [Mafia godfather] John Gotti as an authority on the FBI," the director snapped. Their trips to the jail were considered insulting to the agency.

The backbiting and heel-nipping continued for months between Congress and the CIA. In a closed session before the House intelligence committee, Jeanne Vertefeuille found herself pelted with angry questions. One of the rudest attacks came from Chairman Glickman, who demanded to know why she thought that *she* was qualified to investigate the 1985 losses? Vertefeuille was offended. Had it not been for the persistence and hard work that she and her mole hunters had done, Ames would never have been unmasked. "We were being criticized by people who couldn't track an elephant in six feet of snow," she later said. The criticism of Vertefeuille seemed especially ironic, since she could have abandoned the mole hunt in 1992 during what was perhaps its most critical period. Vertefeuille had reached the agency's mandatory retirement age of sixty, but instead of leaving the CIA, she'd retired and returned to work *in less than one hour* as a full-time contract employee so that she could continue to help with the search.

No one in the CIA was pleased about the barrage of criticism that the agency received, but it was the FBI's actions that upset most of those directly involved in helping catch Ames. The FBI claimed full credit. Photographs of the FBI's Bryant, Wiser, and his team appeared in numerous news magazines and on the front pages of newspapers. At a jammed press conference, Wiser announced that the key to catching Ames had been the FBI's discovery of a Post-it note during an unauthorized search of his trash. "When we got this, we knew we had a spy," Wiser declared dramatically, "and he was active." No mention was made of the CIA's role months before in pinpointing Ames, no credit given to Vertefeuille and her team's discovery of the Swiss bank accounts. Peter Maas, in telling the FBI's exclusive story in his book *Killer Spy*, would write that the CIA's Paul Redmond had begged the FBI to enter the mole hunt in 1991, gushing at one point: "We have blood on our hands!"—a quote Redmond would later dismiss as pure fiction.

The most fierce battle between the CIA and FBI, however, was being waged behind the scenes. The agency lost. President Clinton signed a directive that required that the chief of the counterespionage group at the CIC at Langley always be an *FBI agent*. This unprecedented step effectively put the bureau in control of the CIA's future mole hunts. Congress went a step further by adding a provision to the Intelligence Authorization Act of 1995 that required the CIA to give the FBI access to any files it wished. The agency was also told that it had to notify the FBI immediately whenever it suspected any type of loss of classified information. Riding a wave of CIA-bashing and favorable FBI publicity, Bryant was put in charge of all FBI intelligence matters. His promotion irked many within the agency who saw him as the FBI's point man in its power grab.

At Langley, word of what Vertefeuille and her mole team had done slowly leaked out. Woolsey took Vertefeuille to the White House when Clinton and Vice President Albert Gore met with congressional leaders to discuss whether or not the Ames case should have any impact on U.S.–Russia relations. Before the meeting began, Woolsey told Clinton and Gore about Vertefeuille and her task force. Clinton walked over, shook her hand and gave her his thumbs-up signal. As was her way, Vertefeuille told the president that catching Ames had been a team effort.

Nearly one year after Ames was arrested, the CIA decided to hold an awards ceremony, so employees could congratulate Vertefeuille, Grimes, Payne, and Worthen. Formal invitations were mailed to their friends and relatives, and then, without warning, the entire affair was canceled. By this time, Woolsey had retired as CIA director, his career badly soiled by the Ames affair, and acting director Admiral William O. Studeman did not want the media to find out that the CIA was congratulating anyone about the Ames debacle. After Studeman left, the agency decided to host a private, secret ceremony for the mole hunt team members only. The CIA workforce was not told or invited, nor were family members invited. Both Vertefeuille and Grimes refused to attend. Although it was not widely known, being part of the investigation had personally cost Grimes $25,000. During the investigation the CIA had offered a cash buyout to employees willing to take early retirement. Grimes had wanted to retire, but was told that if she accepted the money, she couldn't be rehired to work as a part-time employee on the mole hunt team. Redmond pleaded with her to stay, and on the final day of the $25,000 offer, Grimes agreed not to accept the cash buyout, but to retire and remain as a contract employee until the agency identified the mole. When Ames was arrested, Grimes was glad that she had stuck it out. She felt that she had helped repay the debt the agency owed to Dmitri Polyakov and the others.

A few days after the private reception at the agency, Grimes received a package in the mail. Inside was a medal and a CIA commendation. She tossed both in a desk drawer.

Rick barely had time to eat and sleep. He had so much to do. At least three days each week after he pleaded guilty, he was taken from the jail to an FBI office to be debriefed. At the start, Les Wiser, Jr., Jim Milburn, and special agents Mike Donner and Rudy Guerin were there from the FBI. Hulkower was the U.S. attorney's representative. The FBI had not wanted the CIA to be included in the debriefings, but it had begrudgingly agreed to let Jeanne Vertefeuille sit through them. She made sure that she was the last person to enter the room on the first day. She didn't want to shake Rick's hand. Once the debriefings got underway, Wiser, Hulkower, and Donner dropped out. That left Guerin, Milburn, and Vertefeuille to do the work. Vertefeuille and Rick often found themselves telling stories and even laughing about some inside jokes that only fellow CIA employees would understand. Sometimes, she even forgot what he had done. Early on in the debriefings, Rick was asked if he had ever suggested that the KGB blame someone else at the agency for the 1985 losses. Rick admitted that he had. He'd given them the name of a person to frame who had known all about the losses. Looking directly across the table at Vertefeuille, he quietly announced that he had given the KGB *her name*.

On the days when Rick wasn't being debriefed, he spent hours trying to help Rosario. He studied the guidelines that Federal judges use when determining prison sentences, and in a twenty-two-page memorandum to the court, urged Judge Hilton to reduce Rosario's sentence from five to a maximum of two years. In his best legalese, Rick claimed that Rosario was being treated much more harshly than the wives of other convicted spies. Barbara Walker had kept quiet for fourteen years before turning in her husband, Rick noted. Yet she was never charged, even though she admitted having gone on a dead drop with him and later using an iron to flatten U.S. currency that had become curly from being hidden in a Coca-Cola can. Anne Pollard was convicted of being an accessory when her husband, Jonathan, was caught spying for Israel. She'd served three and a half years in prison before she was released because of health problems, Rick wrote. Ironically, Rosario was secretly behind Rick's moves to help her. She sent him a flurry of angry and hateful letters demanding that he "save" her. At times, she threatened suicide if he didn't do what she demanded. Rick, meanwhile, suggested that Rosario portray herself as a battered wife. In a letter that Rosario later tore to pieces and flushed down a toilet in the jail, Rick wrote that he would tell reporters that he had used every trick that he had learned from the CIA to manipulate her, including psychological blackmail. He urged her to blame him for everything.

A few days before Rosario was to be sentenced, she fired her court-appointed attorney, and hired John P. Hume, whose firm also represented the Colombian embassy. She paid him $25,000 with the proceeds from the sale of the condominium and beach land that she and Rick had owned in Colombia. Hume warned her that there wasn't much he could do, but he did arrange for Rosario to give an exclusive interview to Sally Quinn of *The Washington Post* and also oversaw another exclusive interview with Diane Sawyer on ABC's *Prime Time Live*. Both raised questions about whether she was being too harshly punished by the government. Hume continued preaching that theme when Rosario appeared before Judge Hilton, on October 23, for sentencing. "Rosario Ames was the victim of the worst form of spousal abuse," he charged. After being lied to and deceived for years, Rosario had "very little choice" but to keep silent when she finally learned about Rick's spying. A pale and exhausted Rosario read from a prepared statement. "I have made terrible mistakes and choices," she said, fighting back tears. ". . . It makes me sick to even think that what Rick did caused people to die." Once she learned that Rick was a spy, her life had become a living "nightmare," she claimed.

> The coercion and duress I suffered at Rick's hands was devastating and totally debilitating. The more duress Rick created, the more dependent I became upon him. Soon I became obsessed with him not getting caught. Your Honor, you must understand that Rick Ames— the CIA-trained spy—had convinced me that my life and the life of my son was in danger if he was caught. So I helped him . . . and for that I am remorseful and ashamed.

As she neared the end of her three-page statement, it looked as if Rosario were about to break down. "Paul needs a mother. . . . my life may be ruined, but my little five-year-old still deserves a life. Rick took mine away, please do not help him take Paul's away, too."

An angry Hulkower hurried to the podium, where he paused, turned and stared directly at Rosario. "There are many victims in this case, Mrs. Ames, but you're not one of them!" There was not a shred of proof that Rosario had ever protested her husband's spying, he declared. "When Rick Ames tells his wife that he's coming back from picking up the KGB package and all is well, the only question she asks him is: 'Financially, too?'" Hulkower proclaimed, quoting from a tape made October 3.

Judge Hilton appeared completely unmoved, some might even say bored, by the forty minutes of emotional statements. He sentenced Rosario to five years in prison, and adjourned the court.

THE WORDS OF RICK AMES

The Rosario you see today is not the woman I fell in love with. You will never be able to see her. My sister remembers what she was like before we went to Rome. There was an innocence and unworldliness to Rosario then, and to my great shame, I am responsible for the transformation. In order to see the Rosario with whom I fell in love, you must understand her past and how she was influenced by me and my deception.

In Mexico, Rosario's assistance to the agency was one of naive friendship, letting a friend use her apartment for a small payment. She had no real idea of what the CIA was and its true purposes. When I announced my true status to her, I am sure she was genuinely surprised and shocked. Desperately in love, she simply put that aside. At various times, I tried to explain some of the basics about my work, my specialty, my career. Rosario was simply not very interested. First, her interest in Russia, the USSR, Slavic culture, literature, et cetera, was minimal—without any particular animus, though. That part of the world might as well have been on the moon. She tended to see the East as a massive, grey, oppressive place, full of dull, grey, and oppressed people. But her lack of interest also allowed her to obscure and avoid talking about her negative view of the CIA and many of my coworkers. Rosario makes quick and strong decisions about people, and many agency people whom she met did not impress her. And my own frankness about my views certainly supported some of her negative assessments. Espionage, spying, betrayal, agents, all of this was very distasteful to her. She could no more identify what she'd done for a friend in Mexico with what I was talking about and doing than to fly. Only her commitment to me, and her belief that I was different, enabled her to get past what she saw as dishonorable, nasty, and, in a somewhat vague but passionate way, serving the most debased ends of U.S. policy. She put my professional life out of her mind, and psychologically this was important because it set a pattern that later proved extremely useful to me.

Rosario and money. A generation or two before she was born, Rosario's family was quite comfortably well off, but as she grew up, she was aware that her mother and father were not wealthy, and by the time her parents separated, her mother's salary and then her own were all that they had. She did not have expensive tastes, but had spent her life surrounded by nice, tasteful and expensive things—the comforts of well-off Bogotá society. This accounts for her aristocratic point of view. But money to Rosario is a bit unreal, abstract, not something you have to think about, plan for, and even go out and get. It is something one just has or not. Up until 1985, Rosario was used to hard work for little money, so when I started producing money, always careful to give vague and off-putting cover stories about its source, Rosario found it very easy to use it. After about a year in Rome, I began telling her I had earned enough that we were close to wealthy and permanently financially secure. I encouraged continually the spending of money and bought expensive presents, but Rosario's own spending habits remained roughly the same: more expensive clothes, things for the house. A lot of money went to Colombia to support her *mother and buy the apartments and land. Expensive restaurants and a few va-cations were about it after that. Little things can eat up a lot. I was the one who decided on and bought most of the really costly toys.*

By the time we returned to Washington, Rosario was used to the idea that we had enough money for just about anything reasonable we wanted. When I broke down and told her, to my eternal regret, that I was a spy, I used several techniques to put off her objections and equally importantly to avoid any de-tailed discussions. I told her I was "consulting" independently with the Rus-sians, but gave her no idea of what I had and was giving them. And I never allowed her questions and fears to penetrate past this. I also blackmailed her, using two basic arguments. First I suggested that I had turned to the KGB in order to make money to support her, our future children, her mother, and to pro-vide a secure financial future. Rosario was especially vulnerable to this, be-cause she knew how generously we had supported her family, and she also feared that she was extravagant. We also both felt that her mother had little sense of how to use the money we had sent her prudently. This form of black-mail, used subtly and skillfully, to my shame, made Rosario hesitant to take a strong stand. She also, of course, found it difficult to envision Paul growing up without the advantages she thought important, and indeed, had also grown to think necessary.

The second blackmail element was my promise that it would all stop soon with my retirement from the agency, and that I had to be careful in detaching myself from the Russians so they would not become angry or vengeful. I also told her that the Russians were holding more than one million dollars for me and I had to be very careful to "resign" in a way that would ensure I'd get it.

Rosario's initial and continuing objections revolved around her conviction that what I was doing was wrong; that I'd done something against the law and dishonorable without ever consulting her; that we were all in terrible danger should I get caught; that the Russians held our fates, too, and that we certainly didn't need more money. I countered by saying that I wasn't doing any harm to anyone; that the law was a technicality; that the Russians and I were com-pletely safe from discovery; that what's done is done; that we did still need the money; and that it would all be over in a year or two. Of course she was unable to answer my repeated and general arguments that "what's done is done" and "we simply have no choice now but to finish it off." I really gave her no real choices, don't you see? A year or so after I told her what I was doing, during one of the infrequent and brief conversations we had about it, she said she had never spent a day without the blackest and most utter fears for the future. Despite her total ignorance of what passed between me and the Russians, and my assurances that it was somehow innocuous and part of the inane spy games that we played, she knew deep down that I was in terrible danger. But I think she never conceived of the danger to her personally, but rather in terms of she and Paul somehow losing me, or the effects of discovery or disaster on me. She was never afraid for herself. Why would she be? I was the spy. This was something I had decided on and done and was insisting and determined to carry on, regardless of what she thought or feared.

So this is what it comes down to: Rosario's inability after I told her the truth to take some forceful action to stop me or to remove herself from danger. That is why she is being punished, and it is unfair. Don't you see? When I told her what I was doing, I already knew that it would be impossible for her to do anything about it. She was already predisposed to blocking out my world, and she felt trapped by my blackmail and the need for the money. So you tell me, who is to blame? And before you judge Rosario, ask yourself what you would do if your spouse announced that he was doing something illegal and blackmailed you into thinking that you had no choice. So there you have it. Rick Ames says his wife is innocent. And he still loves her deeply.

THE WORDS OF OTHERS

Mr. Hulkower sets so much store in his famous tapes, and there was a microphone hidden in the kitchen, so he has to have a tape recording where he can hear: Bang! Bang! Bang! That's me hitting my head against the kitchen cabinets. One day I got so angry at Rick that I couldn't stand it any more.

—Rosario Ames

She was a first-class bitch. She definitely wore the pants in that family and she didn't do a damn thing around the house but boss him around. She had a maid. She had a nanny. She was completely focused on herself. She was both vain and haughty and contemptuous of him. Listening to those tapes—Jesus! It was just pathetic.

—An FBI agent describing Rosario Ames, after listening to conversations between Rick and Rosario overheard by hidden microphones

What is to be gained by keeping Rosario in jail? Hasn't she been punished enough already, deprived of her husband and son, her house, all of her possessions?

—Luciana C. Divine, Rosario's friend

Prosecutors should take a hard look before going after spouses for doing little more than remaining faithful to their mates . . . A wife should not be forced to choose between the state and her marriage.

—John P. Hume and Marc E. Elias, Attorneys for Rosario Ames, writing in *The National Law Journal*

The notion that Rosario Ames chose "family values over flag" is ludicrous. Greed is not a family value.

—U.S. attorneys Mark J. Hulkower and Robert Chesnut, in response to *The National Law Journal* article entitled "Rosario Ames Chose Family Values over Flag"

Paul was to go to a birthday party. . . . Rosario gave him paper and a pencil. [To make a birthday card.] Paul reversed the r in birthday. "Rick!" Rosario shouted. "Come in here and look at this. In Bogotá every child knows how to read and write at Paul's age . . ." She turned her wrath on the boy. "You're so stupid!" And she stormed out of the room. . . . "Let's try again, son," Rick said quietly to the sobbing Paul.

—Peter Maas, *Killer Spy.*

I offer you no excuses for my conduct—only explanations. In order to understand how I got caught up in Rick Ames's deceit, you have to understand that he was, and is, a master liar and manipulator. Exactly those qualities that made him a good intelligence officer for our country.

—Rosario Ames, in her plea for mercy at her sentencing

Judge, Please make mommy come fast, I love her.

—Paul Ames, in a letter asking Judge Hilton for a reduced prison sentence for his mother

The tale she tells is compelling and heartbreaking. She paints herself as a victim, isolated by a controlling husband, caught in an expanding web of secrets. It is the story of the mental and emotional deterioration of a woman, or-

*chestrated by a clever and manipulative man. . . . Whether it is the sponta-
neous truth or a carefully crafted fabrication intended to sway her interviewer,
she tells it with conviction.*

—Sally Quinn, *The Washington Post*

*All these things, these charges people are making about me, are totally
ridiculous.*

—Rosario Ames

CHAPTER 26

MOSCOW

It had been nearly one year since I had first met "Yuri," the mysterious Russian intelligence officer to whom retired KGB general Boris Solomatin had introduced me during my first trip to Moscow. But I recognized Yuri's voice the moment he called me at the apartment I was renting on Vspolny Pereulok, a street not far from the American embassy. He offered to pick me up at ten o'clock the next morning, so we could talk. Yuri arrived in a new black Volga limousine, and I fought back a grin. Yeltsin's government was in such dire financial straits that the Russian navy was afraid that the nuclear cores in some of its older submarines might melt down because the government could no longer afford to keep them maintained. Yet Russian intelligence continued to have enough funds to buy its generals new limousines.

Yuri seemed more hurried than the last time we had met, and when I mentioned it, he waved his hand toward the congested traffic and pedestrians hurrying down the sidewalks. "Look around," he replied, "Moscow is changing. Everyone is in a rush now. People must work two or three jobs just to buy meat." Although he had not told me much about himself, I knew that he had a granddaughter who was about the same age as my teenage daughter—or at least he had told me that he did. I asked if she was well. "Of course!" he replied, sounding a bit offended. "I am financially secure, and her parents—they are part of the new Russia." He was referring to Russia's emerging entrepreneur class, the "new rich" who are the only residents of Moscow who can afford the outrageously overpriced Western goods overflowing from the city's better shops. "It was better before, you know," he told me. "Before your McDonald's and MTV came here."

Our destination was an ornate apartment in an older building near the center of Moscow. It had a balcony that looked out toward the Kremlin. The view was magnificent. A woman brought us vodka. After several toasts, Yuri got to the point.

"Please tell me, how is my good friend Rick?" For nearly two hours, we spoke about Ames and my book. He asked me several questions, which I answered. I asked him several questions, and he answered a few, but not many. I thought we were finished, so I started to rise from my chair, but Yuri motioned me with his hand to stay seated. There was one last item he wished to mention.

"I would like to ask you for a favor," he said. "I want you to give Rick a personal message from me." Without waiting for me to reply, Yuri said: "Tell Rick that we are extremely grateful for what he did for our country. Tell Rick that we have not forgotten him. If we can find an appropriate way to help him, we will. Good friends do not forget each other."

My mind was racing with questions. Ames had told me during one of our jailhouse interviews that the Justice Department had made a critical error when it had drafted his plea bargain. It had seized everything that he and Rosario had owned in the United States and confiscated the money in his Swiss bank accounts. It had even written clauses into the plea bargain that required him to forfeit any money that he might be paid from future book or movie deals. "But they didn't say anything about the money that the KGB is holding for me in Moscow," he had whispered. I had burst out laughing at him. "What makes you think the KGB is going to pay you?" I snickered. Ames had leaned back in his chair and had smiled confidently. "Oh, they will," he replied, "because they will want to send a message to others like me who are still out there working for them. They will want them to know that the KGB always pays its debts."

I asked Yuri what his message to Rick meant. Was he saying that the Russian government was still keeping his money secure for him in some Moscow bank? Was it planning on trying to arrange his release diplomatically—perhaps a future spy swap? Or was his message meant to make Ames feel better by letting him know that his buddies in the SVR still toasted him occasionally?

"Just tell him that friends do not forget each other," Yuri said. "He will understand."

"Why do you still give a damn about Aldrich Ames?" I snapped. My question shocked him, and me. I hadn't meant to be so blunt, but I suddenly realized that I was angry. During my trips to Moscow, I had met with the families of several spies whom Ames had betrayed. These were the faceless wives and children made into widows and orphans by the spy wars. It was their husbands and their fathers who had been arrested and executed. In the 1980s, the Soviet government had confiscated everything that these persons had owned. These women and children had been evicted from their state-controlled apartments, barred from working in state-controlled jobs. They were social outcasts, whispered about wherever they went, embarrassed to say their own names out loud. I had watched these widows and their now-grown children wipe tears from their eyes as they described how they had been abused, scorned, and hated. And I had discovered that none of these persons had ever received a penny from the U.S. government. None of these persons had ever been told, "Thank you for the sacrifice your family made for our country."

I had mentioned this to the CIA and FBI after I had returned in December 1994 from my first trip to Moscow, and I had been warned that I was being simplistic. What could the U.S. government have done differently during the Cold War? It had been too dangerous to reach out to these people after their husbands and fathers were exposed as spies. Even today, I was told, it is still much too risky for the United States to help them. I had accepted this rationale at first, but not now, not any more. Why had it been too risky to pay the widows and the orphans, but not too dangerous to continue making dead drop deliveries to a new generation of agents recruited in the late 1980s in Moscow? And why was it too risky now? Most Russians can travel abroad without restrictions. Most foreigners in Moscow are no longer followed. Western-owned banks can be found in many hotels. Wire transfers are common. U.S. businesses do millions of dollars of business in Moscow each year. Russians use Visa and MasterCard cards issued by non-Russian banks. Here I was, standing in an old KGB guest apartment, talking to a general in the Russian intelligence service, and he was telling me that his bankrupt government wanted Ames to know that it was going to make sure that it kept its promises to him, even though it had already paid him more than two million dollars. Yet my government was telling me that it was impossible for it to help the impoverished families of its dead spies—the same men whom I had heard being eulogized by the CIA, FBI, and Justice Department so eloquently when they were condemning Ames for his treachery. I was ashamed.

"There is something I don't understand," I said. "Your government has never done anything to help John Walker, Jr. You have never reached out to him. Why should I now believe you when you say that you are prepared to keep your promises to Ames?"

Yuri didn't reply.

"I mean, what is it about Rick Ames?" I continued. "Why is he so special?"

Yuri was quiet for several moments, and then he said: "There is a real difference between these two men, my friend. Walker was a good source for us, that's true. He produced a lot, and we appreciate that. I am sorry he is in prison. But Rick, you see, with him it is different. We must keep our commitments to him."

"Why?" I pressed. "Why is he different?"

"Because Rick Ames is a professional intelligence officer. He is one of us. That is the difference."

THE WORDS OF RICK AMES

The anger and indignation and bitterness felt by many toward me is perceived by me in several different ways.

That of the general public, the press, many government officials—all of these "outsiders"—their anger is natural and understandable. When authors such as Peter Maas scream that I killed ten men, I feel very little—whether guilt, shame, or even embarrassment. But I understand why they are reacting this way. It is normal for them based on how little they really know.

When it comes to the "insiders"—people such as James Woolsey, most agency and even DO officers, the FBI and Hulkower and his cronies—their screams of indignation are literally offensive to me. I don't mean their genuine anger at my actions and betrayal—of course, this is natural and justified. I'm talking about their agonizing over the injustice of it all, how I spilt the blood of innocent men, and their amazement over how I could do what I did! What hypocrites! What do they think Gordievsky, Orgorodnik, Varenik, and Polyakov were all about? Prove to me that I am different from your heroes. Their hand-wringing and tears are institutionalized, bureaucratized, and sanitized hypocrisy. People such as Hulkower and Wiser have been helped, they have become media stars, because of what I have done. They are careerists and time-servers, blind to the moral and ethical dimension of their own behavior and motives.

Do I feel guilt? Of course, but it is not their words that bring me my shame. It is when I stand before many of my former friends, colleagues, and bosses that I hide my face. You've talked to many of them—people such as Jeanne, Sandy, Burton Gerber, Milton Bearden. Confronted with their reactions, even in my imagination, which is mainly the case, I feel a deep sense of shame and guilt, one which I revolt against displaying in public—partly for reasons of principle, partly because I have no wish to comfort others, partly no doubt, out of cowardice. I am ashamed for two reasons: I betrayed the personal and professional trust which existed between me and them; and I betrayed the deep commitment that I had made to the agents who trusted me. In both cases it is the personal trust that I betrayed, and for that I have no explanation, only sorrow. Betrayal and trust. Is this not where we started?

So now you have heard my life story, stripped bare for all to judge. Am I ashamed? Of course, but let me be clear. I am ashamed of the harm that I have done to Rosario, Paul, and even myself. I am ashamed of the personal betrayal. But for those who have feasted upon my tragedy for their own glorification, I feel nothing but contempt.

I know we have talked a lot about why I did what I did, but in retrospect I'm still not certain I've really explained it well. My frustration comes from attempts by you and my FBI and CIA debriefers to simplify and find a single, overriding reason for what happened, when, in fact, there is no single reason, but layers upon layers upon layers of reasons, none more pressing than the others, and added to these layers are the events themselves, an almost-never-to-be-repeated coming together of circumstances, which facilitated a fantasy, causing it suddenly to gel, without conscious realization or careful, even painful, thought, into a real plan. If I had been required to plan a trip to Vienna and a sophisticated walk-in plan of some sort in order to volunteer to the KGB, I'm sure I would never have done so. Had I had to work out a plan to meet some Soviet in Washington to provide cover, I'm quite sure I wouldn't have done so. So you see, the events, themselves, come into play: the fact that I was introduced to Chuvakhin; the fact that I had access to materials about our agents; the fact that in the Soviet Union three "double agents" came forward. These unique circumstances were critical. They created the opportunity.

This does not absolve me of responsibility. But in the winter of '84 to '85, who was Rick Ames? More importantly, was he dangerous? Yes, he was. Why? Was the danger in my confusion in my personal life and goals, my marriage to Nan, my upcoming marriage to a foreigner and my frustration over my somewhat out-of-ordinary career progression? Was it in my retiring and somewhat shy personality? Was I dangerous because of my difficulties with alcohol? Was there some basic character flaw in terms of integrity and responsibility, dating back to my youth? You and the others are searching for an easy solution, when in fact it is all of these factors. They are all part of that petri dish culture into which the germ floated.

But wait, there is even more. What made the nourishing soup for the germ to grow in? Here is where my ideas and experience came to play. Ideology is certainly out of fashion, and I'm uncomfortable talking about such things, too, but I think to separate it from the other strands is to misconstrue real life. What was my ideology? I've explained this—my discovery that political intelligence was never used, TRIGON/Kissinger, Angleton, et cetera. I talked before about how there were no barriers left in 1985 to keep me from slipping down the slippery slope. It may be more useful to think of it less as the absence of restraints than the existence of ideas and experiences which, when put into that petri dish stew under sufficient stress and confusion and an almost unique set of opportune circumstances, caused the germ to bloom and blossom into treason. To attempt to rank or segregate or declare that one factor provides the explanation is to deny how a person feels, thinks, and acts.

The other night I decided it was time to look at some positives in my life, and I think they deserve mentioning. Over the course of my nine years of being a KGB mole, I made more money than most crooks, enjoyed myself more, did more interesting things and, during and at the end of those nine years, accomplished some important things which I believe worthwhile. You have heard me mostly moan and groan over regrets and guilt—true enough. But putting them aside for a moment, I can take a fair amount of satisfaction in my life, and in that spirit my biggest regret is that I was too blind to see what was coming during 1993.

I've always been an optimist, accused even of being Pollyanna-y, and I am capable of seeing some good things in my past. Rosario and I were good parents, and Rosario is, and will be, once she is released. Paul was, and will be, as happy and confident a boy as anyone's seen. I think they will be all right materially. I don't know just how, but have few fears on that score. Despite the futility and absurdity of the U.S. war on drugs, I take a lot of satisfaction in my Black Sea Initiative. Many people have shown in one way or another that I have been a good friend. If I can keep my failings in perspective, and that takes some focusing, I believe I can hold my head up high and feel like a normal and decent member of our species in all the critical respects.

So how will you ultimately explain what I did and why I did it? If you must have a simple answer, then here it is. On the first page of Pére Goriot, Balzac speaks of the reader's callousness toward Goriot's secret sorrows because, after all, it is just fiction, romance. Then Balzac breaks into English: "All is true!" Everyone, he writes, can find the elements of tragedy in his own house and his own heart. It is there for the looking.

You want an easy explanation. Here is mine: "All is true."

THE WORDS OF OTHERS

Ames is trying to reinvent himself and will doubtless soon step into the media spotlight as an objective and veteran commentator on the intelligence game.

—R. James Woolsey, CIA

He is a humanitarian. How did he hurt your country? He didn't betray any of your secrets, he simply told us who were the traitors in our midst. I consider him a very fine fellow.

—Viktor Cherkashin, KGB

Do I want him punished? Oh, yes, yes, yes. I'm upset that he gets to read books. I want vengeance for what he did and the people whom he destroyed. The death penalty wouldn't bother me, but if not that, the worst thing that could happen to Rick Ames is for him to be forced to sit in a cell by himself. No television. No radio. No writing materials. No pen. Nothing at all. All alone. Let him just sit there and think about what he has done.

—Sandy Grimes, CIA

I knew the people I identified would be arrested and put in prison. He knew the people he identified would be arrested and shot. That is one of the differences between us.

—Oleg Gordievsky, British agent

Rick and Rosario used to bring out the worst in each other's personalities. It was just the way they were sometimes.

—Nancy Ames Everly, Rick's sister

You know Bob Duncan had a big influence on Rick in high school. Bob killed himself in 1975. There was another kid in our class who committed suicide, too, but I can't think of his name right now. At the reunion we were talking about all the tragedy. For some, high school was the very best time in their lives.

—Jack Seeley, high school friend

As I see it, the money was never important to him, until he met Rosario. If he had found some other woman who was not materialistic and who had said, "Okay, Rick, we've got to live on a budget because you only make this much money and we don't need to eat at expensive restaurants or buy expensive clothing," then he would have gone along with that. He never would have been a spy. He was dominated by strong women. So it was a combination of his weaknesses and Rosario's materialism that caused him to do it.

—Jeanne Vertefeuille, CIA

My mother died right after my father was executed. This man who betrayed them, he destroyed so much, so many, and for what reason? His own vanity, his own selfishness, so that he could be someone important. I read where he called it all a game. My father believed that what he was doing was right. Can this man Ames wash my father's blood so easily from his hands? It is not a game when your father lies in an unmarked grave and his grandchildren cry at night because he is gone.

—Son of an executed spy

I was powerless to do anything.

—Rosario Ames

SOURCES

GENERAL

The skeleton for this book came from my exclusive interviews and correspondence with Aldrich Ames. All our interviews took place in the Alexandria (Virginia) Detention Center. Each lasted three to four hours, was tape-recorded, and was done in the attorney/client interview room at the jail, where we met alone. I interviewed Ames in 1994 on these days: July 1, 4, 5, 6, 7, 9, 10, 13, 14, 15, and 17. After the government discovered we were meeting privately, it whisked Ames away to a federal prison. At that point, we began corresponding regularly.

All Ames's letters to me were read by a CIA censor before they were delivered. At first, this censor deleted an average of four or five sentences in each letter. But after several weeks of corresponding, Ames and I began to grasp what we could and couldn't write, and only a few deletions were made after that. I did receive one letter, however, where every word Ames wrote was essentially blacked out, except for "Dear Pete" and "Best Wishes, Rick." I had asked Ames to give me his opinion of Paul Redmond, Jr., and had assumed that he could do this because Redmond's name already had been published in numerous newspaper and magazine articles. I was wrong. One of the CIA censor's tasks was to make certain that Ames did not make public the names of any current CIA employees, including Redmond. Consequently, Ames was prohibited from writing about Redmond. Of course, he and I both knew that I wanted to learn his opinion of Redmond, so in later letters, Ames simply referred to Redmond as a "coworker" or "the person whose name I can't mention." So much for government censorship.

Ames is an excellent letter-writer—a skill honed, no doubt, by his CIA training. His letters were filled with colorful descriptions, rich details, and intimate recollections. All of his letters were single-spaced and handwritten on legal pads. Here is a list of the letters that Ames mailed me.

1994		1995		1996	
Aug. 23:	2 pages	Jan. 7:	8 pages	Jan. 4:	6 pages
29:	8 pages	13:	11 pages	9:	24 pages
Sept. 22:	1 page	18:	2 pages	Feb. 23:	2 pages
24:	3 pages	20:	3 pages		
Oct. 4:	1 page	25:	10 pages		
14:	1 page	Feb. 1:	1 page*		
24:	2 pages	5:	1 page		
Nov. 12:	2 pages	11:	5 pages		
25:	2 pages	15:	1 page		
Dec. 6:	6 pages	16:	1 page		
7:	3 pages	19:	13 pages		
11:	3 pages	23:	6 pages		
12:	1 page	Mar. 7:	12 pages		
23:	16 pages	14:	6 pages*		
29:	9 pages	25:	12 pages		
		28:	2 pages		
		30:	10 pages		
		Apr. 1:	11 pages		
		3:	6 pages		
		14:	7 pages		
		23:	14 pages		
		26:	5 pages		
		27:	8 pages*		
		May 6:	8 pages		
		12:	14 pages		
		18	4 pages		
		26:	7 pages		
		27:	4 pages		
		30:	4 pages		
		June 1:	12 pages		
		5:	1 page		
		9:	22 pages		
		18:	16 pages		

*Heavily censored by the CIA.

	22:	10 pages*
	26:	10 pages
July	13:	15 pages
	20:	8 pages
	22:	9 pages
	26:	5 pages
Aug.	2:	3 pages
	8:	4 pages
	16:	5 pages
	22:	3 pages
Sept.	8:	11 pages
Oct.	21:	14 pages
	23:	10 pages
	23:	15 pages
Nov.	8:	3 pages
Dec.	6:	2 pages

These 466 pages of correspondence were pivotal in helping me write this book.

I did not pay Ames for his exclusive cooperation. I did not sign any contract with him, nor did I give him any editorial control over my manuscript. One of the questions readers are bound to ask is whether or not Ames has told me the truth. I am convinced that he has, in every area except for one. Ames wants his opinions and criticisms of the CIA to be taken seriously, and he knows that his critics would use any exaggeration or lie that he might tell to attack his already questionable credibility. I have verified nearly all the information that Ames told me, by checking it with other sources. I have also compared the statements that Ames made to me with his comments to the FBI and CIA, which used a polygraph machine to determine whether or not he was lying. In the few cases where I have been unable to substantiate what Ames told me, I have used the words "Ames claimed," to warn the reader that his statements cannot be corroborated. In some cases, I have noted discrepancies in the text and have offered the reader more than one plausible explanation for what may have happened.

While I am convinced Ames was truthful in describing his professional career and his own personal faults, feelings, and attitudes, I do not believe he has told the truth about Rosario Ames. I do not believe that she first learned that her husband was a spy in 1992 after she found a mysterious note in a discarded wallet. Nor do I believe that Rosario was as ignorant or naive about his spying as she and Ames now claim. I also found no evidence during my research to substantiate Rosario's claim to me that she was planning to divorce Ames just before he was arrested. I do not believe that she ever considered herself a battered or abused woman until *after* she was arrested, and it became convenient for her to be portrayed as a victim. Having written this, I must add that I *personally* do not believe Rosario Ames should have been prosecuted or imprisoned for her husband's treason. There is no evidence that she ever did anything to help him spy, other than tell him to be careful. There is no doubt in my mind that Rosario Ames would have immediately surrendered her U.S. citizenship and voluntarily returned to Colombia after her husband was arrested, and that solution, in my opinion, would have been much more just than what has been done.

I interviewed Rosario Ames at the Federal Correctional Institution in Danbury, Connecticut, without a CIA censor being present. The fact that the CIA did not feel it was necessary to have a censor listen to our interviews shows that the U.S. government knows that Rosario Ames knew nothing significant about her husband's spying. I spoke to her for eight hours on January 25, 1995, and met with her again for another eight hours on February 21, 1995.

It is always difficult for an author to "reconstruct" events. People lie, memories are imperfect, prejudices come into play, mistakes are made, people honestly disagree about what was said, agreed upon, done. At various times, I have chosen to let one person recall a specific incident in this book. In such cases, these events were confirmed by at least two other sources, and usually more, before being included. Oftentimes, I chose the story that seemed the most logical.

The most difficult information in this book to corroborate deals with the events that happened in Moscow regarding Ames. Although I have done my best to write the fullest and most accurate account possible, readers should be aware that it was impossible for me to connect every piece of the Ames puzzle. For instance, Ames insists that when he first visited the Soviet embassy in Washington, D.C., on April 16, 1985, he gave a letter to the guard there which had a page from the SE division's internal telephone directory attached to it. Ames has told the government and me that he highlighted his name on that roster so that the KGB would know he worked for the CIA. Yet KGB counterintelligence officer Viktor Cherkashin told me in Moscow that he knew Ames only as "Rick Wells" when they met for the first time in the Soviet embassy. Cherkashin said that he never saw any CIA telephone roster. At first glance, it would appear that either Ames or Cherkashin is lying, yet both may be telling the truth. The letter Ames wrote was given to KGB *rezident* Stanislav Androsov, and it is possible that he removed the CIA roster before showing the letter to Cherkashin. Such comparmentalization was not unusual inside the KGB. I tried to find Androsov, but was unsuccessful. This is one of the missing puzzle pieces.

Another unknown in this book is the name of the KGB general who met with me four times in Moscow. Based on FBI photographs, I have been able to narrow down my list of possible candidates. "Yuri" could be: Aleksandr Aleksandrovich Shposhnikov, a good friend of Boris Solomatin's and a well-respected KGB officer; Igor Shurygin, who was the KGB's counterintelligence chief in Mexico City when Ames worked there; Igor Batamirov, a KGB troubleshooter who helped debrief Edward Lee Howard; and Yuri Karetkin, known to Ames as ANDRE. I suspect that "Yuri" is ANDRE, but I am unable to prove this. I have tried to corroborate everything that "Yuri" told me through other sources, mostly retired KGB officers. Although most of these officers did not know about the Ames case, they were familiar with KGB procedures and the personalities of Vladimir Kryuchkov, Viktor Chebrikov, Vadim Kirpichenko, and others who were key players in the Ames case. Two men, in particular, provided me with insights about Kryuchkov and the Ames case. I have described these men only as "aides" to Kryuchkov. This was done to protect their identities. Both spoke to me only after I swore that I would keep their names a secret. I found the information that these retired KGB officers provided to be extremely useful.

I first met the CIA's mole-hunting team on June 6, 1995, at CIA headquarters. Up until that point, the agency had turned away all requests to interview the team. I was told that the CIA decided to grant me access to the team after John M. Deutch became the new CIA director. I met with members of the team on June 6, 14, 28, and 29, and then met with each member of the team individually. I found the team members to be amazingly candid, even when discussing mistakes the CIA had made. Because Ames had already told me the names of the agents whom he had betrayed and also had revealed details to me about the still-classified ABSORB and TAW clandestine operations, the task force agreed to clarify and, in some cases, provide me with additional information about its former agents, ABSORB, and TAW. Besides the mole hunt team members, I also interviewed a number of retired CIA officials who had worked with Ames. One retired high-ranking CIA officer, in particular, granted me a series of helpful interviews but asked not to be named in my book. The CIA did not attempt to censor my book, nor was it given an advance copy to read.

On my own, I decided to withhold the names of several agents who were not arrested or were arrested and then released. Among these names is the identity of MOTORBOAT. I made this decision without consulting with the CIA. I have no interest in causing the arrest, prosecution, or possible execution of any agent who might have helped the CIA in the past. I have tried to explain my reasoning in the text.

Besides interviews, I reviewed hundreds of pages of documents, newspaper clippings, magazine stories, and other published material while researching this book. This includes the investigations of the Ames case done by the Senate and House intelligence committees and the unclassified versions of the CIA's inspector General Report. I also reviewed more than fifty articles published in Russia about CIA spies who were arrested there. While in Moscow, I was able to obtain two long articles that were written for internal KGB publications. These dealt with the arrest of Adolf Tolkachev and Dmitri Polyakov, and provided me with information that still is secret in Russia. I have identified books that were useful to me in a selected bibliography. I have also listed in the chapter notes that follow, the names of the persons who provided me with specific information that was used in each chapter. In these chapter-by-chapter listings, I have identified the CIA mole hunt team as a source and also individual members of the mole hunt team as sources. This was done when some of the information in the chapter came directly from the team and other information in that same chapter came from individual team members.

SPECIFIC

Prologue
My eyewitness experiences.

Chapter 1
Aldrich Ames, Nancy Ames Everly, two Ames relatives who asked not to be named, Wendy Law Yone, Bryan Law Yone, a close friend of Carleton and Rachel Ames in River Falls who asked not to be named, Charles Wall.

Chapter 2
Interviews with Aldrich Ames, Nancy Ames Everly, Chuck Windley, Margaret "Peggy" Anderson, Wes Sanders, Jack and Susan Seeley, two former students of Rachel Ames who asked not to be named.

Chapter 3
Interviews with Aldrich Ames, Nancy Ames Everly, a relative of Nancy Segebarth Ames who asked not to be named.

Chapter 4
Interviews with Aldrich Ames, Nancy Ames Everly, a retired CIA employee who worked with Ames in Turkey.

Chapter 5
Interviews with Aldrich Ames, Sergey Fedorenko, R. Patrick Watson.

Chapter 6
Interviews with Aldrich Ames, Sergey Fedorenko, a retired KGB officer who claimed he took part in the arrest of Alexander Ogorodnik, a retired CIA officer stationed in Moscow when Adolf Tolkachev volunteered to spy, Russian journalist Dimitri Lekhamon.

A note about Alexander Ogorodnik and Henry Kissinger

Aldrich Ames was the first person to tell me that Ogorodnik had sent the CIA microfilm that contained photographs of a memo supposedly written by the Soviet Union's ambassador to the U.S., Anatoly Dobrynin, about his last meeting with Henry Kissinger. I later discovered that the 1989 nonfiction book, *Widows: Four American Spies, the Wives They Left Behind, and the KGB's Crippling of American Intelligence*, was the first book to reveal the existence of Ogorodnik's microfilm. Beginning on page 93, the authors, William R. Corson, Susan B. Trento, and Joseph Trento, Jr., discuss the arrest of Ogorodnik and quote from an interview, which they published in their book, with Leonard McCoy, the CIA official responsible for investigating how the KGB had learned about Ogorodnik. According to *Widows*, McCoy and a CIA analyst, David Sullivan, tried to determine whether or not the documents which Ogorodnik photographed were legitimate or KGB disinformation. McCoy and Sullivan were unable to tell, but the authors of *Widows* quote Sullivan as saying that McCoy's damage assessment report to then CIA director Stansfield Turner contained this information: "His punch line said that (in McCoy's opinion) the only way to describe Kissinger's actions from what the evidence of this cable showed, if it was valid, was treason." I made several attempts to contact McCoy, but was unsuccessful. On February 23, 1992, Elmo Zumwalt, Jr., writing in *The Washington Times*, also revealed the existence of the Ogorodnik microfilm. Without mentioning Kissinger by name, Zumwalt wrote the Ogorodnik had provided the CIA with a "startling revelation . . . that a former Cabinet official . . . had met with Dobrynin . . . and provided him with tactical and strategic advice on how the Kremlin might best defeat President Carter's SALT II proposal in order to effect a better deal for the Soviets!" Zumwalt continued by calling Ogorodnik's microfilm a "hot potato" for the CIA, "as evidenced by the fact that two of its employees who subsequently attempted to get action taken against the [cabinet member] in question for treason were demoted or had to resign."

The information Ames told me adds a new chapter to this exposé. Ames told me that the negatives of the controversial microfilm had been removed from the CIA's vault. This was confirmed to me by a retired SE division official who had seen that Ogorodnik file and had noticed that the negatives about Kissinger had been removed. Ames also said that the matter was dropped at the insistence of the Carter White House, another accusation that was confirmed to me by two retired CIA officials who were involved in the Ogorodnik case. During my trips to Moscow, I asked "Yuri" repeatedly for a copy of Dobrynin's original cable. While he refused to provide one to me, Yuri and another KGB source confirmed that Dobrynin had written a cable based on his meeting with Kissinger and that Dobrynin had claimed in his cable that Kissinger had given him advice about how to outmaneuver the Carter administration during the upcoming SALT II talks.

Chapter 7

Interviews with Aldrich Ames, Arkady Shevchenko, Margaret Anderson, Nancy Ames Everly, David and Angela Blake,* Thomas Kolesnichenko, a retired CIA official in SE division familiar with the flap caused by the book *Legend: The Secret World of Lee Harvey Oswald.*

Chapter 8

Interviews with Aldrich Ames, Rosario Ames, David Samson, Dewey Clarridge, Irwin Rubenstein, Richard Thurman.

Chapter 9

Interviews with Aldrich Ames, Rosario Ames, David Samson, Irwin Rubenstein, Richard Thurman, Diana Worthen, Oleg M. Nechiporenko.

Chapter 10

Interviews with Aldrich Ames, two former SE division employees familiar with the agency's decision to select Ames as Soviet branch chief. Information about the CIA's human assets and clandestine operations were first told to me by Ames and later confirmed by the CIA mole hunt team. Information about Angleton was gleaned from several publications cited in my selected bibliography.

Chapter 11

Interviews with Aldrich Ames, Rosario Ames, Diana Worthen, David Samson, Nancy Ames Everly, two CIA officials who worked with Ames in New York City when he was on temporary assignment there, a former SE division coworker of Ames.

Chapter 12

Interviews with Aldrich Ames, Rosario Ames, Viktor Cherkashin, CIA mole hunt team.

A note about the list of agents exposed by Ames

The list of agents who were identified by Ames is based on my interviews with Ames, "Yuri," information provided by SVR's public information spokesman, Yuri Kobaladze, and the CIA mole hunt team.

*Not their real names.

Chapter 13
Interviews with Aldrich Ames, "Yuri," Yuri Kobaladze, Dimitri Lekhamon, Viktor Cherkashin, David and Angela Blake, a CIA official in SE division, CIA mole hunt team, Rosario Ames, Diana Worthen, Yuri Shvets. Information about Edward Lee Howard and Vitaly Yurchenko was taken from books cited in my selected bibliography. Both Howard and Yurchenko refused to meet with me in Moscow.

Chapter 14
Interviews with Aldrich Ames, Viktor Cherkashin, Oleg Kalugin, Oleg Gordievsky, Yuri Pankov, Yuri Kobaladze, two aides to Vladimir Kryuchkov, CIA mole hunt team.

Chapter 15
Interviews with Aldrich Ames, a current CIA official, Sandy Grimes, Paul Redmond, Jr., relative of Leonid Poleschuk, Charles Leven, relatives of Gennady Varenik, "Yuri," Dmitri Lekhamon, Ilya Milstein.

Chapter 16
Interviews with Aldrich Ames, Rosario Ames, Diane Worthen, Nancy Ames Everly, David Samson, David and Angela Blake, "Yuri," CIA mole hunt team, Paul Redmond, Jr., a coworker of Ames in Rome.

Chapter 17
Interviews with Spencer Lonetree, Michael Stuhff, Jeanne Vertefeuille, Paul Redmond, Jr., Sandy Grimes, Sergey Fedorenko, Vladimir Potashov.

Chapter 18
Interviews with two relatives of Dmitri Polyakov, Oleg Gordievsky, Oleg Kalugin, Paul Joyal, Sergey Kryuchkov, "Yuri," two aides to Vladimir Kruychkov.

Chapter 19
Interviews with Jeanne Vertefeuille, Dan Payne, Aldrich Ames, Rosario Ames, Nancy Ames Everly, Diana Worthen, R. Patrick Watson, Sergey Fedorenko.

Chapter 20
Interviews with Aldrich Ames, Rosario Ames, Diana Worthen, Sandy Grimes, Paul Redmond, Jr., Jeanne Vertefeuille, "Yuri," Dan Payne, David Samson.

Chapter 21
Interviews with Aldrich Ames, Rosario Ames, Sergey Fedorenko, R. Patrick Watson, Paul Redmond, Jr., Jim Milburn.

Chapter 22
Interviews with two aides to Vladimir Kruychkov, Yuri Pankov, Sergey Kryuchkov, Dan Payne, Jeanne Vertefeuille, Diana Worthen, Paul Redmond, Jr., Sandy Grimes, Aldrich Ames, a CIA official, Jim Milburn.

Chapter 23
Interviews with Aldrich Ames, Rosario Ames, Paul Redmond, Jr., Dan Payne, Jeanne Vertefeuille, Sandy Grimes, Bruce Gair.

Chapter 24
Interviews with Dan Payne, Jim Milburn, CIA mole hunt team, Aldrich Ames, Rosario Ames, Sandy Grimes, Leslie Wiser, Jr.

Chapter 25
Interviews with Aldrich Ames, Rosario Ames, Dan Payne, Jim Milburn, "Yuri," Plato Cacheris, Jeanne Vertefeuille, Sandy Grimes.

Chapter 26
Interviews with Aldrich Ames, Rosario Ames, CIA mole hunt team, John P. Hume, Plato Cacheris, William Cummings, Luciana Devine.

Chapter 27
Eyewitness observations.

Others who provided me with useful information are Amy Knight, Ronald Kessler, Herb Romerstein, Natasha Gevorkyan, Vladimir Snegirev, Igor N. Prelin, Ralf Piechowiak.

SELECTED BIBLIOGRAPHY

Adam, James. *Sellout*. New York: Viking, 1995.

Albats, Yevgenia. *The State Within a State: The KGB and Its Hold on Russia—Past, Present, and Future*. New York: Farrar, Straus & Giroux, 1994.

Barker, Rodney. *Dancing with the Devil: Sex, Espionage, and the U.S. Marines: The Clayton Lonetree Story*. New York: Simon & Schuster, 1996.

Barron, John. *KGB Today: The Hidden Hand*. New York: Reader's Digest Association, 1983.

Beschloss, Michael R. and Strobe Talbott. *At the Highest Levels: The Inside Story of the End of the Cold War*. Boston: Little, Brown, 1993.

Corson, William R., Susan B. Trento, and Joseph J. Trento. *Widows: Four American Spies, the Wives They Left Behind, and the KGB's Crippling of American Intelligence*. New York: Crown, 1989.

Earley, Pete. *Family of Spies: Inside the John Walker Spy Ring*. New York: Bantam, 1988.

Epstein, Edward Jay. *Legend: The Secret World of Lee Harvey Oswald*. New York: McGraw-Hill, 1978.

Gordievsky, Oleg, and Christopher Andrew. *KGB: The Inside Story*. New York: HarperCollins, 1990.

Howard, Edward Lee. *Safe House: The Compelling Memoirs of the Only CIA Spy to Seek Asylum in Russia*. Bethesda: National Press Books, 1995.

Kalugin, Oleg. *The First Directorate: My 32 Years in Intelligence and Espionage Against the West*. New York: St. Martin's, 1994.

Kessler, Ronald. *Escape From the CIA: How the CIA Won and Lost the Most Important KGB Spy Ever to Defect to the U.S.* New York: Simon & Schuster, 1991.

————. *The FBI.* New York: Simon & Schuster, 1993.

————. *Inside the CIA: Revealing the Secrets of the World's Most Powerful Spy Agency.* New York: Simon & Schuster, 1992.

————. *Moscow Station: How the KGB Penetrated the American Embassy.* New York: Scribner's, 1989.

————. *The Spy in the Russian Club.* New York: Simon & Schuster, 1990.

————. *Spy vs. Spy: Stalking Soviet Spies in America.* New York: Scribner's, 1988.

Knight, Amy W. *The KGB: Police and Politics in the Soviet Union.* Winchester, MA: Unwin Hyman, 1990.

Knightley, Phillip. *The Master Spy: The Story of Kim Philby.* New York: Vintage, 1988.

————. *The Second Oldest Profession: Spies and Spying in the Twentieth Century.* New York: Norton, 1986.

Kuzichkin, Vladimir. *Inside the KGB: Myth and Reality.* London: Andre Beutsch, 1990.

LeCarré, John. *The Russia House.* New York: Alfred A. Knopf, 1989.

————. *The Spy Who Came in from the Cold.* London: Victor Gollancz, 1963.

Maas, Peter. *Killer Spy.* New York: Warner, 1995.

Mangold, Tom. *Cold Warrior: James Jesus Angleton: The CIA's Master Spy Hunter.* New York: Simon & Schuster, 1991.

Riebling, Mark. *Wedge: The Secret War Between the FBI and CIA.* New York: Knopf, 1994.

Schevchenko, Arkady N. *Breaking with Moscow.* New York: Knopf, 1985.

Sheymov, Victor. *Tower of Secrets.* Annapolis: Naval Institute Press, 1993.

Shvets, Yuri B. *Washington Station: My Life As a KGB Spy in America.* New York: Simon & Schuster, 1994.

Waller, J. Michael. *Secret Empire: The KGB in Russia Today.* Boulder: Westview Press, 1994.

Weiner, Tim, David Johnston, and Neil A. Lewis. *Betrayal: The Story of Aldrich Ames, an American Spy.* New York: Random House, 1995.

Wise, David. *Molehunt: The Secret Search for Traitors That Shattered the CIA.* New York: Randon House, 1992.

————. *nightmover: How Aldrich Ames Sold the CIA to the KGB for $4.6 Million.* New York: HarperCollins, 1995.

————. *The Spy Who Got Away: The True Story of the Only CIA Agent to Defect to the Soviet Union.* New York: Random House, 1988.

Wright, Peter. *Spy Catcher: The Candid Autobiography of a Senior Intelligence Officer.* New York: Viking Penguin, 1987.

Woodward, Bob. *Veil: The Secret Wars of the CIA, 1981–1987.* New York: Simon & Schuster, 1987.

ACKNOWLEDGMENTS

I would like to thank my parents, Elmer and Jean Earley, who read this manuscript and have always encouraged me to write. Special thanks are also due to George and Linda Earley for their continued support. I would like to thank Robert Gottlieb, my literary agent, and several others at the William Morris Agency, including Johnny Levin, Tracey Keyes, and Brett Smith. Thanks are also due to my editor and publisher at G. P. Putnam's Sons, Neil S. Nyren, and CEO Phyllis Grann. Others who helped me include: Elizabeth Seldes and Mike Marcus at MGM; Bob Beitcher and Brad Weston at Adelson Entertainment; and screenwriter Lorenzo Semple, Jr., who is working on the movie version of this book. In Russia, I am indebted to Boris P. Likhatchev, Yuri Pankov and his assistant Galina, and Boris Solomatin, as well as several family members of the victims of Aldrich Ames. I would also like to thank Terrance Alden, Nelson and Ginny DeMille, Richard Miles, Mike Sager, Tibbie Shades, Thomas Silverstein, Lynn and LouAnn Smith, and Donna and Wayne Wolfersberger. Thanks also to Lisa Austin, Rod Barker, Lyn Ekedahl, Nancy Everly, Tracy Fu, Debra Gabor, Olga Gorlinskaya, Donna Coffman, and Herb Romerstein.

I am especially indebted to Walter Harrington, a gifted author, excellent editor, and longtime friend who read my manuscript, provided me with sound editorial guidance, encouragement, and always wise advice.

Finally, I wish to thank my three children, Stephen, Kevin, and Kathy Earley for their love.

ABOUT THE AUTHOR

A former reporter for the *Washington Post*, Pete Earley is the author of four previous books, including *Family of Spies: Inside the John Walker Spy Ring, Prophet of Death, The Hot House: Life Inside Leavenworth Prison,* and *Circumstantial Evidence.*

For *Family of Spies*, Mr. Earley was the only journalist to speak with all members of the Walker spy ring. The book was a *New York Times* bestseller. For *The Hot House*, Mr. Earley was the first journalist ever given unlimited access by the government to a major federal penitentiary. For *Circumstantial Evidence*, Mr. Earley helped uncover information which led to the release of a black man unfairly sentenced to death in southern Alabama. *Circumstantial Evidence* won the Robert F. Kennedy Award and the Edgar Award.

A native of Oklahoma, Pete Early lives in Herndon, Virginia.